THE FIGHT FOR AUSTRALIA

Also by Roland Perry

Programme for a Puppet
Elections Sur Ordinateur
The Programming of the President
The Exile
Blood is a Stranger
Faces in the Rain
Shane Warne, Master Spinner
Lethal Hero, The Mel Gibson Biography
The Fifth Man
Don Bradman
Mel Gibson, Actor, Director, Producer
Bold Warnie
Waugh's Way
Captain Australia
Bradman's Best
Bradman's Best Ashes Teams
Monash
Last of the Cold War Spies
Miller's Luck
The Ashes
Sailing to the Moon
Bradman's Invincibles
The Australian Light Horse
The Changi Brownlow
Bill the Bastard
Horrie: the war dog
The Queen, Her Lover and the Most Notorious Spy in History
The Honourable Assassin
Celeste

Documentary Films
The Force
Ted Kennedy and the Pollsters
The Programming of the President
Strike Swiftly
The Raising of a Galleon's Ghost

HACHETTE MILITARY COLLECTION

THE FIGHT FOR AUSTRALIA

FROM CHANGI AND DARWIN TO KOKODA: THE TRIUMPH OF BRAVERY, MATESHIP AND COURAGE THAT SAVED US IN WORLD WAR II

ROLAND PERRY

This edition published in Australia and New Zealand in 2017
by Hachette Australia
(an imprint of Hachette Australia Pty Limited)
Level 17, 207 Kent Street, Sydney NSW 2000
www.hachette.com.au

First published in 2012 as *Pacific 360°*

Second edition published in 2014

10 9 8 7 6 5 4 3 2 1

Copyright © Roland Perry 2012, 2014

This book is copyright. Apart from any fair dealing for the purposes of private study, research, criticism or review permitted under the *Copyright Act 1968*, no part may be stored or reproduced by any process without prior written permission. Enquiries should be made to the publisher.

National Library of Australia
Cataloguing-in-Publication data:

Perry, Roland, 1946– author.

The fight for Australia: from Changi and Darwin to Kokoda – the triumph of bravery, mateship and courage that saved us in World War II/Roland Perry.

ISBN: 978 0 7336 3911 1 (paperback)

World War, 1939–1945 – Australia – Defences.
World War, 1939–1945 – Participation, Australia.
National security – Australia – History.
Australia – History, Military – 1945-.
Australia – Defences – History.

940.5426

Cover design and illustration by Luke Causby/Blue Cork
Cover image courtesy of AdobeStock
Text design by Simon Paterson
Typeset in Sabon LT Pro by Bookhouse, Sydney

*To the memory of Don Clarke, Nate Gluck and Trevor Perry,
who fought together in New Guinea in World War II*

*When you go home, tell them of us and say,
for your tomorrow, we gave our today*

Memorial inscription at Thanbyuzayat,
Burma War Graves Cemetery

Contents

Part One *Japan's Mass Attack*
               December 1941–June 1942

1	Curtin Up	3
2	Same Peas, Different Pods	6
3	Wise Council	12
4	Tugs of War	16
5	The Sinking of Innocence	22
6	Mass Attack	28
7	Blow to the Admiralty	37
8	No Holiday for Nippon	43
9	Push to Invade Australia	49
10	Evatt and Curtin Blunder; Churchill's Wrath	53
11	Article of Intent	59
12	America's China Card	65
13	Cable Bickering; Japan's First Setback	70
14	Malaya Falling	76
15	Anderson's Last Stand	80
16	Churchill's About Face; Fall of Rabaul	85
17	The Lull Before	91

Part Two *Australia Under Siege*
               February 1942

18	Singapore's Siege	101
19	Yamashita's Moment	106
20	Operation Australia	110
21	Aftershock	114
22	Attack on Darwin	122
23	A Sense of Isolation	127
24	The Prime Minister Goes Missing	132
25	Japan's Army v Its Navy	138
26	Japanese Base at Lae	142

Part Three *MacArthur and Blamey in Australia March–June 1942*

27	MacArthur Parks in Australia	149
28	Meeting the Australians	153
29	Blamey in the Mix	159
30	Blamey v MacArthur – the Record	163
31	Of Doubtful Character	170
32	Taking Care of the Rear	175
33	Second Enemy Surge	179
34	Battle of the Coral Sea	186
35	Midget Rampage	193
36	MacArthur's Blunt Message	197
37	Midway	201
38	'Australia is Secure'	205
39	Over-Sexed and Over Here	208
40	Essential Essington	213

Part Four *Battle for Australia July–September 1942*

41	Japan's Second Thrust	219
42	39th in Trouble	224
43	Setbacks and Success	230
44	Papua: War on Two Fronts	236
45	The Fighting Withdrawal	240
46	Marvels at Milne Bay	245
47	Austerity Campaign	248
48	Potts' Last Stand	252
49	Rout of Maroubra Force	257
50	Last Razorback Stand	261
51	'Canberra's Lost It'	265
52	Horii's Horrible Dilemma	269

Part Five *Japanese Retreat October–December 1942*

53	Rowell's Howler	277
54	Reversal of Fortune	280

55	The Battle for Eora Creek	285
56	Blamey Fires Potts, Allen	289
57	Kokoda Won; Massacre at Gorari	294
58	Blamey's Rabbits	298
59	Silence of a Mountain Gun	302
60	US Navy's 'No Show'	308
61	The Battle of Brisbane	313
62	Escalation	317
63	Gona: 'Going, Going . . .'	322
64	Tanks for the Advantage	327

Part Six *Battle for Australia 1943*

65	Buna Busted	335
66	Sanananda Sorrow	337
67	War of Opportunity	341
68	The Japanese Keep Coming	345
69	Savige Turn of Events	351
70	Red Herring	355
71	Curtin's Electoral Appeal	360
72	Savige Sets Up Fourth Victory in Papua, New Guinea	363
73	Post-Election Spoils	366
74	More than 'Mopping Up'	369
75	Menzies Thwarted; Finschhafen Sorted	374
76	Sattelberg Breakthrough	377
77	The PM's Many War Fronts	381

Part Seven *Battle for Japan 1944*

78	Reluctant Voyager	387
79	Meeting Roosevelt	391
80	Rendezvous with the Bulldog	395
81	Churchill's Big Distraction	398
82	Checkmate at Chequers	402
83	MacArthur Dumps the Diggers	409
84	The Forgotten POWs	414

85	MacArthur's Farewell; Savige's Way of War	418
86	The Comeback	422
87	Curtin Down; MacArthur Makes Running	426

Part Eight *Japan Defeated 1945*

88	Curtin Recovers	433
89	Borneo Blunders	439
90	Beyond the Call	442
91	Last Call	447

Postscript

92	Japan Capitulates	449

Epilogue

93	At the Centre	459

Notes	466
Bibliography	480
Acknowledgements	485
Index	487

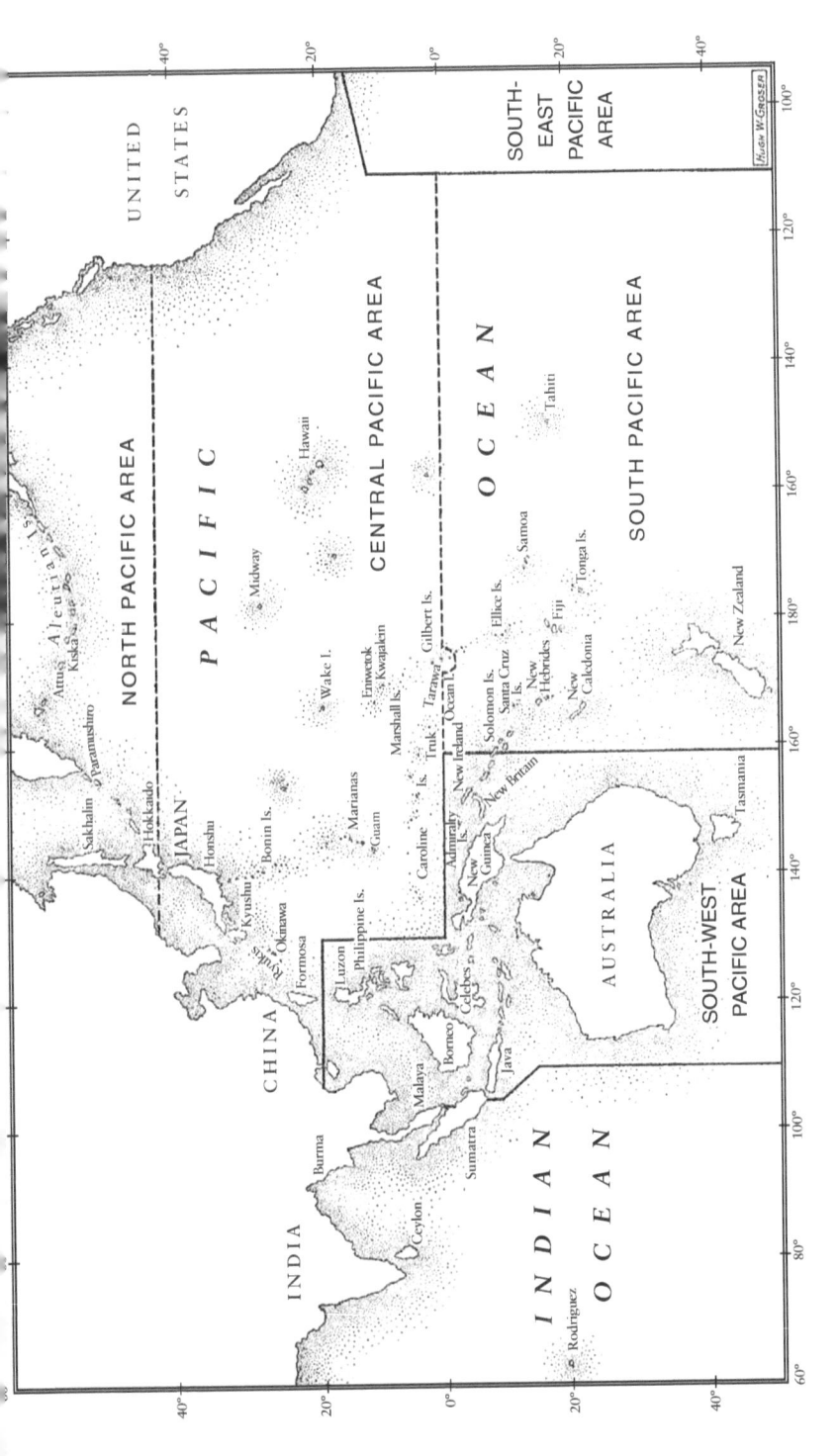

Part One

Japan's Mass Attack
DECEMBER 1941–JUNE 1942

I

Curtin Up

John Curtin was about to slip into the limousine. Prime Minister Arthur Fadden hustled down the steps of Parliament House, gripped Curtin's right hand and shook it. 'In every footy team there's someone on the other side you'd like to have in your team,' Fadden said, 'and as far as I'm concerned, you're the one.'[1]

That pleased Curtin. He liked to be liked. He liked to be fair – too much so for some in his Labor Party. He had handled the slow slide to oblivion of Fadden's forty-day United Australia Party government with patience and resolve. He'd made no grab for power as Australia's conservative political forces disintegrated following Robert Menzies' resignation as prime minister in August 1941. Curtin wanted the natural attrition of the Menzies/Fadden forces to be in full view of the media and public. He wanted Labor to be seen as the only party the people could trust with government at the most critical time in the nation's history.

On 3 October 1941, two independent House of Representatives members, Alex Wilson and Arthur Coles, voted against the Fadden government's Budget Bill. Labor had the numbers to take control of the House and form government. Curtin was its leader.

That night, Curtin was driven to the Governor-General's residence and sworn in as Australia's fourteenth prime minister since federation in 1901. There were big doubts about him, in the nation, in his party and in his own mind. He had an inferiority complex concerning the urbane, eloquent, born-to-rule Robert Gordon Menzies, who had been the nation's leader since 1939. Yet still Curtin felt he was better equipped than Menzies to rule the nation at this time.

Menzies had been close to the British prime minister, Winston Churchill. This made it awkward for him to face down Churchill over certain issues. Prime among these was the situation of two brigades of the Australian 9th Division, which were holed up in Tobruk, Cyrenaica (now Libya), fighting the Germans and Italians. All Australian leaders – from both sides of the political fence – reckoned their soldiers had done far more than enough. They wanted those exhausted troops out of the Tobruk siege. Churchill wished the brigades to stay put.

General Thomas Blamey, the Australian commander in chief, had been ambitious to lead all four of Australia's divisions – the 6th, 7th, 8th and 9th – in battles in the Middle East. His dream had been to emulate General Sir John Monash in World War I. Blamey had been his chief of staff and stood in awe of Monash, the most accomplished commander of that war. He had pulled together Australia's first five divisions and shaped them into the conflict's most powerful and successful army. Blamey saw himself as having the same challenge in World War II.

Blamey's mindset did not allow for defending Australia, as – like Churchill – he believed that any Japanese moves towards Australia would never get past Singapore. Blamey was intent on fighting with the big boys in Europe and the Middle East against the Germans and Italians. Every assessment of just about all Allied commanders in the Pacific and South-East Asian region, including that of the highly regarded Philippines-based US General Douglas MacArthur, downplayed the possibility of a Japanese threat in the region. Japan was already overstretched, most believed, by its invasion of China.

Like Australia's political leaders, Blamey worked hard to pull the two brigades out of Tobruk. But he did not want to return those vital fighting divisions home just in case everyone was wrong about the Japanese. This left Australia isolated and vulnerable.

Curtin would face plenty of problems, domestically and abroad, which would lead him to work up to twenty hours a day. But none would tax him more than the question of Australia's defence. It had also been at the top of Menzies' agenda. Even as Fadden sat at his desk for the last time, not long before Curtin was sworn in as prime minister, he was responding to yet another cable from Churchill, who wanted to keep the diggers in Tobruk. Fadden drafted a reply affirming the Australian position that the brigades would be withdrawn. He showed it to Curtin, who agreed with the wording.

The pugnacious Churchill was a bulldog with a bone of contention. The Australian attitude put more agitation into his step as he paced his war-room bunker deep beneath Whitehall, not far from his official residence at 10 Downing Street. He grumbled to his aides that it would be difficult to extricate the diggers from Tobruk. He complained that Curtin would be trouble. The new Labor PM was a pacifist who had once been jailed during World War I over his opposition to attempts to introduce conscription.

Curtin was a socialist with 'ideals', an irritating rather than dangerous matter for Churchill. He accepted that the Australians were suffering a much higher percentage of casualties than the rest of the Allies in the Middle East. But Churchill looked at the 'big picture', arguing that Australia's contribution to his aim of defeating Adolf Hitler – the overarching strategy for this war – was not so significant.

Churchill had often muttered in private about Australia having 'bad stock' – meaning convicts and Irish. Yet he had witnessed the World War I performance of the Australians at Amiens, 100 kilometres north of Paris. Under John Monash, and aided by the Canadians, they had smashed two German armies in less than forty-eight hours. Monash had been the architect of the success, and Churchill had been the first to congratulate him, aware that his digger army had changed the course of the Great War. Churchill's knowledge of the fighting capacity of this supposed 'poor stock' was one reason he wanted them to remain in defence of Tobruk. Another was to keep Germany's Field-Marshal Rommel distracted in Libya and allow other British forces to be used elsewhere.

Churchill's truculence towards Australia was exacerbated by his hare-brained scheme to fight the Germans in Greece, the so-called 'underbelly' of Europe. Thousands of Australians in the 6th Division had been killed or captured while on the retreat in Crete. Churchill did not care much, but his relations with Australia were at their lowest ebb since the failure at Gallipoli, another ill-prepared campaign he had sponsored that was a catastrophe for the Anzacs, along with the British and French. Churchill's penchant for circumventing the main theatre of war in Western Europe had now led to a terrible waste of men and other resources in two World Wars.

2

Same Peas, Different Pods

Curtin and Churchill had many more character-forming traits in common than they knew. They were both alcoholics. Churchill loved the impact of drink and seemed to thrive on his heavy daily consumption of spirits. It did not seem to influence his desire to work or his capacity to function at his intellectual peak.

When challenged in parliament on his over-imbibing, he remarked, 'All I can say is, that I have taken more out of alcohol than alcohol has taken out of me,' which may have proved true over his lifetime. He had a remarkable constitution. When a female MP accused him of being drunk one afternoon in the House of Commons, Churchill snapped a reply: 'And you, Madam, are ugly. What's more, I shall be sober in the morning.'

He was driven by his emotions, which emanated from quirky, often quixotic inspiration as much as considered strategic and tactical motivations in war, diplomacy and all his working and personal relationships. Yet the moods resulting from his heavy drinking sometimes had chaotic results. Churchill could be engagingly empathetic, solicitous and apparently compassionate. He could also be contradictory, cunning and deceptive. His word could be trusted by some yet not by others. But he was nothing if not consistent in his single-minded effort to defeat Hitler. Every action – futile and fabulous, bumbling and brilliant – was aimed at that goal.

Curtin had a different problem with alcohol. He loved a drink and could usually control his daily consumption. But he had an irresistible desire to binge. In his case, this did not mean a rapid, big-drinking session; rather, Curtin would disappear on benders that might last three days. This was impossible for him in his native Melbourne, where he would be spotted. He preferred Sydney, where he would not be recognised and could drink himself into oblivion.

He felt comfortable and invisible in Sydney. He would go for a weekend with a friend, James Hunter – a conservative MP with the Country Party. Choosing a trusted 'mate' from the other side of politics was important, as Curtin had made pledges to the Labor Party about maintaining his sobriety.[1] Hunter would travel to and from Sydney with him and help Curtin sober up on the train back to Canberra. But Hunter did not appear to have been with the Labor leader on the actual 'bender': Curtin preferred to go alone to pubs he knew.[2] Curtin had promised his wife and key members of his party that he would give away alcohol once in government. But he had made and broken such promises for decades. He was sincere when he said it. Yet no one knew what the pressures of the highest office in the land and the predicament of war would do to Curtin's psyche.

Many reckoned he did not have the constitution for the pressures of the Lodge. He would fall apart in office, some said. It will kill him, others thought. And the booze could accelerate both those possibilities. Curtin's penchant for alcohol had begun when he was in his mid-twenties and Secretary of the Timber Workers' Union in Victoria. Liquid lunches with fellow officials and visiting workers from the bush were mandatory. He rarely missed a day's drinking, even on Sundays, when it was illegal. In July 1911, Curtin was fined a pound when caught drinking on this Christian holy day with brickworkers in Brunswick, Melbourne, at the Union Hotel. It was close to his home and too tempting. The fine did not stop him. He continued to drink there on Sundays, telling his wife he was elsewhere.[3]

Through the years, there were reports of Curtin's long, drunken forays. They threatened his career more than once, and even his life. Big drinking accompanied his campaigning for office.[4] Campaigning brought extra pressures, which drove him even more to the bottle. The Labor Party worried about Curtin but his drinking did not impair his performances, especially on the hustings at rallies and in speeches. Even so, abstinence – which had been suggested both by family and friends and also by Curtin himself – seemed to be a precondition for his taking leadership of the Labor Party in opposition, which he did in 1937.

The need for change was even clearer in October 1941, when Curtin became prime minister, by which time turning away from 'the grog' was an imperative. His health had deteriorated to such an extent that any excesses of drinking and smoking – along with the pressures of leadership, especially in a time of war – would kill him.[5]

Curtin and Churchill would each learn of the other's love of alcohol. No doubt it gave them a certain uncommunicated kinship. But neither would know of the other's manic depression.

Churchill called it his 'black dog': it was an animal that stayed close and meant the darkest of moods. Although it nagged, bothered and bewildered him, his depression could also generate withering energy, bursts of ideas and strong, intelligent, lateral-thinking impulses. Whatever chemical flows this capricious canine released, its results and moments could be exhilarating. It was a part, perhaps a major element of Churchill's political genius, particularly when focused on his great aim of ridding the world of Nazism.

Curtin had no name for his mental condition, but he was aware of it and discussed it with his family, friends and close political contacts. His wife, Elsie, and daughter (also Elsie) attempted to manage his emotional swings. In the down moments they would take him for long walks in the bush or on the beach, or go on a car ride in the country. They removed him from the hustle and bustle, and controlled the 'access' of contacts, the press, parliament and other distractions that could lead to debilitation. To wife Elsie, her husband's depression was not so much a black dog but a more euphemistic 'old bogey'. She said that he was 'coming to terms with it', which was more the observation of a compassionate spouse than a dispassionate psychiatrist.

Before and during the war, it was not only the booze that caused Curtin to isolate himself for days on end. The binge missions would cause him to disappear from view. In moments of depression he would sometimes ensconce himself in a hotel room (and later the Lodge) for up to three days. Those close to him knew where he was but he could not be contacted. Afterwards he would emerge imbued with ideas, inspirations and drive. His mood, too, would be upbeat – gone were the mists of melancholia. He would be jocular and flush with new concepts, determinations and missions, which would flow from him like the Niagara Falls.[6]

Curtin and Churchill had very different attitudes to war. Churchill loved the thrill of combat, taking every chance to report on it – from Cuba to South Africa – and to take part in it – from the Sudan to France. He wrote about it in books and as a correspondent. He fancied himself as a strategist and tactician, but the ill-conceived Dardanelles (Gallipoli) Campaign saw him obliged to leave the War Cabinet, where he had held the post of First Lord of the Admiralty, in 1915. Churchill tried to redeem his image by commanding – reportedly with courage – a battalion of the Royal Scots Fusiliers on the Western Front in World War I. He loved the concept of martial combat, especially if battles won maintained and expanded the British Empire.

Curtin detested war, believing – at least early in his life – it was little more than an excuse for capitalist and imperialist endeavour at the expense of working people. This did not deter him from attempting to enlist in 1915. He realised a loss to Germany, a military dictatorship, would mean the end of democracy in countries of the British Empire and could lead to foreign control or occupation; Australia and Canada, in particular, were juicy targets because of their mineral wealth. But any torment for him was avoided when his poor eyesight disqualified him from active service.

Curtin was not against fighting; rather, he opposed citizens being forced into combat. He struggled against conscription, even going to jail for his cause in 1916, when the Labor prime minister Billy Hughes' efforts to introduce it were twice defeated, in no small measure due to Curtin's protests. In his twenties, he was happy to be called a 'revolutionary socialist', which was a genteel description for communists who were a little insecure about coming out of the closet completely, lest they be seen as totalitarian and anti-democratic. But the fervour for forceful change was nearly but not quite there for young Curtin, especially at the time of the Bolshevik upheaval in Russia in 1917. It inspired all communists and the watered-down version: socialists. He felt strongly about 'revolutionary socialism', where the interests of the worker rather than those of capitalists shaped society.

When addressing a crowd on the bank of the Yarra River in Melbourne, Curtin urged 'rebellion' if conscription were forced on them. This remark earned him a police fine for making a statement 'likely to cause disaffection to His Majesty' and was about as bellicose and militant as Curtin ever got. He had Irish Catholic parents and could not have cared less about offending the British Royals if it meant helping to avoid young men like him being forced against their will into an Imperial war that did not seem to imperil Australia. He believed in the socialist aim to 'control of the means of production and exchange', but he would never have striven for it by means other than the ballot box. A central theme for Curtin was that socialism was the cure-all for society's major ills, particularly poverty and war. It would end them both, he preached.

Churchill and Curtin were both writers and orators. Churchill was educated in England, first at Harrow and later at Sandhurst, the military academy. He was not academic enough for the two top universities of the era, Oxford and Cambridge. He learnt enough Latin at school 'to detest it' but he loved the English language. He was never trained on a newspaper but worked as a war correspondent – from South Africa, Cuba and elsewhere – for top Fleet Street papers. He learned to be tight with copy, and to use less flourish than he would like. He also wrote biographies, fiction and historical works.

As an orator, Churchill penned his own speeches and delivered them with verve – in the House of Commons, on national radio, anywhere. He stuttered but had the will to overcome it. He was never dull. His speech in the Commons on 4 June 1940 will live as long as the English language itself. It lifted everyone who heard or witnessed it, including Curtin, who, like most aware Australians, realised that this European war could soon spread to the Pacific.

Churchill believed in destiny – particularly his. He had the courage, arrogance and conceit to be sure that England, *his England*, would be in peril one day and that he would save her. He confided this to his wife, Clementine, and to close friends. There was no doubt in his mind. Churchill, in his mid-sixties when he became prime minister, would fulfil his life-long sense that he was born to do great things.

This supreme self-confidence spilled over into the British parliament and public. Some admired him for it; others loathed him. But in the 1930s, when leaders were not imbued with great charisma – except for that 'wicked man' Hitler, as Churchill characterised him – Churchill stood out as a curio, a hardliner predicting war, a pugilist with style, a man with the capacity to lead, direct and inspire. His ascension to the prime ministership in May 1940 meant he had the chance to prove himself.

John Curtin, in his own way, was also no slouch as journalist and speaker. His training was at struggling socialist and union papers, hardly in the same league as the grand organs of Fleet Street, yet it was instructive. He would learn to hone sentences and shape themes in a thousand words.

His early prose was wooden and overwrought, but the themes, intent and strength of his guiding ideals were clear. Curtin learned more about the economy of language later, in his editorials at *The Westralian Worker*, where, as editor, he also worked on the copy of others. By the time he was thirty, Curtin could count himself a competent journalist. His thoughts were ordered; his arguments more readable and less rhetorical.

Curtin would never become an attractive writer; the working milieu and his restriction to its socialist aims and ideals were not conducive to developing flair or innovation. But there was another element to his use of language that made him a standout in the Labor movement: his speech-making. Good-looking and tall for the time at about 183 centimetres (six feet), he was well-schooled in oratory by two leading Victorian socialists, Frank Anstey and Tom Mann.

Curtin performed in front of big crowds on the Yarra bank, at street corners and in packed halls and theatres. He was advised to wear stiff collars that would keep his head up, which allowed him to project a strong voice. Anstey and Mann directed him to read Karl Marx, Edward Bellamy and Ramsay MacDonald. None had set the world alight with deathless prose. But they thought originally and stimulated Curtin's fertile young mind to consider how the state and society should be organised and governed. Curtin found their messages more inspiring than religion, which he abandoned, or the Salvation Army, with which he had flirted. Socialism was for him.

Like Churchill, Curtin would have had a sense of *destiny*, a feeling – more intellectual than emotional – that he could one day transform *his* island of Australia. By the 1930s, Curtin had lost his revolutionary zeal, although not his socialist aims. By late 1941, when he was prime minister, a destiny of sorts beckoned, but not the kind he had dreamt of in his twenties. Curtin was now in a position of power and could influence change. But he might have to forsake many of his socialist ideals.

He feared he would again face conscription issues, but that this time he would have to fight for, not against it. He worried he could be embroiled in prosecuting war closer to home. Menzies had declared war against Germany when the United Kingdom did. Curtin dreaded leading in circumstances that would push the nation into a conflict in Asia or the Pacific, where 'the workers' would form the bulk of any Australian armed force. He would rather push for socialist measures that would impact on Australian life. Before that, he would have to be a wartime leader.

3
Wise Council

Curtin's thoughts on where Australia stood in the early war years had been moulded by his experience on the Advisory War Council. Menzies, when prime minister, wanted to have a War Cabinet made up mainly of representatives of the two major parties: the ruling United Australia Party and the Labor Party. This would have given Menzies continuing control of the nation and its path during the war, while keeping the opposition Labor Party under control. Curtin would not agree to this, realising his potency would be reduced in such a situation. Instead, he agreed to join an Advisory War Council. It began on 29 October 1940, with Curtin and three other Labor representatives sitting alongside conservative members, who on most issues would back the British position. Curtin had no power but he did have a voice. More importantly, he was able to assess the thinking of the government at first hand.

Curtin took note of the major influences on this council, which affected the decisions taken by the Menzies government and, in turn, the military. The Chiefs of Staff of the Armed Forces advised the council. Its secretary, the man with most influence, was Frederick Shedden, who was highly regarded by the leaders of both political parties. Shedden had been in favour of the British position, at the expense of the Americans, especially in protecting British interests in the Pacific and Asia. The council's chairman was Arthur Fadden, leader of the Country Party and Menzies' deputy prime minister.

The Advisory War Council's mentality was founded in defending the region through the British base in Singapore. There was no discussion about defending Australia and its interests, which seemed dwarfed by British concerns. Curtin listened and learned, particularly from Shedden. He became less and less convinced of the invulnerability of Singapore, and argued for more troops to be sent there.

In Sydney on 12 February 1941, Curtin told the annual convention of the Australian Workers' Union (AWU) that Australia's plight was 'equally as vulnerable as that of Great Britain'. But the statement didn't create headlines. The Germans had taken Paris; France belonged to Hitler and Britain was there for his taking, if he wanted it. Australia had not been bombed. An attack by Japan was not a threat as yet, only a fear.

Curtin's point was that Australia was undefended. The bulk of its fighting force was a long way from home, defending British Imperial interests. Curtin insisted it was no longer appropriate for Australia to be sending its soldiers abroad. He was not yet advocating that the troops should come home from the Middle East and North Africa, but he did raise the question of who would defend 'this part of the Empire'. This was a broad enough statement not to alarm most of the Advisory War Council or the media; it could have been interpreted to mean Singapore or Australia.

Intelligence from various quarters began predicting that Japan would launch a push southwards. If Japan's military excursions into China were any guide, it would not operate by half-measures. Singapore would be a takeover target. But during the last throes of the Menzies government and Fadden's forty-day interlude, the attention of the council, the military and the government was still focused on North Africa, the Middle East and Greece.

In the latter part of 1941, Major General Gordon Bennett was stationed in Singapore with two brigades (12,000 men) of the Australian 8th Division. He was desperate to have at least two divisions (about 35,000 men) under his command. General Blamey ignored his pleas and flew off to the Middle East. The two had been bitter rivals since before World War I.

Blamey argued that there were 130,000 British military personnel in Malaya and Singapore, which he considered adequate. Bennett's concern was that they were not all fighting men but garrison troops. On top of that, Bennett privately believed that the British and Indian soldiers were not trained or led well enough. He had dealt with the British command and pronounced its members as 'weak'. He feared that the Japanese troops, especially the crack divisions that were having such a devastating impact in China, would be too much for Singapore's defenders.

Bennett had been amongst the bravest frontline troops at Gallipoli and on the Western Front in World War I. He was a forceful commander, imbued with a ruthless, aggressive spirit. He had been described as an 'unconventional' soldier, and indeed he was not conventionally trained: most of his 'training' had been in battle during World War I. Yet most neutral observers regarded him as the best senior military officer in Malaya. According to the Australian war correspondent for *The Times*, Ian Morrison, Bennett could be difficult to deal with and at times lacked diplomacy. A bitter, sarcastic streak did not win him friends. Bennett was fond of speaking his mind, which meant he was offensive on occasions, but few doubted his capacity as a soldier and leader.

Bennett was certain that if he commanded two Australian divisions he would defeat any Japanese force thrown at him. In the treacherous jungle conditions, a couple of brigades or even a complete division was not enough. To Bennett's mind, any battle was about fighting, tactics and will, not mere numbers. But his pleas were blocked by Blamey and some of the regular army command in Melbourne. They may have been schooled in military theory in academies from Duntroon to Sandhurst – and even, in one or two cases, West Point. Yet few had been in battle against a determined enemy. None had led from the front.

Bennett's instincts were more than wary of a Japanese invasion – he expected it. Curtin, without having had any direct contact with Bennett, was coming to a similar conclusion. He argued again for more troops to be sent to Singapore. But the Advisory War Council did not advise the Menzies or Fadden governments to do anything more in Singapore. It was the 'Gibraltar' of the region – as solid as that rock. The focus was still on maintaining the British Empire.

Not long before he became prime minister, Curtin began to broaden his view, especially after speaking to Shedden when he returned from a trip to London. He had spoken to Churchill and come away unsure about Britain's professed commitment to help Australia if Japan attacked southwards. Shedden, who until then had been trenchantly pro-British, was now hedging his bets. He wanted to open Australia to cooperation with the United States. It would mean less need for pleading to Churchill, who seemed disingenuous over the issue.

According to Shedden, Prime Minister Churchill knew the British did not have the military resources to defend the Dutch East Indies, Australia, Hong Kong or any other of its interests, Empire or otherwise, in the 'Far East'. In other words, Churchill was not being honest with the Australian government.

All Allied nations' diplomats, and many of their politicians, were attempting to second-guess Japanese intentions, aims and priorities. General MacArthur in the Philippines still maintained that the Japanese were preoccupied with their war with China, a conflict that had been going on for a decade. The main Japanese army, he argued, was unlikely to be diverted from battle on the Chinese mainland against Chiang Kai-shek's Nationalists and Mao Zedong's Communists.

This prolonged military lunge meant the Japanese were running out of raw materials. Their oil reserves were critical. Their mineral resources had somehow to be replenished, especially if the war with

China went on for another decade, as some in Tokyo were now predicting. The problem of resource supply was exacerbated when US President Franklin D. Roosevelt placed an oil embargo on the Japanese. This was a drastic measure that shocked the Imperial Army, as the United States was by far Japan's biggest oil supplier. Roosevelt was influenced by his Department of State, which had a strong intellectual love for all things Chinese. Now that China was under siege, Japan was very much in US bad books. The embargo pushed the Japanese into a corner. If they wanted to fulfil their expansionist aims, they would have to acquire fuel for their forces from somewhere else. The Dutch East Indies was the nearest main supplier, while South-East Asia, including Australia, held abundant mineral reserves.

In late August 1941, a secret Imperial Conference was held. The generals, with the Emperor's approval, finally decided to attack southwards. Plans for the invasion had to be completed within two months. Japanese diplomats were ordered to attempt to gain drastic concessions from the British and the Dutch, which in effect would have forced them to withdraw from the region. These demands were impossible to meet, and all parties knew it. This left one option: war.

The first signs of Japan's preparations were picked up by Allied intelligence in September 1941, when the Japanese military began easing some of its stock of Class C56 steam locomotives towards its docks for imminent loading onto ships. The locomotives had been adjusted to run on the rail gauges of Burma and Thailand.

4
Tugs of War

One of Curtin's first acts as prime minister was to cable Churchill. He assured him that his Labor Party government would cooperate fully with the British and all governments of the Empire 'in all matters associated with the welfare of [it].'[1] Yet he insisted that the two remaining brigades of the 9th Division at Tobruk be relieved.

Curtin was following the line of Menzies and Fadden. All three Australian leaders had now expressed their fear that Tobruk might be overrun by the enemy and the brigades captured. There were already thousands of prisoners of war in Germany and Austria from the fiascos in Greece and Crete, and Curtin was sleepless at the thought of thousands more being killed or wounded. His feelings were exacerbated by the fact that he had opposed Australian forces going to the Middle East in the first place.

Churchill reacted with predictable anger. This affirmation of the Australian position set him against the new prime minister, and reaffirmed his attitude to socialists: they were half-baked communists, but weaker. Churchill could not override the decisions of a sovereign nation, not even a former colony. Such recalcitrance by Australia was irritating. Pledging allegiance but not complying with the seat of the Empire's aims and wishes was tantamount to betrayal, in Churchill's mind. He didn't see that Curtin was worried for his own island.

Churchill believed that everything should be subsumed for the 'greater good' of defeating Hitler and preserving England and its Empire. It was his obsession. Curtin was nervous about a threat from Japan; despite experts far and wide telling him there was none, his educated instinct was telling him otherwise. Hitler's successes in the Middle East and Europe had to be inspiring another fascist military power in Japan, especially as British forces were so involved a long way from Asia and the Pacific. Singapore was garrisoned, but could it resist a full-on attempt by the Japanese to take it?

Curtin was a natural worrier. His mentality was at odds with the laidback approach of many Australians around him in parliament, the public, even the military. Yet he had a rational, logical mind. When he put his thoughts on paper, he could work through issues with clarity. Like Churchill, he would do everything to protect his island, even if it meant taking troops away from a danger zone, against Churchill's wishes, in anticipation of possibly bringing them home.

Curtin, like everybody else, was impressed by the British prime minister's bulldog spirit. But he had never met Churchill and did not feel beholden to him. Curtin agreed neither with his domestic policies nor his elitist principles. Unlike Menzies, Curtin did not aspire to be like Churchill. Australia was his realm, and that was that. He would not be cowed, bullied, cajoled or swayed by Churchill, especially in cables, where nuance, hyperbole and a persuasive tongue were stripped away and the integrity of a position alone was left.

In the battle of basic needs, Curtin had more integrity than the mercurial Churchill. The British prime minister had to present many faces to many different people and nations. There was the parliament, his constituency, the nation and the United States, which was his prime focus. Then there were all the 'British' nations, including Australia. His presentation to diplomats and government leaders would be different, depending on whether he was cajoling, persuading, intimidating or bluffing. Churchill was also prosecuting war, running the military and influencing other nations' forces.

Curtin's situation was less complicated, although he was always juggling the demands of his union, his party and the nation. Curtin would never dictate to the military. He retained Menzies' choices for military command, unless they proved incompetent. But his prime focus in the weeks after his election was on Australia's increasingly precarious position.

In his second week in power, Curtin made a shrewd political move that signalled his mindset, even if he did not explain his thinking. He offered permission for US aircraft to land in Australia until the war ended, with an extension of at least one year beyond that. This reversed Menzies' protection of British interests: he had not allowed the Americans access, and would not make any such move without British approval.

Curtin did not stop there. He let the United States establish an air route between Hawaii and the Philippines, using bases in Australia and New Guinea. He informed the British of these US/Australian deals *after* they were done, out of courtesy. But the 'mother country' – for the first time – would no longer be consulted about Australian matters. This was not a divorce or separation but rather an act of independence.

It was Curtin's first move as a statesman. Washington's powerbrokers took note. It could do business with this new man 'down under'.

Churchill always sought the grand political gesture. He thought he had made a more than useful one by ordering a most reluctant Admiralty (the chiefs preferred restricting their war to the Atlantic) to send a naval squadron, commanded by Admiral Sir Thomas Phillips, to Singapore. It consisted of the battleship HMS *Prince of Wales* – the pride of the fleet – the World War I battlecruiser HMS *Repulse*, and the aircraft carrier HMS *Indomitable*.

The *Indomitable* did not live up to its name. It ran aground in the Caribbean on its maiden voyage and could not go to Singapore. Churchill was not too fussed. He reckoned the other two big ships would be enough to put the Japanese on notice – even perhaps deter them – and would also appease Curtin. But the importance of the loss of the *Indomitable* did not escape the Japanese. If there were an armed conflict, the other two British vessels would now be unprotected from air attacks, on which the Japanese relied.

Churchill kept up his diplomatic offensive, sending his envoys into the public eye in Singapore. First there was the Far East Commander in Chief, Air Chief Marshal Sir Robert Brooke-Popham, whom Menzies described in his 1941 diary as follows: 'He has borne with the white man's burden from Kenya to Canada and it has left his shoulders a little stooped. His hair and moustache are both sandy and wispy and a little indeterminate.'

Churchill's second envoy was his good friend Duff Cooper, a British Minister of State. In September 1941, Churchill had appointed him Resident Cabinet Minister in Singapore to coordinate Britain's military and political position in the Far East. Cooper, a statesman, soldier, MP and diplomat, was one of those floating emissaries of Britain's powerful elite. He knew everyone who mattered in politics and society. He was a political party animal, and also simply a party animal. Cooper had been a first-hand participant in just about every significant political development that had occurred since 1914.

Cooper and Brooke-Popham were photographed, seen on Movietone newsreels and interviewed about the state of play in the Far East. Their message in every utterance was that there had been a 'great strengthening' of Singapore's defences. Again, this was meant to give the Japanese pause and reassure Curtin.

Brooke-Popham flew on to Melbourne and fronted the Advisory War Council on 16 October 1941. He 'informed' the attentive audience that 'for the next three months she [Japan] would not be able to undertake a large-scale attack in the south'. Reference to nations in the feminine was common, but the Englishman overdid 'she' in referring to Japan, as if this somehow softened 'her' image. Japan was more concerned with the 'north', another euphemism. China wasn't mentioned by name, but that was where 'she' was currently dallying.[3]

The Council was not necessarily reassured. Curtin was now its dominant figure, and Brooke-Popham was questioned hard. There was less diplomacy and more discussion in the Council than there had been under Menzies and Fadden. Both those men were still members but the circumstances had changed. Shedden's scepticism about Britain's intentions had infected the new government's approach. The 79-year-old Billy Hughes, now leading the UAP, asserted himself with blunt queries. Herbert 'Doc' Evatt, the Labor government's foreign minister, was no less direct: under what conditions would the British declare war on Japan? Brooke-Popham hedged a response. What if the Dutch East Indies (Indonesia), with its oil reserves, was attacked? Now the reply was evasive.

When asked about the current state of Singapore's defences, Brooke-Popham was more forthcoming. 'Be assured that the Chiefs of Staff are not neglecting the Far East,' he said. 'Malaya is growing from strength to strength, Burma too. Hong Kong is being reinforced with four to six battalions.'[4]

The mere reference to the 'Far East' – coming from an Englishman who would rather be back in Europe – made the Australians fidgety. The so-called 'Far East' was their 'Near North'. It reinforced their sense of isolation. They were leading a nation of, some would say, seven million misplaced Europeans in a region of more than a billion Asians. One powerful, militaristic nation had become hostile. Europeans were symbolic of white imperialism, which Japan's more vitriolic extreme right would not hesitate in ridding from the region, one way or the other.

It was now Duff Cooper's turn to make anodyne noises in Australia. He went to the Melbourne Cup, expressing mild surprise – but also appreciation – that the nation 'stopped' for a horse race. In Canberra, Curtin paused a Cabinet meeting to listen to the race, having bet on its three Western Australian horses (all were unplaced). On 7 November, Cooper was in Canberra. He too met with the Advisory War Council and reiterated that the British government was prepared to abandon the Mediterranean altogether 'if this were necessary' to hold Singapore.

The peppery Billy Hughes was unconvinced. He had never been enamoured of Churchill and was unimpressed by the smooth, urbane Cooper. Hughes had dealt with the British during and after World War I and had never felt comfortable with their diplomats, especially when it came to comprehending the 'truth' of an issue. Hughes did not call Cooper a liar; that was not his way. Instead, he claimed that British public opinion would never allow the fleet to leave the Mediterranean to defend Singapore.

This was a quaint way of calling Duff's bluff. Hughes knew that Churchill and Cooper would have a feel for public opinion – which really meant the media. They knew that no such move would ever be taken.

Menzies showed similar scepticism in a different way. He admitted that Churchill had always told him of the importance of Singapore, but doubted whether Churchill was 'fully seized with the significance' of the current situation. Menzies was closer to the heart of the British prime minister's attitude. Churchill just did not 'get' it. He was stubborn in his belief that Singapore was impregnable. He *wanted* this to be the case and therefore believed it. It was an irritation for Churchill to have to concern himself with it. Yet despite his dismissiveness, he realised that a Japanese attack would be near-catastrophic for his Empire in the Southern Hemisphere.

Curtin was more placatory. He told Cooper that 'Australia feels it is imperative that there should be a strong battleship force at Singapore. It's the core of the whole problem.' That no doubt pleased Cooper. Churchill was sending two mighty ships. They would arrive at Singapore early in December. The 'problem' – or at least the diplomatic argument between Britain and Australia – would settle down then.⁵

Cooper and Brooke-Popham's unspoken aim was to dissuade Australia from taking its three divisions out of the Middle East. From that perspective, their diplomatic mission had been accomplished. Curtin told parliament that his government did not plan to recall the divisions from the Middle East. The blimpish deputy prime minister and Minister for the Army Frank Forde informed the media that the government was still sending an armoured (tank) division to the Middle East.

However, the courage of the War Cabinet's collective will was noted when General Blamey, in charge of Australia's force in the Middle East, was refused the transfer of the 8th Division to Cairo. It was a temporary measure, Blamey was told, because of the situation in the Far East. His ambition to control the bulk of the Australian force abroad remained on hold.

5
The Sinking of Innocence

On 19 November 1941, the German raider *Kormoran* was sailing north in the Indian Ocean, 280 kilometres south-west of Carnarvon, Western Australia. At 4 p.m. it encountered a bigger Australian light cruiser, the HMAS *Sydney*. The *Kormoran*'s Commander Theodor Detmers altered course and built to full speed, while setting the ship at action stations. As the two ships came closer, the Australian cruiser, skippered by Joseph Burnett, requested that *Kormoran* identify itself. The German ship prevaricated. The *Sydney* persisted, and after some delay, the *Kormoran* gave the call-sign for a civilian ship – a Dutch merchant – and hoisted an ensign.

The ruse drew the *Sydney* closer. It asked for a clearer signal. The *Kormoran* obliged, lengthening its halyard and swinging it around to starboard to face the oncoming *Sydney*. The Australian ship now asked where the *Kormoran* was bound. The response was 'Batavia' (Jakarta), which fitted with the claim to be Dutch. Further questions received more deception about the ship's port of origin ('Fremantle') and cargo ('piece-goods'). The German ship was well prepared, deceiving the Australians at every turn and breaking all the accepted 'rules' of naval engagement on the high seas.

Other exchanges were made. The *Kormoran* sent out further confusing messages, including the deception that it was a merchantman under attack. Still Captain Burnett did not seem to smell a rat. His ship was positioned just off the raider's starboard beam, on a parallel course about 1300 metres away. The *Sydney* may not even have been at 'action stations', although the Germans believed (or later claimed) that the main guns and port torpedo launcher were aimed at them. Commander Detmers warned his crew to prepare to engage.

At 5.30 p.m. after the German ship had failed to respond for fifteen minutes, the *Sydney* signalled it should show its 'secret sign'. It refused. Detmers ordered his *Kormoran* crew to reveal its true identification. Up went the German ensign. Its guns and torpedoes were ordered to fire, just as the *Sydney* did the same. The two blasted away with multiple salvos. One of the German torpedoes struck the weakest part of the *Sydney*'s hull and tore a hole in the ship's side. The *Sydney*'s bow angled down with this mortal wound. Burnett directed the ship hard to port. Detmers thought the Australians might be attempting to ram them, but the *Sydney* passed behind the raider. The Germans let fly with a tenth salvo, doing more damage to the stricken larger vessel.

The entire battle had been going just five minutes and was effectively over. The *Sydney* limped away southwards, its momentum diminishing. Its main weaponry was out of action and its secondary arms were out of range. Fire had broken out in various parts of the ship. The *Kormoran* stopped its salvos, but kept firing its aft guns and scoring hits.

At 5.45 p.m., fifteen minutes into the battle, Detmers made a decision: he would destroy the *Sydney* completely. He ordered the *Kormoran* to turn to port so that four gun salvos could be fired. The manoeuvre was fortuitous for the Germans. It took the raider away from the line of two of the *Sydney*'s torpedoes. Just as the raider completed its turn, its engines failed. It stopped dead in the water. The *Sydney* went on sailing south at ever-reducing speed. The stationary raider kept firing at it. More than 450 shells hurtled at the broken *Sydney*. Maybe half of them hit home. By 5.50 p.m. the *Sydney* was out of range at six kilometres. Detmers launched a final torpedo at 6 p.m. It missed its target.

The battle had lasted just half an hour. The ships were now ten kilometres apart. Both were ablaze and damaged. At 6.25 p.m. Detmers ordered his crew to abandon ship, and 317 of the *Kormoran*'s crew of 397 made it to life rafts and were rescued.

The *Sydney* drifted on for nearly another six hours, its fires visible to the Germans until midnight. The ship lost buoyancy and sank upright. Its bow was torn off as it submerged and descended almost vertically. The rest of the hull glided 500 metres forward as it sank, hitting the bottom stern first. No one survived. 645 personnel were lost. It was Australia's worst naval disaster.[1]

Kormoran sank at about the same time as the *Sydney*, when a mine hold exploded about thirty minutes after midnight.

When the *Sydney* failed to arrive at Fremantle on 23 November 1941, wireless communications stations there sent out signals asking it to report in. Soon all high-power stations in Australia joined in. There was no response and the worst was feared; all ships in the area were sent out to search.

The British tanker *Trocas* rescued twenty-five of the *Kormoran*'s crew in a liferaft. They were interrogated. The Germans told of the fearsome naval battle with an Australian ship, which was assumed to be the *Sydney*. The Australian Naval Board was informed on the afternoon of 24 November. It contacted John Curtin's office.

The loss of the *Sydney* was a massive shock to Curtin. People close to him wondered how he would cope. He felt the pain of all those families who had lost loved ones and couldn't summon the strength to tell Elsie.

Ever selfless, Curtin found a way to blame himself. The *Sydney*'s departure from Sydney had been delayed by industrial trouble. Curtin indulged in self-accusation. His softness with unionists had always been a worry. What if he had been tougher with them? The *Sydney* would have left on time and may have avoided the attack.

This thought distressed Curtin so much that he went to see his one close non-Australian confidant: Lord Gowrie, the British Governor-General. Curtin confessed that he did not have the nerve to make the public announcement about the probable loss of the entire crew. 'I couldn't bear to think of the shock the news would bring to relatives and friends of the crew,' he told Gowrie.

Gowrie advised him to say nothing. Many German survivors from the *Kormoran* had been rescued. There was a fair chance that some of the much larger crew of the Australian ship would also be found.[2]

Pressure mounted on Curtin. The media wanted statements. Rumours circulated. Crew-members' next of kin were sent the customary telegrams informing them that the sailors were 'missing as a result of enemy action'. Navy censors advised the media that no announcements about *Sydney* would be allowed.

On 30 November 1941, six days after he had learned of the *Sydney* disaster and eleven days after it had happened, Curtin forced himself to make the official announcement of the *Sydney*'s loss. The newspapers could now publish the depressing news. Radio stations were ordered to wait forty-eight hours to avoid alerting other German ships off the Western Australian coast. Three Melbourne stations broke the embargo and were suspended for a short time.

The media was slow to comprehend what Curtin and his government knew: for the first time, Australia itself – rather than Australian servicemen abroad – was very close to war.

An atmosphere of gloom pervaded Australia. Those who dared to examine the facts thought that Germany, Japan and their Axis allies were likely to win the war. France had fallen eighteen months earlier, and now almost all of continental Europe was controlled by Axis powers, by their allies (Hungary, Bulgaria and Vichy France) or by countries allegedly 'friendly' to them, such as Spain, Finland and Sweden. The German Luftwaffe had pounded England. The Nazis had invaded Russia in June 1941 in the largest military operation in history – a giant *Blitzkrieg*. The Germans had driven easily across Ukraine. They had taken its capital, Kiev, surrounded Leningrad and were at the gates of Moscow.

Reports and rumours of all this were reaching Canberra, Australia's isolated bush capital. In the Pacific theatre, Japan now controlled Korea, Vietnam and much of northern and coastal China. The Chinese army seemed near collapse, and the Japanese were winning every battle, short or prolonged. Some observers were saying Chinese armed resistance would collapse by early in 1942, helped along by near civil war between the Chinese Nationalists and Communists. Millions of Chinese had already died in the fighting or because of Japanese atrocities over the past four years. Millions more were refugees. Famine and disease were rampant. There seemed few reasons to believe that the Japanese would not conquer China. India was also in their sights.

By late November 1941, intelligence assessments indicated that Japan's intention was to attack somewhere in the Pacific and South-East Asia. Curtin had befriended the Japanese ambassador to Australia, Tatsuo Kawai, but it is unlikely that Kawai would have been privy to the first Japanese campaign of military conquest in the Pacific. Given that the strategies of Japan's navy and army often opposed one another, disputing where, when and why campaigns should proceed, diplomats were generally the last to know. Kawai probably had no idea that the first operational stage had been planned to halt short of New Guinea but to take nearby New Britain and New Ireland, which were Australian territories mandated by the League of Nations. This strategy had been the brainchild of Admiral Shigeyoshi Inoue, Commander of the 4th Fleet, or South Seas Force, which was based in the Carolina Islands, Japanese-mandated territory.

Inoue was the first to warn the Japanese Naval General Staff that it would be in trouble if the Americans were allowed to establish bases in Australia and New Guinea. He urged an offensive against Australia and the British Solomon Islands to prevent the United States from having bases for a counter-offensive against Japan. The Imperial headquarters saw the merit in his advice and added New Britain and New Ireland to their shopping list of Pacific targets, which already included Guam and Wake Island in the northern Pacific.

Unaware of these schemes, Ambassador Kawai tried to reassure the Australian prime minister that Japan was not hostile to Australia or any of its territories. Curtin weighed this against the judgement of his sources in London – two former Australian prime ministers, Earle Page and High Commissioner to Britain Stanley Bruce. Curtin had been happy to leave them in their roles. They were reliable, although Bruce was unpopular with Churchill, who regarded him as an 'appeaser and a busybody'.

The main reason for Churchill's dislike was Bruce's sometimes brusque criticism of him and how he was running the war. Bruce was not alone in calling for a new British war cabinet; he believed Churchill held too much power and did not consult enough on wartime policies and decisions. Bruce had never been impressed by Churchill since the grand misadventure in Gallipoli, where Bruce was a British war hero, winning the Military Cross.

Page was held in no higher regard than Bruce. The British Cabinet was unimpressed by his input and comments. He was called a 'windbag'. Yet this did not detract from the two Australians' capacity to pass on intelligence to Curtin. His two representatives missed little, and their information kept Curtin happy enough.[3]

Intelligence also came from Washington DC, from another reliable diplomat, Richard 'Dick' Casey, who had the ear and confidence of Roosevelt and Churchill. Casey, the son of a businessman, had served on the staff of Colonel William Bridges (the commander of Australia's 1st Division) at Gallipoli, and later under General Monash at the Western Front in Europe. Casey's polished mien and skills made him one of Australia's most impressive diplomats. In 1940 he was appointed Australia's Ambassador to the United States, where he befriended Roosevelt. Curtin could rely on Casey being more adept than any other diplomat in Washington at supplying accurate, insider intelligence on the White House and the Pentagon.

Curtin wanted to remain optimistic. The thought of all-out war with Japan was too depressing to contemplate, especially so soon after the horrible experience with the *Sydney* and the *Parramatta*. He could take some comfort from information supplied by US Military Intelligence, which had cracked the codes of the Japanese Embassy: there was no indication of any imminent attack. The United States was also working on Japan's naval codes.

Deciphering them might tell a different story.

6
Mass Attack

The surprise attacks planned by the Japanese would begin in Thailand, with the main targets being Malaya and Singapore. These air and land offensives on 7 December 1941 would be followed by a further mauling of the US fleet at Pearl Harbor, Hawaii.

Lieutenant General Tomoyuki Yamashita commanded the 25th Army, which sailed from Hainan Island on 4 December. He was a bull-necked, forceful character who would not have looked out of place at a sumo wrestling tournament. Like Gordon Bennett, he had a ruthless streak and was an unabashed risk-taker. Unlike Bennett, however, Yamashita had never commanded in battle, having only led military missions to Italy and Germany between the wars. He was a good student of war and could not wait to pit himself against the British.

Additional Japanese troopships sailed from Saigon in southern Vietnam – French Indochina – which was now a forced Japanese 'ally' due to France's capitulation to Germany. A British Lockheed Hudson aircraft spotted the invasion force on 6 December, as did a Catalina sea plane the next day. The Catalina shadowed the Japanese ships but was shot down, making Flying Officer Bedell and his crew the first casualties of the South-East Asian Pacific war with Japan.

The news of Japanese troop movements reached Curtin in Melbourne and froze him there on the night of Sunday, 7 December. Instead of taking the overnight train to Canberra, where he would be less in touch, he stayed put, anticipating news that would help him ascertain if Japan was going to war or posturing.

He pulled together his closest government confidants: Evatt, Chifley, Forde and Shedden. They gathered among the 'cluttered palms, aspidistras and thick cigarette smoke' in the modest sitting room of Curtin's suite at the Victoria Palace Hotel. The group sat close to a telephone manned by Shedden. After a long wait, it rang. He was given more details about the Japanese moves. They had landed five ships on the east coast of Malaya.[1]

Yamashita carried out a two-pronged attack. He landed the 5th Division on the east coast of Thailand at Pattina and Songkhla. Troops from the 18th Division hit the north-east coast of Malaya, at Kota Bharu. The forces in Thailand were to push through to the west coast and invade Malaya from its north-western province of Kedah. At the same time, the 18th Division would move down Malaya's east coast and into the interior from Kota Bharu.

The British were aware of the Japanese moves. They had a plan – Operation Matador – to destroy the invasion before and during its landing. But Air Marshal Brooke-Popham hesitated to launch it, fearing that the Japanese were trying to provoke a British strike that would give them an excuse to go to war.

The Americans had asked all Allied commanders in the Pacific, including the British, to let the Japanese make the first overt attack. This was a directive from Roosevelt, who wanted a genuine excuse to go to war with Japan. The president believed that if the American public (through the media) believed the United States was the initial aggressor, then they would be less inclined to support the government's military actions.

Brooke-Popham also worried about invading neutral Thai territory. But his lame excuses, caution and desire to play by 'Marquis of Queensberry rules' against an enemy that ignored them proved fatal. The Japanese moved easily towards their planned sweep into Malaya. Their dual moves to the east coast had to be met by the Indian 9th Infantry Division defending fixed beach positions on Malaya's northern coastline. Gordon Bennett's two brigades of the 8th Division would defend the southern coastline.

Yamashita's attacks on Malaya had been underway for half an hour when 353 planes from six Japanese battleships began a two-hour bombardment of an unsuspecting US naval base at Pearl Harbor. Across the international dateline it was a lazy, early Sunday morning on 7 December. There was no concern at first. Onlookers, many going to church, thought it was some sort of large-scale practice run. When eighteen US warships were hit, the Americans knew the attack was real. Those ships were sunk, 188 aircraft were destroyed and 2043 service personnel were killed.

Raw statistics did not reflect the US reaction. The Japanese had affronted this somnolent world power; it had shocked and shaken the American psyche, which pleased everyone wanting the US to fight in the world conflict. The public could now be manipulated into supporting America's entry. This would be backed by an odd collection of American bedfellows from communists who wanted to side with the Russians, conservatives who believed the United States had to stamp its authority on the world, and just about everyone in between. There would be dissent, but it would be minor and ineffectual.

Funding for the US military effort would run into difficulties, but there would be ways to overcome them. The propaganda would always point to the brutality of Japan smashing and killing on American soil. Bold – perhaps foolhardy – Japan had made the most significant move in the world conflagration to that point.

The Australian government's shortwave radio monitoring service picked up news of the Pearl Harbor attacks early on Monday 8

December. Curtin was woken up at 5.45 a.m. in his suite at the Victoria Palace. He was neither panicky nor profane; he was ready. 'Well, it has come,' he remarked.

Curtin would go through a range of emotions. The phony war had ended. Japan had hit British, American and neutral Thai territory. On one level, he had to be pleased that Churchill and Roosevelt would now comprehend his fears. On another level, it chilled him. Japan had made ferocious attacks on China and the United States; it was clear that they would have no qualms about making an aggressive move on Australia.

Curtin adhered to 'process'. He sent a telegram to Bruce, to let King George VI know that, acting on advice from his (the King's) Australian Ministers (that is, Curtin and Co.), he (George VI) was at war with Japan. This was regardless of whether another set of Ministers in the United Kingdom wanted their Monarch so disposed towards Japan. Curtin wasted no time in making a national radio broadcast. He would declare war on Japan without consulting it or the United Kingdom and the United States. He had jumped in before Churchill, asserting his nation's independence which was a break from the past.

'Men and women of Australia,' he began in his nasally yet strong twang, 'we are at war with Japan.' He thumped down hard on the second syllable when mentioning the aggressor.

> *That has happened, because, in the first instance, Japanese naval and air forces launched an unprovoked attack on British and United States territory; because our vital interests are imperilled; and because the rights of free people in the whole Pacific are assailed... We do not want war in the Pacific... I point out that the hands of the democracies are clean ... For the first time in the history of the Pacific, armed conflict stalks abroad. No other country but Japan desired war in the Pacific. The guilt for plunging this hemisphere into actual warfare is therefore upon Japan ...*

Curtin concluded:

> *We here, in this spacious land, where for more than 150 years, peace and security have prevailed, are now called upon to meet the*

external aggressor. The enemy presses from without . . . We shall hold this country and keep it as a citadel for the British-speaking race and as a place where civilisation will persist.

This was Curtin's equivalent of Churchill's 'never surrender' speech. It was less flamboyant, more politically precise and pregnant with barely veiled messages. Reference to 'the British-speaking race' was more about skin colour than language. It was in keeping with the unifying concept of the 'White Australia Policy', which had been part of Labor's platform since Federation. In more prosaic terms, he was saying that Asia's 'yellow hordes' would not touch his nation's fair complexion. The underlying message was for the United States and United Kingdom as much as Australia.

Curtin would have shown this speech to Evatt, Chifley and Shedden for comment. Evatt, a former High Court judge, would always be argumentative as if he were in court. He was never the diplomat. His approach came across as combative in cables, his intermittent influence over Curtin's communications, and the way he bullied others, particularly those in the employ of Foreign Affairs (his portfolio) abroad. Curtin had often apologised for Evatt and his behaviour. He regarded him as clever but unpredictable, once telling Paul Hasluck that Evatt needed 'watching' because he could still 'do good things for Australia'.[2] Curtin often leaned on Evatt for a diverse view, particularly when it came to legal matters.

This speech, however, was distinctively Curtin's in mentality and style. Speech-writing was not a chore or bore, but a part of his profession as a journalist/politician. The business of writing lifted him, refining his thoughts, clearing his mind and making him stronger. The raw emotions had come from within; its honed words were their vehicle. This speech was the most important of his life so far, the culmination of his decades of working on his journalism, his political career and himself. Many observers, especially among the press, whom he cultivated as if he were just a marginally elevated paid-up member of their union, judged that this was the day that John Curtin began to grow into his job.

The nation's leading political reporters were called to a conference in the hotel lobby. They were able to assess the leader at the most critical moment of his short tenure as prime minister. 'Curtin's demeanour throughout was calm,' *Smith's Weekly* reported.

> *He dealt with his interviewers as one journalist to others. [The] PM has not forgotten his early training. He had his information ready. Pithily he told of Cabinet's decisions. Proceedings were as calm as a round table chat on some subject of no great importance. That's John Curtin's way. When another man might be theatrically dramatic on such an occasion, he is himself . . . [He] spoke freely . . . It was 6.15 p.m. when the interview finished. 'See you tomorrow, boys,' John Curtin said casually. Then he pulled down his soft, black felt hat and went to his dinner.*[3]

This was typical of the reporting. Lots of padding and 'colour'. Curtin had given the journalists nothing except an impression. Yet it was favourable. The Canberra press men agreed that he was rejuvenated, and they were close to him in an era when the media – mainly newspaper reporters – mingled daily and nightly with politicians. Canberra was a lonely country town where these two professions interacted as mates or enemies in close proximity. Characters were exposed. There was nowhere to hide.

There was no spin in the press gallery's assessment. It just wanted to be brought into the top person's confidence regarding the real world situation, as far as he knew it. Curtin was not quite ready to do this so soon after the Pearl Harbor attack, which had not yet even been evaluated by the two biggest players on the Allied side: Churchill and Roosevelt.

If he had time for reflection at that moment, Curtin might have considered destiny had been cruel to him. This anti-war, anti-conscription, anti-capitalist, anti-Imperial leader now had to embrace these things he opposed. It had been easy for Churchill; he supported them all. He always believed in his destiny. Curtin would take on the new challenges but with a knotted stomach each time. On top of this, his nation was unprepared for its plight, although it had been predicted by many – including Curtin – for years.

Curtin now discovered Australia's true state of unpreparedness for the war he had just announced, and an unexpected invasion. Part of the Australian militia was ordered to camps in major cities. Waiting for them were only half the numbers of machine guns and anti-tank weapons needed. Australia was producing about 200 Vickers machine guns a month, but more than half of these were contracted to go to the Indian Army. Nor were there enough artillery pieces or rifles. The Chief of the General Staff, Lieutenant General Vernon Sturdee, demanded more. Curtin had to tell him to make a plea to the Indians.

Militia personnel in areas considered less likely to be in any immediate action (Tasmanians, for instance) were told they had to do without weapons for the moment. Many farmers around the country had their own rifles, and of their own volition were buying ammunition. They were preparing for an attack. Australia had no tanks, except six trainers. They had no heavy bombers like those on production lines in Europe and the United States. There were no fighter planes such as those rushed into production in England for the Battle of Britain and the defence of the airways after it. Australia would remain unable to repulse similar waves of attacks. To make matters more desperate, Australian pilots were being trained to fight for the Royal Air Force in Europe, leaving the Royal Australian Air Force severely depleted.

On top of this was one bald fact that now chilled Curtin, his government and the services chiefs. Their entire home force was no more than a couple of brigades – about 10,000 soldiers. In theory, Australia was supposed to have up to seven divisions, totalling about 250,000 soldiers; in reality, in terms of mustering for an all-out war in Australia, it could produce four fighting divisions. They were all overseas. The 6th, 7th and 9th were in the Middle East, and heavily 'engaged'. The 8th was primarily in Malaya, with its third brigade proving a phantom for its commander, Bennett. He was not even told that it had been scattered to islands north of Australia until he went in search of it.

And then there was Blamey. When the debated merits of his capacities were set aside, he was Australia's most powerful and influential soldier. But his mindset, even when Japan attacked Pearl Harbor, was still in making his reputation with all Australia's top divisions 6th, 7th, 9th and the now isolated parts of the 8th – 20,000 kilometres away, in the Middle East and possibly Europe. He still wanted to be the new Monash. But he was slow to realise that there would be now a major problem at home: war on Australia's front doorstep.

It was 'amateur hour' as far as all arms of the Australian military were concerned, especially if Japan turned the attention of any of its heavily armed, trained and experienced divisions, backed by massive air cover, towards the Great South Land. Curtin did not immediately appeal to have the 6th, 7th and 9th Divisions brought home from the Middle East. He too had yet to fully grasp the dimensions of Australia's sudden, naked isolation.

The Japanese also attacked the Philippines on 8 December 1941, just ten hours after the Pearl Harbor raids. First they bombarded the capital, Manila, from the air. There had been plenty of warning time, but General MacArthur, the American in command of the Philippines military, erred by not ordering his air force aloft or away from the undefended airport. The result was the smashing of most of the planes, including a B-17 Bomber force. MacArthur's second blunder was his failure to stockpile food, ammunition and medical supplies for a retreat to the Bataan Peninsula, which had been planned for some time. His aim was to hold out until saved by the US Navy. But the twelve Filipino divisions he had built up since basing in Manila in 1935 were overwhelmed by the Japanese ground troops who invaded from the north and south of Manila.

Douglas MacArthur was highly regarded in Washington DC, sometimes for the wrong reasons, by friend and foe alike. The incident that drew out his true character occurred in the summer of 1932, when 25,000 penniless World War I veterans and their families, calling themselves the Bonus Expeditionary Force (BEF), camped in Washington DC and petitioned the government to pay them a cash 'bonus'. It was during the heart of the depression. MacArthur, then the Chief of Staff of the US Army, took a hard line towards them. He declared the BEF members 'fakes'. But they were not: ninety-four per cent of them had army or navy records, and some had even fought under MacArthur himself in World War I.

President Herbert Hoover wanted the BEF evicted, and MacArthur wanted to please his Republican commander in chief. He took personal charge of destroying the camps. He put on his uniform, including his medals, and ordered the infantry, tanks and cavalry under Major George S. Patton Jr. to line up around the Washington Monument.

One staff member, Major Dwight D. Eisenhower, urged restraint and pleaded with MacArthur not to take charge of the eviction. 'It will offend congressmen,' Eisenhower warned him. 'That will make [getting] approval of military budgets that much harder.'

President Hoover was worried about his public image; unlike MacArthur, he did not want his administration tarred with the opprobrium of an armed attack on former soldiers' tents and shacks. Hoover directed that there would be no assault on the BEF camp. He sent two of his staff to inform MacArthur.

MacArthur brushed the messengers aside, demonstrating breathtaking arrogance and a reckless disregard for anyone with superior power. 'I am too busy,' he told them, 'I don't want me or my staff being bothered by people coming down pretending to bring orders.'

Before Hoover could prevent him, MacArthur led his men across the river and ordered the camp burned. Two babies were killed by tear gas. Many veterans were injured. After the camp was razed, MacArthur, the master of press manipulation, called a conference at midnight. His blatant insubordination turned brazen. MacArthur said the responsibility for evicting the BEF had been the president's. He then praised Hoover for it.

Not long after this incident, Franklin D. Roosevelt, then Governor of New York but soon to be the next US president, told an advisor he believed MacArthur was one of the two most dangerous men in America. (The other, Roosevelt said, was Huey Long, Louisiana's populist governor.) Roosevelt once told MacArthur, 'Douglas, I think you are our best general. But I believe you would be our worst politician.'

When Roosevelt became president in 1933, he worked to harness MacArthur's military capacities and to curtail his political ambitions, especially those concerning the presidency. In mid-1941 Roosevelt put him on the US Army's active list as Commander of United States Forces in the Far East, with the rank of lieutenant general. It was in theory a demotion. MacArthur had been on the Philippines' payroll thanks to the largesse of a friend, President Manuel Luis Quezon, who grandiosely made him a field marshal, a rank no American has held before or since.

After the Japanese assault on the Philippines, there was no hope of MacArthur living up to such a title. But he did have an exit strategy for himself, his family and his staff. It was one plan that he would make every effort to get right.

7
Blow to the Admiralty

While Curtin was considering his limited options, should the Japanese decide to invade Australia too, the Royal Navy's Admiral Phillips had reached Singapore with his fleet. He evaluated the Japanese action on 8 December 1941 and decided to intercept a second wave of enemy landing ships. He sailed off with the *Prince of Wales*, the *Repulse* and four destroyers – the HMS *Electra*, the *Express*, the *Tenedos* and the HMAS *Vampire* – to hunt down the Japanese, who had struck Malaya and Thailand from three points almost simultaneously.

The Japanese planned to ambush Phillips' British fleet when it was without air cover. Phillips had been unperturbed by the inability of the HMS *Indomitable* to join his convoy and provide protection from above. He had long believed such air support was superfluous, but his thinking was mired in World War I strategy. An enemy submarine, the *I-65*, spotted the British fleet as it returned to Singapore, steaming right into the net. Japanese aircraft and submarines tailed the fleet.

At 11 a.m. on 10 December, nine enemy planes were sighted at 10,000 feet, flying in single file along the length of the battlecruiser *Repulse*. A bomb hit the catapult deck and exploded in a hangar. Fire broke out below decks. Fifteen minutes later, Phillips radioed the RAF for assistance. At 11.20 a.m. the *Prince of Wales* was hit by one bomb and four torpedoes, knocking out the ship's propellers and rudder. An hour later RAF air protection had still not arrived, and both ships were in serious trouble as they were smashed by bombs and torpedoes. The *Prince of Wales* flooded. Its power was cut. It began to sink. Its strong hull allowed it to stay afloat for an hour, leading to many being saved, but not Admiral Phillips or Captain Leach, who went down with the ship, perhaps by choice. The *Repulse* fared worse and sank quickly. The trailing four destroyers saved 2081 lives, but 326 men on the two ships were lost.

There was a final, tragic irony. Just as the *Prince of Wales* went under the waterline, RAF planes appeared on the horizon. Admiral Phillips' carelessness about air cover had brought about his own and the *Prince of Wales*' demise. The Japanese had now disposed of the only Allied battleship and battlecruiser in the Pacific Ocean west of Hawaii.

Curtin and his young government reeled for the third time in seventeen days. The sinking of the *Sydney* had been a huge blow. The shock of Pearl Harbor demonstrated that the Japanese were prepared to go to any lengths in this 'new' war in the Pacific. The sinking of these two important ships off Malaya would create a sense of siege in Australia. The enemy was sinking Allied shipping and killing thousands in the Indian and Pacific Oceans.

News of the British ships being destroyed broke in the newspapers on 11 December. Curtin went on the front foot, making a statement that took an indirect swipe at Menzies for his relaxed and benign attitude to war when he followed England in declaring hostilities against Germany in 1939. In this, Curtin was stretching the facts a fair way. That had been more than two years ago; by the end of 1941 Menzies was certainly not taking a 'business-as-usual' approach within the Advisory War Council. What irked Curtin most was how hard it was to stir Australians at home into doing their bit and making sacrifices. He blamed the citizenry's current 'head in the sand' reaction to what was happening offshore on Menzies' earlier attitude.

Curtin said there was a critical need for 'an absolute concentration on war production and war necessities'.[1] The government advised the citizenry in every state and territory to start digging and sandbagging. This was meant to alert the nation to the potential for bombing and invasion. Holes were excavated in backyards; trenches were built around government buildings and could be used as crude air-raid shelters. National emergency services ordered city hospitals to evacuate. Brisbane, Sydney, Melbourne, Darwin and Perth introduced limits on the use of lights at night. Emulating the British experience, women and children began moving to the country. This only encouraged speculators and landlords. Rents in rural Queensland and outside Sydney and Melbourne shot up twenty to twenty-five per cent.

The preparations still seemed half-hearted, despite the government's exhortations to prepare for a Japanese onslaught. Only in Darwin, Brisbane and, to a lesser degree, Perth was there a sense of something like urgency. Military mobilisation meant that all resources, human and material, were needed for the war effort. The states, more than the federal government, decreed whether or not sports would continue, but the prime minister had a responsibility to give firm direction. The sporting world sat up when cricket's Australian Board of Control announced that it was abandoning seven of a planned eight-match 'Interstate Patriotic Competition'. The proceeds would have gone to the war effort.

This was serious. Cricket had been abandoned only once before in Australia since the first inter-colonial games began holding regular annual competitions in the 1850s, and that was for three years during World War I. The last first-class match of the 1941–42 season was played at Brisbane's Gabba ground between Queensland and New South Wales, and it was reduced to three days. A poor crowd of 8000 saw Queensland win in a tight game, despite a nine-wicket haul by great leg-spinner Bill O'Reilly. A new young speedster, Ray Lindwall, impressed with his rhythmic bowling style. But he, like thousands of young men with Test aspirations, had to put his career on hold. Most would go into military service.[2]

Curtin strove for a balance. He appreciated that people – himself included – needed recreational pursuits in tough times. But he did object when two separate race meetings were held on the one day in Melbourne. He called on race clubs to economise, cut the number of races at a meeting, and reduce the amount of food and alcohol on sale.

He was irked by the money spent by big punters. After heavy betting at Randwick and Flemington one Saturday, he spoke out. 'Most of the punters . . . would have done better to have backed Australia than the horses . . . Their money should have been wagered on the Fourth [Government] Liberty Loan. The record investments on the totalisators and the huge turnover with the bookmakers reveal that many men and women were employed as clerks.' He said racegoers should have rested and been fit for work, and the war effort.

'I understand also that many punters pulled rolls of wads out of their pockets, which reveals at once why the Federal Reserve Bank's note issue has gone up,' he remarked with tongue in cheek. 'The man who is reported to have pulled five one hundred-pound notes from his pocket to put on a horse is a thoughtless enemy of this country. That is putting it mildly.'[4]

Curtin was motivated by the losses and sacrifices being made by the armed forces, and also by millions of others in the country. He made many speeches addressing this. In one address at Canberra's Albert Hall, he spoke with feeling about the loss of Patrick Hore-Ruthven, the son of his good friend (and Australia's then governor-general) Lord Gowrie. His words were telling, and reminded people of the loss of a generation of exceptional people in World War I. Curtin feared that World War II would also rob the country of a mass of talent and humanity that could never be replaced.

'We cannot measure the cost of this terrible war in money and material things,' he noted. 'I doubt if there can be any spiritual assessment of the loss. I am certain that just as many a Bradman of the future has lost the chance of development.'[5]

Curtin appeared to turn Scrooge in the lead-up to Christmas 1941. The War Cabinet decreed that factories should keep operating from 24 December 1941 to 2 January 1942, putting an end to the traditional nine-day break. However, Christmas Day, Boxing Day and New Year's Day would remain public holidays. Union leaders objected to the loss of six days' vacation, but Curtin stood firm. Evatt was more aggressive, telling union leaders that the Japanese were still working – Tokyo was taking no days off.

In his address of 11 December, Curtin added a final thought on the sinking of the *Prince of Wales* and the *Repulse*: 'For years I have insisted that a maximum air defence was imperative to the efficiency of land and sea forces – however strong they might be. Now we are faced with the reality.' It was his first 'I told you so' pronouncement in office. It was also a swipe at the British, and in particular at Churchill and his choice of Admiral Phillips.[6]

On 12 December there were more concrete moves than rhetoric. The War Cabinet approved the call-up of 114,000 more men for the army. Australian troops were shipped to what was thought would be the frontline: Port Moresby, Timor and Darwin. The thinking of the Army chief was that the Japanese would have to do some island-hopping, forming air bases along the way. They had to be met on Australia's doorstep, and stopped.

Curtin wanted to blame the conservatives for the feeble state of the military. Yet there was a certain measure of hypocrisy here. He had long been the pacifist, dismissive of any need for Australia to prepare for war. He had been against bigger budgets for a skeletal army or militia. Both sides of politics had been slack, as they had been in England. Now they were paying for that unpreparedness.

The loss of the *Prince of Wales* and the *Repulse* was a huge blow to Churchill. He was awakened in his bunker by a phone call with the news, and later commented that it was the worst shock he ever received in war. He was struck by how 'weak and naked' the Allies now were in the Pacific area.

With a strange twist of logic, he blamed Curtin for pressuring him into action to defend further Singapore and the Pacific. Churchill now bemoaned the fact that 'over all this vast expanse of waters [the Pacific] Japan was supreme'. This would have been the case whether or not Churchill sent two 'Capital' ships (as they were called) to the region.

While he attempted to shift the blame, Churchill perhaps did not have time to comprehend the ramifications of the mighty, swift

Japanese sweep through South-East Asia. When he thought about the new situation more soberly, he proposed that one of Australia's three divisions in the Middle East should be sent to repel the Japanese. But he was not considering the defence of Australia. Churchill was thinking about the Dutch East Indies, or Malaya, and the defence of Singapore, on the remote chance (in his still distracted mind) the Japanese might penetrate that far.

Churchill still considered the Australian divisions under his control. Once they left Australia and lodged in North Africa, Churchill did nothing to suggest he considered them other than 'British'. In his mind, this was always for the 'greater good': defeating Hitler. To that end, Churchill secretly booked a boat across the Atlantic to shore up Roosevelt's support: he did not want Roosevelt diverted by Japan's stunning intervention in the Pacific.

Hitler had helped Churchill's position by declaring war on the United States after it declared war on Japan following Pearl Harbor. This move by Hitler was perhaps a minor mistake. If so, it was another in a growing litany of decisions that seemed based on a combination of arrogance and ignorance rather than sensible consideration. Astute and confident, Churchill would use it in his new 'sell' to Roosevelt.

On the rough ride over the ocean, Churchill created three papers: 'The Atlantic Front', 'The Pacific Front' and '1943'. He wanted to stay ahead of everyone else in directing the war. His Pacific strategy was based on Singapore being held for six months, until at least June 1942, and the Philippines not going under to the Japanese either. He foresaw another Tobruk, with Singapore, as an island, being far more defensible than any place on the North African coast.

Churchill, as he often did, had convinced himself of the small island's impregnability, which meant he would absorb no argument to the contrary. He did concede that much would depend on the United States and United Kingdom regaining supremacy in the Pacific. He believed it would take eighteen months – until the middle of 1943 – for the Americans and the British, with the Russians assisting, to turn the tide against Germany and Japan. Then Allied expeditions could wrest back any countries lost to the Axis powers. This approach meant that Australia would have to be considered expendable.

Churchill's worry was that Roosevelt and his services chiefs would want a policy to recover the Pacific first, something that Curtin also dearly desired. For this reason, Churchill and Curtin were on an inevitable political collision course.

8
No Holiday for Nippon

As Churchill steamed across the Atlantic, Curtin worked round the clock, rearranging Australia's defence and urging everyone to hunker down and accept the coming austerity, including a dampened-down Christmas. But the Japanese, as Evatt pointed out once more, were taking no days off in their advances through the jungles of Malaya towards Singapore. They had stunned the world by attacking the American possessions of Hawaii and the Philippines, along with Malaya, Thailand and Hong Kong.

American troops in the Philippines, primarily composed of local Filipinos, under General MacArthur, were pushed back into a tiny enclave on the Bataan Peninsula, and the island of Corregidor in Manila Bay. In Malaya and Hong Kong, untrained British troops were proving no match for the battle-hardened Japanese soldiers, who had toughened up for years in China. Thailand was invaded by land from Battambang, Cambodia, by air at Don Muang airfield, and by sea in seven amphibious landings from Hua Hin and Pattani on the Gulf of Thailand coast. Despite savage fighting at several points in the south, organised resistance was brief. Thai field marshal Phibun Songkhram ordered a ceasefire, believing his troops had no hope. He signed a 'peace treaty of alliance' with the Japanese on 21 December, which handed Thailand to the invaders.

Following Pearl Harbor and the sinking of the *Prince of Wales*, all remaining Allied warships were combined into a single fleet, under the command of a Dutch admiral, in an effort to defend the Dutch East Indies. After moving troops north to Darwin and New Guinea, Australia now pushed them to several major islands of the Dutch East Indies, including Timor and Ambon. Singapore and Malaya seemed more vulnerable than ever.

These shocks clarified the main problem facing the defenders of South-East Asia that had led to the sinking of Admiral Phillips and his armada. There was no opposition to speak of in the air. Japan's fighters and bombers could attack with impunity anywhere they wished. Sortie after sortie was sent to hammer the ground defences of the British, Indian and Australian troops. The impact lowered resistance.

Added to this were the subtle but effective activities of the Japanese fifth column on the ground. Locals were paid to help the advancing invaders learn where the defences were. Japanese troops disguised as Malayan natives infiltrated Australian positions as the diggers waited for the inevitable clashes.

In addition to this intelligence, there was the much underestimated Japanese military precision. Gordon Bennett noted in his diary the regularity with which the enemy pinpointed British or Indian troops. Japanese reconnaissance planes accounted for some of this laser-like identification.

Bennett's diary entry for 12 December 1941 was typical: 'The [Krocol] Front [in Malaya's north] experienced a black dawn. As day broke extremely heavy bombardment was concentrated on the positions held by the Indians.' Reconnaissance planes had located the Indians' positions. Then the Japanese began a much repeated manoeuvre. They attacked, gaining a foothold on a hill. Using artillery and machine-gun fire, they bombarded a flank facing a river and the Indians' right rear. This was followed by the Japanese moving around the weakened flank and 'threatening to cut off this battalion'.[1] The other flank was hit in the same fashion. Enemy reserves were brought in to cut off the Indians' retreat.

This was Yamashita's basic military tactic. Malaya was his big test. He was determined to make it work. He was ambitious and aggressive. He had been allocated fewer than 35,000 men, which meant he was outnumbered by four to one. He knew that the more he stretched his supply lines and the longer he fought, the less likely he was to pull off a victory. He had to win as quickly as possible.

But Yamashita had a deeper concern that gave him sleepless nights. If his soldiers were drawn into street fights, real hand-to-hand stuff that meant dragged-out encounters right through to Singapore, his army was sure to lose. Yamashita had learnt from his German mission that some of the British troops – particularly the Scots and Australians – revelled in such close fighting. It had to be avoided at all costs. Intelligent strategy, smart tactics and courage were required.

On 16 December 1941 the Japanese hit Burma from southern Thailand, with the aim of capturing the British airfields at Victoria Point and Mergui. The plan was to cross the mountains on the Thai–Burmese border at Three Pagodas Pass and at Mae Sot, and then push the limited British forces west towards Rangoon.

The Japanese had no direct contact with the Australians as the Imperial infantry moved south over the next five weeks. They fought, defeated and pushed back the British and Indian forces with a little too much ease for the Australians' liking. Bennett, with more urgency than ever, was pleading for an extra division to be sent from the Middle East. In mid-December 1941 he wrote to the Australian Army headquarters in Melbourne:

> *The situation in the north [of Malaya] is very grave indeed . . . I have seen a total absence of the offensive spirit [by the British and Indians], which after all, is the only great remedy for the methods adopted by the Japanese. Counterattacks would put a stop to this penetration . . . I am convinced that an advance of more Australian troops to Malaya . . . is a matter of paramount importance.*[2]

In the week since Pearl Harbor, the Japanese had made their intentions in the region even more clear by invading the Philippines and seizing Guam in the Pacific. They also hit Burma running. On

16 December, they were into British Borneo. They planned to take Hong Kong in a few days.

There was time – just – for the Australian government to ship 20,000 soldiers to Singapore to bolster its defences. But Bennett was receiving no support from his British commander in Malaya, the unassuming Lieutenant-General A. E. Percival. There was no doubting the Englishman's strengths as a staff officer, but he was not so impressive in the field. Nor was there support from Churchill, who was far too preoccupied with talking Roosevelt out of focusing American energies in the Pacific.

The Australian Army headquarters was cool to Bennett's request, which was not surprising given Blamey's self-serving ambitions in the Middle East. The last thing he wanted was to lose a precious division – a quarter of his formidable fighting force – to Singapore. That island, in which Churchill had invested so much political capital, would have to live up to his faith with the 130,000 British troops that were already defending it.

Churchill was still assessing Singapore's chances on paper, without proper analysis and consideration of the troops' fighting capacity and the commanders' experience and skill. Churchill's belief that Singapore could not be taken was also based in part on its big artillery guns, which pointed out to sea. But the flaws in that argument had already been exposed – the Japanese had already come a long way on land. A naval attack was irrelevant.

The same day the Japanese entered Burma, they took the island of Penang, on Malaya's north-west coast. The Malayans were wondering which side would win. Now there was further uncertainty. The invaders were making headway. The Japanese turned their focus to the Slim River, another 200 kilometres further south. It was held by British and Indian troops. The roads were clogged with refugees fleeing south and military personnel moving in the opposite direction. There was a sense of panic from the locals, and concern from the defenders.

By mid-December 1941, Canberra – Sleepy Hollow Central – was more frenetic than it had ever had been. 'Even the sheep (in the paddock next to the Parliament) looked more excited than normal,' journalist Alan Reid remarked.³

Every member of Cabinet was receiving advice, solicited and unsolicited, on how to prepare. Some were suggesting a 'Brisbane Line' – a defence perimeter running from that city inland a few hundred kilometres. This meant sacrificing territory, people – everything – in the top half of Australia. The suggestion smacked of desperation.

There was something more like panic coming from the office of deputy prime minister and Minister for the Army Frank Forde, who had been taking advice from a British officer, Major H. H. Irvine Andrews, on how to create and use a guerilla army. Andrews gave him a lecture on how Colonel T. E. Lawrence had defeated a Turkish army at the Hejaz Railway in Arabia and Jordan in World War I. Andrews believed that the fighting conditions in Australia's semi-arid and desert regions would be similar, should Japan attack anywhere along the country's vast northern region. Andrews gave him a copy of Lawrence's epic *Seven Pillars of Wisdom*, which Forde read. Andrews also lectured on how to fight the enemy in the major cities, again guerilla-style.

The impressionable Forde was enthusiastic. He told General Sturdee about Andrews' views. Sturdee was unimpressed, aware that his Australian friend General Sir Harry Chauvel had done far more than Lawrence to defeat the Turks by leading a conventional mobile force of lighthorse, cavalry and cameleers. Chauvel had said that Lawrence was a 'bit player and nuisance' to him during the Middle East War. The steady, calm Sturdee listened to Forde and then put it about that his Minister might have taken on board 'misleading and inaccurate statements'. There would be no guerilla army set-up while General Sturdee had any say.⁴

The chiefs of the armed forces believed Darwin should be beefed up militarily and be retained 'as a fleet operational base'. The city's civilian population was told that they should think about leaving. The E-word – 'evacuation' – was not used initially, but it was present behind the suggestions. The chiefs knew full well that Japan's espionage network would learn of Darwin's changing face. It would become a strategic military base of the utmost importance, and therefore it would also become an important Japanese target.[5]

Parliament adjourned for the summer recess on 17 December 1941, but the key men in the government were in for the most hectic work period of their lives. Evatt finessed the press, giving nothing away about the real state of affairs, which frustrated and concerned journalists. Evatt would leave the details to Curtin. A week after his last impressive but uninformative press conference, Curtin decided to open up a little to the 'chooks', as he called the all-male reporter contingent. At 10.30 p.m. he asked seven of the nation's leading political journalists into his office.

'When are you going to let us know what's going on?' one asked. 'Especially the strategic situation.'

Curtin scrutinised them, smiled and replied, 'No time like the present.'

The room was shut; attendants were asked to leave. The journalists sat in silence. Australia's wartime leader was about to take them into his confidence at a most critical moment. Curtin was alone without minders or advisers. He had no notes. He delivered a comprehensive dissertation, and was interrupted only four times, usually to be asked if a certain remark could be published. He spoke for nearly ninety minutes without faltering. He did not have Menzies' grand enunciation, but it was clear to the listeners that his grasp on all issues was second to none. He was clear-headed, apparently on top of every issue. He communicated without hesitation. Any nagging uncertainties that these informed 'critics' may have had about Curtin were washed away in this conference.

'They felt his greatness,' Lloyd Ross noted. Ross would be Curtin's first biographer, and was a close family friend. As such, his observation would be judged by some as an exaggeration. But Ross kept an acceptable level of objectivity when judging his mate in high office. He seemed sincere when he added that while some of these hard-nosed professionals had been sceptical of Curtin – one even branded him a 'woolly theoretician' – they now had a different appreciation of him. The good impression he had made on the day after Pearl Harbor had been replaced by a conviction that he was the right man for the job. Ross concluded: 'the journalists felt that the Prime Minister had revealed sources of great strength'.[6]

This image was vital for public morale. The journalists would report accordingly, giving the citizenry some confidence at a moment when 'woolly theories', if reported or reflected in media comment, would have had the opposite impact.

9
Push to Invade Australia

The Australian government continued its penny-pinching as Christmas approached. Trains in major cities – the prime mode of transport – were cancelled. Even racecourse 'specials' were stopped, preventing many from taking part in the nation's most popular pastime – betting on horseraces. There was no backlash, which indicated that the population was accepting these restrictions. Curtin went further and appealed to the nation not to buy expensive gifts, which brought a reaction from retailers. City stores advertised big sales and urged customers to 'Spend! Spend! Spend!' Sales went up across the country, before a reaction of sorts. In a swipe at the prime minister, city stores put up signs saying 'We Believe in Santa' and 'We Didn't Let Santa Down'.[1]

High-priced items were featured in store windows. Over the pre-Christmas period, sales were at least as strong as in recent years. The government was puzzled by the reaction, which meant that enemy espionage agents, too, would have been baffled by the psychological state of the nation. It seemed that spending on gifts was sacrosanct. But Curtin held his ground in a broadcast to the nation, making no apology for the 'wowser' Christmas as the nation's leisure-time activities continued to wind down.

Life as Melburnians knew it was about to change in a way that would depress many. The Victorian Football League – the nation's top football code – decided in late December, after meeting with Curtin, a life-long Fitzroy supporter, that it would keep its competition going. He did nothing to discourage it, acknowledging that there were activities that had to continue for the morale of the population. But crowd projections for the 1942 season predicted a big drop-off in fans, and many clubs struggled to form teams. Other codes, including rugby league and rugby union in Sydney and Brisbane, were also scaled down.

Australians would have looked at their future differently had they been privy to the thinking of Admiral Nobutake Kondo, Japan's most experienced naval officer after Admiral Isoroku Yamamoto, who masterminded the attack on Pearl Harbor.

Kondo was a political moderate. He opposed the army's plans to conquer China after the 1937 Marco Polo Bridge incident outside Beijing, when China's National Revolutionary Army fought the Japanese. He was against signing the Tripartite Pact with Germany and Italy. Kondo saw the primary aim of his nation's sudden, violent expansion of its Empire as being to break the British Empire in the region. He saw two alternatives: the conquest of India or Australia.

India was tempting. It was the most prized nation under British control. But Australia was even more enticing. It was not quite the jewel in the crown; not even a diamond in a modest tiara. But acquiring it had one immediate advantage: it would deprive the United States of a base in the Pacific from which to counter-attack – assuming, as seemed likely, that the Japanese would win in the Philippines. There was another factor that was not an urgent consideration, but which would be of future importance: Australia was one of the richest countries in natural resources. If Japan had to be in any protracted war, such as with China (which Japan's extremists believed was more important than any other conflict), it would need all the iron ore, for instance, that it could acquire.

Kondo and his staff had considered the options. Taking India would need assistance from Germany in the Middle East to cut off Britain's oil supply. He was opposed to doing deals with the fascists, whom he did not trust. The Indian operation would be bigger and messier, militarily and politically. Kondo much preferred the Australian option.

'The Australian Operation,' he wrote, 'could be regarded as part of our main operation against America. It would also have a rich chance of taking hold of American task forces.'[2]

The Japanese Admiralty's power and influence was at its peak after smashing the US fleet and also the British off Malaya. It had cleared the seas of Allied navies in the Pacific and Indian Oceans. The admirals were bold, sensing the Imperial navy's ascendancy over its army. Their aircraft carriers had the capacity to knock out Allied ships, with planes – including long-range bombers – that changed the nature of the war. Where the army looked at a problem and declared it too hard or far away, the navy believed that no target was beyond it, at sea or on land.

In late December 1941, people such as Kondo were in a powerful position within the Japanese High Command; they would not have thought that the navy could have attained such a position before its successes between 7 and 10 December. Kondo had strong supporters for the Australian Operation. Among them was the commander of the 4th Fleet, Admiral Shigeyoshi Inoue. This fleet was based at Truk Island and included three light cruisers and a destroyer squadron. Inoue was also a moderate, a man with a passionate dislike for the Nazis. He too saw fascist pacts as being likely to draw the Russians into conflict with Japan, thus stretching the Japanese military further.

Inoue, in turn, had the support of his staff officers, who carried weight under the Japanese way of decision-making, tactics and strategies. There was a bottom-up influence unmatched among the allies, in which junior officers put up plans and ideas to their superiors, who were happy to let them do the hard work in presenting new operations. Some would be taken up, some rejected, but there was no fear among the young officers about pushing hard for their missions.

A third major supporter of the Australian Operation was Baron Tomioka of the Naval General Staff. He would not back the Indian Operation, which would mean more land-based missions in Burma (as a gateway to India), similar to those now being prosecuted by General Yamashita on Malaya. This would reduce the navy's role and influence, which none wished to consider in these heady days of success.

Tomioka and his staff feared the Americans building up a power base in Australia. Japanese intelligence was already informing the High Command (and all the chiefs of the Armed Forces) of important US military personnel, planes, ships, weaponry and equipment being sent to Perth, Brisbane, Sydney, Darwin and Melbourne.

Inoue met with Admiral Yamamoto and requested aircraft-carrier support for a proposed operation to invade Port Moresby, Papua. He raised the idea of invading Australia. Yamamoto was non-committal, which Inoue took to mean that he was, in principle, open to the concept if he and Kondo kept progressing militarily and lobbying. They marked out key areas of northern Australia that should be occupied to deny the Americans access to Australia. They calculated they needed three army divisions – about 80,000 soldiers – for occupation.

Conflict between Curtin and Churchill over the main aims of the war came to a head in the second half of December 1941. Churchill was still in Washington DC, trying to persuade Roosevelt to keep his focus on aiding the Allies' cause in Europe. Churchill was in a perpetual battle with American public opinion, and the primary battleground was the American press. The media had held back from reporting Roosevelt's aid to the Allied effort against the Nazis; now Churchill had to counter its influence over Roosevelt's response to Japan's aggression.

Editorials were urging the president to concentrate more on the Pacific. He had already suspended Lend Lease aid shipments to the United Kingdom. Roosevelt had wanted to put off his meeting with Churchill to the New Year, but the Englishman had persisted. For him, the situation was urgent. Roosevelt did not really want the extra hassle of having to divert his mind to one war front and then to another – especially one to which the Americans were yet to commit.

Some, including Sir Alan Brooke – the new British Chief of the Imperial General Staff – urged Churchill to take a cautious approach. He was not above taking such advice, but this time he did not. 'That is the way we talked to her [the US] while we were wooing her,' he told Brooke. 'Now that she is in the harem [with the Allies in the Pacific war], we talk to her quite differently.'[3]

Despite Churchill's flippant remark, coaxing this large concubine into doing his bidding would still require some seduction. He began by pushing his 18th Division, which was at Cape Town, South Africa, to Bombay instead of Egypt. This gave Churchill a useful 'chip' for use in the Pacific.

10

Evatt and Curtin Blunder; Churchill's Wrath

There were enough 'sightings' of Japanese in Australia in the third week of December 1941 to make a UFO convention envious. Planes of various types and sizes were spotted, especially over the north coast. Supposed battleships were frequently seen, predominantly off Western Australia's coast. There were even reports of chauffeur-driven cars manned by Japanese cruising along dirt tracks in the remote north-west. This, along with the verifiable hourly reports of Japanese aggression in about twelve countries and in the major nearby oceans, was enough to keep Australian government ministers on edge.

The building pressure, and the tyranny of Canberra's distance from everywhere, caused the nation's leaders to fill vacuums and do *something*. There was plenty of time for Curtin and his Cabinet to have meetings and work each other up, if not to fever pitch, then a level that sometimes precipitated unnecessary action.

Russia and its communist dictatorships were very much to the fore in a lot of Cabinet's thinking. Doing deals with Stalin was often discussed. But the increasingly practical and less ideological Curtin considered most of the suggestions either too extreme or too silly to take seriously. But one idea did stimulate the Cabinet members, especially Evatt. He convinced Curtin to see the merit in suggesting to Churchill that Stalin be offered the Baltic States in the Allied carve-up of the defeated Axis powers at the war's end. In return, Stalin would need to attack Japan – now. This, the theory went, would divert Japan from trying to acquire Australia.

The preposterous concept demonstrated a certain parochial naivety, which would never have entered the minds of Bruce in London or Casey in Washington. They were much closer to the action and the main players. Yet Curtin was persuaded that this sacrificing of a slice of Europe as a trade-off for Australia's safety from attack in the Pacific was a more than useful concept. He and Evatt crafted a cable to this effect.

Churchill was furious at the suggestion. He wasted no time in replying. 'I hope you realize that it would be impossible for His Majesty's Government to make a bargain with Stalin involving forcible transferring of large populations against their will into communist spheres,' he wrote. Curtin had underestimated Churchill's distaste for communism, especially the Stalinist kind. He would no sooner do a deal with Stalin than with Hitler. He saw both as hideous dictators, rotten to the core. Churchill added: 'By attempting it we would vitiate the fundamental principles of freedom which are the main impulse of our cause.'[1]

Curtin realised that his suggestion was poor, even thoughtless. He tried to save face by claiming he had been misinterpreted. He attempted to say 'it was desirable to conduct exchanges with Stalin on broadest lines'. By doing so, he suggested, Stalin would not think that he would be blocked from 'his desire to adjustment of frontier claims'. This was a transparent euphemism for Stalin's expected desire postwar to take control of further chunks of Europe. Curtin added: 'So far as practicable, the peoples concerned would have right to choose their own Governments.'[2] This would never be practicable; Stalin had a history of crushing democracy and choice. Curtin had dug himself into a deeper hole, embarrassed by this gross error of judgement, his first in office.

Dick Casey, the Australian envoy in Washington, had learned about the secret Churchill–Roosevelt talks from his British contacts. He cabled Curtin, who had no idea of Churchill's moves, urging him to tell Roosevelt how important it was to hold Singapore. Casey wanted

Curtin to paint a clear picture of what the Pacific and Indian Oceans would look like if the Japanese took the island.

Casey, who was proving an outstanding diplomat under pressure, also informed Curtin that Roosevelt would now push for an active American commander in chief in the Pacific. The president would probably nominate MacArthur, who had the title already. Casey mentioned the American general's 'human frailties'.[3] But Curtin was less concerned with MacArthur's weaknesses than his high reputation as a military commander.

The impact of Roosevelt's thinking was not lost on Curtin, who wished to facilitate any possibility that the Americans would use Australia as a base, perhaps a large one, in its war against Japan. He needed to embed this notion deep into Roosevelt's thinking by making it clear that Australia would be most cooperative. Curtin was quick to put his views on paper for the immediate consumption of Roosevelt and Churchill, *before* they got down to their hard negotiations after Christmas. His skills as a journalist were never more paramount.

Writing was exhilarating for Curtin. It gave him a 'high' that alcohol could never deliver, banishing his 'old bogey' – depression – while he worked to find the right phrase, the right emphasis, without omitting the key points he wished to convey. Early in this letter he wrote: 'I have already addressed a communication to Mr. Churchill on the question of Russia, which I regard of great importance in relation to the Japanese war . . .' He watered down his suggestion about the Russian trade-off. He was no longer proposing that Russia be given a few hapless nations after the war; instead, he pushed the idea that Russia should be cajoled into attacking the Japanese even without mentioning inducements.

But this view would never have any currency with Churchill, who wanted the Russians to concentrate on defeating Hitler. Not that the Russians would have bothered with Curtin's suggestion, whether they were offered anything or not. Stalin was even more focused than Churchill on fighting the German war machine. The Nazis were in Russian territory and preparing for massive efforts to bring it further under their control. Stalin needed to put all his resources into the European war; Japan was never going to be a priority for him.

Nevertheless, Curtin's raising of the issue of Russia and Japan may have been a shrewd way of stressing how concerned Australia was about the Japanese in the Pacific and South-East Asia. Perhaps Curtin wished to show his worry – even his desperation – through this extreme suggestion. He went on:

> [I]t is evident that in North Malaya, the Japanese have assumed control of air and sea. The small British army there includes [two-thirds of] one Australian division, and we have sent three air squadrons to Malaya and two in Netherlands East Indies. The Army must be provided with air support; otherwise there will be repetition of Greece and Crete, and Singapore will be grievously threatened.

This may have been a grim reminder to Churchill about the lack of air power that had led to the demise of the *Prince of Wales*. But Churchill would not have grasped the point just yet. His mind was so focused on his dealing with Roosevelt that he may not have processed the true reasons for that massive setback. Curtin's comment would have grated on Churchill for another reason: The president would be reminded of the British folly in Greece and Crete. The remark about Singapore would be fobbed off as panic, so certain was Churchill of its invulnerability.

Curtin persisted:

> The fall of Singapore would mean the isolation of Philippines, the fall of Netherlands East Indies and attempts to smother all other bases. This would also sever our communications between the Indian and Pacific Oceans in this region. The setback would be as serious to USA interests as to our own . . . The reinforcements earmarked by United Kingdom Government for dispatch seem to us to be utterly inadequate, especially in relation to aircraft, particularly fighters.

These lines had Churchill steaming. Not only was Curtin complaining about the United Kingdom's support, he was appealing – indirectly – for US help.

Curtin continued: 'At this time, small reinforcements are of little avail. In truth the amount of resistance to Japan in Malaya will depend directly on the amount of assistance provided by Governments of United Kingdom and United States.'

Again, in any discussion with Roosevelt, Churchill dismissed this as a colonial loss of nerve. He was certain that the defence of Malaya and Singapore was adequate, despite the sinking of the *Prince of Wales*. Curtin added:

> *Our men have fought and will fight valiantly. But they must be adequately supported. We have three divisions in the Middle East. Our airmen are fighting in Britain, Middle East and training in Canada. We have sent great quantities of supplies to Britain, Middle East and India. Our resources are very limited indeed.*

Then came the pitch to Roosevelt based on Casey's intelligence:

> *It is in your power to meet the situation. Should the United States desire, we would gladly accept a United States commander in Pacific area. The President has said Australia will be a base of increasing importance, but in order that it shall remain a base, Singapore must be reinforced. In spite of our great difficulties, we are sending further reinforcements to Malaya [1800 soldiers were being sent to bolster the 8th Division]. Please consider this a matter of great urgency.*[4]

The most telling line in his letter was 'we would gladly accept a United States commander in Pacific area'. Both recipients would have sat up for different reasons. Churchill was angered and upset. He viewed Curtin's utterance as a betrayal of the United Kingdom, the Empire and the past. To use one of Churchill's most telling similes, the harlot was attempting to switch to another Sultan's harem.

Churchill, with his deep knowledge of British history, would have seen the dangers. If Australia was under US military command, it would have ramifications for the world's imperial powers after the war. Britain's influence would be reduced in the Pacific and South-East Asia, which was what Churchill was fighting hard against. He knew more than most about the acquisitiveness of superpowers after wars.

Curtin's words represented Australia's first tottering steps towards independence in its short history since European settlement. They were also nicely timed. Within a week, the first US military personnel would arrive in Australia and prepare to support General MacArthur's embattled army in the Philippines.

Casey slipped into the White House's East Wing for a meeting with Churchill, whom he had known for twenty years. Casey went through the points in Curtin's telegram, putting his polished diplomatic spin on the thoughts that had upset Churchill. Churchill brought in the chiefs of staff of all the British armed services, who were with him attempting to make the case to Roosevelt for the 'Hitler first' policy. They all refuted Curtin's fears about the fall of Singapore and the intentions of Britain's Far East strategy.

Then Churchill brought Roosevelt into the discussion, along with the US Secretary of the Navy, Colonel Frank Knox. They sided with the British and attempted to reassure Casey that the US, alongside the British, would be most active in the Pacific to restore Allied power. Casey had been outflanked but not bluffed. The president and Colonel Knox left after about half an hour's discussion. A few minutes later, Churchill's team departed, leaving him and Casey alone again.

Churchill vented his anger about Curtin, saying, 'You can't kick me around the room. I'm not kickable.'[5]

Churchill's fury reflected his view of the 'bad stock' down under, especially the new pacifist/socialist prime minister. He had begrudging respect for Menzies, Bruce and Page but regarded them as pests when it came to his war policy. The new lot in power in Australia seemed more odious to him with every cable. His fury also exposed his own insecurity about his Far East strategy, which had been in place for three decades. It seemed that Churchill had talked it up so much that he may have reached a point of self-delusion. No matter how much he and his chiefs defended it, Churchill must have known in his heart it was a fraud and a phantom.

But Singapore was incidental for Churchill at this time. He was concentrating on cajoling the Americans in another direction. As Roosevelt was deceiving Casey, he was promising massive increases in plane (145,000) and tank production (120,000) over the coming two years, which would provide Churchill with a significant boost in firepower as the war reached a decisive point. This would aid Churchill in achieving his main aim.

Meanwhile, Curtin, Bruce and Page continued to plead for just 300 fighter planes for Australia's defence. They were not forthcoming – an indication of Churchill's real intentions.

Curtin was buoyed by knowing that American military personnel were at last beginning to trickle into Australia. The first contingent of US forces – Task Force South Pacific – arrived at Brisbane's outer harbour, Moreton Bay, at noon on 22 December 1941. The convoy's original destination had been the Philippines, but the deterioration of the US forces' situation there caused it to be redirected to Brisbane, where it would be met by US air corps officer Major-General George H. Brett.

About 4600 Americans disembarked, and their first camp – Ascot – was established at Eagle Farm racecourse. Members of the force were also sprinkled in the northern cities of Rockhampton and Townsville. The news that 'the Yanks had arrived' made moderate splashes in newspapers, but the sense of relief was measured, particularly in Brisbane. This inexperienced, small contingent, comprising mainly air force personnel, could do little against a Japanese invasion. But the sight of uniformed Americans coming down gangplanks gave some hope to worried locals.

The arrival also boosted Curtin's confidence, and made him ponder further about pushing for greater US support in the Pacific War. It made practical sense to look to help from the Americans rather than the British, especially as Japan had dragged them into the conflict and might well push the United States out of the Philippines. If that occurred, Australia was the logical major base for any eventual counter-attack.

11

Article of Intent

The news of the Americans' arrival allowed Curtin to relax on Christmas Day 1941. He took the luxury of staying in bed until 11 a.m. before entertaining six West Australian airmen with lunch at the Lodge. Meanwhile, his press secretary,

Don Rodgers, was hard at work putting the finishing touches to a 1500-word commissioned feature for the Melbourne *Herald*.

Curtin wrote his own cables but asked for comment and ideas from his 'inner cabinet' before finalising them. After consultation with Curtin, Rodgers would write the longer pieces, such as this Christmas piece for the newspaper. They were a distraction from the tough cable clashes between Australia, the United States and the United Kingdom over the past fortnight. Rodgers penned the *Herald* piece before showing it to Curtin, who added some touches and inserts that reflected his growing confidence since the advent of the Americans.

Curtin also ran the article past Shedden, who made a couple of suggestions, one of which was ignored. The piece was then passed on to the *Herald*, with no anticipation of a significant public reaction. It was published on 27 December 1941 in the Saturday magazine pages. It was titled 'The Task Ahead', and its first few paragraphs were dull enough. They were followed by some comradely socialist trumpet-blowing about Australia's speed in declaring war on Finland, Hungary and Romania when they were in conflict with the Soviet Union. 'We felt that there could be no half-measures in our dealings with the Soviet when that nation was being assailed by the three countries mentioned,' the piece read.

Curtin was reaching out to the Labor Party's left and extreme left: *we are solid with our communist allies*. The feature then belaboured his proposed Soviet 'deal' – without spelling out his suggestion to hand Stalin chunks of Europe in exchange for his attack upon Japan. The temerity and foolhardiness of Curtin's first cable to Churchill was watered down and given an Orwellian twist:

> *Similarly, we put forward that a reciprocal agreement between Russia and Britain should be negotiated to meet an event of aggression by Japan. [The original idea was to have Russia attacking Japan.] Our suggestion was then regarded, wrongly as time has proved, as premature. [Curtin was saying here that Japan's attacks on 7 and 8 December justified his requests. Churchill disagreed.] Now, with equal realism, we take the view that while*

determination of military policy is the Soviet's business, we should be able to look forward with reason to aid from Russia against Japan.

Once over that hump of misleading self-justification, there was a little more linking of arms with the Soviet communist regime, which, in another sop to the extreme left, was designated a 'democracy' on the same level as all the other Allies: 'We look for a solid and impregnable barrier of the democracies against the three Axis powers . . .'

The preamble took up about a quarter of the feature. A sentence later, those who were not asleep or put off at this point were alerted: 'The Australian Government therefore regards the Pacific struggle as primarily one in which the United States and Australia must have the fullest say in the direction of the Democracies' fighting plan.'

This was different, if not odd: there was no mention here of the British. Then came the jolt: 'Without any inhibitions of any kind, I make it quite clear that Australia looks to America, free of any pangs as to our traditional links or kinship with the United Kingdom.'

These were Curtin's thoughts and words, direct. The *Herald* editor who subbed the piece got the message. This paragraph appeared in black bold type, indented left and right. Curtin later reflected he should have used the phrase that Shedden suggested, which was ignored. Instead of 'free of any pangs', Shedden wanted 'without any lessening of the bonds'.

The discarded phrase was more diplomatic, more sensitive to the British reaction, particularly that of Churchill, the Empire man, who feared the US postwar empire becoming greater than the British. Yet the impact was the same. In Curtin's Pacific, Australia wanted a big brother to protect it. The other, 'traditional' link was to the 'mother country'. And this mother seemed, beneath all the rhetoric and promise, to be abandoning her distant child. Australia could not fend for itself against the powerful bully in the region.

Curtin's next lines confirmed these feelings of abandonment: 'We know the problems that the United Kingdom faces. We know the constant threat of invasion. We know the dangers of dispersal of strength. But we know too that Australia can go, and Britain can still hold on.'

Go where? some may have asked. The answer really only could be to hell in a handbasket or under Japanese control. They were the same. After this eye-catching declaration for the power elite – the United Kingdom, the United States and Japan – came an exposition that clarified, in an almost naively open way, Curtin's strategy for the war from this point on:

> *We are therefore determined that Australia shall not go, and we shall exert all our energies towards the shaping of a plan, with the United States as its keystone, which will give to our country some confidence of being able to hold out until the tide of battle swings against the enemy.*

Curtin's attitude and direction could not be clearer. This was an argument of independent, realistic thinking. It was a declaration that the brilliant Menzies, with all his intelligence, clearheadness, articulation, ambition and political skill, could never have written. He was too wedded to the British link. Curtin's background – Irish, Catholic and socialist – allowed him to brush aside what he considered ephemeral. He had not met Churchill in the flesh, but he was intelligent and strong-willed in an unobtrusive manner. Unconnected to the 'mother country' mentally, physically or in background, he could make hard decisions about what he considered to be in the best interests of Australia, which was not necessarily in the best interests of the British Empire.

The *Herald*'s sub-editor again chose indented, bold type for the next paragraph, which ranked all the key countries on the Allied side, as Curtin saw them: 'Summed up, Australia's external policy will be shaped toward obtaining Russian aid, and working out, with the United States, as the major factor, a plan of Pacific strategy, along with British, Chinese and Dutch forces.'

Curtin's use of the name 'Russia' was calculated; the harsher sounding 'Soviet Union' smacked of an empire, and a communist one too. Stalin could not be mentioned. This was a clever way of signalling to Australia's far left that the Soviet regime was still a priority, just in case they were upset that Australia would be throwing in its lot with the capitalist United States. Curtin here downgraded the British, lumping them in with the Chinese and the Dutch. This, too, represented a monumental shift away from Australia's past.

At times, this remarkable, watershed article drifted towards being something of a rambling internal intelligence report. Curtin spoke of the 'psychology' of selling the seriousness of the Japanese invasion threat. He had to overcome the 'lackadaisical Australian mind'. He believed he had succeeded. It was all about preparing for war in 1941, when no war was in sight until 7 December. He was 'heartened' by the production and conservation of supplies. Curtin warned – again in bold type – that 1942 would 'impose supreme tests. These range from resistance to invasion to deprivation of more and more amenities . . .' In short, the country had to go onto a 'war footing'.

'I demand,' Curtin added, 'that Australians everywhere realise that Australia is now inside the fighting lines.' The seven million people of Australia had to comprehend that the enemy was 'hammering at our frontier'. He may well have been tempted to say 'front door' rather than 'frontier', but he did not wish to be alarmist. Curtin wanted a nation of thrifty coast-watchers, on guard against 'raid or invasion', and against 'spending money'. He wanted the nation also to be vigilant against 'hampering by disputation' – a warning to part of his union power base not to go on strike. 'Idle, irresponsible chatter' was also out.[1]

In this article, Curtin was making an unconvincing reach for the ideological drive of his earlier years. He had thought, in the minuscule time he had to reflect, about how to create social change through the fog of war, especially in the final year of war, when and if that came. He mentioned in this end-of-year message that he wished to revolutionise 'the Australian way of life'. He wanted 'every citizen' to 'place himself, his private and business affairs, his entire mode of living, on a war footing'. He spoke of 'austerity' and groped for a pathway to a new era – a chance, perhaps, for his revolution.

At that point Curtin's call for serious change was too obscure to be taken seriously. But war would offer an opportunity for the federal government to take powers away from the states and make significant reforms. If Labor stayed in power, there would be moves towards an evolution in policy.

No article in Australian history – apart from Keith Murdoch's piece exposing the folly of the Gallipoli invasion in 1915 – had such an impact in high places elsewhere. And it was Murdoch's *Herald* and the man himself who now turned this hidden Christmas message into a major revelation. It was an old-fashioned 'scoop'.

Murdoch wrote a piece for the high-circulation *Daily Mail* and a letter to *The Times*, ensuring both wide and 'important' coverage in the United Kingdom. Pushing for an outcome in Australia's interests, he mentioned but downgraded Curtin's apparent 'break' from Britain in the Pacific in favour of the United States. Murdoch claimed the prime minister wanted high-level consultation in the Allied war councils. His letter to *The Times* called for 'the entry of stout Dominion minds into the [British] War Council'.

The editor of *The Times* agreed that this was the correct interpretation of Curtin's apparent outburst. He editorialised accordingly. It was almost as if the integrity of the prime minister's Christmas message was not to be taken seriously; it had to be code for something more *sensible*.[2] The sentiment in London was that Curtin could not be serious about dumping the Empire for the Americans. But he was.

There was also a vital psychological element to Curtin's article. It appeared on 27 December and was circulated all over Australia and the world. On 28 December General George Brett, the US commander of the troops being sent to shore up MacArthur's forces, slipped into Melbourne, where his headquarters would be. The media was not informed. Brett was preparing to help MacArthur but, like all good commanders, he already had Plan B in mind. If MacArthur's force was defeated, the Americans would not be able to use the Philippines as a base for the eventual counter-attack against the Japanese. The next best base would be Australia. Brett and all his staff were more than pleased to learn the attitude of this ally towards the United States.

Roosevelt read the piece too. Curtin's attitude matched his action of a few weeks earlier, when he had opened up air routes in Australia to the United States, against British interests. The president felt well disposed towards this apparently independent-minded prime minister, even though they had never met and he knew little about him. But he had to keep any such thoughts to himself, in order not to upset Churchill.

It may have been just a passing consideration late in 1941, but the US political and military power elite now knew it had a stable ally in the Pacific – one that was so far unmolested by the Japanese, and one that could be trusted, regardless of its historical allegiances to Britain.

12

America's China Card

In Washington, Churchill was cabled the most important paragraphs of the Melbourne *Herald* article; he had no doubt that Curtin was not simply posturing for more say in the war councils. He saw it as a declaration of independence of sorts, but an ill-timed one. It hurt and angered him. In Churchill's view, the public pronouncement would give succour and confidence to the enemy, who would seize on any dislocation or uncertainty in the Allied ranks. Curtin had also exposed Britain's meaningless Far East strategy: he had split the Empire's solidarity, called into question Churchill's integrity, and made his task of bringing the United States into the fight against the Nazis in Europe far more difficult.

Churchill dictated a furious response, threatening to go over Curtin's head with a radio broadcast to the Australian people. This was Churchill at his most arrogant, and it may or may not have worked. Perhaps he thought twice about interfering in a sovereign nation's governmental decision-making, despite being unable to believe that Australia had anything but a parochial, upstart socialist government.

In the end, Churchill did not send his 'hot' cable.[1] But he let everyone know his feelings. He claimed that Curtin's words impacted in 'high circles' in the United States – which indicated the president. This was because Churchill himself complained to him about Curtin.

Roosevelt summoned Casey. 'If you think that this statement will ingratiate Australia with the United States,' the president told him, 'then I assure it will have the opposite effect. It tastes of panic and disloyalty.'[2]

President Roosevelt's reaction, especially his references to panic and disloyalty, reflected Churchill's attitude, and would have been parroted by Roosevelt to be agreeable and placatory to him.

There was a mixed, if minor, public reaction in Australia to Curtin's call for a link to the United States. Some thought it necessary; others resented the prospect of a US connection above Australia's traditional British affiliation. In the United States, the media took a superficial, critical stance, which was rumoured to have been organised by the British, or even some in Australia.

Meanwhile, the war continued. On 2 January 1942, the Japanese bombed Rabaul, New Britain, just to Australia's north. The next day the British chiefs of staff asked Curtin if he would shift his 7th and 6th Divisions from the Middle East to the Dutch East Indies' island of Java. The British wanted to help keep the Dutch oil interests from the Japanese. Curtin agreed on 5 January. It was better to have these crack troops closer to Australia, just in case they were needed at home.

The talks in Washington over Christmas 1941 and into January 1942 were resolved very much to Churchill's satisfaction. The United States would join the Allies in Western Europe in the fight against Hitler. In the negotiations, Churchill had been shrewd, quick, adaptable and fluid in order to get what he wanted. He had quickly appreciated Roosevelt's desire to help China in its struggle against the Japanese.

Churchill was surprised to learn the US State Department's key officials were obsessed with China, and that they had captured the president's thinking on foreign policy. The department was split in its passions. Some supported Chiang Kai-shek's Nationalists and wanted to give them a $1 billion loan. Others, including a raft of secret communists such as Owen Lattimore, supported Mao Zedong. They were prepared to do much to help him defeat Chiang Kai-shek, even while China was at war with Japan.[3]

Churchill held back as much as he could in the discussions. He was intrigued to learn as much as possible about the reasons for this apparent split in the State Department over the two Chinese extremes. 'I believe, Mr President, that you may be overestimating the contribution which China could make to the general war,' Churchill said.

'Ah, Winston, I suppose India is a great contributor to the "general war"?' Roosevelt replied, with more than a trace of cynicism for the British obsession with the 'jewel in the Empire's crown'.

Churchill did not respond. He wanted to gauge the president's thinking, as directed by his Sinologists at the State Department.

'What would happen if China's enormous population developed in the same way as Japan has done in the last century,' Roosevelt asked, 'and they got hold of modern weapons?'

But Churchill was focused on his immediate challenge in Europe. 'I'm speaking of the present war,' he replied, 'and that is quite enough to go on for the time being.'[4]

This was a telling comment, indicative of the different mindsets of the two men. For many years, Churchill had put all his considerable being into saving his nation and Empire. Roosevelt had been doing much to avoid conflict and the massive pressures it brought to governing. Although he had now been dragged into it by the Japanese destruction of Pearl Harbor, he was still reluctant to abandon the intellectual meanderings of the theorists at the State Department for the cut-through practicalities of war.

Roosevelt changed tack. He pointed out that supporting China would keep several Japanese armies tied up in fighting. 'If China goes under,' Roosevelt said, 'how many divisions of Japanese troops would be freed – to do what? Take Australia? Take India?'[5]

This was a secondary argument. Churchill wanted to concentrate on the 'present war' involving the United States and the United Kingdom in the Pacific and Europe. Resources were limited, and diversions to assist China would not defeat their direct enemies.

But Churchill held his tongue. Realising that the president was a captive of American Sinologists, he became agreeable about the United States' policy towards all things Chinese. He wished to keep Roosevelt – and anyone or anything influencing him – onside.

Now it was Churchill who changed tack. He offered to send a division to Burma to tackle the Japanese there. It bordered China and had an important supply road on its west coast, running from Rangoon. This offer kept Roosevelt happy. Churchill left the talks ecstatic and, as one observer noted, 'drunk with power'. He had pulled off one of history's greatest diplomatic coups, and he knew it.

The Washington talks did nothing to improve Australia's position. The US military chiefs of staff, led by General George Catlett Marshall, drew up plans for combating the Japanese in South-East Asia. In other words, the plans were limited to where the fighting was going on. The strategy did not allow even for immediate contingencies, such as if Singapore were to fall. Marshall's mind was on the war in Western Europe, for which he was creating a new plan that was aimed at Allied victory, in accord with Churchill's wishes.

Australia was not considered to be a part of this South-East Asian theatre of war. It and New Zealand would have to defend a vast area: themselves, Papua, New Guinea, New Britain, the Bismarck Archipelago, the Solomon Islands, the New Hebrides and New Caledonia. In the eyes of the United States and the United Kingdom, this was adequate. From Australia's perspective, the strategy left it and New Zealand in a precarious position.

Curtin was irritated and despondent. On 5 January 1942 he wrote to Elsie:

The war goes very badly and I have a cable fight with Churchill almost daily. He has been in Africa and India and they count before Australia and New Zealand. The truth is that Britain never thought Japan would fight and made no preparations to meet that eventuality. In addition they never believed airpower could outfight seapower. Now they (Britain) will not risk ships uncovered by air support and there is no early possibility of air support. In

Australia we have to produce our own aircraft. Notwithstanding two years of Menzies we have really to start production.[6]

Curtin wrote as though he were still in opposition, and perhaps, in the deeper crevasses of his mind, he was rooted there. He had yet to fully grasp the levers of power and pull away from the foibles of the previous administration. He had been right about air power, but the time taken to design, manufacture and test any new flying machine was prohibitive. And who would test them? The best Australian pilots had been trained in Canada and the United Kingdom and were in combat in Europe in planes such as the Mosquito. Those under instruction in Australia at the end of 1941 would – at best – be novice fighter pilots in a year. Curtin's desire to 'produce our own aircraft' had more than a whiff of wishful thinking. If that were accomplished inside eighteen months, it would be most impressive. But by then the war could well be over.

In the 1930s, Curtin appeared to be in transition from his pacifist days to his more hardheaded days as the nation's leader and commander in chief. In the 1937 federal election, the electorate had not been convinced by him; he had not been able to dodge the conservatives' accusation that he was an 'isolationist'. For a potential prime minister, that was a step up from being branded a pacifist, but not enough to get Curtin elected.

Since then, he had thought through what he saw as a solution: he wanted to focus on building the Royal Australian Air Force. Given Australia's vast territory and shoreline, this aim had some merit. Perhaps also he was hoping, naively, that if Australia had enough planes – even the local Wirraways – he would not have to send huge numbers of troops into battle. He would always fear such a decision. This reflected his humanity, but not his fitness for all aspects of leadership.

Now that Curtin had the nation's top job, the thought of directing men to fight and die for their country, no matter what Australia's predicament, would literally make him ill.

13
Cable Bickering; Japan's First Setback

Churchill, now aged sixty-seven, was drinking as heavily as ever, smoking incessantly and working horrendous hours under perpetual pressure. He knew that the fate of the free world rested on his shoulders. In early January 1942, he and Stalin were the only two anti-fascist leaders with the will and power to crush the Nazis, and Churchill was attempting to rope in Roosevelt, the third figure who could have an impact against this formidable foe.

The exhausted Churchill was amenable to a small break. President Roosevelt had agreed to an all-out fight against Germany, and a 'holding operation in the Pacific' – exactly what Churchill wanted. He could retreat to a warm clime – Florida – before heading back into the northern winter.

The small break did Churchill's health and demeanour much good. He had set a clear course to defeat Hitler, with support from the world's most powerful military force. He could now deal more equably with the lesser problems, such as Curtin in Australia. Churchill mumbled again to Wilson about 'bad stock' and said he had sent Curtin a 'stiff' cable. It was far less than that, and quite mild. Churchill informed Curtin of the carve-up of various war theatres. Concerning the 'defence of Australia', Churchill remarked – disingenuously or cynically – 'I thought you would prefer it to be in the hands of the Australian Commander-in-Chief.' 'It', meant the vast territory that Curtin had been left to defend without remotely adequate manpower, or air and naval strength. He added as a concession, 'The United States would be quite willing, I believe, to reinforce your home defence troops with 40 to 50,000 Americans.'

Churchill was showing his power in the relationship with the United States. Curtin would be thrown what bones from the American table Churchill considered adequate. Rather than causing Curtin to back off, this simply increased his determination to push for more concrete concessions.

Churchill then asked, 'Do you think you are in immediate danger of invasion in force?' He had in mind, but did not say, six to ten Japanese divisions – about a quarter of a million enemy troops – on Australian soil. He knew that Curtin would not be able to reply, because no one knew the Japanese intentions. 'Immediate', in the rush of this war, could mean next week. Churchill then implied that Curtin should be more resolute. 'It is quite true that you may have air attacks,' he said, 'but we have had a good dose already in England without mortally harmful results.'[1]

Churchill was not only aiming at a holding position with Japan. He was attempting to do it too with what he viewed as his Empire's most recalcitrant member.

While Churchill recuperated, the Japanese fought down the west coast of the Malayan peninsula. They had not had it all their own way. Yamashita had nail-biting moments as, here and there, the British forces put up stiff opposition and delayed his determined force. But one by one the key places fell to the Japanese in December 1941 and the first half of January 1942: Jitra, 11–12 December; Balor Star, 13 December; Gurun, 14 December; Sungei Patani, Penang, 16 December; Taiping, Port Weld, 23 December; Kuala Kagsar, 24 December; Ipoh, 26 December; Kampar, 30 December; Kuantan, 31 December; Telok Anson and Slim River, 2 January; Kuala Selongor, 3 January; Port Swettenham, 10 January; and Kuala Lumpur, 11 January.

Outside Malaya, the British had capitulated to the Japanese in Hong Kong on 25 December. Early in the new year, the enemy had taken Manila and the US naval base at Cavite, and had attacked Bataan in the Philippines. On 11 January 1942, the same day that Kuala Lumpur had fallen, the Japanese invaded the Dutch East Indies and Dutch Borneo. They began by attacking Tarakan Island, off the coast of East Kalimantan, Borneo, where there was a major oil field. The Dutch were overwhelmed and massacred. It was an important acquisition, given that the shortage of fuel had been one factor of many driving the Japanese to war. Their next aim was to take Java, the most important island of the Dutch East Indies. Japanese troops began a methodical pincer movement towards their objective.

That week, they planned an advance on Burma. Japanese diplomats were on their way to Berlin to sign a military agreement with the other fascist powers, Germany and Italy. The intensity, ferocity and spread of their invasions, attacks and advances were frightening for an unprepared Allied world. So far, the Japanese had not received the predicted setback in Malaya that could turn a battle. Yamashita's high-risk strategy was working.

Gordon Bennett, with his force of not quite a division, was now in charge of the southern state of Johore, the last region in Malaya before the straits that led to Singapore. He felt the pressure hourly. He knew that his Australian force would be the last hope for Malaya, if not Singapore. He still agitated for an extra division of soldiers, but he realised it was probably not forthcoming. Bennett was an attacking commander. It was his instinct since Gallipoli and always his first option. He believed the indecisive British commanders' lack of a plan to counter-attack had imperilled Malaya. He decided to take the war to the Japanese for the first time.

The Japanese tactic of flanking through the cover of jungle – Yamashita's specialty – was working well. Bennett would attempt to counter it two ways: first, by attacking rather than waiting to be caught in the Japanese web; second, by spreading his defensive flanks to make it tougher for the enemy to creep past. After the fall of Kuala Lumpur, he chose Gemencheh Creek – about eleven kilometres west of Gemas village in Johore's north, and fifty-five kilometres north-east of Malacca, on the west coast – as the place not just to make a stand but to counter-attack.

In Tokyo on 10 January 1942, there was a joint liaison conference of the Japanese Imperial Headquarters staff and the government. Australia and New Zealand were on the agenda. The conference decided to proceed with 'southern operations' in the Pacific, which included naval conquests and military moves against Australia (initially against Papua), New Guinea and Guadalcanal in the Solomon Islands. Simultaneously, the Japanese would blockade supply from Britain and the United States. The aim was to increase pressure on Australia, and isolate it. The conference put it quaintly: ultimately, the aim was to 'force Australia to be freed from the shackles of Britain and the United States'.

Noticeably, the Japanese had edited the 'Great' from Britain. They had a masterplan to control Australia. It was called, euphemistically, Operation FS (Fiji–Samoa). Its aims were twofold. First, the Japanese wished to sever Australia's lines of communication with the United States. This would deny the Americans access to Australia, from which to launch a counter-offensive against Japan. Second, the plan would prevent the United States from supporting Australia. This blockade would be accompanied by fierce military pressure on Australia, at first by aerial bombing and naval attacks. The purpose here was to break the Australian government with psychological warfare, and ultimately to cause Australia to break from the Allies and surrender.

Curtin learnt of the continuing Japanese advance by intelligence, and not directly from the British. Bennett and his 8th Division would be called on to make a last stand in Johore. Curtin was unhappy not to have been informed of this worrying development. He fired off a cable (which smacked of Evatt's combative instincts) to Churchill, urging him to leave nothing 'undone to reinforce Malaya to the greatest degree possible in accordance with my earlier representations and your intentions'. He predicted a 'violent public reaction' if the follies of the Greece and Crete campaigns were repeated.[2]

This was the wrong approach to a refreshed Churchill, who on 10 January 1942 had taken a special train from Florida to Washington DC, accompanied by Casey, for whom he had high regard. On 12 January Churchill repeated his confidence in his Singapore fortress and believed that the Australians would stop the Japanese, especially as the British 18th Division was about to arrive in Singapore 'to take their stand with their Australian brothers'. He had faith in General Archibald Wavell (the overall commander in the region), who was suggesting a combined British/Australian force would be able to mount a counter-attack in late February.

Churchill, buoyed by his success in Washington, was floating on a cloud of optimism without properly examining the Malaya situation. His penchant for commanding everything in the political and military decision-making, strategically and tactically, had caused him to take his eye off the Far East. He was not alone in underestimating the Japanese, who, although outnumbered by British troops, had dominance on the seas and in the air. And in the ongoing land battle, Japan's ruling of the skies was becoming increasingly vital. Yamashita had 600 Zero planes, the best fighters in the region, and competent pilots, while the British had only about 250 inferior planes. Churchill made much of his sending fifty more Hurricanes (disassembled in crates and not in sight by mid-January) to Singapore. But in light of the rapid Japanese advance, this looked like being too little, too late.[3]

The constant cable bickering between Canberra and London was being picked up by Japanese spies in both cities. It may have been second-hand espionage – agents hearing persistent rumours – but it provided more than useful propaganda for the military-controlled press. In Tokyo, the *Nichi Nichi* daily newspaper of 13 January splashed the headline 'Canberra is indignant'.[4]

The accompanying article noted that Curtin's government was 'desperate'. Noting editorials in Australia, the paper further claimed that the public was dissatisfied with the lack of support from the United Kingdom. Local agents did not have to look too far to sense the disquiet. Curtin's historic message of 27 December was being quoted and embellished, just as Churchill predicted.

The *Japan Times* kept the scuttlebutt going with its own headline: 'Australia Feeling Uneasy as Premier [Prime Minister] Asks for War Material'. The piece claimed that Curtin felt Australia had been let down by Britain. 'The Australian people will no longer allow its sons to shed their blood in North Africa, nor even Malaya, while the Australian continent itself is bared of every means of defence.'[5] With the hyperbole taken away, this was more or less accurate.

Preoccupied with a counter-attack plan, Gordon Bennett had studied World War I sites from Gallipoli to Flanders and Northern France. He considered the wooden bridge across the Gemencheh Creek as a good spot to stop the enemy. The road on which the Japanese were expected to come twisted through dense jungle for about half a kilometre. Once the enemy force crossed the bridge, it had to travel another 250 metres in the open, with no cover either side of the road, before reaching more jungle. Bennett considered it perfect for an ambush.

He put Lieutenant-Colonel Frederick 'Black Jack' Galleghan, the commander of the 2/30th Battalion, in charge. His nickname came from his part West Indian background, and misleadingly indicated a cavalier approach. Galleghan was a careful planner and a good leader. His initial reaction was that the bridge area was too small for a battalion (about 1000 men). He opted for a company of 250. All his company commanders wanted to lead the mission; the only fair way to make a choice was to put names in a hat. D Company, led by Des Duffy, won the draw. Galleghan put the rest of the battalion across the road a further five kilometres back. They were geared up for the inevitable stealth by the Japanese. Indian troops were kept at the ready on both flanks.

It was raining on the night of 13 January 1942. The diggers crept to their positions. Sappers moved to the bridge and set it up with explosives. The entire battalion waited all night. Finally, at 4 p.m. the next day, the Japanese appeared. There were about 1000 soldiers on bikes, riding eight abreast. They began to cross the bridge, smiling and chatting. They were relaxed and enjoying themselves.

Duffy and his men were hidden close to the winding road. They let 300 of the happy throng pass by and over the bridge, leaving 700 in the vulnerable zone. Duffy signalled. His engineers blew the bridge. Wood, men and bikes were hurled in the air. Duffy's men tossed grenades and opened up with machine guns. The Japanese had nowhere to run. They were cut down, the dead and the dying littering 300 metres of road among the debris.

The initial action took nineteen minutes. Duffy's men made it back to the Battalion position five kilometres away west of the bridge. Only one Australian was killed, making it in every respect one of the most successful ambushes in the war to that point.[6] Bennett's counter-attack mentality, evident since the early days of Gallipoli, had worked.

14
Malaya Falling

Curtin was hopeful when he learned of Bennett's counter-attack, but there was no jubilation in Canberra. The battle had taken place in the southern half of Malaya, which meant the Japanese were in striking distance of Singapore. It was a battle win, not victory in the war in Malaya.

Curtin was preoccupied with another problem: some miners had gone on strike in thirty mines in New South Wales. These actions were ill-timed, and calculated by communist union leaders to cause Curtin the maximum embarrassment at a moment when he did not need any vexing distractions. The dispute over retirement pensions had merit, but not at this time, when coal supplies were critical.

Curtin enlisted federal and state union leaders to appeal to the New South Wales miners' union, but this achieved nothing. The prime minister reacted by bringing in national-security regulations that threatened tough penalties for anyone disrupting coal production. Miners would be expelled from their unions or have their exemption from military service cancelled. The latter penalty carried the greater threat, especially with the daily reports of casualties among the Australian ranks. The number of people asking for exemption from military service had increased. Press editorials and comment called for those avoiding call-up to be pressured, and decried those who thought that the Americans would come to Australia's rescue. Such help might be a long way off, perhaps a year, the reports claimed.[1]

Some strikes continued. The press generally backed Curtin's move, knowing it would hurt him personally to take such stringent action against workers. But media owners and journalists also protested, without striking, against government censorship, which they considered too harsh. *Smith's Weekly* was fined for reporting on 'fifth columnists' – spies or agents of a foreign power – and publishing a photograph of Queensland's fascist leader in his black shirt. Other papers were cautioned.

National focus returned to Malaya as the Japanese recovered after the Gemas upset. Other contingents of Yamashita's force kept coming. They reached the Muar River, about sixty-five kilometres south of Gemas. It was 500 metres wide and the last hurdle before the causeway at Johore. The Japanese gathered north of it. They engaged two Indian companies and overran them. At night the Australians attacked with heavy artillery fire. But it could not stop the enemy, who used boats they had brought with them. By the end of the day they had crushed their terrified Indian opposition on the southern bank of the river. The Japanese also made it across the river fifty kilometres further south of Batu Pahat. Bennett's sensitivity at being one division short was at its most intense. He would somehow have to stiffen his defences at Johore. He committed the 2/19th and 2/29th Battalions to battle.[2]

The enemy sent patrols forward. When they discovered the Australian positions on 17 January 1942, they hit them with accurate mortar fire, which the diggers were forced to endure through the night. It did some damage to the guns of the 2/4th Australian Anti-Tank Regiment, which indicated that Japanese intelligence was as pinpoint as ever.

At first light on 18 January, the Japanese sent tanks down the Muar Road, heading for the digger battalions. The Australian gunners fired armour-piercing shells, which ripped right through some of the lightly built tanks. Yet three kept sliding forward and passed the frustrated gunners, who were looking down the road for the next group of tanks. But the commander of the 2/4th Regiment, Lance Sergeant C. W. Thornton, ordered his men to keep firing at the first three, this time using high-explosive rounds. The tanks became trapped in a cutting. They tried to manoeuvre out. The anti-tank shells roared at them. One struck home and exploded inside, then another. The tanks blew up, ammunition and metal flying off like a catherine wheel. The third tank endured the same fate.

In all, ten tanks were obliterated over the next few hours. The Japanese infantry, shocked and demoralised for the first time, were beaten off. They brought in fresh troops, unscarred in battle, who attempted many assaults but were repulsed. Yet the Japanese were relentless. Their expertise at jungle flanking moves was successful again, with the inexperienced Indians unable to defeat them.

The Japanese built a roadblock between the positions of the 2/29th and the 2/19th Battalions. A valiant attempt by commander Lieutenant-Colonel J. C. Robertson to link the battalions failed. He was cut down by Bren gunfire from the roadblock and died an hour later. This stunned the battalions. The Australian soldiers were demoralised by their leader's demise. But they regrouped and held off assaults from the south and west. The Japanese continued to mass around them, like angry hornets. The diggers, with no support on the flanks, were left vulnerable.

Curtin was under great stress, worrying about what would happen in Malaya and about the recalcitrant unions at home. The industrial stoppages were pushing him to take actions that he hated. Once more he threatened transport workers that they would be called up if they didn't go back to work. He called in the navy to unload goods when waterside workers went on strike, claiming an additional two shillings an hour. A fresh problem arose when the Waterside Workers' Union in Darwin refused to unload artillery from a US freighter, the SS *Holbrook*. The union would not let soldiers do the work, and the big guns remained in crates on board for three weeks.

Curtin sent a minister to Darwin to negotiate with the unionists. Given that most Australians, especially in this northernmost port, knew it must be a target for the Japanese, this stop-work appeared to be the most disruptive and stupefying act of the war so far. Artillery would be Darwin's main defensive weapon if and when the Japanese made their move.

On top of this, the far left of Curtin's party, led by his most difficult colleague – the Minister for Labour and National Service, Eddie Ward – was pushing him to nationalise Australia's basic industries. Curtin had chosen Ward for the job, which seemed a shrewd enough move because it was thought he could negotiate with union bosses. But it had not worked to the government's satisfaction. Ward, a firebrand in parliament, was weak in the face of extreme left and communist opposition. Union militancy ruled in vital industries such as the wharves and coalmining, and production had fallen with Ward as Minister. He failed to make them choose between the war effort and their demands.

Ward had another, bigger agenda. He saw the war as an excuse to move the country hard left, aiming for a form of communism. Curtin had no mandate to do this. His dream of a socialist state was not a priority, although he would push for new legislation to do with health and welfare if the chance arose. The extremists, careless of the consequences, saw early 1942 as their moment to strike.

Curtin resisted all these challenges but they took a toll on his health. His fear that he would be an inferior prime minister to Menzies in wartime had not been justified, yet when the heat was on, his physical frailty would show. This concerned his family and close friends.

Churchill finally appreciated the dire situation in Malaya in mid-January 1942. He cabled Wavell, asking what would happen if the British forces had to withdraw onto Singapore. How many troops would be needed to defend it? How would the Japanese be stopped?

Wavell replied, 'Little or nothing has been done to construct defences on the north side of the island to prevent [the Japanese] covering the Johore Straits.'[3]

Churchill was stunned. The Australian fears over a long period had proved correct. He was angered by not having known, and by his advisers failing him. He railed against his chiefs. But he knew that he was wriggling away from his own careless disregard for the warnings. In what would have been seen as high farce had it not been so serious, he exhorted the troops on Singapore to make up for his blunder: 'The whole island must be fought for until every single unit and every single strong point has been separately destroyed. The city of Singapore must be converted into a citadel and defended to the death. No surrender can be contemplated.'[4]

Everyone would have to die for the Empire, and Churchill's folly.

15

Anderson's Last Stand

The 8th Division's fight on Malaya was no longer about holding the Japanese; it was a rearguard action to escape obliteration or capture. Lieutenant-Colonel Robertson's place was taken by the no-less-distinguished commander of the 2/19th Battalion, the bespectacled Lieutenant-Colonel Charles Anderson. Aged forty-four, he served in the King's African Rifles in World War I and won a Military Cross fighting pro-German Askari tribesmen in the jungles of East Africa. That experience prepared him better than most for war in Malaya.

He also shot big game in Kenya for pleasure. Now instead of being the hunter he was the hunted. Anderson was given the tough task of leading a night withdrawal to the bridge at Parit Sulong, eight kilometres away. On 20 January 1942, the battalions were to retreat through swamps and go wide of roads where the Japanese had set up roadblocks and prepared ambushes. Anderson's aim was to clear each roadblock so that his force's vehicles – ambulances and trucks – could move forward.

It was slow going. The fatigued men dragged themselves through the mud. They had gone two kilometres when they sighted around 100 Japanese troops dug in on a marshy knoll fifty metres off the road. They would have to be removed to allow trailing vehicles through. Anderson swung his forward company into action in an attempt to remove the enemy. A battle ensued. The Australians could not make headway. Anderson ordered another company to assist in the conflict.

A digger began singing 'Waltzing Matilda', and soon a huge chorus of voices lifted above the mangroves as the two companies attacked. The inspired force of the assault dislodged the Japanese, who were soon surrounded and forced to retreat into the jungle. The vehicles carrying the growing number of wounded troops rolled forward.

Anderson and his men waded on. They were soon faced with another obstacle: some Japanese on a hill. Armed with a pistol and several grenades, he led seven handpicked men around the south side of the enemy while others created a diversion to the north. Anderson's group crept up close behind the Japanese. Then they tossed grenades at their position. Anderson himself then led the charge, firing his pistol. The action cleared the way again.

There were other blocks on the road that had to be cleared. The diggers were struggling. Casualties were mounting, filling the convoy of trucks and ambulances. About 400 were wounded, some in need of urgent treatment. Anderson ordered his medical officers not to leave any wounded in the 'hot' battle areas. The Japanese were known to show no mercy to prisoners, especially the wounded, who were regarded as liabilities and executed.

Ammunition was low. To preserve it, Anderson had to order his force – comprising the 2/19th and 2/29th Battalions, and the Indian 45th Brigade – to make fixed-bayonet charges. After eighteen hours on the move, with stop-start 'marches' and battles, he and his depleted force reached the outskirts of Parit Sulong, about 130 kilometres from Johore Bharu and the causeway to Singapore.

The Japanese now controlled most of Malaya's west and spine. They had leapt ahead of the Australians. They were fortifying at Parit Sulong, waiting for these desperate diggers.

The Curtin–Churchill cables descended into bitter claim and counter-claim, culminating in a thousand-word justification by Churchill for his entire political career from 1930. Yet he concluded in a conciliatory tone: 'We must not be dismayed or get into recrimination but remain united in true comradeship. Do not doubt my loyalty to Australia and New Zealand . . .'[1]

He then contradicted himself again, switching his strategy to promote the protection of India. He now wanted his chiefs to consider evacuating all British forces from Singapore to Burma. Churchill worried that India would receive 'a tremendous shock' if Singapore and Corregidor (in the Philippines) fell.

There was anxiety in Curtin's Cabinet. Its members were at least consistent in their views, while Churchill was erratic. From Canberra, it seemed clear that it would be dangerous for the men of the 8th Division, who had not yet made it out of Malaya.

Anderson's aim was to smash through one last roadblock, at a bridge in a village on the road that would take them north to brigade headquarters on the coast at Yong Peng, sixty kilometres away. The men rested through the night of 20 January. Anderson planned an assault on the town at 11 a.m. the next day.

In those fourteen hours, the Japanese dug themselves well in, and waited. Anderson's force attacked for two hours but could make no headway. He sent news to a British contingent moving close by. It made a move from the west but failed to distract the Japanese enough. Anderson pulled back his men. They were outnumbered and running out of supplies. He sent an urgent message to Bennett to rush him ammunition. A message came back: 'Look up at sparrowfart.' This would have had the enemy interceptors scratching their heads, but the Australians understood. Supplies would be dropped into the region at first light.

At dawn on 22 January, five old planes – two Albacores and three RAAF Buffaloes living up to their name – lumbered into the sky and followed the road to Parit Sulong. They dropped cases of tinned food, morphine and other medical supplies by parachute, then doubled back to drop bombs on the Japanese manning the main bridge. But they had forgotten something even more important than food and medicine: ammunition.

Anderson faced an agonising dilemma. The alternative to the road was through the jungle. He attempted to liaise with the Japanese, in the hope that they would let the truck and ambulance convoy carrying the wounded pass over the bridge to Yong Peng. The enemy refused. He considered his dwindling options again. His men would have to leave the road and all the vehicles and heavy equipment in order to make a detour north to the Australian base. This would be through jungle all the way.

This decision meant Anderson would have to leave the most incapacitated soldiers behind. Only those who could walk would be taken, if a mate would assist them. After medics had comforted the 110 diggers and thirty-five Indians who could not be moved, they left them with food for a week and plenty of morphine. In an act braver than any of the fighting, ten of the slightly wounded volunteered to stay with their mates and act as medical orderlies, knowing that they would soon be taken prisoner by the Japanese.

Anderson ordered his fit men, and the wounded who could be helped, to slip away from Parit Sulong and into the swampy, malaria-infested jungle, leaving the ill and wounded to the whim of the enemy.

Bennett at Yong Peng headquarters was concerned that Anderson and his men had been isolated and would be defeated. He sent a message to Canberra saying his battalions had been cut off 'without possibility of relief'. This seemed desperate, although he did not rule out that they might somehow escape.

Not for the first time, Bennett doubted the capacity of the Indian troops, who had failed to stop the Japanese flanking manoeuvre. This reinforced his endless pleas for more troops. His argument had been consistent long before the Japanese attacked on 7 December. Now there were traces of bitterness and despair in his communication. Everyone, it seemed to him, had let him down, from Blamey and Churchill to Curtin and Sturdee. His disrespect for Percival and the British command had grown monthly. Bennett, a hero at Gallipoli, could see the edifice of his career and reputation collapsing.

A Japanese contingent crept over the bridge at Parit Sulong the day after Anderson and his men left. It surrounded the vehicles, unsure if trucks were booby-trapped. Realising that they were full of wounded men, the Japanese approached with fixed bayonets. They ordered the men out of the vehicles. Those who were too sick to move were dragged out and pushed to the ground. They were left for several hours.

The captured men were placed in the remnants of a farmhouse nearby, where they were left for another night. The rough treatment and delays indicated that the Japanese were unsure of what they should do. They had captured 145, a big haul of prisoners. Activities the next morning indicated a renewed urgency. Soldiers bustled about. A guard formed outside the farmhouse. Half an hour later a car pulled up. The bulky General Yamashita stepped out.

He was escorted around the building. The General peered in through windows at the wounded men. There was urgency in his step and manner. He grunted a few observations, then returned to his car and conferred with his senior officers. Yamashita ordered that there should be no delay to the push to the causeway and the attack on Singapore. All the POWs should be 'disposed of'.

Yamashita was then driven away. The prisoners were clumped together in groups of five, tied with wire and dragged, pushed or carried outside to a clearing. They were machine-gunned and bayoneted until there was no movement among them. Similar acts were repeated in the clearing until the end of the morning. When the carnage was over and all seemed dead, petrol was doused over the bodies. They were set alight.

Some had faked their deaths, but there was no faking the screams that followed as the diggers and Indians were incinerated.[2]

Anderson and the 'fit' remnants of the battalions – about 500 Australians and 400 Indians – pushed their way through swamps and staggered over open ground here and there. The enemy noted their movements. Unaware that the diggers were out of ammunition, the Japanese, recalling the diggers' aggression near Gemas a week earlier, thought this was another manoeuvre to attack and decided to withdraw. This left a 400-metre escape route for the Australians and Indians, who reached Yong Peng just before the base had to be vacated. The Japanese were closing in fast. From there, transport trucks drove the fleeing soldiers east and then south, down to a 'safe' Australian brigade position.

Lieutenant-General Percival later said Anderson's effort was 'one of the epics of the Malayan campaign'. It would earn the Australian leader a Victoria Cross (VC) to accompany his Military Cross. His VC citation read: 'For setting a magnificent example of brave leadership, determination and outstanding courage. He not only showed fighting qualities of a very high order but throughout exposed himself to danger without any regard for his own personal safety.'

Anderson and his men deserved every accolade. But their efforts were swamped by news that the Japanese had also taken North Borneo.

16
Churchill's About Face; Fall of Rabaul

Curtin was close to a nervous breakdown in the second half of January 1942. The cable battle with Churchill, his concern for the 8th Division, his worry about the probable fall of Singapore, and the infuriating behaviour of unions threatening or going on strike all conspired to make him ill. Stress brought on his manic depression and a craving for solace in alcohol. Even although he had sworn off the 'grog' as prime minister, the self-denial was itself another pressure – a push towards a mental abyss. Friends, family and colleagues urged him to go on holiday.

Curtin decided to go across the country to Perth with wife Elsie. Their four-day train journey, via Adelaide, began on 21 January. Before the train left Canberra, his office put out a comment for the media in response to a question about the Japanese bombing off Rabaul, New Britain, the island just north of New Guinea that was administered by Australia under a League of Nations mandate. Rabaul was one of the best natural ports in the south-west Pacific, and an Australian battalion was stationed there.

The newspapers the next day quoted Curtin as yet again warning Australians against any complacency. The press was kept away from him, although he put on a brave face in Adelaide. Curtin covered up his illness well, always managing to look authoritative in front of a welcoming crowd. Unaware of his real condition, many observers became critical of him vacationing at this vital time, and so far from Canberra.

Although on holiday, Curtin still carried out a round of speeches and engagements, unable to avoid the media. A newsreel company parked outside his modest Cottesloe home and filmed him walking through the front gate. He looked towards the crew, smiled and disappeared into the house. Some of his minders wondered whether this might be a lapse in security, but Curtin took the view that it was better to appear 'natural' during these tough days.

Curtin was proved correct. Servicemen in Perth and Darwin clapped and cheered when the film was shown. They were responding not to anything he said but to the image he projected. This bloke was unostentatious, the newsreel showed; he lived modestly; he was homely. Along with Curtin's ability to grip an audience through his oratory, this view pointed to a growing potency in his electoral appeal as the nation slipped towards a possible crisis. In truth he was struggling, but only his tight inner circle of family and friends knew it.

The media was looking for any signs of weakness or a lack of resolve in the still new prime minister. Curtin did not appear incapacitated but he was away from the 'action', leaving his government without its leader and perhaps its shrewdest and wisest mind. Evatt, the most forceful and ambitious minister in Cabinet, attempted to fill the vacuum. He had been vocal in putting his case about what should be said in cables. Without Curtin's tempering influence, he dominated.

Deputy Prime Minister Frank Forde called for an emergency Cabinet meeting on 23 January to discuss Bennett's alarming and cryptic message from Johore. Forde's concerns were compounded by a report from the Australian representative in Singapore, who said the 'British position was desperate and perhaps irretrievable'.

This new shock followed intelligence from Page in London concerning Churchill's Plan B. He would abandon Singapore and concentrate on the British fight in Burma. The Australian government had to respond in some way, although no one was sure how. Curtin's leadership and his common-sense command of the issues were missing. Cabinet began trying to compose a message. It was always going to have a disjointed look, with Forde, Chifley, Evatt and, later, Shedden all wishing to make a point.

The cable began diplomatically: 'Whilst we have no intention of suggesting any criticism of the Indians who are fighting the common foe, we hope you are not placing too much reliance on the mere numerical strength of the land forces you are sending [to Singapore] without regard to their qualities.' This was transparent: Cabinet was blaming the Indians for the collapse in Johore, and suggesting that the 18th Division on its way to Singapore had better be experienced and capable. Next, Cabinet let Churchill know they were aware of his plan to sacrifice Singapore in favour of Burma.

Then came the punchline, which had Evatt's imprimatur and his signature legal 'argument': 'After all the assurances we had been given, the evacuation of Singapore would be regarded here and elsewhere as an inexcusable betrayal.'

The term 'betrayal' would make Churchill both annoyed and uneasy. Leading Australian politicians of all political hues, along with historians of both world wars, had wanted to say this word to him ever since Gallipoli, and more recently over Greece and Crete. Now it had been said. But, as he had vehemently told Casey, he was 'unkickable'. Churchill's self-righteousness, continued sense of destiny and recent 'win' in America would see his anger subside into indignation.

Nevertheless, the accuracy of the Australian reaction touched him. He knew he had done everything to keep the Australians in the dark about his evolving plans. 'Betrayal' was a strong description, but there were elements of truth that gave Churchill pause. He had ignored Australia's overtures concerning Singapore when he believed in its impregnability. Now that it was not the fortress he had believed it to be, the 'bad stock' had a good grievance. Churchill could see that his about-face on Singapore would indeed look like betrayal.

The Evatt-influenced tough line continued: 'Singapore is a central fortress of the system of Empire and local defence. We understood it was to be made impregnable; and, in any event, it was to be capable of holding out for a prolonged period until the arrival of the main fleet.' In other words, Churchill's belief in Singapore's soundness, especially without air cover, had been a gross tactical error.

The cable added: 'On the faith of the proposed flow of reinforcements, we have acted and carried out our part of the bargain. We expect you not to frustrate the whole purpose by evacuation.'[1]

The mention of 'evacuation' had resonance. Churchill's strategic folly over Gallipoli had led to the Anzacs and British creeping off the Turkish Peninsula, and was a reminder of that military failure.

The cable went on to demand, rather than suggest, that if Churchill was going to divert his 18th Division, it should be to the Dutch East Indies rather than Burma. This confronting cable reflected a disappointment at Churchill's sudden, staggering flip-flop.

Curtin's illness, Churchill's perplexing change of mind and the collapse of Malaya caused the Australian government to feel confused and isolated. Its woes were increased as ministers learned more about what was happening in Rabaul. The Japanese, it seemed, were coming from everywhere, and nothing could stop them. If Rabaul and New Britain fell to the Japanese, they could use it as a base from which to hop across to nearby New Guinea, and advance towards Port Moresby. A glance at the map showed that the next move after that was to Australia.

Rabaul was garrisoned by 1400 soldiers led by Lieutenant-Colonel John Scanlan. There were 716 frontline members of the 2/22nd Battalion, which had been deployed for ten months. The force included a local militia unit, the New Guinea Volunteer Rifles, a coastal defence battery, an anti-aircraft battery and the 2/10th Ambulance Unit. It was linked with the 130-member 2/1st Independent Company garrisoned on the nearby island of New Ireland. The New Britain garrison's main job had been to protect an RAAF airfield near Rabaul and a flying boat anchorage.

Its moment of truth came on 21 January. Eight of the ten tiny and lightly armed RAAF Wirraway training planes scrambled skyward to meet 109 Japanese Zeros. Squadron Leader John Carew summed up his situation by sending a Latin motto to RAAF headquarters in Melbourne: *'Nos Morituri Te Salutamus'* – 'We who are about to die salute you'. Six of the inadequate Wirraways were quickly disposed of. The Japanese lost just one plane as they smashed the Australian coastal artillery. An RAAF flying boat spotted an enemy invasion fleet carrying a Japanese assault brigade, led by Major-General Tomitaro. The Australians signalled their discovery before being shot down. The vulnerable ground forces were withdrawn from Rabaul.

On 22 January, Tomitaro's Nankai Shitai Regiment struck New Ireland and took the main town of Kavieng without opposition from the small 2/1st Independent Company, which had dispersed throughout the island. Five thousand Japanese attacked Rabaul at 2.45 a.m. on 23 January. The swiftness of the night assault and the superior numbers of the Japanese helped the invading force break the defence. Before dawn, Scanlan realised his garrison troops had no hope of defending Rabaul. The order to his men was 'every man for himself'. Soldiers and civilians split into small bands of forty or fifty men. Eight hundred soldiers were captured. Four hundred retreated into the interior jungle.[2] News of Rabaul's fall was relayed to Forde, Evatt, Chifley and co. on 23 January, reaching them as they were working on their forceful response to Churchill. It prompted an insert in their communication: the attack on Rabaul, they wrote, has given rise 'to a public feeling of grave uneasiness and Allied impotence to do anything to stem the Japanese advance'.

The Australian people, the cable concluded, having volunteered 'for service overseas in large numbers, find it difficult to understand why they must wait so long for an improvement in the situation, where irreparable damage may have been done to their power to resist, the prestige of the Empire and the solidarity of the Allied cause'.[3]

While the politicians sent each other cryptic, confrontational messages, the RAAF's response to the fall of Rabaul was swift. It bombed Japanese shipping and installations in Rabaul from airstrips in Port

Moresby, Lae and Salamaua. Admiral Inoue, who was emerging as the Imperial Navy's leading strategist, urged that Japan should capture these bases, along with the island of Tulagi in the British Solomon Islands. On 29 January, then, Japan's Naval General Staff ordered the Commander in Chief of the Combined Fleet, Admiral Isoroku Yamamoto, to take these Allied bases.

Churchill's strong inclination to evacuate Singapore in favour of Burma was intended to appease the US State Department's infatuation with China. Placing British troops in Burma to defend China's border would show the Americans that Churchill was supporting their foreign policy, but his mind was still on Europe. Even moving the British 18th Division to Singapore had been done to keep Roosevelt happy. But the 'squeal' (as Churchill characterised it) from the Australians about his betrayal of them caused him, he later claimed, to stay with the idea of fighting it out in Singapore.

It's probable that all the generals under British command at Singapore, including Bennett, would have agreed to an evacuation. Bennett had seen the result of his counter-attack at Gemas: it had given the Japanese a blood nose, not a mortal wound. After the invaders recovered, they outflanked their opponents. The hard-headed Bennett was a realist. He kept pleading for an extra division of Australians. Any faith he once had in the British and Indians had evaporated. The expected advent of the 18th Division did not imbue him with any extra confidence.

Since the Australian support he wanted was not forthcoming, he was resigned to finding an exit strategy for his troops digging in at Singapore. Bennett wanted to fight, but he preferred an even playing field on which to do battle. By departing with some honour and many lives – like the defeat at Gallipoli – he and his troops had the prospect of living to battle another day. Now it was too late.

The Australian government's quite rational response to Churchill's switching of emphasis to Burma influenced Churchill to 'stay the course'. It flushed out his lukewarm approach to evacuating Singapore. He now feared that a British 'scuttle', coming at the same time that the United States was fighting on at Corregidor, would give the British (and him) an image 'all over the world' too 'terrible to imagine'.[4]

The sad result, however, was that a stubborn defence of Singapore imperilled the entire 8th Division, which was exactly what Curtin and his Cabinet did not want.

17

The Lull Before

Churchill's response to the Australian government's blistering cable was to play both the statesman and the gutter-fighter. He told Curtin he would not allow Australian discourtesy to cloud his judgement or lessen his efforts on Australia's behalf. Then he complained that Page had passed intelligence to the Australian government. He said it would now be tough for Page to be allowed to attend 'our most intimate and secret councils' if just parts of 'sensitive discussions' were reported to Curtin to 'make the basis for the kind of telegrams you have sent me'.[1]

Churchill had already abused Page, who said Churchill had gone 'off the deep end' about Australia generally.

'If you are going to squeal,' Churchill threatened, 'I shall send them all back home again out of the various fighting zones.'

This was Churchill at his most arrogant. Australia was not entitled to learn about any decisions that might affect it until after he had put them in place. It made a nonsense out of consultation. And while in this latest telegram he took a swipe at 'Colonials' (as he disparagingly referred to the Australians in private), he could not resist some patronising remarks about Curtin's *Herald* article of a month earlier, which had hurt him.

'You have made it clear in public that you place your confidence in the United States,' he wrote. 'We are very glad you should consult with them and set up any arrangements necessary for that purpose.'

Disingenuously, Churchill added, 'Pray continue to invoke our assistance in securing [US] attention to your views.'[2]

The relationship between the United Kingdom and Australia had reached a low ebb. Not since the cricket fiasco of the 'Bodyline' Ashes series of a decade earlier had it held such enmity. The rancour was far more serious in 1942, and some suspected it might cause permanent dislocation.

On 27 January 1942 General Wavell was given permission by Churchill to withdraw the entire British force in Malaya to Singapore. It was a humiliation for everyone from Churchill down to the lowliest private, and a massive psychological boost for the Japanese.

The impatient Yamashita was thrilled: his promise to Japan's Emperor to deliver Singapore to him now had a strong chance of fulfilment. Yet still his concern was time. As ever, his nightmare was the thought of his so-far triumphant force being caught in the street-by-street brawling that would impede his supply lines for everything from fuel and ammunition to food and arms.

This nagging fear caused Yamashita to be even more aggressive. The Japanese airforce would bomb everything on the island without discrimination. Hospitals would be targeted rather than spared. The civil population would be attacked just as forcefully as Britain's military bases. Prisoners would continue to be savaged: machine-gunning, beheading and torture would be increased. Yamashita's aim was to force the British command to capitulate.

The cunning tactic was to target the British commanders' humanity – their desire to spare civilians, the wounded and the fatigued soldiers. If they did not surrender, the Japanese promised to annihilate both civilians and soldiers alike. No one would be spared.

Going on the history of the war so far, no one believed this to be an idle threat. The British commanders, especially the vacillator Percival, would be forced to consider their place in history. If there were a massacre, it was put to Percival, he would be held responsible for it.

The news of Yamashita's huge success in taking Malaya initiated a feverish round of meetings in Tokyo as all sections of the armed services hastened to propose plans for the next conquest. Yamashita's victory was a euphoric moment for the army, especially since the admirals had taken a prestigious leap ahead of the generals after Pearl Harbor and the sinking of the *Prince of Wales*.

Not to be outdone, on 28 January the navy's operational planners put forward a plan to Navy General Staff. The highest priority, once Ceylon was taken (with German assistance), was that 'Darwin must be taken'. This could only mean an invasion, albeit a modest one, with perhaps no more than a brigade (5000 men). Unlike Darwin, 'Fiji and Samoa need not be taken, only destroyed', the 'Combined Fleet' planners stated. They appeared sanguine about Hawaii: 'We should like to take Hawaii, if possible.'[3] They proposed this should be done before the middle of 1942, which was not overly ambitious, given the fleet's record so far.

The navy was jumping in first, before Yamashita could boast he had taken Singapore. If that eventuated, the Japanese leaders' confidence in the army rather than the Navy might be consolidated forever. Pressure on the Imperial headquarters in Tokyo was at a peak. Because of the speed of acquisitions and battle victories on land and sea, no one, including the very top of the military dictatorship, was certain of what to do next. Yet there was an urgency to do *something*. Success in war, it seemed, spawned too many bright ideas. Imperial headquarters had no time to reflect, only to react.

Emperor Hirohito, Japan's Supreme Military Commander, liked the navy planners' ideas about acquiring Darwin. On 29 January, on the advice of his High Command, he affixed his seal on an order for the Combined Fleet to capture Lae, Salamaua and Port Moresby. These were the first steps of the plan to isolate and attack Darwin. After Japan's massive efforts in China, Pearl Harbor, Thailand and Malaya, gobbling up little Darwin was hardly a major operation. But it would be the first step of a grander mission to deny the United States its big base in the Pacific.[4]

On 30 January 1942, General Tojo, Japan's prime minister and war minister, met with the army's head of operations, Colonel Takushiro Hattori. Hattori told Tojo about the navy's plans to invade Australia. Tojo demurred. He approved a general plan to invade Fiji, Samoa and New Caledonia, but indicated there was no agreement between the High Command and government ministers, including himself, over Australia.

General Tojo was concerned about the navy taking such initiative, and articulated the army's general objections. Australia was an operation too far away for Tojo and the soldiers. They did not have the navy's new perspective where its aircraft carriers could use long range bombers to flatten a city like Darwin and then send in troops via carriers to fight and take control. Tojo preferred battles such as Yamashita's operation in Malaya, which had gone on for only two months. He refused to accept the navy's argument that with a sea and air attack, operations could be even quicker and just as effective.

Tojo was also forever looking over his shoulder at Russia. He had to make provision that it might attack Japan, which would stretch his armies. Ever since defeating Russia in the war of 1904–05, the Japanese had been confident about repeating the feat, especially if Germany attacked Russia through the Caucasus, as was rumoured to be planned for May and June 1942. This was a further reason for easing the Australian option aside for the moment, although the Russian option was equally vague. All plans had a fluidity that only war could create.

Tojo and his chiefs would reconsider all possibilities if and when Yamashita took Singapore. In the meantime, he approved the invasion of eastern New Guinea and the Solomon Islands.

There was a British rush to cross the one-kilometre-long causeway linking Malaya with Singapore, which was just twenty metres wide at the waterline. Churchill's 'fortress' island was flat, apart from three hills. The main one, Bukit Timah, rose 176 metres and sat just north of a village of the same name, which was nearly at the centre of the island. Another hill lay north of that. A long ridge about thirty metres high ran along the south coast towards the town of Singapore.

The rest of the island was low-lying. Outside the built-up areas it was covered with jungle, rubber and other plantations. Small *kampongs* (villages) were scattered every few hundred metres. On the southern shore, Singapore town merged inland into areas of well-manicured parkland, interspersed with the homes of the rich. Bukit Timah road ran from Singapore north across the island to the causeway, and beyond into Malaya.

The worst sound of all on Singapore came at 8 a.m. on Saturday 31 January 1942, when the island's already tense residents were unnerved by a massive explosion in the north. It rattled windows and caused chairs to jump. The city had been hammered for two months. But this detonation was as loud as it was symbolic. It came from the charges set on the causeway linking the island to Malaya. It signalled Britain's concession that it had no hope of defeating the Japanese in Malaya. Singapore was to be the last stand.

The Japanese wanted the excellent harbour in Singapore's south; the naval facility in its north-east; and the prestige of defeating the opposing Empire at its Asian stronghold. The British command, in permanent disbelief and even shock that Malaya had slipped from its Empire so quickly, would not give away Singapore quite so readily. It carried prestige as the British Empire's 'Asian Gibraltar'. The lives of one million people on this small sea-bound outpost, just forty kilometres long and twenty-three kilometres wide, were at stake.

Bennett's Australians would be part of the defence. His troops included the two AIF Brigades and a recently landed Indian Brigade, the 44th. They had made their final withdrawal from Malaya the night before the blast. The Australians felt a real stand should be made from their bridgehead in the southern tip of Johore. They believed their defensive positions were well-sited for a shootout, despite the disadvantage of a lack of air cover and support. That was not going to be possible on the island.

Bennett, too, was stunned but in a different way from the British generals. Withdrawals hurt his military pride, especially after his World War I experience. He had been part of the evacuation from Gallipoli, where 30,000 diggers lived to fight another day without disgrace. And he had been in the victories of 1918 on the Western Front. This was a new experience.

His diary entry for 31 January 1942 reflected his incredulity: 'Thus ended the retreat to the Island. The whole operation seems incredible: 550 miles in 55 days, forced back by a small Japanese Army of two divisions, riding stolen bicycles and without artillery support.'[5]

He expressed his disappointment at not being allowed to hold Johore and blamed the British and Indian troops for its demise. Bennett was certain the war would have gone a different way had the Australians been allowed to fight the Japanese from the start. But once Singapore became their last bastion, it was too late. The Japanese had lost just 2000 men, with another 3000 wounded. But they had annihilated three of the seven Indian brigades, with their combined Indian and British battalion make-up. Bennett knew the momentum was with the enemy.

By 3 February 1942, there seemed to be nowhere to hide from the Japanese air assaults and artillery. The skies had belonged to the enemy in the last two months. Most of Singapore's planes had been withdrawn to the Dutch East Indies (Indonesia). Two of its three airfields were within Japanese artillery range, which made taking off and landing hazardous. Air support for the defence of Singapore had to be forgotten.

The Japanese had an observation balloon tethered near the Sultan of Johore's palace on the mainland. This afforded a fine view of Singapore and indicated where to shell the British forces, to sever communications and interrupt its defensive preparation. Percival directed that the palace, now occupied by Yamashita and his command, was not to be fired on, mainly because he wished to preserve his ammunition. The Japanese commander, worried by supply issues, took the opposite approach. He was gathering all his ammunition and artillery for one all-out assault. Each of his 168 guns had up to 1000 rounds to fire.

Three months would perhaps be two months too long for him. Yamashita, the risk-taker, was betting everything on the success of a quick and decisive strike. He reckoned he had no choice. He was stretched to the limit down the Malayan peninsula as it was. A prolonged battle would end in defeat for him and a major psychological setback for the entire Imperial Japanese Army.

Percival had 85,000 fit troops (about half of them experienced combatants) for the defence. He had two choices: he could fight the Japanese on the beaches or allow them to come ashore and then counter-attack with a strong and mobile reserve force. The British commander in chief opted to meet them on the beaches. His reasoning was simple: there was no room to move a reserve force around. Percival was not confident about the British forces' ability to fight in the jungle, which covered most of the island's centre. Nearly all the battles had gone the enemy's way in Malaya's mangroves and dense undergrowth, where stealth and encirclement had defeated the Allies.

Repelling a mass Japanese attack on the beaches presented its own problems. The force would have to be thinly dispersed unless intelligence could be sure where the assault would come from. The experienced Wavell, who had flown in to assess the situation, reckoned it would come from the north-west, where the Australians were stationed. Percival thought it would be too tough for the Japanese to invade there. He was convinced the attack would be from the north-east where he had placed the bulk of his artillery.

Wavell and Percival dropped into Bennett's headquarters in the western sector of the island. In the middle of the meeting, Japanese planes dive-bombed the building. 'The unedifying spectacle was seen of three Generals going to ground under tables or any other cover that was available,' Wavell noted. 'There was a good deal of debris and some casualties outside, but the party of VIPs escaped untouched, though I lost my car and my field glasses.'[6]

The accuracy of the attack was no fluke. The Japanese fifth column had been working overtime to locate the Allied generals' meeting places. Wavell was in no doubt about the seriousness of the situation. He must have been more than pleased when he flew out of the war zone again that evening.

Communications were tough in Bennett's area of command. It was part-jungle and dissected by rivers, and he had half as many men as the north-east sector. He placed the 27th Brigade in the causeway sector, with the 30th and 26th Battalions forward and the 29th at the rear. The 22nd Brigade was west of the 27th; the Indians were further west still.

The positions brought a quiet despair for all officers and men. Most faced areas thick with mangroves, with streams converging on the foreshore. Unless the diggers stood at the water's edge, there was no way to see the enemy coming, and there were no natural fortifications. The terrain was unsuitable for defence in every way. There were just a few foot-tracks on which to move; they wound through the wilderness and provided no sense of direction or protection.

Because of the size of Bennett's western sector, battalion posts were several hundred metres apart. There was thick jungle in between the posts. Each one was isolated and vulnerable. The vegetation afforded the Japanese the perfect cover for their method of fighting by stealth. Despite Yamashita's haste, his officers were doing everything right as they prepared for the invasion of Singapore. Gun emplacements were being dug fifty metres back from the Johore Strait, and in rubber plantations on the Malayan coastline. Big kitchens were being trucked in to feed the troops before their assault.

Intelligence on these developments was passed to Bennett, who agreed with Wavell that his sector would be the target. Percival still disagreed, arguing that the same build-up was going on opposite the north-east sector.

The first semblance of an Allied counter-attack in the Pacific occurred on 1 and 2 February 1942, when US forces raided the Japanese-held Marshall Islands and Gilbert Islands in the Pacific, sinking sixteen ships. The victory was token, however, in view of the expanding Japanese war machine. As if to make a point, Japan bombed New Guinea's Port Moresby on 3 February. They also bombed Burma, with the expected invasion of that country a few days later.

Part Two

Australia Under Siege
FEBRUARY 1942

18
Singapore's Siege

Curtin returned with his daughter Elsie to Canberra by train early in February 1942 after his two-week absence in the West. He was refreshed and over his near-breakdown. He attended a wedding on 7 February. He was relaxed enough to invite a woman who had sung at the wedding to have tea with him the next day at Parliament House.

Chifley joined them, and both leaders were in a good mood. Perhaps they wished to put on a confident front, or maybe they were unaware of the true military situation in Singapore. Their spirits would have been lifted by the news that the British Admiralty had at last assembled a convoy at Suez to ferry the 18th Division to Java via Aden and Bombay. A quicker vessel, the converted liner *Orcades*, sailed first to Java, carrying 3400 diggers but without their weapons, which inexplicably were put on a separate boat. It had taken the Admiralty a long time to organise the troopships. It was almost as if it were delaying the movement of the diggers away from the Middle East theatre, just in case Churchill needed them there.

With his staff, Lieutenant General John Lavarack, the commander of Australia's I Corps (the 'new' combined force of the 6th and 7th Divisions, comprising some 64,000 soldiers), flew to Java to set up his headquarters. Lavarack met with General Wavell, who wanted to split the divisions for missions along the Dutch East Indies (Indonesian) archipelago. Lavarack opposed this. Such division of Australian forces was a sensitive area in this war and the war of 1914–1918. Wavell had the same argument with General Blamey in the Middle East.

The roots of the negative Australian reaction went back to World War I, when the British refused to allow Australia's first five divisions to combine as one Australian corps. The divisions had been tacked onto British armies on the Western Front in Belgium and France, often for battles that ended in defeat or stalemate and massive loss of life. It had taken a lot of political activity behind the scenes to have the divisions link up under Australian command – of General Monash – in May 1918. The impact of this force had changed the course of the war.

Blamey's experience as Monash's chief of staff caused him to fight to keep the Australian divisions together in World War II. But it was a different conflict, and Blamey was not Monash. Lavarack, who had also been a staff officer under Monash, had had bitter experiences under British command and did not want it repeated in this war.

Instead of upsetting Wavell by saying this, Lavarack told him that if these divisions were kept together, their fighting capacities would be at least doubled, even if they lined up back-to-back. Wavell left the issue unresolved. Lavarack got in touch with Blamey, who was still in the Middle East, and informed him of the British request. Blamey cabled Curtin, warning him against letting the Australian force be scattered this way. Curtin then cabled Wavell, emphasising that 'the concentration of the AIF in one force under its own command is a principle of cardinal national importance.'[1]

Curtin's strong line was laudable. But given that the Australian forces were already split between Egypt and the Indian Ocean, along with the fact that most of the diggers would not reach Java for weeks, the matter was theoretical in any case.

While Curtin was worrying about when and if his crack troops would return home, Emperor Hirohito was signing another order pertinent to Australia's immediate future: this time, the Combined Fleet was to attack the island of Timor, just north-west of Darwin. According to Hirohito's biographer, American Herbert P. Bix, the Emperor was 'as intoxicated by victory as his senior commanders'.

Hirohito was keen to receive news from General Yamashita, who had vowed to him that he would gift him Singapore.

The Japanese invaded Burma on 8 February and simultaneously began their intense barrage of the Australian sector in Singapore's north-west. The artillery fire was accurate all through the first day. Lieutenant-Colonel A. L. Varley, the commander of the 18th Battalion, said he had never seen a heavier pounding, and he had served on several World War I fronts.

Despite the ferocity of the attack, Percival at first refused to fire a counter-battery from the heavier British guns. The position was so critical that the artillery liaison officer with the 20th Battalion said simply, 'Bring down fire everywhere.'[2]

Percival and his jittery command guessed that the shelling would continue for several days and shift to the causeway in the middle, and then to the north-east. The Japanese accuracy came from their aerial reconnaissance but also from their infiltration of the island. Some Japanese on Singapore had been 'sleepers', waiting for the instruction to attack; others had come across by boat at night. They were in their element in the thick jungle on the coast, spreading out to avoid detection. The secret invaders in the first week of February had been hard at work mapping the Australians' positions and passing them back to the artillery commanders on the mainland. The defenders' slit trenches and the soft soil saved many lives, but there was chaos when communications were cut by the shelling.

On the night of 8 February, the Japanese invaded in big numbers, crossing the Johore Strait in barges, armoured boats and rafts. They landed in the western sector, just as Bennett and Wavell had predicted. The fierce day of relentless shelling had been the key indicator.

The 20th Battalion was the first defending force to encounter them. Gunners of the 4th Machine Gun Battalion were parked right on the shoreline, barely in the jungle. Burning oil tankers in the strait afforded them just enough light to see the silhouettes of the Japanese invasion vessels. The gunners' commander waited until the enemy was just thirty metres from the shore. Then he ordered his men to fire. The Vickers machine guns opened up, shredding the barges' flimsy sides. But they had less impact on a second wave of armoured landing craft. Those who survived the first Australian attack scrambled away and headed further west. Their invasion vessels kept coming across the strait from every angle, right across the north-west coast.

The Australians kept their weapons spitting into the dark at the unwelcome shapes throughout the night. Yamashita's two best divisions – the 5th and the 18th – poured out 13,000 men at night and another 10,000 at dawn. This huge invasion was being held up by about 1000 Australians, who inflicted heavy casualties on the Japanese.

There was a cost for the Australians' fierce defence: 334 were killed and 214 wounded. The forward battalions, who took the enemy head-on, fared worst. One company of 145 diggers right at the front had fifty-seven killed, twenty-two wounded and sixty-six taken prisoner. The 22nd Brigade's forward posts were similarly overrun. Its survivors were forced back behind the Tengah airfield, six and a half kilometres from the coast. It had been shelled from Johore throughout the night. Its commander, Brigadier Harold Taylor, formed a defensive position.

By 11 February the defenders had been pressed back into a shrinking perimeter around Singapore town in the south. The hill and village at Bukit Timah, with its considerable oil and food supplies, were in Japanese hands.

Wavell was away from the battle zone after another fleeting visit the day before. Churchill had reminded him in a cable that he commanded 100,000 men, half of them British Empire soldiers (33,000 British and 17,000 Australians) and the balance Indians and Gurkhas. He wrote:

> *There must be no thought of saving the troops or sparing the population. The battle must be fought to the bitter end at all costs. The honour of the British Empire and the British Army is at stake. I rely on you to show no mercy to weakness in any form. With the Russians fighting the way they are, the Americans so stubborn at Luzon [the Philippines], the whole reputation of our country and our race is involved.*

Wavell was not ruthless enough to send out such a directive. Instead, he delivered a plaintive 'Order of the Day' via a dispatch rider to all troops at Singapore: 'In some units the troops have not shown the fighting spirit which is to be expected of men of the British Empire – the spirit of aggression and determination to stick it out must be inculcated in all ranks. There must be no more withdrawal without orders.'

These platitudes, a watered-down version of Churchill's bulldog blustering, did nothing to boost morale, especially as they came from an absent commander. They demonstrated either a lack of comprehension of events or an attempt to circumvent criticism of Churchill or of Wavell himself and his command, should the Japanese succeed in taking Singapore. The implication was that the Australians had run from the battle. Waiting for 'orders to withdraw' would have ensured that every one of the soldiers and non-combatants of the 22nd and 27th Brigades was slaughtered. Wavell's hollow cry was thrown in a bin.

There was much fighting at close quarters, just what the Australians wanted and the Japanese did not. But by the evening the weight of numbers facing the 22nd Brigade told. The invaders seeped around to the south and isolated the brigade, which had to be withdrawn after dark. The Australians, Percival noted, fought 'a gallant action for 48 hours and had done much to hold up the enemy's advance'.[3]

A conference of Percival's generals, including Bennett, was held at Fort Canning in south-eastern Singapore on the morning of 13 February. It was agreed that further resistance was hopeless. Morale, especially among the Indians, was disappearing as fast as the ammunition. The command generals were sure the Japanese would take the fight right into Singapore town, which meant the civilian population would be wiped out. They could not escape the Japanese cordon. The heavy bombing and artillery fire had already created severe dislocation among the people, killing and wounding thousands. The generals decided to send a message to Wavell, seeking permission to capitulate.

Gordon Bennett planned to escape among the 100 AIF personnel of all ranks allowed by the senior command. His world at that moment had come crashing down. Instead of being involved in the first defeat for the enemy marauders of the Asia-Pacific region, he was a key part of a humiliating loss. The Japanese, so long degraded in the propaganda as 'little yellow men', were having a golden moment.

They had proved superior in planning, strategy, tactics and fighting techniques for the terrain.

Bennett escaped on a *sampan* – a light boat – that took him to Java. From there, he flew to Australia. This act would ensure he remained a controversial figure, with many questioning whether he should have abandoned his men.

19
Yamashita's Moment

General Yamashita was on Singapore on 13 February, having left his safe haven, the Sultan's palace. His troops had captured much of Singapore town's water supply. The Australian troops and the rest of the British forces were now squeezed into a tighter and tighter semi-circle. They were running out of ammunition, weapons, food and water. All the British planes had flown away. There were very few means of escape from the island, and certainly not for more than 70,000 troops. There could be no face-saving mass evacuation, no Gallipoli.

The experienced 6th and 7th Divisions arrived at Bombay to learn that they would not be going to Java after all. The Dutch East Indies was also not far from collapse after Japanese assaults. Wavell cabled Churchill that they should be deployed to either Burma or Australia. He copied the message to Curtin, who sent a message of his own to Churchill, arguing for Australia to be their destination.

Curtin took the opportunity to push for the return of the 9th Division as well. Without it being expressed, the concept of 'forward defence' – of taking on the enemy in the islands to Australia's north – had effectively been abandoned by the Australian government. The impending defeat in Singapore had forced them to rethink everything. It would be better, it was now believed, to use home as the strategic base for as many diggers as possible. Together with the now hoped-for US force, they could prepare for a counter-attack or defence.

Just after lunch on Saturday 14 February 1942, Japanese soldiers burst into the grounds of the British Alexandra Hospital in Singapore. They headed first for the sisters' quarters. A British lieutenant in the reception area was warned of their approach. He assembled a white flag and waved it as soon as the first three soldiers charged in. Ignoring the surrender, they bayoneted the lieutenant to death and rampaged through the hospital.

Staff waved Red Cross signs and cried, 'Hospital!' 'Hospital!' but it had no impact. There was no stopping the invaders, who seemed intent on barbarity. Ten medical staff were herded down a corridor, then – apparently on a whim – were bayoneted and shot. The mayhem continued over several floors and more than 200 were murdered. Nothing in the underworld of Chicago in the 1930s could match the horrors of this St Valentine's Day massacre.

The severity of this indiscriminate killing of non-combatants and wounded soldiers drove home the danger to all as the Japanese seeped into the town. There was enormous pressure on the British command to capitulate. While the feverish acts were being perpetrated against British medical staff, across town St Andrew's Cathedral was being converted into a hospital by the Australian Field Ambulance for civilians as well as troops. Pews were removed. Apartments were transformed into surgical operating theatres, first-aid wards and recovery units. The Adelphi Hotel across the road was seconded. A special section for traumatised patients was set up in its basement, with the aim of lessening the nerve-shattering noise of bombs and artillery.

The Japanese were swarming closer. Snipers had infiltrated the town. They were firing at any target. No civilian, not even a child, was safe to wander the streets. Japanese artillery and mortar fire was more penetrating with every hour. The shells rained in on the St James Cathedral grounds. On the night of 14 February, all the avenues appeared blocked off.

Singapore was at cracking point on 15 February. Heavy shelling and bombing of the defended parts of the town began at daybreak. The British artillery batteries and anti-aircraft gunners were active, bringing down three Japanese planes. But it did not deter the attackers, whose artillery inched closer. The hospitals at St Andrew's Cathedral, Cathay and Tanglin Road were hammered. The Japanese were targeting non-combatants. They sent planes to bomb a battery located 300 metres away from the cathedral. Two bombs landed in its grounds.

Early afternoon, perhaps because of the devastation at the cathedral, Percival realised his fight for Singapore was over. A deputation of military and civilian leaders approached the Japanese front along the Bukit Timah road. Yamashita, revelling in his moment of glory for the Emperor, sent a message back that Percival himself would have to make the surrender. This was most important for the Japanese general's own image in front of the ubiquitous Imperial Army camera crews and journalists. No second-rate major bending his knee to General Yamashita, and therefore to the Emperor, would do. Forcing the top British commander into the picture, literally, also ensured maximum humiliation for the vanquished, and a lowering of the Allies' morale. Such subjugation had been rare in Britain's 400 years as the most powerful nation in the world. Especially unusual was that some 70,000 British Empire prisoners would be taken. Yamashita, with his keen sense of history and his place in it, viewed this moment when one empire transferred power to another.

By mid-afternoon the fighting began to stop. A strange silence descended on Singapore town. The only army in operation now was the corps of doctors, nurses, orderlies and ambulance drivers. Their war – against injury and death – had to go on. For them, a cessation of hostilities meant only that they could continue their courageous work without the interference of bombs, artillery, snipers and crazed enemy soldiers.

Yamashita's request for Percival to turn up with the British flag and another of surrender caused a delay. But in effect, Japan on the afternoon of 15 February 1942 had taken control of Singapore. It had added to its euphoric and frenetic run of territorial acquisitions in the last ten weeks: Hong Kong, New Britain and Malaya. The Japanese occupied Manchuria, about 30 per cent of China, Korea, French Indochina (Vietnam) and Thailand. Their plans in 1942 were to control Burma, the Dutch East Indies (Indonesia), the Philippines and New Guinea. Australia was now also in their sights.

With their spies working overtime in Darwin, the Japanese were aware of the build-up of the military there and the decrease in the civilian population. Since 16 December 1941 about 2000 women and children had been moved away by sea, while others had departed by plane, road and train.

On Sunday 15 February, the last hot and over-crowded ship – the *Koolama* – carrying female and child evacuees, left Darwin with everyone on the lookout for enemy mines.

At the very time those on board the *Koolama* were observing a blackout to avoid Japanese air detection, the British were officially surrendering Singapore. It was 8.30 p.m. The capitulation stunned most of the Allied troops. Silence in the Australian camp spoke volumes. The 8th Division had 1919 men lost or unaccounted for since the Malayan conflict began on 8 December; another 6000 personnel were wounded or ill. In all, it was a heavy price to pay for a campaign the world would view as an abject failure.

Stories about Japanese behaviour in Malaya caused great fears in Singapore, not to mention their barbarous acts in Nanking, Hong Kong and many other countries. Would they continue to murder, rape, loot and pillage? Probably not in front of their own huge media throng and countless witnesses. The Japanese acts of inhumanity would be confined to war in remote regions where there were no observers.

Yamashita had made it clear to his troops that anyone caught committing crimes such as abuse of the female population or looting would face the death penalty. There had already been countless atrocious acts during the siege of the island, mainly against the local

Chinese. Many had been decapitated, their heads placed on poles outside villages as a deterrent. But in Singapore town Yamashita was making sure the Imperial Army was seen by the world as 'benevolent'. It was the image the face-saving conquerors craved, even if it did not tally with the integrity of events and Yamashita's own brutality, exemplified by his order to liquidate the wounded and ill Australian and Indian soldiers in Malaya.

Churchill's focus on defeating Hitler had, in part, led to the fall of Singapore. He had misjudged events there, gambling – like many others – that the Japanese would not enter the war. Now, just seventy days after attacking to the south, they had swept all before them. The Allies' defences in South-East Asia and the Pacific had crumbled. Just a few 'outposts' such as Australia and New Zealand were not yet in their keeping.

Yet Churchill did not deserve all the blame. Australian military advisers (although not Blamey) had been warning successive governments that they should be preparing a far stronger forward defence in the islands to Australia's north. But they had been ignored. Japan's capacities had been downplayed. Singapore had been vaunted as the great fortress of the Far East. Australia had relied too much on its protection by the British Empire, which, when tested, proved inadequate.

20

Operation Australia

Yamashita, the so-called 'Tiger of Malaya', became the first army commander to urge that Australia be consumed by the Imperial war machine. Prime Minister Tojo and most of his key planners, staff and commanders had yet to bother much about Australia. Again, first glance at a map would make any army observer think stretching that far south would present supply-line problems. They refused to countenance the navy's attitude that the fleet and its long-range bombers could attack any country and win. If the army did accept the approach of its rivals in the Admiralty, it would mean surrendering its pre-eminent position within the Imperial Force, and with Japan now giddy with acquisition and power in the region, no army general was going to accede to being subordinate to the navy. Yet Yamashita gave the High Command and Tojo pause. At last the army had a battle commander in this war with a definitive success, and against the odds. Yamashita's prestige rocketed. It upset his main rival, Tojo. Now Yamashita was urging him to let him take Australia.

'Singapore, the great British bastion in the Far East, has fallen into our hands,' he wrote in a letter to Tojo. 'The Allies are effectively sealed off.'[1] Yamashita wanted Tojo to abandon his plan to take Burma and India in his bid to destroy the British Empire. Instead, he suggested they garrison Malaya and Burma, and then attack Australia.

Yamashita was most confident. He had forced the British into submission with an army far smaller than that of the vanquished. His plan was to attack Australia as he had Malaya. This time, Yamashita's two-pronged strategy would follow a series of dummy landings in remote parts of the northern Queensland coast, which would force the Australians to send the best of their limited combat troops there. This would leave the centre of Australia and the east coast exposed and ripe for Yamashita's plan.

He seconded Admiral Yamamoto to help him lobby Tojo to order the invasions. Yamamoto would provide the carriers from which to bomb Australian cities and land troops. Yamashita would land one division at Darwin, after it had been pulverised from the air, then he would land another north of Brisbane. Yamashita may have underestimated the difficulty of going through Australia's 'dead heart', but he had faith in his troops after the ease of his recent victories against the British. He was aware that Australia's crack troops were in the Middle East and southern Europe – and also, because of him, incarcerated at Changi on Singapore.

After taking Darwin, he would move his force of about 30,000 men by road and rail about 300 kilometres to Larrimah, just south of Katherine. After camping there overnight, he would then embark on the next leg, about 980 kilometres by dirt track to Alice Springs. This would need considerable transport, but Yamashita again intended his troops to go by bicycle. He reasoned that they had moved through 900 kilometres of tough terrain in Thailand, Malaya and Singapore by bike, with considerable back-up transport; it could be done again in the different, just as challenging terrain of the Australian desert. He would insist on air protection.

Alice Springs would host a main Japanese army and air base. From there, he would use road transport, bikes and the cumbersome train routes to get his troops to Adelaide. The first – 400 kilometre – leg of the troop movement would be to Maree, in the middle of South Australia. The train journey would be on narrow-gauge tracks. From Maree, it would be on to Quorn, where every train had to reverse and change direction to reach Terowie. The invading force would then switch to a train on a broad-gauge line for a four-hour trip to Adelaide. Finally, Yamashita planned to move the division a further 800 kilometres to Melbourne, again using the broad-gauge rail and the road. Yamashita was thinking in weeks rather than months for this operation.

Simultaneously, the other Japanese division would take Brisbane and then move on Sydney. A pincer movement around each city would see them cut off. Without substantial troops to defend these cities, they would be captured in much the way he had taken Singapore. If there was resistance, cities would be bombed, civilians would be targeted. Yamashita was prepared to do anything, including massacring prisoners, the sick and the wounded, to hasten Australia's capitulation.

There was debate over how many divisions would be needed. Admiral Inoue and Admiral Konda, who were more or less in accord with Yamashita, had reckoned in December on three divisions. Yamashita, worried as ever about his supply lines, suggested that two divisions would be enough for his two-pronged invasion. Yamamoto, who was less concerned about supply lines, saw the operation needing five divisions. Even this was a far smaller number of troops than the Allies believed would be needed: they felt six to twelve divisions would be required to subjugate Australia. Yamashita's estimate was double the number of men he had used to take Malaya and Singapore.

He believed he would be fighting a quarter of the troops he had faced there.

Yamashita had thought through his plan well, and argued that 'there were hardly enough Australians to have organised a resistance to the Japanese Army. All they could ever hope to do was to make a guerilla resistance in the bush.' Once Brisbane and Sydney were under his control, he believed, it would be relatively easy to 'subdue Australia'. He never intended to take over the entire country. 'It was too large,' he said. 'With its coastline, anyone can always land there exactly when he wants.'[2]

Once he had occupied Australia, Yamashita believed it would be easy to defend, precisely because of one of the reasons Tojo had been loath to move against it: it was too far for Allied supply lines to attempt to recapture it. This was particularly relevant given that the Allies had other areas to attempt to recapture and defend in the Asia-Pacific region. Yamashita boasted that he could have called on sufficient troops to rebuff any Anglo-American 'invasions' of his newly conquered Australian territory.

He was disdainful of Tojo's argument that Japan's supply lines would be over-stretched. Australia was such a vulnerable target in the eyes of the Tiger of Malaya that once it was snaffled, the length of supply lines would be a bigger problem for the Americans or the British. He felt they would most likely abandon Australia altogether. The unthinkable for Australians was an afterthought for the now bombastic Yamashita.

The Japanese admirals, too, with their power and praise from the Emperor and the media, were a threat to Tojo. He was forced at least to consider that Australia might become the main US base in the Pacific for a counter-attack. Admiral Yamamoto insisted that Darwin, the northern-most Australia city and its port, now growing into the Americans' most functional military base in the Pacific, had to be obliterated. For this mission, he wished to send the same carrier-based force that he had used to smash Pearl Harbor seven weeks earlier. The same pilot, Captain Mitsuo Fuchida, would lead the attack. His squadrons would take off from the same aircraft carriers with the same air crews in support. But the intensity of the attack on Darwin would be greater.

The Japanese believed that they had erred at Pearl Harbor in not having more planes in the first attack wave. There were also more target ships in Darwin than there had been at Pearl Harbor. The second wave of planes would come not from aircraft carriers this time but from land. They would be heavier aircraft carrying bigger bombs. Another difference was that the attacking planes would target the ships in port, the airfields, and also town buildings such as the post office. This would endanger civilians, something that had not occurred at Pearl Harbor.

The Japanese, it seemed, were less concerned by the reactions of Australians if civilians were killed. The destruction of Darwin would prove to Japan's leadership that Australia could be taken with little fuss. Yamamoto, his staff and the key naval planners would wait for an appropriate moment to push hard again for their original plan.

For the moment, the admirals were exhilarated by the thought of another Pearl Harbor.

21

Aftershock

Curtin reacted to Singapore's collapse, putting out a media release within hours of Percival's surrender. It was aimed at all Australians, and he hoped it would at last set the country on a war footing.

'The fall of Singapore can only be described as Australia's Dunkirk,' he began. '[The] fall of Dunkirk initiated the battle for Britain. The fall of Singapore opens the Battle for Australia.'

This was a well-considered comparison. It linked Australia to the plight of the seat of Empire. There was no newsreel footage of boats full of soldiers, nurses and other escapees leaving Singapore. But everyone had seen the Dunkirk images and could make the connection.

His words had a Churchillian resonance: 'What the Battle for Britain required, so the Battle for Australia requires . . .'

His concern since taking office four months earlier was that many of his countrymen were not truly aware of the dangers the nation faced. Now that Singapore had fallen to the Japanese, Curtin took the opportunity to shake the nation from its reverie with blunter speech. 'Our honeymoon has finished,' he declared. With his eye again on the communist elements in his party and the unions, he concluded, 'It is now work or fight as we have never worked or fought before.'

The day after the collapse of Singapore, the Australian chiefs wanted all three divisions – the 6th, 7th and 9th – brought back from the Middle East. Curtin cabled Churchill on 17 February 1942, just as the Japanese occupied Palembang, Sumatra: 'If possible all Australian forces now under orders to transfer to the Far East from the Middle East should be diverted to Australia.'[1]

The Japanese took control of New Britain on 23 January. From Rabaul, they sent a sortie out to bomb Port Moresby, New Guinea and Papua's administrative centre. Now the Japanese were beyond hammering at the 'new frontier' – they were attacking Australian territory and its nearest neighbour.

More trenches were dug in Darwin, Brisbane and Perth. Bomb shelters were built. Shops, buildings and homes were boarded up as if a cyclone was coming. Drills with gas masks had more meaning than before. Hundreds of Queenslanders began rushing south to New South Wales. Brisbane residents were dispersing to the hills outside the city.

Unofficial defence force planning envisaged a Japanese attack in the Newcastle/Sydney/Port Kembla region. General Sturdee believed that Lithgow, Brisbane and Melbourne would be next hit. There did not seem to be any point in invading across Australia's vast northern coastline, and there was little discussion about the Japanese sending troops down the country's centre by train, bicycle and truck. The top echelons of the Australian military believed that any enemy invasion force would struggle in the desert and semi-arid regions.

The army decided that the services personnel already in Western Australia, northern Queensland and Tasmania should not be augmented by more troops and equipment. In effect, those areas should be 'sacrificed' in order to protect a line running from Brisbane to Melbourne. These were sobering thoughts for Curtin and several of his Cabinet. It meant abandoning their own electorates. Curtin had the final say on the armed services' unofficial plans, and he would not countenance them at this time. He was banking more than ever on US military aid.

Churchill's attitude to Australia was not changed by the fall of Singapore: he still treated all Australian divisions as if they were his own. A substantial part of the 6th Division had been used up in Crete and Greece. The 9th had been kept at Tobruk much longer than the Australian chiefs and Curtin wished. Now Curtin had asked that the 7th and 6th be returned home (and not dispatched to Java, as the British chiefs requested on 3 January) to take on the Japanese.

Churchill wanted these two crack forces to be diverted to Burma to keep Roosevelt happy. Curtin and his Cabinet were confused. The snappy cable exchanges had rarely seen Burma mentioned; now it was all about Burma and it was not clear why. Did it mean support for India or China – or both?

Curtin had to shore up Australia's defences, as intelligence was suggesting that the Japanese were poised to attack. It was time to share with the public just how much the enemy had advanced since Pearl Harbor. He had advertisements placed in newspapers. A map showed Japan with arrows springing from it running west to China, east to Hawaii, across many islands in the Pacific, and south to several countries including Vietnam, Burma, the Dutch East Indies, Thailand, Malaysia, Singapore and parts of Papua and New Guinea. The inference was clear: Australia was next.

Curtin, in his now-familiar direct style, wrote, 'The spearhead of the Japanese hordes reaches south – always south. Australia faces the darkest hour in her history.' Since the collapse of Singapore, he explained, he sensed that states south of Queensland were at last waking up to the seriousness of the war. 'For many the working pace of peace time has not given place to the pressure appealed for in war production.'

He took aim at unions who seemed to be striking for no apparent reason. When Hitler and Stalin had a non-aggression pact – a stalling process that suited both – it was understandable, although treasonous, that communist unions would try to disrupt Australian industry and war production. But the Germans and Russians had now been at war for nine months. By default, Stalin was on the Allies' side. There was no excuse, treasonous or otherwise, for their stop-work actions on wharves, in the coalmines and in other industries. The extreme left was relying on the forlorn hope that communism would somehow be installed in Australia regardless of events in the rest of the world. Curtin added: 'For many, readiness to provoke strikes or lockouts suggests an ignorance of, or disregard for, national security. Those things cannot continue.'[2]

This straight talk was what the public wished to hear. Now that it was alert to the dangers ahead, Curtin had the nation's attention as never before. Whenever he appeared, there was an appreciative crowd. There was a sense that the former tub-thumping politician was an increasingly effective leader. Curtin's oratorical skills were now more important than ever. His apparent steadiness and calm (which belied his weak physical condition), his sincerity and his strong, vowel-crushing speaking style were gaining wider appreciation.

On Tuesday 17 February 1942, Curtin took a train from Canberra to Sydney for the public launch of a war loan in Martin Place. He became ill on the journey, experiencing severe stomach pains and vomiting. Curtin had a nightmare that night and awoke anxious, telling his wife, 'I saw the shape of ships in the dark. Then torpedoes hit. Flames lit up the sky. Men jumped into the sea. There was screaming.'[3]

Elsie feared an attack of 'old bogey'. She called for a doctor. Curtin was examined in Sydney. He was diagnosed with having 'gastritis', or inflammation of the stomach lining, brought on by a virus or bacteria. This illness, both physical and mental, came only weeks after his near breakdown. Both had most likely been brought on by stress as his nightmare reflected.

But Curtin remained stoic in public. He braved his condition and went on with the war loan launch. Since becoming prime minister he had become aware that image was nearly everything when dealing with the public. If he had gone to hospital instead of turning up to this 'event', where he was flanked by a contingent of soldiers in battle-dress, he would have missed a chance to raise funds. It would have called into question also his capacity to lead in moments of crisis.

A little panic was seeping into some Sydneysiders' psyches. Suburbs and towns on the coast were nervous. Some residents were selling their houses. Prices were dropping in places such as Manly. Those who could afford it, and some who couldn't, were moving inland. The Blue Mountains was a popular retreat. House prices there and in nearby places such as Bowral were on the up.

Certain areas of the coast, such as the Manly Peninsula, including North Head, were requisitioned by the Department of Defence. A girls' school was taken over on the foreshore. Machine guns were set up, and Norfolk pines were chopped down to clear the line of fire. Some beaches were covered with barbed wire.

In Melbourne, the entire population of exclusive Toorak girls' school St Catherine's was evacuated to Warburton, in country Victoria. Sir Norman Myer, the executive chairman of the Myer emporium, lived with his family at 'Heymount', a magnificent home across the road from the school. He built an air-raid shelter and stocked it with tinned goods, a water tank and sleeping quarters.

Shortages of military equipment around the country led to desperate measures. In Sydney, dummy gun pits were erected with painted green down-pipes sticking out through netting – imitating gun barrels. There was no obvious panic, just most unusual 'activity' that seemed a little bizarre even to Sydney's more phlegmatic citizens, and Melbourne's population, which was, as ever, more distracted by spectator sports. There was still an attitude that something *might* happen 'up north', but not in old Sydney or Melbourne towns.

Curtin didn't want to spread fear, but he did wish for more dedication to the war effort. With this in mind, he performed at his best at the war loan launch, despite the pain that could double him up.

His speech and body language were forceful as a big crowd gathered, press photographers clicked and journalists scribbled.

'Australians,' he began; he reserved his usual 'men and women of Australia' for radio broadcasts and their unseen audience. 'You are the sons and daughters of Britishers! You have come from England and Scotland and Wales and Ireland. There is, fused in you also, the best qualities of the other races.'[4] There was no explanation of how this selective DNA infusion was achieved, but it did not matter. The PM sounded good; he looked good; he appeared as a leader. Anyone in Martin Place that day would have been surprised to learn that the vigorous orator they had witnessed had to be put into St Vincent's Hospital after his performance.

Curtin's condition would not have improved had he known that, only five hours before he appeared in public, a single-engine Japanese 'float' plane had flown over Sydney. Its pilot, Nobuo Fujita, had circled the city, taking pictures of the war ships in the harbour. He had then flown back to the Japanese submarine *I-25*, which was waiting 185 kilometres off Sydney's coastline.

Curtin was too sick to attend a meeting of the War Cabinet that afternoon and would remain too ill for any meeting the next day, Wednesday 18 February. But he left written instructions for action with his deputy, Frank Forde. The most important issue on Curtin's list was 'urgent consideration' for the recall of the 9th Division from the Middle East, and the return of two RAAF squadrons from Britain. He also wanted some troops from the returning 6th or 7th to reinforce Darwin before all other areas in the country.

This directive clashed with Churchill's new policy to defend Burma. Curtin had sent a cable the previous day requesting this, but Bruce and Page had decided not to pass it to Churchill. Instead they took it upon themselves to attempt to change Curtin's mind. The issue was most contentious. Those supporting the Empire's position over Australia clashed with Curtin. Churchill's 'Burma Road' was supported by Menzies and others on Australia's Advisory War

Council, along with the government's key representatives in London, Bruce and Page. Churchill had won them over, specifically against the wishes of their own government. He had used the same finessing technique on Menzies over the diggers fighting in Greece.

Bruce was now advocating that the 7th Division should go to Burma. Unaware that Curtin was laid up in hospital, he sent a cable to him on 18 February, arguing Churchill's points. The Dutch had abandoned Java. Bruce portrayed this as courageous and statesman-like, reflective of the 'character and toughness of the Dutch people'.[5] These descriptions, which Australians liked to apply to themselves, were meant to touch a nerve in the Australian prime minister. But it was empty rhetoric. The Dutch government was in exile in London: it was not in Batavia or Canberra, attempting to shore up defences against the encircling Japanese war machine.

Bruce continued with the 'Burma Road' line. The 7th Division's presence in Burma, he said, 'offered the best hope of keeping open the Burma Road to China'. Bruce, like the Dutch government-in-exile, was far away in London, unaware of the uneasiness in Canberra over the need for the troops to be 'home'. He added that sending the troops to Rangoon was of paramount importance in the fight against Japan. The explanation for this was again pure Churchill as he evoked the China argument. The Allies had to keep up China's morale at all costs. If China threw in the towel, it would lead to an 'incalculable disaster'. How an extra division being sent to Rangoon would even marginally impact on the Chinese nationalists and communists in their separate battles against the Japanese was not explained. Once more, these remarks reflected Churchill's adoption of the American State Department line in order to keep President Roosevelt happy.

With Curtin incapacitated in hospital, Bruce's cable reached Forde, who was at an Advisory War Council meeting in Sydney. When there was no reply, Page decided that he too would send a message to Curtin reinforcing the 'Burma Road' attitude. But instead of making it appear that the advice was his (as Bruce had), he invoked the names of Churchill and Roosevelt: 'Churchill expressed great anxiety about the effect on China if Burma was not reinforced, especially if troops so near the battle-front [the Australian 7th Division], and the only troops available, are not allocated at this critical moment.' Page added that Churchill and Roosevelt were certain that 'China is the ultimate key of the whole Asian situation'.

This sounded academic, and indeed it was, when compared to Australia's plight. Most members of the Advisory War Council, and certainly Curtin, would not have hesitated to say that Japan, not China, was the immediate and ultimate 'key' to what would happen in Asia. For more than two months now, every other nation in the region had been reacting to what Japan did.

Page reminded Curtin that Churchill would arrange an American division be sent to Australia to cover for the non-return of the 7th.[6] But this missed the point of Curtin's request. The Australians and British regarded these divisions as the best frontline Allied troops. With no disrespect to any American division, tried or untried, Curtin wanted the battle-hardened Australian diggers of the 6th and 7th Divisions defending their homeland.

Page finished drafting his cable late on 18 February London time (with the intention of sending it early the next day) just as events in Australia would dictate a response from Curtin. The non-government members of the War Council – Fadden, Hughes, Menzies, Percy Spender and Jack McEwen – decided to back Page's request.

'The Australian Government should be asked to agree that the 7th Division already on the water should ... go to Burma,' they said at the next Council meeting, in Sydney on the morning of 19 February. 'The position of this convoy [in the Indian Ocean] makes it imperative that permission should be given to this course within 24 hours.'[7]

Curtin would make the final decision on such an important change to the 7th Division's destination. The extra emphasis from seven weighty conservatives – including five ex-prime ministers (Hughes, Menzies, Page, Bruce and Fadden) – put extra pressure on him. But in the very hour they were documenting their advice, action to Australia's north-west would give a different complexion to the issue.

22
Attack on Darwin

Just before dawn on Thursday 19 February 1942, four Japanese aircraft carriers – *Akagi*, *Kaga*, *Soryu* and *Hiryu* – were arming their aircraft and warming their engines 350 kilometres north-west of Darwin. Blue smoke billowed from the decks. The jumbled growl could be heard 100 kilometres across the sea, with the more shrill sound of the brutish little Zeros splitting the warm early-morning air. The four carriers were escorted by the battleships *Hei* and *Kirishima*; two heavy cruisers, *Tone* and *Chikuma*; the light cruiser *Abukuma*, and nine destroyers. It was the same armada that had been used to attack Pearl Harbor, but for two fewer aircraft carriers. The fleet itself would not be engaged; the strength of the assault would come from the air.

At 8.45 a.m., with the weather fine, Vice Admiral Chuichi Nagumo launched the first wave of 188 aircraft, led by Captain Fuchida. It comprised thirty-six Zero fighters, seventy-one dive bombers and eighty-one torpedo bombers, which would take off from land. All the pilots were primed to attack Darwin's major installations, oil storage tanks and forty-six ships at anchor in its port. The force sighted a US Catalina flying boat. Nine fighters swooped over the northern tip of Bathurst Island. They disabled the Catalina. Its pilot, Lieutenant Thomas Moorer, was forced to crash into the sea, making this plane the first strike. Fortunately, its crew, including four wounded men, was rescued by the merchant ship *Florence D.*

The Japanese force was spotted first by a naval reservist at a communications station at HMAS *Coonawarra*, the naval shore base nine kilometres west of Darwin. It was 9.15 a.m. A few minutes later, Father John McGrath, at Bathurst Island Mission, eighty kilometres north of the target city, radioed his sighting to Darwin's military HQ, just as six fighters swooped low and strafed the area. They damaged buildings and destroyed an aircraft. But both these reports were lost in the system and not passed to the appropriate commander. This meant that Darwin would not be aware of Fuchida's force until it struck.

The aircraft crossed the Northern Territory coast near Koolpinyah, east of Darwin, then swung to the north-west and flew over the Noonamah area. At 9.58 a.m., two minutes ahead of schedule, the 188 planes were over Darwin. The Japanese encountered five US Kittyhawk planes, which had returned from an aborted mission to Timor. Four of them were overwhelmed and shot down by the superior numbers of the agile Zeros. The eighty-one torpedo bombers concentrated on attacking the forty-six vessels in the harbour. The seventy-one dive bombers, escorted by the thirty-six Zeros, attacked RAAF bases, civil airfields and two hospitals. The one remaining Kittyhawk pilot, Lieutenant Robert Ostreicher, instead of landing, threaded through the clouds for thirty minutes. He spotted two dive bombers aiming for Batchelor Field.

'Intercepting them at 1500 feet, I fired and saw one definitely burst into flames,' Ostreicher said. 'The other was smoking slightly as he headed for the clouds.' Ostreicher lost him but this plane also crashed, giving the American two strikes in an otherwise miserable day for the Allied pilots. They had been caught unaware and overwhelmed before they could take off from the RAAF bases. Crews scrambled to be airborne but too late. Many planes were destroyed or disabled.[1] These included nine Australian planes – eight Hudson aircraft and one Wirraway – and eleven American aircraft.

Captain Fuchida reported that:

The job [of flattening Darwin] seemed hardly worthy of Nagumo Force. The harbour, it is true, was crowded with all kinds of ships. But a single pier and a few waterside buildings appeared to be the only port installations. The airfield on the outskirts of town, though fairly large, had no more than two or three small hangars. In all there were only 20-odd planes of various types scattered about the field. No planes were in the air. A few [the five Kittyhawks] attempted to take off as we came over but were quickly shot down, and the rest were destroyed where they stood.

Anti-aircraft fire was intense, but largely ineffectual, and we quickly accomplished our objectives.[2]

Another 'effectual' instance occurred when four Zeros duelled with four machine-gun posts at Winnellie army camp, east of the RAAF airfield. The Zeros swooped and manoeuvred away, making them near impossible targets for the light machine-gunners. The shirtless gunners had to stand their ground and fire as the planes swept so low that they could see the cocky Japanese pilots 'giving them the finger'. This arrogant gesture riled the Australian gunners, especially Corporal Max Grant. He had tracked several planes coming in at him but had failed to strike. This time he held the Zero in his sights as it reeled away, then he fired. The plane wobbled. Smoke billowed from it. The gunners cheered as they watched the plane spiral to earth about two kilometres away.

A third Zero was hit in its vulnerable oil tank, spilling its fuel until the engine seized. The pilot, Hajime Toyoshima, glided his machine to a wood on Melville Island. He survived and was captured by a Tiwi Islander. Gunners manning bigger anti-aircraft weapons were firing from the Darwin Oval out over the harbour, in the hope that a scatter of shrapnel might catch one of the dive bombers. Jack Mulholland 'scored' when a shell burst close to a plane, causing it to crash into the sea. That made just seven retaliatory hits – two in the air and five from the ground – leaving 181 Japanese planes to fight again.

Eighty minutes later, there was a second attack wave, with high-altitude bombers targeting the RAAF base at Parap. It appeared so orderly, so disciplined, that some observers likened it to an air display. Twenty-seven bombers droned in from the south-west. The same number lumbered from the north-east until the two formations created a perfect V, passing over the RAAF airfield. Those still at the base would have loved to send fighters aloft to upset this exhibition. But there were no serviceable craft left after the damage of the first wave.

As the second wave manoeuvred over the main airstrip, the fifty-four planes released their initial mass load of 13,000 kilograms of bombs. They hit the airfield with almost faultless cohesion, causing a sound like one mighty bomb with aftershocks. The force of the high explosives broke up the entire area. Those crouching in slit trenches and in flimsy shelters felt the blast-oven heat. Buildings shattered, sending concrete flying in every direction. Aircraft damaged in the first raid now disintegrated. Personnel in slit trenches some distance from the tarmac were nearly buried. Windows five kilometres away shattered from the massive vibration.

The Japanese mission was to make the airfield, if not Darwin itself, inoperable and irreparable. The destruction of the Parap airfield by the second wave of bombers was frightening and clinical. This approach was reminiscent of the Japanese pulverising of Singapore. They were making a point: if you do not submit to us, we will kill all of you, military and civilian alike.

But the gunners' work was fruitless. The bombers, which continued their attacks back and forth in their immaculate formation, were too high. Mulholland would have relished another 'crack' at dive bombers and Zeros but there were none. Japanese intelligence reported that there would be no opposition to this second, smashing raid. No escort planes were needed. The RAAF base – the only target of this attack – was at the invaders' mercy. There was none.

The Japanese bombarded Dili, Timor, from two destroyers off the coast on the night of 19 February. Then they landed 4000 troops a few kilometres to Dili's west. About 1000 Japanese soldiers prevented any retreat from the city. Two thousand enemy troops attacked the aerodrome, where the Allied forces – one Australian company and 600 Dutch troops (Indonesians) – were camped. After a fight, the Australians destroyed the aerodrome with pre-set mines and escaped the town.

The official Darwin casualty figures were 243 killed and more than 300 wounded. But on-the-spot anecdotes tell a grimmer story, with the death toll climbing to more than 1000. One priest, Padre Richards, scoffed at the official number. 'Two hundred and forty-three?' he said.

'I buried more than that myself.' He believed the rumoured army intelligence figure of 1100 was about right.

Soldiers and police were detailed to do the grisly work of cleaning up and removing bodies, which had decayed in Darwin's debilitating heat. The remains of the dead, it was alleged, were buried in mass graves at Mindal Beach. All involved claimed that the number of those killed was four or five times higher than the government's official tally.[4] Eight Australian, American and British ships were sunk in Darwin Harbour.[5] The destroyer USS *Peary* lost most personnel – ninety-one sailors. More than forty wharfies were killed.

The attacks caused a further exodus from Darwin. No one could believe that such devastation was not the prelude to a full invasion. About half of Darwin's 5000 population fled and streamed south, heading for Adelaide River, where there was a train leaving for the interior. The race to leave the stricken port city became known as the 'Adelaide River stakes'. Officers at the pulverised Parap RAAF base ordered servicemen to flee; 278 took the opportunity to desert.

The chaotic rush out was disorderly as could be expected, when there was no plan. 'Houses were abandoned in haste,' Darwin's administrator, Charles Lowe, noted. He observed the scene in the deserted Darwin Hotel. Drinks remained half-consumed on tables. 'Letters started but not finished; papers strewn about; beds unmade . . .'[6]

Shops were looted, mostly to grab food supplies for the hurried exit. Some of it was opportunistic and criminal, and would go on for weeks. Trucks, including military vehicles, were backed up to shops and loaded with goods. Groups of servicemen grabbed refrigerators, stoves, clothes, even pianos and toys.[7]

The nation was left uninformed of the extent of damage, but the federal government had a shocking foretaste of what would happen everywhere if Australia was left undefended, disorganised, leaderless and poorly equipped. It would be helpless against a highly organised, determined and ruthless war machine, which was being fed on victory after battles on land, sea and in the air in every country it attacked.[8]

23

A Sense of Isolation

Gladys Joyce, Curtin's personal secretary, and Don Rodgers were stunned when the Sydney teleprinter made its staccato printout from Darwin. Rodgers ripped it off. He read the list of ships and buildings that had been hit, and the estimate of casualties. 'Oh, God,' he cried. 'Oh, God!'

He rushed up two flights of stairs to the Advisory War Council, which was meeting, although still without the stricken prime minister. The military chiefs were in attendance. Breathless and white-faced, Rodgers handed Forde the printout.

Shedden recalled the reaction of the council members, who jumped from their chairs to read the printout themselves. 'They were like a lot of startled chooks,' he said.[1] The nation was under siege. Forde's first move was to alert the prime minister.

Curtin was nervous but did not panic. He checked out of St Vincent's, looking pale and gaunt, and took a train to Canberra. On 20 February he addressed a jittery closed joint session of parliament. If anything, he appeared calm and deliberate, which belied inner tension. Close friends felt the strain was affecting him, but he had not lost his warmth and charm.

Curtin received hourly updates on Darwin and decided to keep published information on the attack to a minimum, in the hope that there would not be hysteria around the country. Some in the press immediately claimed the attack was one of the major events of World War II for Australia. The *Sydney Morning Herald* editorialised the morning after the bombing: 'The opening shots in the Battle of Australia were fired on the mainland yesterday.'

Yet the tabloids seemed just as concerned that race meetings had been curtailed by the government. The Darwin 'event' was played down by the censors, which would have satisfied Curtin on one level. But without dwelling on Darwin, he had to galvanise the nation.

Addressing a press conference, he said, 'There will be no more looking away now. Fate has willed our position in this war . . . We accept the issue and follow our destiny.'[2] Curtin's apparent honesty, always appreciated by the vast majority of Australians, was now a big asset at a critical moment in the nation's history. If he faltered or attempted to hoodwink the people, it would be noticed. Rightly or wrongly, the populace believed their fate was in his hands. As ever, Curtin, unlike Churchill, did not relish this destiny, but he faced it nevertheless. His body was frail but his resolve was not.

He read the cables coming in from London. While he might once have changed his mind on the Burma issue, the attack on Darwin strengthened his position. A Japanese invasion was now obviously imminent. The 6th and 7th Divisions had to return to Australia, or the nation would be left without any real defence. Curtin was backed by General Sturdee, who threatened to resign if the diggers were diverted to Burma. Curtin had been polite and deferential towards Churchill in his requests about Australian troops, giving the impression that he might be won over. Darwin changed all that.

On Friday 20 February, the busiest day of Curtin's life to that point, he learned that the Japanese had invaded Portuguese Timor, 650 kilometres north-west of Darwin. A few months earlier this would have been shocking news, but it was hardly in Curtin's thoughts. He responded to Page's cable backing Churchill and Roosevelt about the diggers' destination. Page had ended his 19 February missive with 'no instruction had been sent to the convoy'. Curtin ordered Page to 'act at once to ensure that convoy should not (repeat not) be committed to Burma.' This left Page and Bruce with no alternative. They had to tell Churchill.

Curtin next communicated with Blamey in Cairo: 'With Singapore, the bastion of Empire defence gone, and with N.E.I. [the Netherlands East Indies – Indonesia], the outer screen to Australia indefensible, they [the British] propose to leave Australia bare . . . Return here as speedily as possible.'

General Blamey's dream about a unified 2nd AIF under his command in the Middle East and Europe evaporated. But he now realised that his biggest fear – the AIF's fragmentation – would occur unless he acted to hold it together. Better to keep it intact, he thought, even if it were in the Pacific theatre. He moved to make sure the divisions were sent to Australia. Churchill was now aware of Curtin's intransigence.

'I suppose you realize,' Churchill began a cable, 'that your leading division . . . is the only force that can reach Rangoon in time to prevent its loss and the severance of communication with China . . . There is nothing else that can fill that gap.'

Emotional blackmail was another Churchill specialty. If Curtin insisted the convoy change direction, he was implying, he would be responsible for the fall of China, the collapse of the Allied strategy in the Pacific/Asian region, and quite possibly the loss of the entire war. In reality, this was heavy-handed and not a little hypocritical. Less than a month earlier, Churchill had been happy to accept Chiang Kai-shek's offer of three Chinese divisions to fight the Japanese in Burma. It was very much in China's interests to keep Japan from taking Burma and to maintain supply lines. General Wavell had rejected the offer. Only British Imperial troops, he said, should be used to defend the Empire. Now, when the situation was desperate and British troops had failed, it would fall to Australian troops to fight for Burmese territory and China.

Churchill claimed he supported the idea that the Australians should return home to defend their country. But he added that in 'a vital war emergency', troops heading one way should be ready to be turned around and sent into battle. He offered a carrot. If the 7th continued on to Burma, Churchill would do his best to have it relieved as soon as possible and then sent home.

Even Curtin, not a military man, knew by now how hollow such offers were. If the Australians became bogged down or even captured – as the 8th had been – they would never make it home. Churchill claimed that the Americans were thinking of sending all Australian divisions abroad – the 6th, 7th and 9th – to Burma. This was highly unlikely. Roosevelt was far less sensitive than Churchill to Australia's plight, but it is doubtful he would suggest trampling over Australia's sovereign right to such an extent.

Churchill was trying to tell Curtin that his directive to send the 7th to Burma could be worse. Wishing to make Curtin feel guilty, he reminded him, falsely, that he (Churchill) had put the 18th Division into Singapore rather than Burma, to please the Australians. Curtin may well have believed this to be true. Churchill accepted, in typical political style, 'full responsibility' for that decision. But then he added, gratuitously, that Curtin also bore 'a heavy share' of the decision because of a telegram he had sent urging more British support for Singapore.

This was as brazen as it was duplicitous. Churchill knew full well that the telegram in question arrived weeks after he had made the decision to send the 18th to Singapore – to please Roosevelt. The point was made clear: Curtin should send the 7th to Burma to make up for the fact that the 18th would have been saved if it had not been sent to Singapore.

If Curtin were not already convinced, Churchill played what he considered his winning card by mentioning the United States, Roosevelt and the China obsession. The message was pointed: if Curtin wanted American military support, he had better comply by fighting the Japanese in Burma to help prop up China. If he didn't comply, 'a very grave effect will be produced upon the President and the Washington circles on whom you are so largely dependent'.[3]

Churchill wanted a quick reply. He sent a slanted cable to Roosevelt, inviting the US president to add his voice to the demands. He told Roosevelt that the offer of American troops to aid Australia gave him the right to push not just for the 7th but the 'movement of Allied forces' in general. In effect, Churchill was saying he regarded Australian troops as his and Roosevelt's, to use as they wished in the fulfilment of their 'big ideas' – Churchill's obsession with Hitler, and Roosevelt's with the preservation of China. Roosevelt played along, sending Churchill an appropriate 'prod', which he tacked on to a cable to Curtin.[4]

Roosevelt also went one better. He himself wrote to Curtin, spelling out the importance of holding the 'left flank against Japan – Burma, India and China'.

Before facing another sleepless night, Curtin was informed by Sturdee of the Japanese invasion of Timor. It added to a sense of siege that gripped Curtin and the government. He was told that the small, under-equipped Allied contingent of Australians and Dutch – known as Sparrow Force – had little hope of holding out.

Curtin's daughter was staying at the Lodge when Darwin was hit and Timor invaded. She recalled his demeanour and felt his concern for the nation, the armed forces, his family and himself. He could not quite steel himself to be immune from growing death tolls of fellow Australians. He could also see 'what would happen if the Japanese had won', she said. 'They would have crucified him. I don't think dad would have ever pretended to be the greatest hero in the world.'[5]

Curtin, however, was determined not to crack under the pressure, especially in public. He fought against the image of being a beleaguered prime minister. What kept him from succumbing was his focus on his principles and his policy regarding the defence of Australia. Under the circumstances, this required an unconventional kind of heroism.

On the night of 20 February Curtin walked the grounds of the Lodge. He managed to slumber fitfully. He woke the next morning to cables from Churchill and Roosevelt. The two most powerful men leading the Allies were both urging him to change his mind over Burma. This could well have been the most isolating and pressured moment in his life to that point. At first glance, these cables would have been intimidating in the extreme. A second read would have shown Curtin that the thoughts of Churchill were behind the arguments. He was using the US president, even if Roosevelt didn't fully realise it.

Yet President Roosevelt was going along with Churchill, not once but twice. First there was his message to Churchill concerning the issue. Secondly, there was his message direct to Curtin. If Burma was to go, Roosevelt wrote, 'it seems to me our whole position, including that of Australia, will be in extreme peril'. This statement was as sweeping as it was uncertain. Roosevelt was reinforcing his (State

Department-induced) obsession over China. If he had truly believed his statement, he would not have begun with 'it seems to me'. He added an unconvincing line: 'If [the 7th Division] would get into the fight at once, it would, I believe, have the strength to save what now seems to be a very dangerous situation.'

This was almost as if Churchill had written it for Roosevelt. The expectations of the supermen of this fighting unit were enormous. The way the two cables put it, the main direction of the war was dependent on their performance in stopping the Japanese, well advanced now, in Burma. And if Curtin dared not support what Churchill and Roosevelt wanted, the responsibility for the enemy advance was his.

Roosevelt added, 'I cannot believe that, in view of your geographical position and the US forces on their way to you or operating in your neighbourhood, your vital centres are in immediate danger.' This comment may well have gone too far. It was the view from Roosevelt's own safe 'geographical' position. Curtin, shaken by Singapore's fall less than a week earlier, and shocked by the smashing of Darwin less than forty-eight hours ago, was in despair. If he had even two experienced divisions to defend Australia, he would have felt better. But he had no soldiers of the experience and toughness required for more than a token effort against an invasion.

Roosevelt concluded with the summarised pitch: 'I . . . want to ask you in the interests of our whole war effort in the Far East if you will reconsider your decision . . .'[6]

24
The Prime Minister Goes Missing

Curtin was under more stress than he could handle. He responded to Roosevelt, justifying his position and telling him that Australia desperately needed the 6th and 7th Divisions to defend 'the only white man's territory south of the equator'.[1] This cable was punched off to Washington DC. By midday of 21 February

1942, Curtin was exhausted and depressed. He asked Evatt to write a draft response to Churchill, which was the tougher job. Curtin then attended another closed session of parliament, which finished at 4 p.m. The prime minister walked out into the late-afternoon sun and disappeared.

Evatt worked at the response to Churchill, consulting Sturdee and Shedden. He had a sharp draft ready by 4.30 p.m. Curtin was not in his office; Gladys Joyce and Don Rodgers had not seen him. Rodgers rang the Lodge, then the Kurrajong Hotel, Curtin's favourite place to relax. He would lie down for an hour in a darkened room, which alleviated his ailment and often saw him emerge with the solution to a problem. But there was no sign of him.

All Curtin's good mates and confidants, including Ben Chifley and the governor-general, were contacted, but they had no idea where he was. The hours slid by. Curtin's staff knew how hard the Churchill and Roosevelt cables had hit him, on top of Singapore and Darwin. It had been the toughest week of all their lives. The impact on the prime minister could barely be imagined.

Shedden, carrying Evatt's draft cable, was irritated and flustered. A reply had to be sent, especially as the convoy carrying the troops was by now in the Indian Ocean and steaming south. Its course had to be confirmed. No one could trust Churchill's reaction if he didn't receive a reply, especially when he and Roosevelt had made such attempts to persuade Curtin to change his mind. If no response from Australia was forthcoming, Churchill might order the convoy to change direction and head for Burma.

Saturday night in Canberra began to fall and still there was no sign of Curtin. The police were contacted and began a search. Shedden contacted Canberra's cinemas, asking them to put messages on the screen. One was to Curtin: could be please return to his office? The other was to the public. Bemused cinema-goers were asked to report to the police if they had seen John Curtin, their prime minister.

Evatt wanted to send his draft as the cable. He had discussed it with Curtin that morning, and the message was clear: the government wished the convoy to sail to Australia and not Burma. Sturdee and the other chiefs of staff wanted this. Only conservatives in the Advisory War Council wished the convoy to change direction, but they had no say in governmental decisions.

The police, the public and Curtin's friends and family could not find him. Some feared the worst. Curtin had wandered off before, but never as prime minister – at least, not without telling anyone. In the past, a disappearance could lead to a bender, when he got blind-drunk for days. But even though he craved this, he had so far stayed true to his word and kept off the 'grog' while he ran the country. Elsie feared that he may have succumbed to 'old bogey'.

At midnight, Curtin returned to the Lodge. He had been missing eight hours, wandering around the 842-metre Mount Ainslie, a few kilometres away from parliament across Lake Burley Griffin.

His depression had taken a toll on the functioning of his government at a critical moment, when the fate of 64,000 Australian troops in the convoy was at stake. Canberra had been in a flap. Worse, Curtin had lost vital hours in replying to Churchill. As was feared, during the delay Churchill had ordered the convoy to change direction and head for Burma.

Oblivious to this, Shedden and Curtin refined Evatt's cable reply, which, as usual, needed toning down. This required full mental application. The final communiqué was temperate and reasoned, yet firm. The long hike around Mount Ainslie had been therapeutic enough for Curtin to function the way a prime minister should.

'If it were possible to divert our troops to Burma and India without imperilling our security in the judgement of our advisers,' he wrote, 'we should be pleased to agree to this diversion.'[2]

Curtin was suggesting that he was an open-minded, cooperative ally, who nevertheless acted on advice. His chiefs' reckoning was that the troops would be needed first in Australia. The message predicted that if the troops ended up in Burma, they would be lost, as they had been in Greece and Crete. Curtin feared that Japan's superior sea and air power in the Bay of Bengal would lead to another debacle. The impact of the problems caused by a lack of air support had been driven home at Singapore and Darwin.

The cable was sent off at 3 a.m., arriving late on Saturday afternoon, London time. Churchill replied within minutes, confirming that he had turned the convoy towards Burma. It did not now have enough fuel to make it to Australia. If Curtin still wanted it in Australia, Churchill wrote, the convoy would have to stop at Colombo, Ceylon (Sri Lanka). The round trip would take three or four days. This, Churchill added, would give Curtin time to reconsider.

Bruce, who had been pushing for the Burma destination, thought Churchill was 'arrogant and offensive'. Yet he advised Curtin to be circumspect in his response and to accept the fact that the convoy would end up in Burma. Churchill was 'near the end of his tether'; it was best not to upset him. Page agreed.

Curtin was shocked by Churchill's intervention and unimpressed by the thinking of Bruce and Page. In an odd way, however, they may have confirmed Curtin in his decision. It was clear that they were under Churchill's influence in this instance; Curtin realised that his distance from that considerable power and magnetism was paramount if he was to make an objective decision. For him, the battle was down to argument and debate on paper. Emotions and personalities were kept in check and had minimal impact.

Curtin stayed with his decision to bring the convoy to Australia. It was now not just a matter of the defence of Australia; it was also an issue of sovereign independence. Curtin had been forced to make a stand over who controlled Australia's forces; he had to break with the past. Despite his condition, Curtin called Churchill's bluff. It was the most important decision of his short tenure – less than five months – running the country.

In the middle of the 'battle of the cables', Curtin received word that Timor had fallen to the Japanese on 23 February, after three days of intense fighting. He learned that most of the Allies surrendered, but about 400 Australian commandos had withdrawn to a mountain village thirty kilometres inland from Dili. They were determined to resist Japanese calls to surrender. They were aided by local Timorese and sympathetic Portuguese. The commandos had to get word to Darwin that they were alive and prepared to fight.

The fall of Timor only stiffened Curtin's resolve not to allow the 6th and 7th Divisions to go to Burma. As the end of February approached, his decision appeared to be the right one, although Churchill would hold a grudge over it for the rest of his life. While the cable debate was going on, Churchill's advisers were telling him that Burma's capital, Rangoon, was likely to fall. Had the lead ships of the convoy carrying the 7th Division steamed on there instead of to Australia, the first of the troops would have poured into the city on 27 or 28 February, just as the Japanese were attacking. The British were already making plans to retreat into the city's jungle surrounds. By early March, the Japanese had surrounded Rangoon.

The 7th Division could not have stopped the advance of two enemy divisions. It would have joined the evacuation, with no choice but to be part of the British retreat to the mountains and jungles of Burma's north. India would have been its ultimate destination. If the 7th Division had opted to stay and fight a guerilla action against the occupying Japanese, it would have been tied up there for years. Although not captured, as the 8th Division had been at Singapore, it would still have been lost to the immediate defence of Australia, which was Curtin's responsibility.

It is doubtful that Curtin would have remained in office had the 7th been 'lost' in this way. As it was, he agonised for a fortnight as the 6th and 7th sailed home, leaving him sleepless. Banned by his family and advisers from bushwalking alone around Mount Ainslie again, he wandered the Lodge's grounds at night, fretting over the Australian soldiers' passage through the submarine-infested waters of the Indian Ocean. He even resorted to long hours of prayer with a religious member of his staff, Fred McLaughlin. The fact that the troop convoy seemed to be wending its way home unhindered opened up Curtin a fraction to spiritual input, after having rejected his faith decades earlier. He was now drifting between belief and agnosticism.

While Curtin was concerned by the troops in the Indian Ocean, the light cruiser HMAS *Perth* – with its crew of 686 Australians – was sailing in an eleven-ship ABDA (American–British–Dutch–Australian) convoy in dangerous Javanese waters. It was on its way to Surabaya, on the northern shore of East Java.

Dutch Rear Admiral Karel Doorman, the commander of the convoy, received intelligence that Japanese forces had been sighted in the north. He ignored the original plan to refuel at Surabaya and sent his fleet north to intercept the enemy. A twenty-strong Japanese convoy of cruisers and battleships was protecting an invasion fleet of fifty ships heading for Banten Bay, Java.

At 11.06 p.m. on 27 February, the ABDA ships spotted a vessel about eight kilometres away, close to St Nicholas Point in northern Java. It was challenged. It was a Japanese destroyer. The ABDA ships engaged it. Minutes later, other enemy destroyers were sighted to the north. Each of the ABDA ships attempted to engage more than one Japanese boat. But there were too many of them. They attacked from every direction. The Japanese, using long-range guns, torpedoes and better teamwork in the night clash, sank or damaged most of the Allied convoy. Only the *Perth* and the USS *Houston* survived the initial action.

Just near the end of the Battle of the Java Sea, as it became known, the *Perth* was hit but not disabled. After an hour's action, the ship had used up all its ammunition. Its Australian skipper, Captain Hector Waller, had no choice but to make a run for it through the Sunda Strait to Tjilatjap, on the south coast of Java. After a day's sailing, the *Perth* was torpedoed by a Japanese destroyer. It sank, losing 328 men (324 sailors, including the Captain, three RAAF officers and one civilian). Survivors were pulled from the water or caught on land and sent to POW camps, mostly on the Thai–Burma railway. A further 105 would die in captivity. After the war 214 would be repatriated to Australia.

It was a tragic day for a six-year-old cruiser that had served its country with distinction in several oceans and against four enemies – the Italians, the Germans, the Vichy French and finally the all-conquering Japanese. Even the USS *Houston,* also using up all its ammunition, was on fire. It was hit by a torpedo shortly after the *Perth* went down, and it too sank but much closer to shore.

The Royal Netherlands Navy, severely disabled, limped off to

Australia and Ceylon. The massive Japanese fleet of seventy vessels lost a minesweeper and one transport. Four other ships had serious damage. The Battles of the Java Sea and the Sunda Strait spread over three days. It was another comprehensive victory for the Japanese. They ruled the waves around the Netherlands East Indies archipelago, in the Timor Sea, around New Guinea, and over the rest of the Pacific.

25
Japan's Army v Its Navy

In Japan, debate over the Australian question descended into outright argument. Tojo had been ambivalent until now. But when he saw that both Yamamoto and Yamashita, the Imperial force's most successful battle commanders, were pushing even harder for an invasion of the Great South Land, he expressed his doubts. He claimed it would cause manpower problems at this time. He informed his subordinates to make the case against invasion. Then Tojo sidelined Yamashita to a garrison command in Manchukuo (Manchuria), which was a blatant humiliation after his success. Worse still, Tojo issued him with travel orders that prevented him from receiving a hero's welcome. Yamashita was also disallowed an audience with the Emperor. He was out of the main decision-making loop and rendered impotent.

At a joint operation meeting at Imperial Headquarters in Tokyo on 27 February 1942, the army representatives tried to dismiss the plan to take Australia. How could the navy contemplate invading a country the same size as China, and *twice* the size of the territory that Japan occupied in China? They argued that at least twelve infantry divisions were needed to successfully invade and control Australia (which was closer to Churchill's assessment).

These arguments reflected the army's experiences in China, where it was fighting two different forces. They ignored the point that Australia was undefended; and a very soft target in comparison to the population then about 500 million and its capacity to organise guerilla defences in remoter regions.

The debate reached a crescendo when the army's chief of operations, Colonel Takushiro Hattori, became agitated when faced with telling points made by the navy's more eloquent Baron Tomioka, who said, 'The enemy [the United States] has to be denied the use of Australia as a base. As long as the enemy has no foothold there, Australia can be taken.'

The Japanese had done their research on Australia. Its sparseness was both a strength and a weakness. But the intelligence was clear. The nation was at present poorly defended and the Japanese had scant regard for the civilian defences which would be brushed aside.

Tomioka added, 'If within the next two years the United States concentrates rapidly on aircraft production and makes full use of Australia, Japan would never be able to resist the material onslaught which would follow.'

This forceful prediction, at a moment when Japan was drunk with success on sea and on land, was confronting. Hattori was furious. He reached for a cup of tea on the round table at which the planners of the opposing military arms sat. Picking it up and holding it stiff-armed away from the table, he said, 'The tea in this cup represents our total naval strength.' He then tipped the cup upside down, spilling the tea on the floor. 'You see,' he said, 'it goes just so far!' Hattori stood up and, glaring at Tomioka, added, 'If your plan is approved I will resign.' He then bowed and left the room, followed by the army planners.[1]

This fit of pique reflected the concerns of Tojo and the army that the admirals could take the ascendancy if Australia was acquired in the way they were urging. In those euphoric days of late February 1942, Tojo had a dream to take Burma, then India, and then link up with Hitler's forces somewhere in northern India. He feared that this plan would be wrecked if his forces were diverted south.

Reports of the horrific loss of the *Perth* reached Curtin late on 2 March 1942. His immediate reaction was to ask his naval chiefs how many men were on board, and how many were lost. The figures were unclear but he braced for hundreds more Australians dead. Such bad news ensured that the pressures on him were incessant.

He had not even finished morning tea the next day when he was informed of another Japanese air attack on Australia. Just after 9 a.m. on 3 March, twelve days after the mass bombing of Darwin, a force of nine Zeros flew towards Broome's port and airfield. Broome had recently become a destination for refugees and retreating military personnel from Java and Timor, but it was defended only by a couple of machine-gunners. Fifteen Australian, Dutch and American flying boats, which had been evacuated from Java, were on the water in the port. A tidal wave and problems unloading the flying boats meant that many of the passengers were still on board as the Zeros split the clouds and swooped low.

All the flying boats were destroyed. Fifty-eight men, women and children were killed. At Broome airport, seven civil and military aircraft, including four American heavy bombers, were attacked. One American Liberator bomber with twenty-one people on board, most of whom were wounded, managed to take off. It was stalked by a Zero, which hit the Liberator. The bigger plane returned fire and brought down its tormentor, but it then crashed.

After destroying Broome, the Zeros then swooped on a Dutch KLM DC-3 airliner over Carnot Bay and shot it down. It crash-landed eighty kilometres north of Broome, killing four passengers. The plane was carrying $500,000 worth of diamonds.[2] On the way home, the Zeros strafed the airfield and port of Wyndham. There were no casualties but a boat, the *Koolama*, was sunk. The next day, in the late morning, for reasons known only to the Japanese, one of their flying boats – a Kawanishi H6K – returned to strafe the wreckage of the KLM airliner.

Early on 4 March Darwin's RAAF airfield suffered another brief Zero attack, but there were no casualties. At almost the same time, the sun rose over the HMAS *Yarra*, which carried 158 sailors. It was south of Java and escorting a convoy to Fremantle: the depot ship *Anking*, the tanker *Francol* and the motor minesweeper MMS 51. All the ships were aware of the destruction wrought in these waters in the preceding days, having picked up two lifeboats full of exhausted survivors from the carnage of the Java Sea battle. There had been plain sailing through the previous thirty-six hours as the small fleet chugged south-east at a steady 8.5 knots. But the night before they had been shadowed by a plane at high altitude.

The *Yarra*'s lookout spotted the topmasts of a Japanese heavy cruiser squadron emerging over the horizon from the north-east. The sight of three cruisers, each with eight-inch guns, and two destroyers sent a chill through every Allied sailor. Lieutenant Commander Robert Rankin remained calm and ordered his ships to scatter. Then he placed *Yarra* between his convoy and the Japanese and prepared to engage.

It was the bravest of acts. The *Yarra* had no chance. This 81.1-metre sloop had just three four-inch anti-aircraft guns, four three-pound guns, an anti-aircraft machine gun, and depth charges. The enemy ships were far better armed, and faster too. Yet Rankin made no move to surrender. One by one, each ship in his fleet was sunk. Only the *Yarra* was still afloat after one hour. But it too was doomed.

The Japanese boats circled closer, hammering the stricken vessel. At 8 a.m., after holding-out for ninety minutes, Rankin ordered his beloved *Yarra* to be abandoned. He remained on the bridge. At 8.05 a.m. an eight-inch salvo hit it and Rankin was killed instantly. Leading Seaman R. Taylor had been on one of the anti-aircraft guns. When he was out of ammunition, Taylor hurried forty metres along the deck to man the sole machine gun. He kept firing it until he was struck and killed. The *Yarra*'s guns fell silent. Two Japanese destroyers moved closer, shelling her until she sank.[3]

The Japanese were wreaking havoc in the air and on the sea, with next to no opposition. Again and again they demonstrated the vulnerability of Australia's remote north.

26
Japanese Base at Lae

A few days later, on 8 March 1942, the Japanese 15th Army exhibited its superiority on the ground by taking control of Rangoon. The same day, the remaining Australian, British and Dutch forces on Java surrendered to Japanese divisions. Among them were 3000 Australians from the advance units of the 7th Division that had travelled on the *Orcades* to Batavia. These soldiers became POWs known as D Force, under the Command of Lieutenant-Colonel Edward 'Weary' Dunlop. They were sent to Changi. Later, they would join survivors of the *Perth* and thousands of POWs from the 8th Division in the labour camps of Thailand and Burma.

Japan's surprisingly quick mastery of the Dutch, British, Australian and American forces in the region had given it an unexpected bonus. Tens of thousands of extra slaves could be driven, without concern for whether they lived or died, on various road and rail projects in Japan, Thailand, Burma, Malaya and Singapore.

---

8 March 1942 also marked the start of the Japanese 'Operation SR', which aimed to occupy the Salamaua–Lae area on the northern coast of New Guinea. The base would allow the invaders to bomb and strafe Port Moresby in the south, softening it up for an infantry invasion. Once Moresby was under Japanese control, they could easily attack Australia's northern and eastern coasts.

It was a simple campaign on paper, but the Allies were determined to make any attempts at invasion difficult. The small detachment of New Guinea Volunteer Rifles and RAAF radio station staff demolished key infrastructure. Then they withdrew into the hills towards Mubo. The Allied Pacific Command, at Blamey's instigation, ordered the joint US and Royal Australian Navy (RAN) fleet to counter the enemy movements.

The RAAF's 32 Squadron, from Port Moresby, bombed the landing force but failed to stop barges disgorging Japanese troops. Four US B-17s from Garbutt Airfield, Townsville, were sent to help. One had engine trouble. The other three ran into heavy cloud and almost zero visibility – often a hazard in the region – and could not find the landing beach. This failure led to the US Navy being notified. It began patrolling closer to Moresby.

Two US aircraft carriers – the USS *Yorktown* and the USS *Lexington* – went into action on 10 March. They were supported by eight B-17s from Garbutt, and another eight Hudson bombers from Port Moresby. These sixteen Allied planes hammered the Japanese fleet, sinking three transports and damaging several other ships.

But this did not stop the invasion. The Japanese began the construction of a forward air base at Lae on the coast, eighty-five kilometres west of Finschhafen, just 120 kilometres from New Britain's western coast. They also occupied Salamaua, fifty kilometres south of Lae, in order to protect it. Both these villages provided access to New Guinea's lucrative goldfields and its main town of Wau, which had an airstrip. If enemy troops were to travel south from Wau along the Lakekamu River, they would have another point from which to strike at Port Moresby. But the Imperial Force's first option was to take that vital port from the sea.

During February and March 1942, the US presence from various arms of its mighty and building military force was beginning to show, particularly in Australia's west. Advance contingents of the US 197th Coast Artillery (machine-gunners and artillery men) arrived without warning aboard the USS *Pinegrove*. Its 'D' Troop had moved with alacrity to Rottnest Island to augment the run-down 'Bickley' Battery there with fifty-millimetre anti-aircraft guns. A huge wireless mast had been erected in the grounds of the University of Western Australia. Almost in secret, the US Army had set up headquarters in Perth's RAAF building. More than 1500 airmen were noticed by locals at this time in and around the RAAF Rendezvous National

House building in William Street, Perth. The US Navy had a headquarters at Fremantle. Americans were putting up more anti-aircraft guns on Fremantle wharf. They had come in stealthily but with intent. Their presence in the west had been hastened by the continuing air attacks on Australia's northern and north-western coast.

The US airmen were not long in Perth. Soon they were on their way to build or improve airfields in Australia's north-west, which were out of range of Japanese strikes, at least until the Americans were settled in. Places as remote as Corunna Downs near Marble Bar and Forrest on the Nullarbor were alive with construction activity.

The small US Army presence in Perth was destined to move on sooner rather than later; the city was just a staging post. But the US Navy established something more permanent in Fremantle. Unlike the US Army, which arrived under escort, the US Navy came battle-scarred and running from the Japanese advance, which now was threatening invasion of Australia's north-west. The American Asiatic Fleet had been based in the Philippines. But MacArthur's departure, heavy bombing of Manila Bay and the imminent fall of Java had forced it to retreat south. Darwin's vulnerability had seen the fleet limp to Fremantle, which was to become a relatively safe base.

This old sea port would have to beef up for the increased 'foreign' presence, but it had everything the fleet needed: food, medical and energy supplies, accommodation, transport and communications networks. There was also entertainment and women, who were thrilled, in the main, to see them. The sailors represented security and excitement, and the well-heeled American military personnel meant a big new slice of business. Perth was far more attractive to the Americans from all these perspectives than the once proposed bases in Darwin and the Gulf of Exmouth.[1]

By early March 1942, the Americans had decided unilaterally that Fremantle would be the base for twenty fleet submarines and five light 'S' Class submarines. A week later, the US decided to set up a second base further south at Albany. On 15 March, the tender *Holland* and five submarines sailed there, escorted by the USS *Parrot*, two minesweepers and the tender *Childs*. Albany would provide maintenance facilities for flying boats – Catalina patrol aircraft from the US Navy Patrol Wing Ten.

But the weather proved too rough for the first three. The flying boat base was switched back to Crawley Bay on Perth's Swan River. Nine more Catalinas were expected in a few weeks' time. The Catalinas' main base would be on the Swan, while advance bases were proposed for Geraldton, Exmouth and Port Hedland. They would patrol the Indian Ocean and northern Australian waters. The flying boats were slow but their role was important: flying low over the coast, searching for Japanese submarines. If they spotted one, they would call in surface vessels to attack them, or drop bombs and fire depth charges themselves. The Catalinas could fly up to fourteen hours before needing to refuel.

This shoring up of Australia's west would be inadequate if the Japanese admirals could cajole Emperor Hirohito and persuade or bully the army chiefs and Tojo into depriving the United States of its mightiest aircraft-carrier base – Australia itself – by invading it. Japan would have to make its move by mid-1942; otherwise, if Curtin had his way, Australia would have part of its three hardened divisions – the 6th, 7th and 9th – back in the country to defend it. These would be supported by the numerous but less experienced American troops. April, May and June 1942 would be critical to the course of the war in the Pacific.

Part Three

MacArthur and Blamey in Australia

MARCH–JUNE 1942

27

MacArthur Parks in Australia

The collapse of yet another Pacific nation to Japanese invasion seemed inevitable with the news that General Douglas MacArthur, his wife, young son and staff of sixteen, had made a hurried exit from the Philippines on 11 March 1942. They had taken a PT boat from the island of Corregidor ('the Rock') to Del Monte Airfield on the island of Mindanao. In the dark of the first hour of 17 March, the MacArthur escape party was then flown on to Australia in two fortress bombers, which had managed to avoid destruction when the Japanese had first struck on 8 December.

MacArthur had been reluctant to leave his 22,000 troops. But if he wanted to avoid death or capture by the Japanese – for himself and for his family – he had to leave. He could always claim that Roosevelt had ordered him to depart, yet he did have a choice. He could have stayed to command his troops but chose to leave them in a mess that was largely of his own creation.

The flight to Darwin covered 2500 kilometres in five hours. They hit strong turbulence over the Celebes Sea, making many airsick aboard the two planes. 'Below them lay strongholds of Japan's new empire,' William Manchester wrote in his biography of MacArthur, *American Caesar*, 'the conquered [Netherlands East] Indies, Timor and Northern New Guinea – where every sign pointed to an imminent enemy thrust against Australia. Zeros were based at captured aerodromes, and Japanese coastwatchers were scanning the skies for Allied aircraft.'

Manchester said that 'the worst of [the flight] came at the end': one of the pilots had picked up a radio warning. 'They could not land at Darwin because an enemy raid was in progress.'[1] There was concern that the airport could be hit when MacArthur and his entourage landed. They were diverted eighty kilometres to Batchelor Field just as the Zeros made another brief strike.

On alighting, MacArthur asked an American air force officer about the build-up of US troops in Australia 'to reconquer the Philippines'. The officer looked bewildered. As far as he knew, there were very few troops in the country. MacArthur could not believe this. He understood that American divisions would be waiting for him, ready to begin a fightback.

Meanwhile, in Washington DC, the US military chief of staff, George Marshall, phoned Curtin, suggesting it would please Roosevelt if the Australian government nominated MacArthur as the 'Supreme Commander of all Allied Forces in the South-west Pacific'.

Curtin was ecstatic. After all the mayhem to the north, this was the best piece of news in 102 days – since 7 December 1941. It cancelled out the disappointment and anger he felt when he learned that Churchill had 'poached' a willing and ambitious Dick Casey, Australia's Minister in Washington, to become Britain's Minister to the Middle East, which would give him a seat in the British War Cabinet. Churchill seemed to have given in to Australian government pressures to have a dominion representative in the War Cabinet. But as Casey would be travelling a lot and missing many meetings, it was doubtful that he would contribute much, or pass back more information than Page and Bruce were already dispatching.

On top of this, Churchill had removed Australia's best ear and voice in Washington DC. Casey had a rapport with Roosevelt, the US chiefs and the most important politicians and bureaucrats. It would take a very good new diplomat a decade to reach the same level, and that would be of no use to Curtin.

It was a small 'win' for Churchill, whose distaste for Curtin and 'colonials' was at its peak. In an act of short-sighted petulance, he decided not to allow Curtin to cable him directly. Every communication would now come through Bruce.

Curtin let Casey know he was displeased but was soon preoccupied with the news that MacArthur was in Australia. No one could tell him where he was until Brett reported that MacArthur had landed in Alice Springs.

Again, the new 'Supreme Commander' was not supremely happy with flying: he would wait for the next train to Adelaide. The four-year-old Arthur MacArthur – saddled with his grandfather's Christian name – was on a drip. The MacArthurs were to have an enforced overnight stay in Australia's sweltering, fly-dominated 'dead heart'. The Americans in the party groped for a description of 'The Alice' and fell back on the hackneyed view of it as a one-horse place resembling an Old West town, complete with a rowdy saloon and a cinema. Appropriately, a western was playing. But MacArthur didn't like it. He sent his staff ahead by plane and took a three-car steam train on the 1600-kilometre journey, which was to take some seventy hours.

The train arrived at Terowie Railway Station, 220 kilometres north of Adelaide, at 2 p.m. on 20 March. The casually attired MacArthur addressed a crowd of locals. They had gathered to greet the famous traveller, who thought his trip was top secret. There were no reporters there. Someone asked what he was doing in Australia, and MacArthur had a ready reply. Adjusting his laurel-wreathed peaked cap, he said that President Roosevelt had asked him to 'break through the Japanese lines' and head for Australia.

'The purpose, as I understand it,' he said, 'was to organise an American offensive against Japan.' The main aim of this, he claimed, was 'the relief of the Philippines'. Then he added the immortal line: 'I came through and I shall return.'

The small crowd cheered and MacArthur saluted. It was a ham line for a test audience. But he liked the response. He would perfect his delivery when he used this line again, with the media in attendance. (When [later] President Eisenhower was asked if he knew MacArthur, he replied: 'Yes, I studied drama under him for some years.')[2]

The following day, his spirits were dampened when one of his staff officers, Colonel Dick Marshall, boarded the train at Kooringa, 130 kilometres from Adelaide. 'There are fewer than 32,000 Allied troops – American, British and Australian – in the whole country,' Marshall reported.

MacArthur was shocked. The officer at Batchelor Field had been right. He asked about the air force and learned that there were fewer than 100 aircraft, mainly 'Australian Gypsy Moths. They're pretty primitive – flimsy fabric-covered wings. You have to hand-start them by spinning the props.'

MacArthur shook his head. 'God have mercy on us,' he muttered.[3]

He changed to a special train, courtesy of Curtin and the Australian commissioner of railways. It had a touch of luxury appreciated by the MacArthurs after their cattle-class experiences on the 6000-kilometre journey from Corregidor. The train pulled into Melbourne's Spencer Street Station at 9.30 a.m. on 22 March. MacArthur was welcomed by a cobbled-together party of 360 American engineers and signalmen wearing tropical helmets. More than 6000 Melburnians gave him a rousing reception. An Australian army band struck up the US national anthem. This was more like it.

MacArthur appeared to be over the stunning news about his phantom army. He believed in self-fulfilling prophecies. He would elicit that army from Roosevelt, no matter what. He tried out his 'I shall return' line again. No one in the audience was quite sure what he meant. The press reports of fighting in the Philippines had been scant. But it sounded good and MacArthur looked the part even if the greeting party didn't know where he had come from or where he was returning to.

MacArthur had created myth and legend around himself all his life. He was now embellishing it, aided by Roosevelt, who bestowed the Congressional Medal of Honor on him to counter the enemy's media attacks. In Berlin, Hitler's propaganda minister, Goebbels, referred to MacArthur as the 'fleeing general'. Mussolini called him a 'coward'. The Japanese chimed in via the state-controlled *Japan Times and Advertiser*, accusing MacArthur of being a 'deserter' who had 'fled his post'. The Allies now scrambled to fabricate the image of a great general regrouping his army for a counter-attack.

But there was no army, just the amateur actor MacArthur, who addressed the newsreel cameras rather than the crowd. He projected a Caesar-like image. He might have compared himself to General Custer with his 'last stand' against the Indians. MacArthur, however, had survived to fight again. He had a willing Australian audience who wanted to believe in this image of a man of power. In the mood of increasing fear, he gave them hope.

28

Meeting the Australians

MacArthur's entourage took up the entire sixth floor of Melbourne's smart Menzies Hotel. The general had a piano installed in his suite, where he relaxed before setting up his headquarters in the city.

President Quezon and his party had also escaped the Philippines and come to Melbourne. They were put up at 'Heymount', the home of Sir Norman Myer. A large villa on three-quarters of an acre, it was the nearest thing to palatial in Melbourne. It featured Louis XVI furniture and large baronial Italian chairs. Crystal chandeliers hung from high ceilings. A white Beckstein grand piano stood in the drawing room. Blue Persian rugs covered the parquetry floors. Two large Axminster rugs lay in the entrance hall. 'Heymount' also featured Myer's well-stocked air-raid shelter, which appealed to the Filipinos. MacArthur spent much of his first days in Melbourne with the bewildered Quezon in the villa's smoking room.

'General MacArthur's arrival at Heymount was always announced with the clicking of heels and a loud "Attenshun!",' according to Pamela Myer Warrender, Norman Myer's attractive seventeen-year-old daughter. 'Leaving his heavily braided cap on the sofa in the hallway, he would disappear into the smoking room with President Quezon, [Philippines] General Romulo and [US] Colonel Willoughby,' who 'had wall-to-wall medals and was the rage of Toorak society women. Between cocktails and top-secret meetings with the President, he avalanched my mother with white orchids.'[1]

MacArthur was introduced to Australian and American military officials at Victoria Barracks on 25 March before being driven to Canberra. On 26 March, he met Curtin. It was important for

Australia that these two had a rapport; it was in their mutual interests. By the end of that first meeting, the American general knew he could rely on Curtin to support his every request in Australia, and on the US for all he required in the fight against the enemy.

Curtin, too, was impressed. MacArthur had the right image, said the right things and had an unmatched air of authority. The American's props – an ornate cap and corncob pipe – added a light touch to his heavy demeanour. His unfashionable dark sunglasses were even thought acceptable by Australians who otherwise regarded them as 'showy' and a sign of insecurity. The glasses added to his aloofness. This, and his too 'correct' manner, speech and dress, did not bother the more grounded Curtin, who was happily without flair or airs. He had dealt with Australia's social spectrum and could always find common ground. MacArthur was too dignified and humourless to qualify as anyone's 'mate'.

He demanded idolatry and could not cope with criticism. He had true enemies in Washington DC but his paranoia invented many in different places. He was big on vendettas. MacArthur's ego needed perpetual massaging. His subordinates obeyed his orders, bent to his ideas and bowed (figuratively) to him. MacArthur connived and lied shamelessly and never let the truth get in the way of anything, especially a story of bravery about himself.

Curtin abhorred idolatry. His ego was intact, but he needed nurturing from his family and bolstering from his mates, particularly Chifley. Curtin always invited views from those in his inner circle and 'kitchen cabinet'. He coped with criticism and rarely took it as a personal attack, even when it was. He was not a natural liar, but he did attempt to manipulate the public if he felt it was in their interests.

All this was incidental, though, to Curtin's appraisal of MacArthur. He liked 'the general' (who was never 'Doug', even to his wife) for his optimism. The American, in turn, was impressed by the prime minister from this white outpost of Empire, who was direct, honest and pliable.

Curtin and MacArthur learned that they had just two things in common: defeating the Japanese and poetry. Both liked to drop a line from Byron or Shakespeare, which was a start. There seemed no reason why their relationship would not serve their mutual goals. Curtin was colourless yet had integrity to spare, while MacArthur was all about self-aggrandisement. He was flamboyant, with an eye to having an exalted place in history. Curtin's dream was to transform Australia into a more equitable, fair, socialist society.

Curtin was image-conscious only insofar as he knew he had to project confidence in a crisis. His one concession to his appearance was to worry about his 'wall eye', which seemed to be turning further outwards as he aged. Curtin once asked a newsreel cameraman if he could do something about that look when he filmed him. He wore drab suits and had only six ordinary ties, one of them a tatty Fitzroy Football Club memento he had kept for thirty years. He always presented in white shirts with starched collars; it did not do in his three professions – union official, journalist and politician – to appear other than drab and grey.

MacArthur was a fraction shorter than Curtin, but in just about every photograph of them together, the general with the aquiline nose and raised chin looked taller. He had been blessed with strong, lean and handsome features. Every photograph of him – from teenager to maturity – was a study in dour, superior good looks. He developed an unmatched vanity and a character devoid of humour, especially about himself. MacArthur played his part as a general to perfection. He was straight-backed and saluted at every opportunity, especially with newsreel cameras rolling. He loved to wear his different uniforms and decorations, and kept his shirt open at the neck.

At sixty-two, there seemed little possibility of fun in MacArthur's expression, and this gave him the appearance of severity. He watched what he ate and worked on a tan, striving for a slim, healthy look. He wanted a Hollywood image for political purposes. He considered himself infinitely better suited to be US president than anyone, including the incumbent.

The two men's closest relationships reveal clues as to their characters. MacArthur, like Roosevelt, was a 'mummy's boy'. His autocratic Southern mother urged him to aim as high as possible in life and be ruthless in achieving his ambitions. She always kept an eye on him, even staying in a hotel close to his US military academy. She wrote letters to his superiors demanding his promotion. Perhaps in defiance of his mother, or possibly because he craved maternal influence, MacArthur married an older divorcee, but they split after a few years. Between marriages, he kept a Eurasian mistress in the Philippines and Washington DC in the 1930s, an era when such relationships were risqué. MacArthur, fifty-four at the time and by now a general, was worried his mother would learn of this liaison, especially after feeling her wrath over his first marriage. He bought off the mistress. After his mother died he pursued a younger woman, Jean, and at last found stability.

Curtin's one marriage was stable from the start, although he did have extramarital 'relationships', primarily with Belle Southwell, who ran Canberra's Kurrajong Hotel, his home away from home. These affairs seem to have been more for company than for any innate lust.

While Curtin loved a drink so much that it was a problem, MacArthur drank in moderation. He despised those who couldn't 'hold their liquor' or who drank too much. He would not tolerate any excesses among the officers in his command. MacArthur spoke often about situations in terms of 'life or death' and invoked references to 'God'. Yet he never hinted that he truly worried about losing American soldiers in battle. His elevation to general confirmed his view that any such attitude was 'softness' or 'weakness'.

MacArthur felt directed by his God, who had a clear destiny mapped out for him. Curtin by now certainly believed in destiny, even if it was not what he had dreamt of as a young socialist firebrand. Whether it was destiny or not, these unlikely bedfellows were now united by a common and all-consuming cause.[2]

Blamey's imminent return to Australia sparked the so-called 'generals' plot' of March 1942, when a group of militia and regular army staff corps approached Army Minister Frank Forde, with the aim of replacing Blamey and his staff. Forde and Curtin viewed this as nothing more than some disgruntled and power-hungry senior officers seeking advancement. It was not done with the nation's interests at heart. The approach was dismissed. Cynical observers reckoned that such struggles within the Australian army meant more energy was aimed at rivals within than the enemy without.

The advent of MacArthur to Melbourne and Canberra coincided with internecine riots of American forces in formerly somnolent Brisbane.

The town was being transformed into Little America, as more and more troops arrived without fanfare. This brought all the features of American culture, good and bad, including a virulent racism.

White troops of the US 208th Coast Artillery, mainly from the segregated South, clashed with African-Americans from the 394th Quartermaster Battalion. It began over the whites resenting the blacks being allowed into dance halls and skating rinks. They were upset by 'cool' and charming blacks mixing with local women in the streets and in the brothels. Bordellos were doing a brisk trade, especially the twenty or so around Margaret and Lower Albert Streets – the old 'Frog's Hollow' quarter of the city. The brothels' madams and prostitutes were colour-blind: the Americans had plenty of money to spend. The braver local women liked flirting with the African-Americans as much as the Caucasians.

The US military authorities tried segregating the Americans in different parts of Brisbane to lessen the chance of confrontation. But the blacks resented this. They rioted and defied the ban to enter certain areas where there was more 'action' at dances and other meeting places. They grouped to beat up white American soldiers they encountered.

These clashes prompted the Australian Inspector-General to recommend that no more black servicemen should come to Australia. This was not accepted, and instead the authorities separated the two groups further, now placing the blacks south of the Brisbane River. Special brothels were set up for their exclusive use. Some blacks were stationed at outposts such as Ipswich, Redbank and Wacol, where more 'houses of ill repute' sprang up.

But these moves did not stop the fights. One turned into a race riot at Wacol. There were further fierce confrontations when blacks tried to cross the Brisbane River to enter the more enticing dance halls in the north. This led to knives being used in a fight in Anzac Square. American military police attacked the blacks, shooting and killing some and beating up others. These incidents were hushed up and went unreported.

The trickle of Americans of all backgrounds would soon become a flood. They easily outnumbered local males, and this created resentment, especially as many Australian servicemen were away from their Brisbane homes. The Americans already had a six-storey building on the corner of Adelaide and Creek Streets. It was called the American PX (for 'postal exchange'), and was an up-market general store. Its ground floor was overflowing with American goods, which were seen by the locals as luxuries. All their favourite cigarettes and alcoholic drinks (beer and bourbon being the most popular) featured. Ham, turkey, ice-cream and chocolates were there in abundance. Then there were other items, such as nylon stockings, which endeared the Americans to the local ladies, whom they were trying to woo. Australian servicemen and civilians had no access to these goods, which were either too expensive or rationed.

On 26 March, as Curtin met MacArthur, the battles in New Guinea were in full swing – in the air. An American air force squadron of Douglas Dauntless dive bombers arrived in Port Moresby, adding to the bombing capacity of Australia's 75 Squadron, led by John Jackson. He set the pattern for the inferior Kittyhawks to tackle the Zeros, which he had learnt from his short time in the Middle East, when he fought against German Messerschmitts.

Jackson instructed his pilots to fly above the enemy planes, and to power down on them with all guns blazing. His flyers were told to then ease away, knowing that the Messerschmitts could not match their speed. It hurt his squadron pilots that they could not engage in dog-fights. But they were disciplined. It still took enormous courage to dive on planes that were better fighting machines.

Jackson's brother Les demonstrated the classic way to take on the Zeros. When doing routine defence reconnaissance, he approached an enemy contingent of thirteen Zeros and bombers heading for Port Moresby. He broke from his squadron and climbed high above the enemy, then he swooped down through the group, his guns firing. The bombers were stunned. They dropped their loads a long way short of Moresby and fled, escorted by the confused Zeros, which chose to stay with the bombers rather than climb into the clouds to find this fearless rogue Kittyhawk. The Japanese rule of the Pacific airways was being challenged for the first time.

29
Blamey in the Mix

Curtin was jaunty – for him – for the first time in months at the War Advisory Council meeting in Canberra on 26 March 1942. The US cavalry had arrived. Curtin made sure any media reports on Brisbane's problems with the Americans were suppressed and did not spoil the image of the American supreme commander.

Curtin introduced MacArthur, R. H. Henderson (Chief of Staff) and Dick Marshall (Deputy Chief of Staff) to the council's members. The full council, except for the Australian military chiefs, sat in awe of the American military power as MacArthur set out his views on the current situation.

There were few interruptions. Even Billy Hughes, who genuflected to no man – and very few women – was mute. MacArthur covered territory, geographical and figurative, that few of the council members had been near. All the negative descriptions that had filtered through about this prominent, controversial American were forgotten. Apart from his sometimes pompous style, MacArthur was respectful to all of them, particularly Curtin, but also Menzies, whom he had met before. It did not hurt that he was mostly saying things they wanted to hear.

MacArthur began by explaining that Roosevelt's order for him to leave the Philippines had come as a 'complete surprise'. At the time he was 'in a desperate struggle against the Japanese'. This was meant to dispel any slurs about his hurried departure. MacArthur spoke of the strength of the Japanese military, whose navy, army and air forces 'worked as one machine'. He had been 'greatly impressed by their complete co-ordination'. It helped explain how his force had been overwhelmed.

'The Japanese were formidable fighters,' he informed the council. 'The vast number of their common soldiers was one degree removed from savages.' They were also 'front runners'. They could be beaten if opposed by well-organised troops. 'The European Theatre [of war] is not predominant,' he told them, 'the Pacific is the real centre . . . Australia must stand firmly in its view that the Pacific is the predominant theatre.'

MacArthur then tried to put their minds at ease: 'It is doubtful whether the Japanese will undertake an invasion of Australia. The spoils don't warrant the risk.' But he had repeatedly been wrong about the Japanese attacking Pearl Harbor and taking Malaya, Singapore, Thailand, Burma, Timor and his beloved Philippines. So just in case he had misjudged the enemy yet again, he added a little out-clause: 'The Japanese might try to over-run Australia to show their superiority over the white races.' He thought that 'the main danger was from [air] raids'. The Japanese would also attempt to secure air bases in Australia.

No one on the council spoke during the frequent pauses in MacArthur's sometimes melodramatic delivery. This was chilling news. But MacArthur had a counter-measure: 'Anti-aircraft defence will need to be increased for the main cities and air stations,' he told them.

Near the end of the meeting, MacArthur turned to Curtin and said, 'We'll see this thing through together. You take care of the rear, and I will handle the front.'[1]

This was like a Mozart symphony to the prime minister's ears. He had not had such credible reassurance since taking office. It made him feel that the burden of the business of war was to be shared for the first time. Curtin never thought he could slip away from the pressures of his office, but this American military 'giant' had removed some of them.

The War Council dispersed, satisfied that they had at last heard a comprehensive, thematic appraisal of their situation, and the options they had for the future. MacArthur's manner and certitude delivered credibility. It did not matter that they'd heard similar advice from their own chiefs; hearing it so succinctly from MacArthur gave them and the nation a semblance of security.

That night Curtin held a dinner at Parliament House for the MacArthurs and the general's staff (known as the 'Bataan Gang'). The highlight occurred when the American Ambassador to Canberra presented MacArthur with the Congressional Medal of Honor. His gushing speech mentioned the general's 'gallantry and intrepidity', his 'heroic conduct', 'calm judgement in each crisis' and 'utter disregard of personal danger under heavy fire and aerial bombardment'.

MacArthur manufactured some suitable humility, saying that the medal was 'not so much for me personally as it is a recognition of the indomitable courage of the gallant army which it is my honor to command'. Liberating the Philippines was his obsession. 'I have come as a soldier in a great crusade of personal liberty as opposed to perpetual slavery,' he said, gripping everyone, especially the press, with his slow, deliberate and emotional delivery. 'My faith in our ultimate victory is invincible.'

'There can be no compromise,' MacArthur said, his chin thrusting. 'We shall win or we shall die.' He paused, letting the drama of this stark truism of war sink in. Then, with a further flourish, he added, 'To this end I pledge the full resources of all the mighty power of my country and all the blood of my countrymen!'

This was a dedication that not even Roosevelt would dare say, and he was the only American in a position to say it. But the press lapped it up. One Australian reporter wrote that the speech was 'terrific', which was not such a cliché in this instance. It was terrifying and electric.[2] It was also called 'Churchillian', which was a description then becoming fashionable. Yet MacArthur had none of Churchill's dry humour, sharp wit or power in the use of language.

MacArthur turned often to Curtin as he spoke. Photographs show the prime minister with an expression that suggested full attention, yet also curiosity. Was this character authentic or not? He would find out. For the moment, MacArthur was inspirational and optimistic. This mattered.

The next day, General Thomas Blamey, back from the Middle East, met his new 'boss' MacArthur, now officially confirmed by Curtin and Roosevelt as Supreme Commander of the South-West Pacific

Area. MacArthur and Blamey were not destined to embrace each other; the best Curtin could hope for was an uneasy alliance. They were very different men.

Aged fifty-eight in 1942, Blamey had led a life that had etched itself onto his face and body. He was rugged, short and stocky, with the kind of stomach that reflected good living and little exercise. He had fleshy jowls, a wispy grey moustache and a devilish grin that bordered on the debauched. There was a recklessness in his nature. He was a big drinker with a sense of humour, however unrefined. Whether alcohol-fuelled or not, he had an aggressive mien. He would be direct and blunt with anyone. Blamey was careless about his manner and image. Fellow military commanders disdained this. Soldiers were unsure that they really wanted a leader who drank and behaved like the larrikins amongst them. On the one hand, it made him seem like one of the boys – which he was not and never had been. On the other, it was not the image they wished to see in a commander in control of their lives in battle.

MacArthur had contempt for Blamey's style, even appearance. He and his staff sneered at Blamey's penchant for uniforms with short pants and long socks. They believed this was the attire of schoolboys, not generals, despite the conditions in the jungles of New Guinea, Borneo, Thailand and Sumatra requiring cooler clothes.

In allowing MacArthur to play his role, Curtin had conceded all to the Americans, and was not cognisant of everything this entailed. MacArthur now had operational command of Australian forces and was responsible for Australia's strategic direction. Curtin believed he would place Australian officers in his Allied headquarters. Even Roosevelt and MacArthur's superior officer, General Marshall, expected this. But MacArthur excluded Australians, saying no suitable senior men were available. It was a remarkable blend of conceit and mendacity.

But as Curtin had accepted MacArthur's legend without question, there would be no challenge from anyone with the power to get the balance right. All eleven senior positions at MacArthur's headquarters were filled by Americans. Eight were Bataan Gang members. If

Blamey had been allowed to select a first XI, there is no doubt that every single selection would have had a superior record to that of any member of MacArthur's team. But this was precisely why MacArthur chose his inferior squad without any interlopers: this way, he could not be challenged. Nor could his officers' inferiority be on display.

The lines of authority were thus clear from the start, which in theory augured well for strong leadership. MacArthur would have control over all Australian, American and Dutch forces in the region. There was one qualification: the reaction of US generals and admirals in the combat zone. But for the moment, MacArthur had most clout in the region.

Blamey became commander of the Allied Land Forces. Reporting to MacArthur, he was responsible for the land defence of Australia and the offensive operations planned by the Bataan Gang. What would happen if and when American soldiers came in force into the region would be another matter.

30
Blamey v MacArthur – the Record

Curtin established the Prime Minister's War Conference, which in practice concerned two people: himself and MacArthur. It would be the senior 'body' for the war's direction. MacArthur would become the government's main war strategy adviser. Shedden would act as secretary for the War Conference and also liaise between the two men. In effect, Shedden became a third member of the conference as it began operating.

Curtin reserved the right to invite whomever he liked to it. This quaint body, comprising a prime minister, a public servant and a foreign general, contravened almost all conventions. It had more power than the usual centres of executive authority: the Cabinet, the War Cabinet and the Advisory War Council. In practice, MacArthur would have all the say in matters of strategy.

This odd arrangement cut Blamey out of the power loop and placed Shedden, the Secretary of the Department of Defence, above him and all the Australian chiefs – an absurd development, given Shedden's meagre record in military matters. He overrated himself as a military and strategic expert. Shedden had spent six months in World War I as a lieutenant in the pay corps. Later, he attended the Imperial Defence College. Curtin's lack of interest in military business put Blamey at a distinct disadvantage.

Blamey threatened to resign, and Curtin wished to placate him. He wanted this tough Australian, who was not going to bend to MacArthur, somewhere in the structure. There was no one else with quite the savvy and strength to act as a counter-balance to MacArthur if he got out of hand or didn't deliver.

Curtin was abrogating all sovereign power to do with war and defence to a foreign general. There could be problems if this arrangement failed, or if MacArthur was not up to the job. Criticism emerged early from within and without the Labor Party, and especially from the far left, which resented any American connection. The conservatives hated the idea of Americans usurping the power vacuum in the Pacific left by the British. Curtin had been decisive, even if he had not carefully considered the ramifications of his decision. At a critical moment for Australia, he had not dithered when he considered the country was in jeopardy.

Curtin had shifted Australia into a position independent of the United Kingdom but dependent upon the Americans.[1] He knew that if he had shared power with the conservatives in a War Cabinet he would have been strongly opposed by Menzies, which would have led to division, an unhealthy state for any government, especially in wartime. Menzies and co. would always have sided with Churchill. On the question of Burma, Curtin would have lost, since the conservatives would have supported the British position. Relying on the British at the expense of the Americans would have meant the Pacific power vacuum remained, leaving an opportunity for the Japanese to strike and take Australia.

Blamey's record was far more impressive than that of his new commander. MacArthur had languished in the Philippines, hoping the Japanese would do nothing, and then was caught unprepared and had to leave his fiefdom in an embarrassing hurry. A month after World War II had begun, Blamey had been promoted to lieutenant-general and appointed to command the 6th Division, the first raised for the new 2nd AIF. When the 7th Division was created, there were enough diggers to call the force an army corps, and Blamey was made its commander in the Middle East.

He was preoccupied with keeping its divisions intact. He had to duel with British commanders such as General Wavell and General Sir Claude Auchinleck. Blamey failed to inform the Australian government quickly enough about the disastrous Greek campaign, into which Churchill had pushed the Australians. Blamey made up for the error to some extent by adroitly commanding the Australian withdrawal down the Greek peninsula. He also oversaw the evacuation from beaches that he had reconnoitred.

On 23 April 1941, Blamey was appointed Deputy Commander in Chief of the British Forces in the Middle East. He involved himself in the strategy of the Syrian Campaign, in which the Australians defeated the Vichy French. Blamey aimed to bring all four Australian divisions together under his command in the Middle East. He demanded that the fatigued 9th Division be relieved at Tobruk. His career seemed a mixed bag of success, errors and defeats, but he was most active in defending Australia's forces.

Blamey's experience in World War I meant that he would not allow British World War II generals to misuse his troops. Wavell and Auchinleck were forced to respect his determination and energy. He upset them with his feistiness. After Blamey had left the Middle East, Wavell, never one to heap praise on Australians, said, 'He was not an easy man to deal with but probably the best soldier we had in the Middle East.' This was in accord with British World War I General William Birdwood, who made way for Monash when he took control of the 1st AIF in May 1918. The diminutive 'Birdy', who was one of the few British generals acceptable to the diggers, called Blamey 'an exceedingly able little man, though by no means a pleasing personality'.

Blamey never cared much for what the British thought. He had learned from Monash to put Australian interests ahead of anything else. In World War II, Auchlinleck liked Blamey but was less impressed than Wavell, saying he wouldn't choose him for an operation. This had more to do with Blamey standing up to him at Tobruk than with Blamey's capacities as a commander. Blamey upset Churchill so much over the same issue that it seemed likely that Churchill would ask the Australian government to remove him from his post. Then Japan attacked Pearl Harbor on 7 December 1941 and Blamey was inevitably on his way home anyway.

Compared to MacArthur's unimpressive efforts in the Philippines, Blamey's record meant that he would never be comfortable in a subservient role. Blamey had other reasons for being aggrieved. Even his performances in World War I, two decades earlier, could be seen as having greater merit than MacArthur's – in leadership, effectiveness, experience and impact. There was no doubting MacArthur's bravery, but there was something dubious about the way he set about gathering glittering ribbons regardless of whether or not he merited them.

He had begun World War I in 1917 as the first US Army public-relations appointment. He employed many journalists, who were not averse to gilding MacArthur's on-field achievements. His mother ('Pinky') pulled her considerable weight in influencing General Pershing, Commander in Chief of the American Expeditionary Force in Europe, to promote him to brigadier general.[2] MacArthur lobbied shamelessly for every award going, right up to the Congressional Medal of Honor, which he did not gain on merit.

By the time MacArthur was near the frontline in World War I, Blamey had been in Gallipoli and on the Western Front for three years. From mid-1918, he was chosen by Monash, the most outstanding battle commander of World War I, to be the chief of staff for Australia's 1st AIF. While MacArthur was in fringe battles of little consequence in the context of the war's outcome, Blamey was assisting Monash front and centre, preparing battle plans that would damage the Germans and lead to the finish of hostilities. He was at Monash's side as the diggers liberated 116 French towns and villages. They took on thirty-nine German divisions – one million soldiers – and defeated every one of them.

Monash taught Blamey everything there was to know about planning, preparation and winning. If MacArthur's obsession was gaining chest baubles, Monash's (and thus Blamey's) was detail, so much so that when he (Monash) served under British generals, they complained about it.

In the decisive Battle of Amiens on 8–9 August 1918, Monash first had the enemy artillery destroyed so that his 102,000 diggers could move forward without being monstered by incessant shelling. On 8 August, the Germans had the biggest loss of men in any single day of the war: 27,000. After such destruction, General Ludendorff, Germany's military dictator, was on the verge of capitulation. He began angling for peace, while withdrawing. He said, 'It was the blackest day of the war for the German Army. It could not now win the war, it could only defend.'

Blamey had a lingering contempt for US fighting techniques (as opposed to the Americans' courage) after World War I. Monash had asked the British (and de facto Allied) commander in chief, Field Marshal Douglas Haig, for 50,000 Americans to fight under Australian command. The request was granted and he received soldiers from the US 27th and 28th Divisions, under the command of Major-General G. W. Read. First, Monash had to train them.

He enlisted 217 Australian officers to instruct them on warfare tactics in Western Front conditions. They needed training in all areas – from discipline to understanding weapons to explosives. There was no comprehension of the clear communication of orders needed right down the line. American officers underestimated the need for a good food and water supply system. They didn't have a clue about how to attack and then protect themselves from unnecessary losses. None knew the concept of 'mopping up': once a position had been secured after battle, a contingent was assigned to keep control of the area while the rest of the force moved on. Blamey was on hand as Monash laid out a battle plan in a three-hour lecture. For once, the brilliant military communicator failed.

On 29 September 1918 Monash had given the Americans the honour of 'going over the top' first, before the diggers. The Americans swept over and past trenches, but did not anticipate the Germans bobbing up behind them from their shell-proof dugouts. Monash and

Blamey lost contact with the Americans and could not shell the area for fear of hitting them. Monash was in despair over the Americans' failure to stick to the plan.

Blamey had tongue-lashed an American divisional commander over the near fiasco. The battle was ultimately successful, but the experience left Blamey with a thinly veiled contempt for American officers, although he recognised the US frontline solders as 'courageous, willing and cheerful'.[3]

Blamey would not have been impressed by MacArthur's 42nd Division, made up of National Guardsmen from across the United States. Guardsmen were regarded as inferior in training and commitment to regular soldiers, since their official role was to 'guard' the United States rather than to fight abroad. But MacArthur had lobbied successfully for this division to go to the Western Front. Blamey believed its officers, including MacArthur, would have struggled more than the 27th and 28th to comprehend the huge, highly coordinated formation battles that Monash thrived on.

MacArthur rose to be a colonel and a chief of staff. This was a vastly inferior position to Blamey's in its impact, influence and size. Blamey was responsible for ten times the number of soldiers in the eight divisions under Monash. Indeed, in September 1918 he had twice as many Americans under his control than MacArthur ever had during World War I.

Blamey's experience under Monash was the most important recommendation of his ability, regardless of his significant flaws. There was no more exacting commander than Monash, the perfectionist. He handpicked everyone under him in any field of endeavour, from building and the law to academia and the military. Once he became commander in chief of the 1st AIF, he selected five generals – Hobbs, Sinclair-MacLagan, Rosenthal, Glasgow and Gellibrand – to run his five divisions. All were outstanding soldiers who would sit well in any military company in history. He demanded and bred organisational skills that tested the most meticulous.

Blamey's most treasured possession was a letter from Monash after World War I. It became a passport for the rest of his professional life. It impressed everyone, including prime ministers such as Menzies and Curtin, both great admirers of Monash. It read:

He [Blamey] possessed a mind far above the average, widely informed, alert and prehensile. He had an infinite capacity for taking pains. A Staff College graduate, but not on that account a pedant, he was thoroughly versed in the technique of staff work, and in the minutiae of all procedure.

He served me with exemplary loyalty ... He had an extraordinary faculty for self-effacement, posing always and conscientiously as the instrument to give effect to my policies and decisions. Really helpful whenever his advice was invited, he never obtruded his own opinions, although I knew that he did not always agree with me.

Blamey was thirty-six years old when this was written. Clearly, much of his character and personality was already shaped, and his capacities and abilities developed. Monash went on:

Some day the order which he drafted for the long series of history-making operations in World War I which we collaborated on will become a model for Staff Colleges and Schools for military instruction. They were accurate, lucid in language, perfect in detail, and always an exact interpretation of my intention. It was seldom that I thought that my orders or instructions could have been better expressed, and no Commander could have been more exacting than I was in the matter of the use of clear language to express thought.

Monash concluded by writing of Blamey's substance, emotional support, 'inexhaustible industry' and his acceptance of 'every task with placid readiness'.[4]

In short, Monash was saying that Blamey had carried out his orders to perfection. Two decades after this assessment, this capacity would be tested as never before with the advent of MacArthur. Blamey would have to accept being subordinate to a man whose measure he felt he had in every respect, but especially in strategy, tactics and commanding and organising an army in battle.

31
Of Doubtful Character

Douglas MacArthur had studied World War I. He was well aware of Monash and his successes over a devastating three-month period from July to October 1918, from Hamel and Amiens to beyond the Hindenburg Line. Those events had been forgotten in American military history. That a general from a small, former British colonial outpost could command and win with so many Americans serving under him was an inconvenient fact that had to be buried. MacArthur realised that, by association, Blamey was also a formidable soldier, especially relative to MacArthur's own experiences so far.

Curtin's acceptance of the chain of command now in place in Australia would have been a relief to the American. Typically, MacArthur planned to cut Blamey out of the decision-making loop. MacArthur had proposed to Washington that he should have two land forces commanders: an Australian for the Australians, and an American for the Americans. US General Marshall refused to agree to this. In the meantime, MacArthur did what he could to undermine Blamey's image. Privately, he summed up his Australian rival as 'a tough commander likely to shine like a power-light in an emergency. The best of the local bunch.' But he prefaced such faint praise with the comment that he found him to be a 'sensual, slothful and doubtful character'.[1]

This remark was as patronising as it was hypocritical, and reflected MacArthur's sense of inferiority to Blamey. The American had turned a blind eye to the activities of his Bataan Gang officers, several of whom had acquired Australian mistresses, all on the Australian government's payroll. All of the Bataan Gang had war experience vastly inferior to that of Blamey. None approached his level of service in either World War.

MacArthur's assessment was based on rumours that had swirled around Blamey since 1925. 'Sensual' was meant in a narrow sense: Blamey was a man of the flesh, someone who had consorted with prostitutes from Melbourne to Cairo. There was a degree of hypocrisy here too, as MacArthur had had his own 'sensual' period in the Philippines – at least between his marriages, and probably during and before them. It is highly unlikely that a man of fifty-four, as he was at the end of his first marriage, who loved the life of a European in the most exotic outpost in the world, would have ignored the available pleasures of the flesh. His Eurasian 'mistress', whom he had bought and then sold like a sleek vehicle that was past its use-by date, was testimony to this. The alacrity with which he had dispatched her indicated that she was not the first. This perhaps reflected a misogyny – either permanent or temporary – brought about by his humiliation over the breakdown of his first marriage. MacArthur had what psychologists call a 'Madonna complex', in which mothers were deified and wives were meant in some way to replicate this deification. Mistresses were for 'sensual' pleasure.

MacArthur and his staff would have recalled all the stories about Blamey – still current – every time he was analysed in the press or discussed in private. First, there was the story from when he was Chief Commissioner for Police in Victoria. On 21 October 1925, the year of his appointment – thanks to Monash's recommendation – police raided a Fitzroy brothel and a found a man with Blamey's police badge (number eighty). Afterwards, Blamey was rumoured to have been the individual caught *in flagrante delicto*, cavorting with two young prostitutes. He claimed publicly that the badge had been stolen, which was untrue. In private, he said he had lent his keyring, including the badge, to a friend, but refused to name him.[2]

Stan Savige, an outstanding soldier of World War I and a founder of Legacy, provided a credible alibi by claiming that he had dined with Blamey at the Naval and Military Club in Melbourne on the night of the incident. This piece of 'evidence' quelled press curiosity at the time as Savige was an individual of the utmost integrity, highly respected as both a brave soldier and a man of compassion. But even if the dinner finished at midnight, it would have taken Blamey five minutes to travel by car to Fitzroy to take part in his favourite leisure pursuit.

The story did not lead to Blamey being sacked, but it lingered like an unwanted odour. This was partly because of his attitude to the press. He may have curried favour with the proprietors and others in Australia's power elite, but he rarely courted reporters, preferring to ignore them. He thought he could control the newsmen through his links to newspaper barons. But this was not easy in Australia, where hungry journalists had long memories.

Reporters were fascinated by Blamey's alleged link to a right-wing 'White Army', a secret force prepared to 'defend the state' if there was an attempted communist takeover. Being involved with any unauthorised army would have appealed to Blamey's born-to-rule mentality. Yet if he was a member, he kept it secret, knowing that Monash was dead against any military-style coup to overthrow the federal government. In fact, Monash, the only man in 1920s Australia who had the power to command such a corruption of democracy, had been approached then by both the far left and the far right to lead coups of ex-WWI diggers, but had rejected categorically all overtures. When Monash died in 1931, Blamey was running his police fiefdom in Victoria and the steam had gone out of any ideas to overthrow an elected government.

Nevertheless, Blamey's rumoured association with a clandestine para-military operation was at least partly inspired by his autocratic nature. Also it would have had something to do with him not being in command of the nation's authentic military. He had been well placed early in 1925 as second chief of the general staff but there were about six more senior military officers ahead of him, including Sir Harry Chauvel and Sir Julius Bruche. They and others would block his advance.

In running the police in Victoria, Blamey acted more like a military commander. He improved standards but he disliked the union. There had been none in the army and he saw no need for one in the police, an attitude that did not endear him to the rank and file. He tended to handle public rallies by meeting violence with violence. His ruthless streak became even more evident than in war. Nevertheless, the

Victorian premier, Sir Stanley Argyle, obtained a knighthood for Blamey in 1935, the year his first wife died.

Another of Blamey's rumoured 'sensual' pursuits had been exposed in May 1936. He was in the backseat of a Daimler car with a prostitute in a street known as 'lover's lane' near Melbourne's Zoo, Royal Park. John Brophy, the head of Victoria's Criminal Investigation Bureau, was in the front seat with another prostitute. According to the former chief of Melbourne's homicide squad, Bill Donnelly, 'Blamey was drunk and had stripped off a prostitute. He was engaged in a sex act with her. He had his head "down" when three men surrounded the Daimler.' Brophy got out of the car and pushed one of the men to the ground. Shots were exchanged. One of the 'criminals' shot Brophy three times. His right arm was shattered. He had wounds to the cheek and above the heart. All the time, Donnelly claimed, Blamey had his head well down, which helped him avoid being shot too.

Brophy survived but Blamey's decade-long tenure as Chief Commissioner of Police was in trouble. At no stage did Blamey admit that he was anywhere near the scene of the crime or involved in any acts with a sex worker. Blamey first claimed that Brophy had accidentally shot himself. But three wounds suggested otherwise. Blamey then changed his story, admitting that Brophy had been shot by criminals.

The state government held a Royal Commission, in which Brophy and Blamey were cross-examined. Brophy said that he had driven to Royal Park to meet a police informer. In the car with him were 'two women friends and a chauffeur employed by one of them'. While waiting for the informer, Brophy claimed that two masked and armed men tried to hold them up. Brophy drew his pistol and fired two shots. The men fired back and Brophy was wounded.

There were strange, incredible elements to Brophy's statements. Why was he with two women and a chauffeur meeting a police informer? Who was this mystery 'chauffeur'? Supposedly, a woman having her own driver meant she was reputable rather than a prostitute. The initial lies and then this implausible, even ridiculous story were believed by no one, especially the presiding judge at the enquiry, Hugh Macindoe. A Scot, he had been Victoria's senior crown prosecutor for seven years before moving to the County Court bench. He knew much about police methods. Macindoe found that Blamey 'gave replies which were not in accordance with the truth'.[3]

The scandal forced Blamey to resign. He was fifty-two and his life was at its lowest point. He let go his six-year command of the 3rd (Militia) Division as a major-general. His career seemed over. He spent a couple of years in a comparative wilderness. Then, in September 1938, Shedden – at the time secretary to the Department of Defence – with support from Prime Minister Joseph Lyons, appointed Blamey chairman of the Commonwealth's Manpower Committee and controller-general of recruiting. The next year, his stocks rose again when the new prime minister, Robert Menzies, appointed him as the army's national commander. In 1939 Blamey also met his new partner, Olga Ora Farnsworth, an artist twenty years his junior; they married in April that year.

Menzies, along with Casey and Shedden, thought the strong-minded Blamey the best man to run the Australian Army, much to the chagrin of many in the regular force and of other aspiring officers. Menzies said he appointed Blamey because of his toughness and willingness to take on anything or anybody.[4] There was a swagger, even an arrogance about Blamey when he was negotiating with leaders from the mother country. None of its leaders fazed him, in either the political or military spheres. He was disliked by the British leaders and commanders, but they all respected him.

Blamey had proven to be a good choice. He'd kept a sharp eye on Australian troops in North Africa and the Middle East and had resisted pressure from his British superior officers to disperse the Australian forces for their needs. He had insisted that the battle-weary 9th Division be rested after its fighting in Tobruk, which the British from Churchill down opposed. No one but Blamey could have stood so firmly, at the risk of making himself most unpopular. But he often got what he wanted.

32

Taking Care of the Rear

After three years as commander in chief of the Australian Armed Forces, Blamey now had to work with a man with an inferior military record. He remained undaunted: he would do his duty. After all, a few years earlier he had been written off by his critics and even his supporters.

Curtin had inherited Blamey from Menzies, but he'd had no hesitation in keeping him as Australia's army chief, despite some in his party, and not a few in the regular force, protesting his position. It did not hurt that he and Blamey got along. Curtin's appreciation of the Australian character, however raw it was, allowed him judge what was best for the country. He more than once told journalists – off the record – that he did not want a Sunday school teacher running the army.

On 31 March 1942, Curtin hosted a reception at the Melbourne Town Hall to welcome Blamey home from the Middle East. With MacArthur present, he said Blamey would have complete control in his new command. 'Military matters are for military men,' Curtin proclaimed. 'Neither the government nor the parliament will override their decisions.'

It was not in Curtin's nature to dictate, bully or control. He recognised that he had no experience or expertise in military matters, and abhorred the thought of making decisions of life and death. Curtin would take advice on war matters, not give it. In this, he was being true to himself but it also happened to be clever politics. Whereas Churchill would step in to fire generals and admirals on a whim, Curtin reckoned it was better to have the very best people in charge from the start, and to leave them to make their own mistakes. He reserved the right to intervene if things went too wrong, but he saw his role as running the country to support the military's needs.

Curtin saw the problem with the definition of MacArthur's role as 'Supreme Commander' when Blamey drew his attention to it. Washington's directive empowered MacArthur to deploy all Australian forces *outside* Australia's territory. Blamey pointed out that Curtin (and Blamey, as his proxy in the Middle East) had always had the right to protect the position of Australian forces even though they were essentially given over to Churchill's needs. If MacArthur enjoyed the same powers in the Pacific, then Australia's troops had to be similarly protected. Curtin realised immediately that Blamey was right: as the US–Australia agreement stood, MacArthur could indeed put local troops into action anywhere in the Pacific or Asia.

Curtin put Evatt and Shedden to work constructing the quasi-legal argument against this state of affairs. Shrewdly, they concentrated on accentuating the positive, attempting to appease MacArthur by feeding his ego and vanity. He would be given every support to counter-attack against the Japanese. The Australian government would uphold its promise to 'take care of the rear'. The country would be turned into a strong base for MacArthur's offensive. Curtin pledged to back him 'to marshal the strength required to wrest the initiative from the enemy'. Crucially, he spoke of the Australian forces 'joining' the Americans in the 'ultimate' offensive – as opposed to being under MacArthur's total control – 'to bring about the total destruction of the common foe'.[1]

'Taking care of the rear' brought its own problems, though, such as legislating for 'industrial conscription' – meaning the legal enforcement of labour for the building of roads, rail, airfields and other construction essential for Australia's defence all over the country. This was tough for Curtin. He had successfully opposed such forced labour during World War I; now he had to convince his doubting colleagues in the ALP to change as he had. But again he had a good argument: Australia had not been under direct threat of invasion in the 1914–1918 war. Now it was.

Curtin also made good his vow to MacArthur to use his key negotiators (led by Evatt) to visit the United Kingdom to lobby for more military support. This was a tough assignment, given Churchill's hostility to the Australian government. Curtin made a compelling radio broadcast to the British, which aimed at shoring up Evatt's efforts. He pulled out every emotion about connections to the 'motherland' and 'kinship', while reminding the British of Australia's disproportionate sacrifice in World War I. He also mentioned Australia's recent fighting for the Empire in the Middle East, and the courage of its airmen in the skies over Europe.

He compared Australia's position in early 1942 with Britain's in 1940. 'Australia is a land preparing to meet an invasion,' he said. Metaphorically putting his hand out, Curtin added that his nation was short of planes and munitions.[2]

Making Australia a suitable springboard for MacArthur's counter-offensive was a huge operation and drained the prime minister even more of his emotional reserves. He considered everything that could bring his fellow countrymen and women into line. Curtin wanted pleasure and leisure time restricted further, which was difficult for a man who was far from the 'wowser' he now appeared. He even toyed with introducing a seven-day working week, which shocked the party faithful and unions. Where was 'Jack' the fervent socialist, who had fought to reduce the length of the workers' week? Curtin appeared to have morphed into a consultant for big business and industry.

There was such an angry reaction to this proposal – not least from the churches – that Curtin dumped it. But he kept making speeches about working harder for the cause. Late in March 1942, he stopped the production of a number of cosmetics, including perfumes, eye shadow, nail lacquers, bath salts and beauty masks. Natural looks and fragrance had to be endured.

Curtin issued plenty of press releases. One said that 800,000 tons of coal production had been lost in three months of strikes at the coalmines of New South Wales. Most were trivial actions by the unions. More than 400 men had gone on strike in a Lithgow factory that produced Bren guns. Communists were working overtime to take advantage of the government's vulnerability at this time of national crisis.

A secret government scorched-earth policy for Australia was drawn up in March 1942. If implemented, it would disrupt a

Japanese invasion. The Navy would immobilise all ships. Airstrips and bridges in northern Australia would be mined with explosives. Essential facilities on the east and west coasts were also readied for destruction. They included naval and army bases, power, wireless, cable and telephone stations and exchanges. Next on the list were petrol and oil installations and refineries, harbour facilities and water supplies. These were followed by coal and raw material stocks. Even food and alcohol stocks were marked for destruction. In effect, the federal government was preparing to bomb Australia itself, to make it unsuitable as a base for the Japanese. Contingencies were made for military and para-military forces to fight as guerillas around all major Australian cities and country centres. Signing off on these desperate measures must have been one of the most difficult acts for Curtin. As a young man, he had imagined an Australian utopia; three decades on, he was forced to imagine Armageddon for his beloved country.

Blamey advised Curtin that the Japanese would hit from the west, through Albany and Perth. MacArthur thought it would come from air strikes and naval attacks on the east coast. Rumours abounded that a group of defeatists and pacifists in Sydney were drawing up plans to sue for peace with the Japanese. They argued that Paris had been saved in this way – why shouldn't Sydney, too, avoid destruction? There was a call for Sydney to be an 'open city' – in other words, the Japanese should be invited in to take over. Curtin heard the rumours and was hurt by them.

The messages coming into his office had no consistency. Some wanted him to capitulate; others urged him to be more Churchillian and call for Australians to be prepared to fight to the last man. Still others called for Draconian measures. Mailbags arrived at his Canberra office stuffed with letters of appeal, admonition, inspiration, threat, advice, anger, fear and demands.

'Mr Prime Minister, you must act now to save Australia,' the Reverend Dr C. N. Button, moderator of the Presbyterian Church wrote. 'On the streets of our great cities, scenes of drunkenness the likes of which have not been known before, are being witnessed daily, to the utter disgust of every respectable citizen. Money and petrol badly needed for the country's defence are being wasted on amusement, much of it of a degrading kind . . .'

The Reverend's parting shot was typical of the moralists' despair: 'Your appeals in regard to these matters have fallen on deaf ears.'[3]

Bombarded with conflicting advice and attitudes that varied from lethargy to panic, Curtin was in a perpetual quandary. He turned daily to his inner circle of relatives and friends for solace and inspiration. His wife, Elsie, was mostly in Perth, looking after the family home. Daughter Elsie gave comfort, but Curtin never wanted to burden her with his woes. His need for feminine understanding was filled more and more by Belle Southwell at the Kurrajong Hotel, a five-minute walk from Parliament House.

Curtin's male friends were never more needed. Fred McLaughlin would often shut himself in a room with Curtin and they would pray. Whether their prayers were answered or not, these minutes of spiritual focus were calming, and the prime minister became dependent on them. The path to Governor-General Lord Gowrie's residence, Yarralumla, became well-worn. Increasingly, Curtin turned to his closest mate, Ben Chifley. They opened up to one another like few males of the era could. More than once in the early months of 1942, Curtin left notes for Chifley at his room at the Kurrajong, imploring him to see him. Once Curtin wrote that he was 'spiritually bankrupt'. The calm, pipe-smoking Chifley was warm and solicitous. Curtin was never left in despair after these meetings.

They recharged him.

33
Second Enemy Surge

Admiral Yamamoto was at a special meeting in late March 1942 with seven submariners onboard the *Yamato* at Hashira Island in Japan's Inland Sea, south of Hiroshima. They were about to embark on sabotage operations in Sydney and Madagascar, which most likely were suicide missions. The fourteen young sub-lieutenants and ensigns would operate seven midget submarines. Yamamoto spoke and pleaded for their 'safe return'; they then formally drank farewell cups of *sake*.

After the ceremony, ships and submarines carrying the two-man midget subs left the Inland Sea. One fleet sailed for the Indian Ocean, heading for Madagascar. Another set off for the Japanese island of Truk, before sailing for the east coast of Australia.

The Japanese had watched the build-up of shipping in Sydney Harbour. Yamamoto and the navy were keen to see the progress of this raid on Australia. The ongoing air attacks on Australia's northern and western coastlines had caused destruction and disturbance. But this would be the first attack on a major city – indeed, Australia's biggest city.

It would be a more than useful trial. First, it would test the feasibility of a long-range ocean attack. Would the modest flotilla and submarine squadron, complete with its midget subs, be detected so close to Sydney's coast? Second, major damage would be attempted, especially on US shipping. Third, the experiment would show how much damage such a terror attack could do to Australia's morale. The attack would require the utmost stealth and would take two months to set up. Then the midgets would be released.

At about the same time, in late March 1942, Japanese Vice Admiral Nagumo, commanding a powerful Japanese force, sailed from Starling Bay in the Celebes to attack Ceylon. It included five fast carriers, four battleships, two heavy cruisers, one light cruiser and eleven destroyers.

He was confident. Japan ruled the Pacific. His naval intelligence operatives had informed him that the British fleet was weak in the Indian Ocean and would be no match for a well-organised Japanese formation. The Allies seemed to have no capacity, given Churchill's focus on the fight against the Axis in the northern seas, to reinforce the Indian Ocean.

Late on the afternoon of 4 April, a patrolling Australian Catalina flying boat spotted Nagumo's force but was shot down before it could report its strength and direction. An unsuspecting British fleet, including the Australian Navy's destroyer, the HMAS *Vampire*, had been operating south of Ceylon without any trouble. British Admiral

The new prime minister – John Curtin with his wife, Elsie, In Canberra in November 1941.

John Curtin with his family: wife Elsie, son John, and daughter (also Elsie).

Curtin with his immediate predecessors as prime minister, Arthur Fadden and Robert Menzies.

Current and future prime ministers – John Curtin with Ben Chifley.

Winston Churchill with Dr H. V. Evatt, in London in 1943.

General Douglas MacArthur, General Thomas Blamey (centre) and John Curtin.

Douglas MacArthur and his staff arriving at Spencer Street Station in Melbourne in March 1942.

After what looks like a tense meeting... Thomas Blamey, Douglas MacArthur and John Curtin.

John Curtin with the Canberra press gallery – Don Rogers (his press secretary) is to the right.

A feature in *Pix* magazine: 'John Curtin – The Nation's Leader'.

John Curtin, hard at work in The Lodge.

The surrender of Singapore. The Japanese commander,
General Yamashita, is seated at left.

During the bombing of Darwin.

A shelled house in Bellevue Hill – one of the results of the Japanese submarine raid in Sydney Harbour in 1942.

The 'golden stairs' on the Kokoda Track.

A view of Imita Range – at the beginning of the Kokoda Track.

Somerville headed for Addu Atoll, a base in the Maldives, to restock with water. He sent two cruisers and the HMS *Hermes*, an aircraft carrier, to Colombo. The *Vampire* was sent to Trincomalee, a port city on the eastern coast of Ceylon. They were to prepare for operations near Madagascar, off the south-eastern coast of Africa.

Nagumo planned to attack Ceylon on 5 April, Easter Sunday. His armada was sighted less than an hour out from its target. In Colombo, the British commander directed the two cruisers in the harbour to move out to sea, but the Japanese aircraft sank them within fifteen minutes. The *Hermes* and *Vampire* were told to leave Trincomalee before the expected follow-up attack, and the two ships escaped south on the night of 8 April. The next morning, fifty-four bombers from Nagumo's carriers struck Trincomalee, smashing its dockyard and airfields.

Once the Japanese Zeros and bombers had done their damage, the *Hermes* and the *Vampire* set sail back to the beleaguered port. But they were visible and vulnerable. At 10.35 a.m. on 9 April, off Batticaloa, Ceylon, Japanese planes swooped out of the sun from 10,000 feet. With no aircraft, the two Allied ships were helpless as the Zeros swept down and the bombers let their loads go. The *Hermes* fired back but went down in twenty minutes. Some 296 men were lost or died of their wounds.

The moment this ship vanished, the dive bombers turned their attention to the *Vampire*. It too fought back with its anti-aircraft guns, bringing down one Japanese bomber, but it was soon broken in two. It sank in ten minutes. Its commanding officer, Jack Donovan, and eight ratings went down with the ship. Most of the other 600 were rescued by the hospital ship *Vita*, with some picked up by local craft. A few sailors swam ashore.

News of this fresh naval setback reached Curtin a few days later. He was upset but thankful that nearly all the Australians had been saved. His relief soon turned to fury, however, and he called a press conference on 16 April. Curtin could not hide his anger at Churchill and Roosevelt for not strengthening their Indian Ocean naval forces. He told reporters that the British and Australian fleets were being eaten up, piecemeal. 'It's wonderful,' he said with cynicism, 'how Churchill gets absolution for every mistake.'

Curtin was annoyed by Churchill's offer to send two British divisions to Australia if there was a threatened or actual invasion by the Japanese. Churchill had chopped and changed on this offer, which had eventually been watered down; by March 1942, just one armoured division was rounding the Cape of Good Hope, South Africa. It was now mid-April and no troop carrier had been spotted. Curtin feared that even if it were sent, it would never arrive. The Japanese were ruling the waves and such shipping would be easy for them to pick off. The reporters left thinking that Curtin did not believe Churchill could or would send any forces.[1]

Having taken control of the Indian Ocean, the Japanese Navy turned its attention in the Pacific to Midway Atoll, where the United States had a stronghold. When this was taken, the Japanese would have a defence in the Pacific running 3700 kilometres to the east, putting them within striking distance of Hawaii, which they coveted. The commander in chief of Japan's Combined Fleet, Admiral Yamamoto, believed that such an attack would draw out the US fleet. It would have to meet the Japanese in the 'decisive battle' of the Pacific War.

The Japanese Army did not want the Navy to take Midway. But Yamamoto had so much intrinsic power that he would go it alone, if necessary. If the Japanese won, they would be unassailable. If they lost, their control of the Pacific and Indian Oceans would be in jeopardy.

The attack would also decide Australia's fate. The Japanese Navy believed Australia had to be isolated before it could be taken. The British had already been evicted from the Indian Ocean and would have no chance of getting soldiers to Australia, even if Churchill had the will to do so. The Americans would also be blocked from sending more troops into the Pacific. If Midway Atoll fell and Hawaii was under Japanese control by the end of May, then Australia would be in the Japanese Navy's sights – again whether or not the Army approved.

Admiral Tomioka was in no doubt that Japan should take Australia next. With Hawaii under Japanese control and the United

States defeated in the Pacific, he would consolidate Japan's position in the region. Tomioka was adamant. The US should not be allowed to build up its troops and bases in Australia. He told the Japanese High Command that if this happened, Japan would most likely not be able to resist a massive US counter-attack.

Tojo was unconvinced, but with the continued success of his admirals, he was feeling the pressure to bend to the Navy's will. Tomioka's plan would have a far better chance of implementation if the United States were eliminated from the Pacific. But Tomioka's urgent point was that taking Australia would have to be done fast – by June/July 1942 – to give the United States no chance of using it as a base. Time was running out while American soldiers were sailing in.[2]

The small number of US troops in Australia, which had so upset MacArthur, was now being rectified in Melbourne. It was almost as if the thousands of the 41st Division pouring in were to make him more comfortable, especially in the light of the US forces' surrender in Bataan on 6 April. There was not the fanfare for the soldiers that there had been for their commander in chief. Apart from MacArthur's determination to soak up all the publicity, he did not want the Japanese to know about his troop build-up.

There is no evidence that MacArthur knew of Yamashita's plan to take Australia. Like everyone else, he was guessing how and where the Japanese might invade the Australian mainland. It could happen at any time, anywhere. In the meantime, Australian-based Allied bombers dropped some loads on Japanese strongholds in the Philippines on 15 April, signalling that MacArthur would not sit back and let the enemy dictate all the terms of the conflict.

Three days later, on 18 April, US war planes bombed Tokyo, Kobe, Yokohama and Nagoya. This delivered the first shock of the war to the Japanese nation and the Imperial Forces, who considered their country inviolate from such attacks. On 22 April, US forces arrived in India. It was clear that the Americans were preparing for wide counter-attack measures against Japan.

On 23 April, at a meeting of the War Conference, MacArthur repeated to Curtin and Shedden his two-way bet about the enemy's intentions. A large-scale invasion of Australia was possible, he said, but not probable. Again he claimed that Japanese predatory raids were likely. 'The enemy's previous operations had been designed to achieve definite objectives,' he said, 'bases, oil, rubber etc. The inhabitants would give no assistance to an invader here.' MacArthur discounted an attack south of Java. He thought a carrier-borne attack on the west coast was 'unlikely', at least until the base at Surabaya was constructed.

Japan's 'interest' in acquiring iron ore was also discussed. But the War Conference concluded that the risks involved with such a move 'would not repay a Japanese attempt to exploit it'.[3]

In reality, everyone was guessing at Japan's intentions. This included even the Japanese forces, since the Imperial Army was not fully informed about the Navy's moves, and vice versa. The two were increasingly in competition to be Japan's dominant military arm.

On 30 April, Japan's army occupied Lashio and entered Mandalay. Not to be outdone, Japanese reconnaissance planes from carriers flew over Townsville on 2 May. Was this a preparation for invasion? Soon afterwards, Japanese army units moved up the Burma Road, which Churchill had so wished to protect, and reached China.

The continual concern about the possibility of Australia being invaded increased MacArthur's desire for protection, not just from bodyguards and police but from an army. The number of US troops seeping into Melbourne approached 30,000. If Yamashita got his way and the Japanese attacked down through the centre of Australia by train, there would now at least be a fight.

The US troops settled around inner Melbourne, so that people in the outer suburbs hardly even knew of their presence. The South Melbourne Cricket Ground became US Camp Robinson. The inner-city area of Royal Park became Camp Pell. The Americans were treating central Melbourne as if it were their own. Roads were built through, in and around Royal Park and named after US generals. The biggest was MacArthur Drive.

There was excitement in the inner-city area about the American presence. One local, twenty-year-old Barry Shackleton, rode from Brunswick to Port Melbourne, having heard the rumour that the Yanks were in town. Sure enough, three weeks before it was officially announced, Shackleton came across six US soldiers guarding the entrance to Station Pier. He joined about fifteen other Australians who were looking on in silence. He was thrilled to see four US ships at anchor. Another four were at Princes Pier. Shackleton came across American servicemen everywhere in Melbourne after that. He was impressed. They had money. They were friendly and generous.

A seven-year-old paperboy, Bernard Barnett, was thrilled by them. 'They were the first foreigners I'd ever seen,' he said, 'and they really were *foreign,* quite a different culture from us. They spoke more loudly. They had strange accents, cute expressions. They were really very exotic.'[4]

'They threw money at taxis,' Barnett said. 'They had a big impact on women.' He believed they introduced to Australia the gifting of flowers to girlfriends. He also noted that one of his seven-year-old mates was left at home alone while his mother dated Americans.[5]

Melbourne women loved the charm offensive. Eighteen-year-old Dulcie Wood recalled sitting and drying her hair on her parents' porch in South Melbourne, near the big football ground camp. Two Americans drove by in a jeep. They noticed her, turned the jeep around, drove up to her house and, ever so politely, asked her to come to the movies. Dulcie went. One of the Americans was a well-mannered nineteen-year-old from Kentucky. He became a regular visitor to the Wood home, where Dulcie's mother baked him apple pie.

Romances like this sprang up all over the city. Diana Gollar, an attractive eighteen-year-old actress, worked part-time as a receptionist at Kraft in the city. She recalled being asked to visit a badly burnt American soldier who had been fighting on Guadalcanal. He was being nursed at the Windsor Hotel. A lieutenant from Milwaukee, Lloyd Miller, came and sat beside her in the room.

After that, 'he never left my side', Diana recalled. 'But it was an innocent relationship and not the only one. The Americans – at least the ones we met – were all moral, respectful and well-mannered. We all went out with them. The Australians were mostly away. There were plenty of "do's" to go to – a lot of parties. There was also the Marine Club for commissioned US officers on Russell Street.'[6]

Melburnians' experience of the Americans soured on 3 May, when Mrs Ivy McLeod was found strangled in the doorway of a shop next to the Bleak House Hotel, in beachside Albert Park. The newspapers dubbed it a 'brownout crime', claiming that electricity cuts, which darkened streets, had made the city more vulnerable to crime. The 'foreigners' came under suspicion for three reasons: they were not locals, the nature of the crime – a brutal throttling – was uncommon, and it had been committed not far from Camp Pell.

On 9 May a similar murder, of Mrs Pauline Thompson, happened at night in another darkened city street. The police began talking to the American base commanders. Melbourne was suddenly fearful. Women were given torches and advised not to walk the streets at night.

'My father would meet me at the Kew tram terminus after work and walk me home,' Diana Gollar said. 'We were all terrified.'[7]

34
Battle of the Coral Sea

The Japanese Navy's main focus was on Midway, but in the meantime it moved to cut Australia off from its US supplies by occupying Fiji, Samoa and New Caledonia. By 10 May 1942, Japan aimed to take Port Moresby on Papua's southern coast, just north of Australia. It was an important air base, Papua's administrative centre and a strategic port; taking it would isolate Australia further. Moresby's occupation would also protect nearby Rabaul, which was in Japanese hands. If Moresby and Midway fell to Japan, Australia would be at its most vulnerable. The Japanese would have an ideal base from which their navy and army could invade.

The Americans and the Australians had enough intelligence from US naval codebreakers to learn of Japan's plans for Moresby and the Pacific islands. In response, the United States built its army and marine strength on New Caledonia, south of the Solomon Islands. Blamey had shifted Australian air and ground forces to Port Moresby. Two US aircraft carriers steamed across the Pacific to counter the invasion force heading for Moresby.

MacArthur stationed a bomber squadron in northern Queensland, which began searching the Coral Sea, east of the Australian coastline, trying to spot the enemy convoy. It would be made up of three fleets: the invasion force of soldiers for the Solomons and Moresby; a support contingent of two aircraft carriers from the Pearl Harbor attack (the *Shokaka* and the *Suikaka*); and a smaller carrier, two heavy cruisers and supporting craft. US naval intelligence picked up the southward movement of Japanese aircraft.

All up, Vice-Admiral Inoue had twelve troop transports and fifty-one warships to protect them. The Allies could muster only twenty ships, but they included the two aircraft carriers, the *Yorktown* and the *Lexington,* which had made it across the Pacific. The ensuing fight would become known as the Battle of the Coral Sea. It would be the first naval engagement in history fought without the opposing ships making contact.

Australia had a significant presence, consisting of a heavy cruiser, the HMAS *Australia*, and a light cruiser, the HMAS *Hobart.* Australian and American crews flew aircraft from Queensland bases. Admiral Sir John Crace commanded the local squadron, along with the US cruiser *Chicago*, and the US destroyers *Perkins*, *Walker* and *Farragut.*

Early on 7 May 1942, the US oil tanker *Neosho* and an accompanying destroyer were sunk by Japanese planes. Five hours later, at noon, US search aircraft sighted the Japanese carrier *Shoho* and an escorting light cruiser. Planes from the US carriers attacked and sank both vessels. At the same time, Crace manoeuvred his squadron to cut off the enemy troopships headed for Moresby. He had no air cover, so he moved his ships into a diamond formation to concentrate their fire on the Zeros and dive bombers.

In the early afternoon, eleven Japanese bombers hit Crace's

formation with bombs, torpedoes and machine-gun strafing. Crace was ready. His Allied squadron countered with a powerful barrage, hitting at least five bombers. The other six planes failed to deliver a knockout blow to the *Australia,* which was skilfully manoeuvred by its commander, Rear-Admiral H. B. Farncomb. The attack was over in five minutes, and none of Crace's ships were fatally damaged. Three Americans and six Australians were killed.

Shortly afterwards, the Japanese came at them again, this time with accurate pattern bombing from high altitudes. This turned the sea into a mass of jumbled waves that threatened to engulf the *Australia.* The ships received a huge drenching but all survived. Crace was able to ease his ships away in the night, even avoiding damage from some US B-17s, which mistook his squadron for the enemy and bombed them.

That night, Japanese Admiral Inoue decided to delay his invasion of Port Moresby by two days. Round one had gone to the Australians and the Americans.

The next day was fought out by opposing aircraft from the carriers. A US dive-bomber pilot, Lieutenant J. J. Powers, swooped low over the deck of the *Shokaku.* Waiting until the last possible second, he released a bomb over the flight deck, then crashed into the sea and was killed. The Japanese carrier caught fire and was badly damaged. One hundred and fifty men were killed or injured. Powers would later win a posthumous Congressional Medal of Honor.

Japan's bombers retaliated, damaging the *Yorktown* and setting ablaze the *Lexington,* which had to be abandoned. More than 2700 crew were picked up. The USS *Phelps* had the thankless task of sinking the *Lexington* to avoid its being salvaged by the Japanese.

Curtin, unable to rest, was up until 4 a.m. on the night of 7–8 May, reading R. C. Robertson-Glasgow's *The Bright Side of Cricket,* which had been lent to him by the Australian Test leg-spinner Arthur Mailey. He later told the former cricketer that it had 'freshened him up' for a speech he planned to broadcast on the evening of 8 May. The address was to be an appeal for the Austerity Loan,[1] but events in the Coral Sea would see it modified.

In the House of Representatives that night, Curtin sat before the dispatch box, absorbing the news from Blamey about Australia's involvement in the struggle. He rose to speak to an almost empty parliament. It was a Friday, and most members had left for the weekend. His solemn tone garnered attention, and the press gallery filled as he spoke.

Curtin informed the parliament that a 'great naval battle' was taking place off Queensland's coast. The outcome would be of 'crucial importance to the conduct of the war in this theatre'. His words moved many witnesses to tears, but he appeared stoic and strong. He mentioned that Australian and American servicemen were sacrificing their lives as he spoke. He had warned of this critical moment for months, he said, and now it had arrived. The 'devotion to duty' of the sailors and airmen had to be matched by 'every man and woman of the Commonwealth'.

Many observers felt this was Curtin's finest speech. He had his own style, marked not by shrillness or histrionics but by sincerity. After seven months as prime minister, Curtin was revealing more of his character to the public. He was projecting himself as a national leader. His inspirational manner was beginning to gain traction and override public cynicism that would have hampered the performances of other leaders. The nation was paying attention.

The weight and import of his 8 May message lifted every listener. Instead of instilling fear, he motivated. It was an opportunity to push for more austerity measures. That evening he repeated his message in a prearranged national radio broadcast. Millions of Australians around the nation huddled close to radios to hear his report on the Coral Sea battle and his request for Australia to move to a 'total war economy'. Australians had to sacrifice 'their peace time things', since Japanese invasion was a 'menace' capable 'of becoming a reality'.[2]

Curtin moved to ration certain civilian goods. He planned extra taxes on alcohol and tobacco, which would have hurt him. He slapped more taxes on cinema and theatre tickets. He carried his attack on the alleged profligacy of the racing industry and punters by advocating the reduction of greyhound and horseracing meetings. There were also restrictions on meals at restaurants and cafés.

Curtin was still having trouble with the coalminers' union, despite having lifted a ban on the Communist Party. Germany and Russia were in a titanic struggle. Regardless of this, the menacing, problematic far left was still hindering the federal government's war effort. The irascible Eddie Ward still seemed to be unwilling or unable to handle the communist-controlled unions.

By the end of 8 May, after five days of skirmishing and battles, the United States and Japan totted up the damage. Both reported 'victories' in the ensuing propaganda war. In reality, there were big losses on both sides. The Allies had had one carrier destroyed, one almost crippled, one oiler and one destroyer sunk, sixty-six aircraft lost and 543 men killed or wounded. The Japanese lost one carrier and had one crippled, one destroyer and three small naval ships were sunk, seventy-seven of its aircraft went down and 1074 men were killed or wounded.

The Allies had delivered the Japanese their first major defeat of the war, not so much in the Coral Sea battle itself, but in what they had prevented the Japanese from achieving. The Americans, with the Australians in solid support, had stopped the enemy landing a force in New Guinea and the Solomon Islands. Japan's sustained, efficient and brutal onslaught in the Pacific and South-East Asian region had received a setback. When Allied morale in the region had been at a low ebb, the Imperial army had been shown to be less than invincible.

At first, the Advisory War Council was unsure of the outcome of the Coral Sea conflict. Its members, including Curtin, had expected a more emphatic result for the Allies. But critical remarks in the council were tempered by the knowledge that the Japanese had been forced to put off their invasion of Moresby.

As the days rolled on, observers began to appreciate the significance of that naval encounter so close to Australia's north-east. It was almost half a year since the Japanese had first attacked in the Pacific, and this appeared to have been the first block on their operations. In reality, the Battle of the Coral Sea was a minor setback for the enemy, but it provided a brief respite for Australia. MacArthur, still Melbourne-based, confirmed this to Curtin: Australia was unlikely to be invaded 'for the time being'.

MacArthur put it in perspective by noting that the Japanese navy was still very much intact. This meant that the enemy was still able 'to strike with a preponderance of force on any chosen objective'. Australia remained open to attack. The US had sent its ships back to Hawaii for repairs in anticipation of a further Japanese move through the Pacific. Australia's real protection was not its own armed forces. It was the US's capacity to break Japanese naval codes, which told it where and when the Japanese were likely to strike next.

Evatt was learning on his trip abroad about the secret agreement between the United States and the United Kingdom to fight Hitler first. There would be no extra troops sent specifically for Australia's defence. This confirmed Curtin's belief that he had to rely on the US using Australia as a base for its counter-attack on the Japanese. That way, at least there would be massed Allied troops in Australia, even if they were on their way north.

The US build-up was made more likely with the fall of Corregidor and the Philippines on 9 May. MacArthur was now even more determined to take back his Asian paradise, which had been stolen from him so embarrassingly. The Japanese navy had been thwarted, but the so far invincible army had only been temporarily diverted from its mission. The Port Moresby invasion force remained intact. It was in Rabaul, building up once more. Japan still ruled the South-West Pacific and the Indian Ocean.

The strength of Japan's hold on the area was demonstrated when Blamey airlifted to Wau a special contingent, known as Kanga Force, which included the 2/5 Independent Company. It would act as a guerrilla unit to harass the Japanese, who had a tight grip on the Markham Valley, New Guinea territory just 300 kilometres north of Port Moresby. New Guinea was under Australian jurisdiction, yet because of limited resources the AIF was reduced to hit-and-run operations. Many in the command considered this a possible glimpse into the near future. If the Japanese decided to occupy part of northern Australia, Blamey would have to resort to guerrilla tactics against a vastly superior enemy force.

The outcome of the Battle of the Coral Sea helped MacArthur shape his thoughts on how the Japanese might be deterred from attacking Australia using naval, land and air forces. It demonstrated, he said at a meeting of the War Conference in Melbourne on 11 May, that the essential 'backbone of the striking power that had given this victory was the aircraft carriers'.

But he reminded those present – Curtin, Shedden and MacArthur's deputy Richard Sutherland – that carriers did not come under his command, but only 'entered it for this [Coral Sea] operation.' MacArthur's immediate objective in the South-West Pacific area was to provide naval, land and air forces to make the region 'secure as a springboard for the ultimate offensive' against Japan. MacArthur said he had cabled to Roosevelt and Marshall his conception of possible Japanese courses of action, how they were to be 'frustrated', and the additional forces necessary for Australia's defence.

Yet MacArthur's view of what was essential to fight off the invaders differed from the Australians'. Earlier discussions by Australia's chiefs of staff claimed that twenty-five divisions (about half a million soldiers) were needed to defend the country; MacArthur believed that if the Japanese had superior naval and air power, no amount of Allied land forces would be adequate to take them on. 'Air forces, both sea-borne and land-based,' MacArthur said, 'were a vital necessity.'[3]

35
Midget Rampage

Despite the minor setback of the Coral Sea battle, the Japanese continued their various missions in the western Pacific. Their intention to terrorise Sydney and disrupt shipping off Australia's east coast by destroying as many vessels as possible remained.

Before daybreak on 14 May 1942, the Japanese submarine *I-29* cruised towards Sydney and emerged in the blackness. Once above water, ratings bustled about on the deck, assembling the wings and floats of a dark-green plane in a covered hangar. When it was ready, the sub began to submerge, pitching its bow down to give the plane a better run along the deck to reach flying speed. With its radial engine purring, it was launched into the dark sky, the first of five reconnaissance flights to gather information on the shipping in and around Sydney Harbour.

Just when the Allies needed all the harmony they could muster, the 'Brownout Strangler' struck again on 18 May, when Mrs Gladys Hosking was killed in Royal Park. The crimes had a pattern. The victims were all strangled. Each one was left with her genitals exposed but none had been sexually assaulted. The crime scenes were all within walking distance of American camps. All the victims were mature women, not the age group of the average US serviceman.

Detectives worked faster after a third murder. They examined the records of all Americans who had been on military charges. One man came under immediate suspicion: Edward Joseph Leonski, aged twenty-five, from New Jersey. It was discovered that this fair-haired, boyish-looking but strong man had attempted to throttle a woman while stationed with the 52nd Signal Battalion at San Antonio, Texas.

He had been drinking heavily, lacing his whiskies with hot peppers. Leonski was powerful enough to strangle anyone. He had a bar trick: when intoxicated, he would jump onto the bar and walk the length of it on his hands. For some reason, Leonski's Texas assault was hushed up. He was slipped back into the army and shipped to Australia in January 1942. The Melbourne police, with the US Army's cooperation, questioned Leonski's acquaintances. One claimed Leonski had confided his crime to him.

'We learned that he went for women with beautiful voices,' Diana Gollar recalled. 'They turned him on. One of the victims was a waitress at the Wentworth Hotel on Collins Street. He must have been there for a meal . . .'[1]

Leonski remained oddly cheerful through the interrogation and was arrested on 22 May. Curtin was alerted and spoke with MacArthur. They agreed that Leonski could be tried first by a US court martial. Parliamentarians, the press and the public all objected, but Curtin held firm. US Army psychiatrists examined the accused. Some suspected he was insane, others said he was not. In the end, the Americans decided he was sane. He was ordered to stand trial on 17 July 1942.

By late May, the Japanese were ready for an assault on Sydney Harbour, having sighted a US cruiser under repair at Cockatoo Island, along with five destroyers and at least six merchant ships. The people of Sydney were oblivious of the threat.

Japan's fifth and final floatplane reconnoitre took place in the early hours of 30 May, flying from a sub thirteen kilometres out from Sydney Harbour. The city and surrounds were lit up beautifully for this spying. Harbour lights outlined its contours, discernible from the air. The Department of Defence had not thought a blackout necessary. Cabinet had decided instead on a brownout, which was more about saving fuel and electricity than hiding from an enemy. No one had heard of a floatplane, at least not in the Japanese style. The Australian military did not think an air attack could come from anything other than an aircraft carrier, which would always be spotted by the air force.

The Japanese air crew noted the American heavy cruiser, the USS *Chicago*, in the harbour about 400 metres east of Garden Island. This intelligence was radioed back to the sub, one of a fleet of five clustered off the New South Wales coastline. The floatplane also observed several other largish vessels – cruisers and a troopship. This was enough for the Japanese admiral to make a decision: three midget submarines would be launched the next evening, 31 May, from three of the 'mother' subs.

Each midget carried two torpedoes and was manned by two of the submariners sent off so ceremoniously by Yamamoto late in March. Each was prepared to die for the Emperor. In fact, each one expected not to return. Despite Yamamoto telling them to return safely, all knew this was a suicide mission. The men planned to shoot themselves rather than be caught or fail in their mission.

Just before 5 p.m. the next day, two thin, young submariners in each 'mother' sub climbed through a tight hatch in the midget's floor. Then they squeezed through a chute above the hatch, gaining access to five cramped, watertight compartments. Each midget's clamps were removed. The three mother subs dived, releasing compressed air, and the three midgets floated away.

In half an hour their motors came to life. A few hours later, the three midgets made it through Sydney Heads. One was picked up by electronic detectors but was thought to be either a ferry or just another surface vessel passing by. At about 9 p.m. a Maritime Services Board watchman spotted an object caught in an anti-submarine net. No one was disturbed, or even suspicious. A full-size submarine would have caused panic, but this strange object caused more curiosity than worry. It was bigger than a shark and more like a whale, although whales rarely entered the harbour.

After investigation, it was found to be a foreign midget sub; the general alarm was raised just before 10.30 p.m. A few minutes later the midget's crew blew it up, killing themselves. At 11.45 p.m. sailors on board the *Chicago* spotted a second midget. They turned a spotlight on it and opened fire, but it escaped. Later, gunners on the corvette HMAS *Geelong* also shot at what they believed was a midget sub. Naval search parties were hampered by limited vision at night, and normal shipping – including passenger ferries – continued to operate.

The Japanese submariners on one of the two remaining midgets lined up to torpedo the *Chicago*. Alerted, the ship put on its searchlights, aiming the beams where the midgets had been spotted. The heavy cruiser HMAS *Canberra* was moored close to Bennelong Point. Its sailors could see one of midgets bobbing up and down. Machine-gunners on board the *Chicago* began firing, spraying bullets that pinged onto buildings and walls ashore. The midgets fired, missing their target but scoring a direct hit on a naval depot ship, the HMAS *Kuttabul*, a converted ferry that was anchored near Garden Island.

An eighteen-year-old able seaman, Colin Whitfield, was on board the *Kuttabul* when it was struck. He dived under a table on the deck. In shock, he did not at first realise the extent of his injuries. 'I tried to stand but couldn't,' he recalled. 'Every bone was broken in both ankles. My feet were just hanging by the skin.'[2]

He slid down the gangway, where he was knocked unconscious and fell into the harbour. He was later rescued and rushed to hospital. Other survivors were hauled from the sinking vessel. Twenty-one of Whitfield's fellow sailors – nineteen Australians and two Britons – did not survive.

The submariners shot their second torpedo but were off-target again. This time, the wayward weapon ran aground on the rocks on the eastern side of Garden Island. It did not explode and was later found intact. The submariners took off for their mother submarine, waiting for them in the ocean. But the midget that had damaged the *Chicago* never reached its destination, struggling and then sinking.

There was panic in parts of the harbour. Orders went out to douse the tall floodlights on Garden Island, which illuminated a wide area and presented clear views of targets for the remaining midget. Several hundred workers, some of them below water, were rushed out of the area.

The third midget failed to make it far into the harbour. It was spotted in Taylor's Bay and attacked with depth charges by Naval Harbour Patrols. The two submariners on board shot themselves.

Meanwhile, the five larger submarines shelled Sydney's suburbs through the night. This diversion was meant to terrorise the people and weaken the Curtin government's will. At the time, Japan's Prime Minister Tojo was calling for Australia to become 'neutral', which would deny the US and British a base. He had misread the intelligence coming to him about the cable battles between Curtin and Churchill, believing that the rift between them was serious enough for the Australian government to break away from the Empire.

The bodies of four of the Japanese submariners were recovered. They were cremated in a ceremony with full Naval Honours at the direction of Rear-Admiral Muirhead-Gould, who was in charge of Sydney Harbour's defences. The ashes were sent back to Japan. Muirhead-Gould's actions brought criticism in the Australian press, but he hoped that showing respect to the submariners might improve conditions for the Allied POWs under Japanese control in various parts of Asia and the Pacific. In fact, his actions had no impact. The POWs' conditions worsened throughout 1942.

36
MacArthur's Blunt Message

On 1 June 1942, the day after the chaos in Sydney Harbour, Curtin was in Melbourne to launch another Liberty Loan. He made no reference to the midget subs and seemed intent on avoiding the subject. The last thing he wanted was panic. While he mourned the loss of life, his early judgement was that it was not a major attack.

Curtin decreed, on the navy's advice, that all media references to the attack should be censored, even though many people had witnessed the fire-fight and heard the machine guns. Although some titbits of information slipped out during the day, Curtin concentrated on the positives of the Battle of the Coral Sea. 'Japan's program of expansion,' he said in his fund-raiser speech, 'has at least suffered a stalemate.'

Perhaps referring to the previous night's mayhem in Sydney, or to the Japanese failure to reach Port Moresby, he added, 'The enemy's thrusts at our soil have been repulsed.' Now sounding like his Brunswick football coach in 1901, he defied Japan 'to land forces in Australia'.[1]

This was a change of tack. Curtin's confidence was growing. The Americans were slowly building up their forces in Australia's cities, either for immediate action or a later counter-attack. There were now about twelve divisions in Australia – sufficient numbers to take on a serious Japanese attack from land and sea.

That same day, the War Conference of MacArthur, Sutherland, Curtin and Shedden met to discuss the midget subs' attack. Curtin began by speaking of his discussions earlier in the day with the Chief of the Naval Staff, who did not want a public statement made about the harbour attacks. MacArthur disagreed. 'This attack happened in Sydney Harbour and was known to the whole population,' he said. 'If there was to be any public faith in the reliability of [MacArthur's] communiqués, one should be issued in this instance.'

MacArthur further surprised Curtin and Shedden (but not Sutherland) with a blunt and revealing monologue. He wanted to speak of the differences between the United States and the United Kingdom in their relationships with Australia.

'Australia is part of the British Empire,' MacArthur said. 'It is related to Britain and the other Dominions by ties of blood, sentiment and allegiances to the Crown.' The United States, on the other hand, was an ally whose aim was to win the war. It had no sovereign interest in the integrity of Australia. Australia was only important to the United States strategically, for its plans to defeat the Japanese. It was just a big base, nothing more or less.

These words jolted Curtin. MacArthur was telling him that the ties of race, blood and sentiment, to which Curtin had been referring in his speeches about Australia's links with the United States, were irrelevant. Australia was no more important to the United States than Fiji or New Guinea.

MacArthur clarified his views: 'As the British Empire is a Commonwealth of Nations, I presume that one of its principal purposes was jointly to protect any part that might be threatened. [Any perceived] failure of the UK and US Governments to support Australia therefore has to be viewed from different angles.'

MacArthur acknowledged that the American people were 'animated' by a 'warm friendship with Australia'. But he reiterated that building up forces in Australia was not so much from an interest in protecting it, but 'rather from its utility as a base with which to hit Japan'.[3]

It didn't matter who occupied Australia, he said. Australia's location was the key to America's interest in it. This was a way of telling Curtin that if the United States had not been at war with Japan, it would never have considered coming to Australia's aid. Even now, it was not defending it from Japan. The United States was simply using Australia as a stepping-off point from which to attack the enemy.

MacArthur was scathing about the lack of British support:

The fact that the British had carried out an attack on Cologne with 1000 heavy bombers, showed that she must have reserves behind this force of anything up to 4000 bombers. Yet the Commander-in-Chief in the Southwest Pacific Area had a total of 40 heavy bombers, of which a large number were unserviceable.[4]

It was a telling observation. Curtin would have felt a further cruel sense of isolation after the abandonment by Churchill. Wasting precious men and equipment to preserve or save Australia was just not going to happen: Churchill's main aims remained in Europe. Retrieving any lost Empire nations in the Asia and the Pacific could happen later. This left the Australian government nervous, uncertain and in despair.

Now, any naivety about Australia's link to the United States was torn down. Churchill had at least paid lip-service to the historical kinship between Britain and Australia; the United States would not even do that. The British had been in Singapore in order to protect the far-flung parts of its Empire, including Australia. The United States had no interests west of Hawaii.

Curtin and Shedden took note of MacArthur's words. Neither interrupted or contradicted him. The message was clear.

After his 'lesson' in the realities of US–Australian relations, MacArthur turned his comments to the brazen midget sub attacks and their consequences. He urged Curtin to try again to recall the 9th Division, which was still in the Middle East. But with Rommel's forces pushing the British back towards Cairo, Churchill would not want the 9th to leave. MacArthur also suggested Curtin demand that British aircraft carriers came to the South-West Pacific. Again, Churchill needed them in the Mediterranean.

MacArthur's opinion that Australia was little more than a useful base for the American push was exemplified in the west, where the US Air Force was creating the foundations for a long and lasting presence. In April, May and June 1942, fighter aerodromes were built, upgraded or planned at Arrimo, Moora and Northampton. Bomber aerodromes were being assembled or used at Corunna Downs, Cue, Tammin, Narrogin and Wagin. Fuel storage sites were installed at Merridin, Kalgoorlie, Northam and Norrogin.

This widespread, well-planned investment demonstrated to Curtin that his new, powerful ally meant business despite the professed lack of 'kinship'. These developments were also examples of the cooperation between MacArthur and Curtin. The Americans oversaw the remote work and the WA Lands and Surveys Department undertook the surveys. The Commonwealth Department of Interior paid for everything, fulfilling Curtin's promise to 'take care of the rear' – in these instances, this meant looking after the foundations for the big fights to come with the Japanese.

37
Midway

MacArthur informed Curtin that a massive, probably decisive battle was looming in the Pacific. The Americans' naval intelligence had continued to break Japanese codes, which revealed that their huge armada was punching its way through heavy seas en route to Midway Atoll.

MacArthur put it succinctly: 'If it is successful it will relieve the pressure on Australia. If it results in a draw it will decrease the pressure, but if it results in a Japanese success, it will be followed by mopping up operations against the islands.' This would be 'on the line of communications between Australia and Hawaii, in order to isolate Australia from America'.[1]

MacArthur usually loved melodrama, but this was not one of those occasions. Curtin, however, was confident that the Japanese would be defeated. He briefed the press, hinting that a battle of unsurpassed significance in the Pacific conflict was looming.

Yamamoto was steadfast in his belief that this new attack would eliminate the United States as a military power in the Pacific. He assumed that after Pearl Harbor, the Philippines and the Battle of the Coral Sea, the Americans had lost their will to fight. Japan would have free rein in the Pacific Ocean. This would allow the Japanese to create what they called 'the Greater East Asia Co-Prosperity Sphere' – a euphemism for the complete subjugation of all nations in the region, including Australia.

Yamamoto and his admirals expected the United States to capitulate after losing Midway Atoll. There was an aspect of revenge in Japan's motivation. Tokyo and other Japanese cities had been hit by B-25 bombers launched from the USS *Hornet* on 18 April 1942. It had not been a significant attack but it had inflicted a deep psychological shock on the Japanese people, who until then had felt invulnerable.

Retaliation was outside the army's scope, much to Tojo's disappointment. This gave the Imperial Navy a chance to perform. Its plan was complex and perhaps overly ambitious. The Japanese would entice the few remaining US aircraft carriers into a trap. Once overcome, they would occupy the US bases on Midway.

Again the Allied codebreakers in Melbourne and the Pacific knew every aspect of the Japanese plan. They knew the date and location of the attack, and the size and components of the armada heading towards Midway.

The US admiral in command of the counter-attack was the square-jawed Chester W. Nimitz. At fifty-seven he was the most experienced admiral in the US fleet, having commanded submarines, destroyers, and cruisers for thirteen years. Ten days after the Pearl Harbor attack he had been appointed commander in chief of the US Pacific Fleet. On 30 March 1942, the Pacific theatre had been divided into three: Nimitz took the so-called 'Pacific Ocean Areas' (POA), which initially was the greatest area of responsibility.[2]

Nimitz planned to prepare a naval contingent for an ambush on the unsuspecting Japanese force, which was led by four carriers and commanded by Admiral Nagumo; Yamamoto was in overall control but was well away from the battle zone. Nagumo was compelled to obey his superior's command with dispersal, where his armada would be broken up into four distinct forces. Yamamoto's tactic was to deceive the Americans. His battleships, he hoped, would not be discovered before they struck. But the flaw in this approach was massive: the distance between the Japanese fleets meant that it was tough, if not impossible, to support each other once the battle began.

Throughout May 1942, Admiral Nimitz had scrambled to pull his ambush force together, with the Pearl Harbor Naval Shipyard working around the clock to have the designated ships battle-ready. The codebreakers had presented him with the date for the Japanese strike: probably 4 June or possibly 5 June.

More importantly, Nimitz knew the complete Japanese order of battle. Never had a naval commander had such devastating intelligence for such an important battle. Nimitz calculated that he had roughly the same number of carrier 'decks' as the Japanese. He had three afloat, all of which were able to carry more planes than the enemy, and another at Midway. Yamamoto had four on the ocean.

Given this balance of forces, Nimitz reasoned, the side with the element of surprise had the advantage.

At 4.30 a.m. on 4 June, Nagumo made his first strike on Midway, unaware of the American fleet lying in wait. He launched thirty-six dive bombers, thirty-six torpedo bombers and thirty-six Zeros. With them went a further squadron of combat planes and eight search aircraft. US radar – another technical advantage – picked up the assault from ten kilometres away.

The US fighter pilots had to defend Midway with just sixteen flimsy and obsolescent planes. They intercepted the Japanese squadrons, knocking out four bombers and four Zeros before being overwhelmed. Just two remained operable. The US anti-aircraft batteries on the ground on Midway did better, destroying more than forty Japanese planes, about a third of the assault squadron.

Meanwhile, US bombers flew from Midway to attack the Japanese carriers. Despite the enemy's blitz, they were able to fly back to the air base, reload and take off again. Midway was battered yet still operating.

The US bombers and torpedo bombers were joined at 10.22 a.m. by those from their three aircraft carriers. They bombarded the four Japanese carriers. In just six minutes, three of the enemy's carriers – the *Kagu*, the *Soryu* and the *Akagi* – were ablaze. Nagumo himself had to escape the burning *Akagi*, transferring his headquarters to a light cruiser.

The Japanese retaliated. Submarine *I-168* torpedoed and sank the disabled *Yorktown*. The *Hiryu* was catapulting its bombers to attack the surviving American carriers – the USS *Enterprise* and the USS *Hornet*. But the *Hiryu* had been hit by twenty-six torpedos and more than sixty-five bombs in the first round of attacks, and it limped away to the north, only to be spotted by a second wave of US bombers. They dived in for their fourth big kill of the day. The *Hiryu* was soon listing and ready to sink.

In command was Admiral Tamon Yamaguchi, who had been part of the attacks on Pearl Harbor and Darwin. He had been an unrelenting and fierce advocate for smashing Midway, then Hawaii and Australia. In true naval tradition, this aggressive commander decided to go down with his ship, a loyal servant of his beloved and equally bellicose 'god-king', Emperor Hirohito.

After a 72-hour fight, which had been effectively won in six minutes on the morning of the first day, the enemy was beaten down. It had lost four irreplaceable fleet carriers, while the United States had lost just one. The base at Midway was damaged by Japanese air attacks but remained operational. The casualty figures were telling. The Americans lost 340 men, the carrier USS *Yorktown*, the destroyer USS *Hammann* and 145 aircraft. The Japanese had nearly ten times more men killed: 3057. Apart from the four aircraft carriers that were sunk, the heavy cruiser *Mikuma* also went down. They also lost 228 aircraft.

Hirohito was told in secret of the true losses of the carriers and pilots. Amazingly, Prime Minister Tojo was not fully informed, nor was the Japanese media or public. By all reckoning, the US Navy had won its first major victory in the Battle of Midway. Coupled with the Battle of the Coral Sea, Japan's strategic initiative in the Pacific had been thwarted.

The Pacific War was a long way from its end, but Churchill may have judged it as the 'end of the beginning' of the battle for supremacy in the region.[3] Whether the Japanese had been robbed of their offensive capacity and desire remained to be seen.

38
'Australia is Secure'

On 11 June 1942, four days after the Battle of Midway petered out, MacArthur met Curtin in Melbourne and told him something that must have been a massive relief, but also perhaps too good to be true: 'The security of Australia has now been assured.'

He overstepped the line by telling Curtin that he should cease his efforts to ask for reinforcements from the United Kingdom and United States. Australia 'no longer needed the aid', MacArthur told him. He wanted Curtin to help him increase the size of his force and equipment for his offensive against Japan.

Curtin said little at this meeting. He was grateful for MacArthur's presence and views, but here and there he was off the mark. Was he overstating the US success at Midway? Had he, for the third time in a year, underestimated Japan's military machine?

The American was sure he could now take Rabaul from the Japanese. Blamey told Curtin that this was probably impossible.[1] But MacArthur persisted. Blamey was obliged to prepare the 7th Division for an attack on Rabaul, despite his misgivings.

Curtin was elated by the victory at Midway but remained unsure what he should tell the Australian people. The pressures on him eased, now that he knew the Japanese were far less likely to invade Australia. But he was not about to impart a false sense of optimism. The enemy was not retreating from the countries it controlled. Curtin felt that if he told the Australian public what MacArthur had advised him, he would be abrogating his responsibility as prime minister to keep the nation on alert, just in case Macarthur was influenced by his urgent desire to counter-attack.

Instead, he commented on the situation from his perspective. However, he was ebullient in an off-the-record press briefing in which he told Canberra journalists that Midway had 'removed the danger of a large scale effect on Australia for the time being'. The 'Nips', as he called the Japanese, had retreated, at least from that area of the Pacific. 'The submarine campaign along our coast,' he told reporters, 'which had been costly for them, should not be taken too seriously.'[2]

On 17 June, Curtin broadcast an appeal for contributions to a war loan that looked likely to be left well under-subscribed (at about one-third received of a hoped-for £35 million). It was costing the government a million pounds a day to prosecute the war. Curtin invoked his capacity for the telling human metaphor. 'A soldier who leaves his unit and his mates without authority is branded and dealt with as a deserter,' he said with force. 'A civilian who selfishly deserts his fellow Australians and his country is no less a traitor.'

Pacifists did not quite agree, but Curtin's rhetoric worked. His speech did not trumpet the situation after the battles of Midway and the Coral Sea. He maintained, accurately, that that these battles had merely frustrated the Japanese. In spite of MacArthur's view, which was not shared by Blamey, Curtin said the nation still faced invasion and the 'horrors that accompanied it'. He compared Australia's future with the present state of the Russians.

The loan was fully subscribed within two weeks.[3] In another talk a few days later, he noted that the nation had 'had a taste' of submarine warfare. 'Australian steamers have gone to the bottom. Our forces struck back successfully. But who can foretell the future?'

Curtin maintained that Australia could still be 'lost', and added a geographic perspective not mentioned before:

> . . . *Hawaii and the whole North American coast, from Alaska to Canada down to Mexico, will be open to Japanese attack free of any threat from any base in the Japanese rear . . . the combined effect of the Coral Sea, Midway Island and Aleutians battles, while frustrating from Japan's point of view, are far from decisive in the struggle through which we must pass if we are to reach our men locked up in Singapore . . . and if we are to strike at the very heart of Japan.*[4]

This was Curtin's first public comment about liberating the 23,000 Australian POWs – among more than 70,000 British prisoners – incarcerated at Changi and being used as slave labour in Singapore, Thailand, Burma, Borneo and Japan. It reflected a shift in his thinking: for the first time, he was considering a counter-attack.

Curtin's overall message, however, was still that Australia had to be prepared for a prolonged conflict. Continued economic rigour in the home was enforced. Clothing and footwear coupon rationing was introduced on 15 June 1942. Curtin told the pressmen in a briefing that he was thinking of lumping in several items – such as tobacco, cosmetics, spirits and confectionaries – on the one ration ticket. Ticket holders would have to choose which of these luxuries they preferred. The lukewarm reaction among his reporter mates to this idea gave him pause.

Soon afterwards, the government turned fashion guru by introducing 'Fashions for Victory'. Double-breasted suits were out, as were vests, sleeve buttons, and cuffs on sleeves or trousers. Women, too, were targeted. Manufacturing of evening wear was discouraged and it became impossible to buy gowns or children's party 'frocks'. Dry-cleaners were banned from taking in dinner jackets or evening dresses, ensuring that they would be worn less and less.

At this time, another piece of news filtered into Darwin, boosting the collective confidence of the Australian military and government.

It had been assumed that the small contingent of commandos in Timor had also been captured. But then a radio transmission from the island was picked up. Max Lawrence, a radio technician in the commando group, had rebuilt a smashed transmitter and receiver. The commandos had been forgotten in the chaos surrounding the bombing of Darwin, the big naval battles and all the other calamities, but they were still at large.

The commandos were being protected, hidden and supplied by the Timorese, making it possible for them to harass the enemy. Timorese boys, some just twelve years old, served with the Australians. 'They provided information,' writes Paul Cleary in *The Men Who Came Out of the Ground*, 'yodelling communication from the mountain tops, providing food and also carrying [the Commandos'] heavy gear. This way they became a vastly more mobile and effective force than the Japanese.'

Over the first five months of 1942, the commandos' guerrilla actions meant that several thousand Japanese troops had to remain on Timor, instead of being shipped to New Guinea or Guadalcanal. The commander of the Australian force, Bernard Callinan, sent a message to Darwin. If they could be resupplied from the air with food and arms, they could keep the Japanese at bay for months more.

Believing that there was a considerable force of Australians on Timor, the Japanese called for further reinforcements, until 5000 enemy soldiers were on the island. The Australian guerrillas would do much more than provide a boost to the government's morale: they would play a part in the overall attempt to counter-attack the Japanese in the Pacific.

39
Over-Sexed and Over Here

The immediate threat to take Port Moresby from the sea seemed over but Blamey went ahead with his plans to fortify it, on the highly unlikely possibility that the Japanese would land on New Guinea's north coast and advance south. A guerrilla group (known as 'Kanga Force') was put in charge of about 300 kilometres of the north coast, from Lae to Salamaua, inland about 50 kilometres to Wau, and further east on the coast to Buna.

Kanga Force was to act as a reconnaissance and sentry group. No one really expected the Japanese to attempt to take Moresby by travelling across the inhospitable mountains of the Owen Stanley Range. The region featured a series of rising ridges covered by thick jungle, and the highest peak was Mount Bellamy, at 2300 metres. The only way through this forbidding morass was by a tiny path, a metre wide at most, known as the Kokoda Track.

The path struggled up slippery ridges, over spurs made dangerous by moss and phosphorescent fungi, around hefty gorges and across fast-flowing streams. The steps cut into the mountains – often simply uncovered tree roots – were uneven, sometimes treacherous. Every three or four kilometres the Track emerged from the gloom onto a small patch of kunai grass. Torrential rain made any march along the Track worse. Downpours came at noon and at night, creating eerie mists and odorous vapours. Yellow sludge covered the Track on every mountain, ridge and spur, transforming it into waist-deep slop. Flat areas morphed into pools of mud. The roughness of the geography was accentuated by the hot, humid days, which contrasted sharply with the cold nights.

The consolations of this hellish terrain were few. In the morning, for a couple of hours, sunlight glistened through the trees at a low angle. Large coloured butterflies flitted around the heads of any trekkers concentrating on their arduous trudge. Birds were unseen but constantly heard; the screeching cockatoos warned of any humans advancing below.

Despite the near impassability of this terrain, Blamey decided that Kanga Force, which was not a fighting unit, would have to be supported by troops. He directed Major-General Morris to assemble Maroubra Force, mainly made up of the 39th Militia Battalion, along with AIF reinforcements. It was sent to garrison Kokoda, a small village with an airstrip that was located about 150 kilometres north of Port Moresby, on the lower northern slopes of the Owen Stanley Range in Papua's peninsula. A walking track and a rough road connected Kokoda to Buna, sixty kilometres away on the northern coast. Another track led south from Kokoda, over the range to Uberi. From there, a walking trail and a dirt road covered thirty-nine kilometres to Port Moresby.

In June 1942, a fit soldier could negotiate the Uberi–Port Moresby route in twelve days. The way forward was exhausting and painstaking. The lead soldier in the single-file 'march' would use a machete to hack through the thick undergrowth along the steep, slippery, root-tangled trails. The grass, which was more than two metres high, could cut a man's hand like a scalpel.

Major-General Morris was unenthusiastic about Blamey's order; he'd had enough trouble supplying Kanga Force over rough jungle mountain tracks. He now had to provide for the much bigger Maroubra Force, over longer routes and through thicker jungle.

Morris could not believe the Japanese would take the Kokoda route to attack Moresby. If the enemy army landed on the north coast and took the Kokoda Track south from Buna, Morris reasoned, they simply would not make it, no matter how well resourced and prepared they were. If attrition of men and equipment didn't stop them, disease would. The torrential rain exacerbated health problems and made soldiers susceptible to tropical diseases. Anyone spending even a few months in the region was likely to contract malaria.

It was impossible to drag heavy guns in these conditions. Morris believed that even if the Japanese somehow crossed the Owen Stanley Range, they would be vulnerable when they closed in on Port Moresby. It was surrounded by open, lightly timbered country and had no natural cover. He thought that the lack of artillery would be such a handicap that a well-equipped garrison defence would repulse any Japanese approach.

Morris felt that to move Allied troops towards Kokoda was to invite the very problems that he predicted for the Japanese. Vehicles could not go more than a few kilometres. He didn't have enough aircraft to supply Kokoda, even if they could negotiate the weather and the mountains. Horses couldn't cope in the slippery, muddy terrain. Native carriers proved the most reliable transporters, but they could carry just twenty kilograms each.

If the Japanese did manage the unlikely move across the mountain barrier, Morris concluded, his force should attempt to strangle their supply lines. It was best to meet the Japanese 'on ground of our choosing' – as close to Port Moresby as possible.

Curtin's growing confidence was boosted by the news that 60,000 soldiers of the 32nd and 41st US Divisions had come into Australia in the last couple of months. After Midway, MacArthur had directed these troops to Queensland. The 32nd was camping west of Brisbane, which in the past half-year had basically become an American city. The 41st moved to a site between Rockhampton and Yeppoon, on Queensland's central coast.

After a luxurious time at Melbourne's Menzies Hotel, MacArthur in early July 1942 prepared to move 2000 kilometres north to Brisbane. His family and officers would take over Lennon's Hotel. His headquarters would be the AMP Insurance building. Now that the immediate danger of a Japanese invasion was over, there was no reason for MacArthur to be so far from the action.

There had been a mixed reaction from locals to this friendly foreign invasion. On the one hand, the Americans were seen as an insurance policy against a Japanese attack. On the other, the social dislocation of a quick imposition of one culture on another caused friction. Melbourne, a far bigger city than Brisbane, had absorbed 32,000 Americans with very little social upheaval; the impact on Brisbane was much greater. MacArthur's decision to make it his base turned the city into a major hub of US military command, and brought tens of thousands more American servicemen. Army personnel dominated, while the navy and air force would also use it as an important base.

For the locals, everything was changing fast. Food and drinks were different. Women found it hard to resist the Americans' polite invitations to eat hamburgers and hotdogs and drink milkshakes and coffee. More American movies were playing in the cinemas, which now commenced not with 'God Save the Queen' but with the American national anthem, 'The Star-Spangled Banner'. The flag of the United States was seen more on buildings than the Australian flag. New music such as jazz and country was played in Brisbane's halls. Brisbane women were introduced to dances such as the Jitterbug, the Jersey Bounce and the Jig Walk. The foreigners' talk – 'jive' – was fresh and inventive.

The Americans brought in books not published in Australia. Tomes such as D. H. Lawrence's *Lady Chatterley's Lover* were whispered about.[1] The women loved the new experiences. It all seemed so exhilarating, especially amid Curtin's wartime restrictions, and the Americans had more style than their Aussie counterparts. Their uniforms were smarter and their manner was more confident. Some, of course, were after sex, but it was the way they went about it that appealed.

Two Jewish sisters, Shirley and Grace Barnbaum, recalled the American occupation as the most exciting time Brisbane ever experienced. 'It was even better than Expo in 1988,' Grace remarked. She fell in love with Calman Feinstein, a 23-year-old naval intelligence officer from New York, and they had a six-month 'friendship'. Because of censorship, Grace would write to his family for him. Some of the newcomers were just teenagers, and lonely.

The sisters found the Americans romantic, and the Barnbaums opened their home to the visitors. They would bring a corsage or present when they arrived for a date. 'I could have been [married] in the US with about seven of them,' Shirley said.

'One of the boys brought my mother a big jar of pepper,' Grace remembered. 'It lasted twenty years!'

Not all the Americans worried about the niceties of romance. Shirley recalled seeing a long line of US servicemen stretching from a brothel. But the sisters dated men with similar backgrounds to them, who comprehended the sensitive mores of romance and courtship better than their Australian counterparts. The Americans wished to appear gallant. 'The most risqué thing said to us,' Grace recalled, 'was "do you know the facts of life?"'[2]

Just before MacArthur's arrival in Brisbane, a journalist went into a Queen Street movie theatre. He counted 152 local women in the company of 112 uniformed Americans. Only thirty-one women were with the sixty Australian soldiers. His report of the 'takeover' of Brisbane by the Americans demonstrated the local sensitivities well.

40
Essential Essington

The Germans' advance into the Middle East in mid-1942 led to the British asking the Australians to postpone delivery of Spitfires that had been promised to them. Curtin agreed, with reservations.

The forty-two planes would now be unloaded at Freetown, Sierra Leone, where they would be assembled and flown to the war zone. The Australians were concerned that they might be delayed indefinitely, especially with Churchill's attitude to the Pacific War.

But the British were not the only ones disappointing Canberra. At a War Conference meeting on 19 July, Curtin showed MacArthur a letter from William Stix Wasserman, chief of the United States lend-lease mission to Australia. Wasserman had made a recent visit and had overstated Australia's 'war strength'. Because of his influence, Washington believed Australia was coping and didn't need financial assistance for its defence.

Curtin was not impressed, saying Wasserman talked like a movie star, full of gestures and fine words. Wasserman was heavily critical of Blamey, both personally and professionally.[1]

MacArthur commented that he viewed the attack as 'cowardly'. 'I am quite satisfied with General Blamey as Commander of the Allied Land Forces,' he said. Blamey was 'the best of all the Australian Generals and above the average ability of Generals . . . He is a first-class army commander.'[2]

This was generous, but MacArthur could hardly say anything less, given Blamey's far superior record in both World Wars. MacArthur told Curtin that he was not concerned 'with any personal idiosyncrasies which General Blamey might possess' – in other words, Blamey's weaknesses with booze and women. MacArthur could not resist telling Curtin that he had heard much criticism of Blamey from

Australian officers. But he put it down to their coveting the job of commander in chief.

This was all true, but by airing these ideas before Curtin, MacArthur was cementing his own image as the more stable and popular man at the top.

The lack of equipment from the United Kingdom and the United States was, to a degree, compensated by the grand efforts of handsome, tall and broad-shouldered Essington Lewis, the powerful industrialist and Director of Munitions. He had a seat on the Defence Committee and had the same access to the War Cabinet as the chiefs of staff. Unlike them, he was exempt from the rules that regulated officers of the Crown, in particular the Public Servant Act (1922).

Lewis could acquire any material or building, and issue contracts without calling for tenders. He had £250,000 at his disposal for any project. In effect, Lewis was Australia's industrial czar, with almost unlimited authority.

Lewis's factories made grenades, land mines, ammunition of all types, .303 rifles, machine guns, including the Owen gun and several heavier weapons. Advanced optical aids were produced, as were tanks and torpedoes. Most importantly, Lewis quickened the output of Beaufort planes to replace the outmoded Wirraways.

After the bombing of Darwin in February 1942, Lewis stepped up production of the new Boomerang fighter plane. His extraordinary business skills could never be matched by a bureaucrat. It was the key reason for Curtin maintaining this original Menzies appointment (in 1940).

By the end of the first week of July 1942, Curtin was able tell journalists at his regular briefing that Australia had seventy-six Beauforts in operation. He considered this a fine achievement, since Australia had been thrown back on its own resources after England cut aircraft supplies to it. Curtin told the reporters that engineers were still trying to improve dive-bombing and fire-power capabilities. He expected the Boomerang to be ready for action by the end of the year. Curtin anticipated it would be superior to the Zero and equal to the Spitfire.

This was a premature pronouncement, and in reality may have been intended for the Japanese.³ But the Boomerang had defeated the Kittyhawk and the Air Cobra in climbing trials: it could reach 30,000 feet if it used a 'supercharger'.⁴ The plane had gone from blueprint to test flight in a record fourteen weeks. It was now expected to come off the production line like 'sausages'. All except one item in the plane had been produced in Australia.⁵

Lewis had 150,000 men and women working for him in the munitions program. His report to the War Council on 9 July 1942 was, according to the prime minister, 'nothing short of amazing. We are now on the verge of producing tanks more efficient than those of the US in Australia and the British in the Middle East, and those of Rommel.' Again, this was more propaganda than fact. The tank was never going to carry a 25-pound gun, despite Curtin's claims. Lewis promised more than fifty tanks would be operational in the next year. More could be made if needed.⁶

Curtin recognised Lewis's unparalleled importance to the war effort and wanted to recommend him for a knighthood. Lewis refused; such decorations meant little to him. His main concern was to make sure an independent Australia could defend itself.

MacArthur reaffirmed this at a mid-July background briefing of journalists. He also expressed 'great satisfaction' with Australia's munitions. 'Australia should never let her industrial potential die down,' he said. Instead, the country should, after the war, continue to manufacture arms with which to defend itself. This time, MacArthur was saying Australia should rely upon itself rather than the United Kingdom or United States.⁷

Despite the setbacks Japan had suffered in the battles of the Coral Sea and Midway, it had not been deterred from its main objectives regarding Australia. After expressing concerns about the increase in Allied air strength in and around New Guinea, an intelligence analysis of 9 July said 'the capture of Eastern New Guinea, especially Moresby, has become of immediate importance in order to carry out our air operations. We must capture advance bases in order to further our attacks on the enemy, and prepare for operations against Australia by controlling the Coral Sea.'[8]

On 16 July 1942, David Ross, Australia's representative in Timor, arrived unexpectedly in Canberra. At a secret meeting with the press, he told of his escape. He described the morale of the 450 Australian troops who were still living in the hills and harassing the Japanese with guerrilla tactics. Some had been stricken with malaria, but most had recovered. Their ammunition was intact. They had plenty of food. They were in wireless contact with Australia and even had a mail delivery. Ross said their only fear was that the Japanese might send in big troop numbers to drive them out. He admitted they could be evacuated from the island with ease, but felt they should stay so that they might 'one day' be a valuable force on Timor.

On 17 July, the trial of Edward Leonski – the triple murderer – took place in Melbourne under US military law. He confessed and was convicted and sentenced to death.

Part Four

Battle for Australia
JULY–SEPTEMBER 1942

41
Japan's Second Thrust

At 4 p.m. on 21 July 1942, Father James Benson looked out to sea off Gona on Papua's north coast. He could see a 5000-tonne Japanese transport ship flanked by two destroyers. The invading fleet had made its way through the shallow reefs and was anchored less than a kilometre from the beach.

Yorkshireman Benson was one of the few whites left in Papua. He and two women – one a teacher at Gona's three schools – had decided to stay rather than evacuate. Along with 1.8 million locals, there were now just 689 foreigners in the country, including 121 missionaries and twenty-one children.

There was no protection from the invaders. Allied armies and navy vessels were elsewhere. American ships were in the Solomon Islands and other parts of the Pacific, preparing to aid a marine attack on Guadalcanal. The defeat of the Japanese at Midway and the Coral Sea had lulled the Allies into believing that the Japanese had given up on the idea of taking Moresby.

Just fifteen minutes after he spotted the fleet, Benson heard its guns firing at Buna and Gona. After 'softening up' the coast for around forty-five minutes, about a quarter of the 2000-strong invading force climbed into barges. Benson led his little group – the two women, four Australian soldiers and two wounded American airmen – into the jungle. As they scurried away, they could hear and see Allied airmen in planes inferior to the Zeros battling it out in dogfights.

As night fell and the sky fights abated, the Japanese advance force, led by General Yokoyama, finishing disembarking at Gona. This marked an important moment in Australian history. The Japanese had invaded Papua, which was sovereign Australian territory, having been ceded by Britain in 1906.[1] By dawn on 22 July, the Nankai Shitai Regiment had secured Papuan beachheads at Gona, Buna and Sanananda.

Blamey and MacArthur disagreed about the significance of the Japanese attack. US and Australian intelligence sources were warning that the Japanese were planning a sizeable invasion; this modest landing was just the beginning. The data was clear and consistent: an increased force of enemy soldiers would soon follow, which would attempt to cross the Owen Stanley Range.

Newly arrived in Brisbane, and more concerned with settling in to his new headquarters, MacArthur dismissed the fresh intelligence. He refused to believe the enemy would take on such a hostile environment. Blamey was more pragmatic. Why would an army land a big contingent if it did not mean to take a sustained action? He was concerned that the Australians had only two militia brigades at Port Moresby. He reckoned that politicians – such as the feisty former prime minister Billy Hughes – and the media would be most critical of this inadequacy. During the Paris Peace Conference following World War I, Hughes had won for Australia the mandate over New Guinea.

As predicted, Hughes complained loudest when news reached Canberra of this unexpected new threat to Australia. Blamey thought it would be wise to divert the 7th Division from Townsville where it was in training for the retaking of Rabaul, and deploy it to Port Moresby. MacArthur did not agree, but he was soon under pressure from Washington, where the US chiefs were receiving the same intelligence. They wanted action to stop the Japanese.

Curtin was stunned by this new threat. His public caution in the face of optimistic advice from MacArthur, Blamey and all the other Australian chiefs had been justified. The military scrambled to meet the threat. While MacArthur, in discussions with Blamey, planned Australia's reaction, the two opposing forces began to engage.

On the evening of 22 July, Lieutenant John Chalk, with his unit of thirty indigenous soldiers from the Papuan Infantry Battalion (PIB), carried out an ambush from a hill on the Gona–Sangara road. It was a quick hit-and-run mission, but it showed the Japanese that they would face opposition. A day later, Major Bill Watson, leading a unit of twenty PIB soldiers, fought the Japanese at Awala before withdrawing across the Kumusi River and destroying the bridge over it. Watson's unit was reinforced by a platoon from the Kokoda village base, sixty kilometres away.

Five hundred and twenty Japanese marines began crossing the river supported by heavy mortar and machine-gun fire. The Australians were forced to pull back five kilometres. 'B' Company commander Captain Sam Templeton mustered a unit of thirty young raw diggers and PIB soldiers. They waited for the advancing enemy.

Templeton had two Lewis machine guns, with which he hoped to hold back the Japanese stealing along the banks of the Gorari Creek. Before the ambush took place, Templeton hastened back to Kokoda to consult with Lieutenant-Colonel William Owen, the 39th Battalion's commander, who had flown in to assess the crisis.

The ambush took place on 24 July but it was not effective. The Australians, outnumbered almost ten to one, had to withdraw to higher ground at Oiva, about twenty kilometres east of Kokoda. The Japanese kept coming, with Kokoda and its airstrip their initial target.

The Australian reinforcement from Port Moresby either underestimated the intentions and strength of the Japanese push or – in keeping with Major-General Morris's attitude – did not want to risk too many of the 39th Battalion. On 26 July, two transport planes with just thirty-two soldiers arrived at Kokoda and set off for the action at Oiva. The Japanese attacked the small defending force over six hours but could not break through, despite using their trusty flanking movements. By 5 p.m. the Australians' position worsened. The Japanese managed to surround the Allied soldiers and Templeton was captured.[1]

The track west to Kokoda was now cut off. The Australians and Papuans regrouped in the night at Deniki, ten kilometres south of Kokoda. Lieutenant Colonel Owen took charge. He made a critical decision on 27 July to keep control of the airstrip. He expected that reinforcements would arrive in time to aid him.

Owen and a contingent of seventy-seven soldiers moved back along the path towards Kokoda, having radioed Port Moresby for help.

They secured the airfield by midday on 28 July, just as two Douglas transports arrived with reinforcements from the 39th Battalion. But the two planes were unable to judge who controlled the airstrip. They flew back to Moresby, leaving Owen and his troops in a predicament.

The Japanese were cautious but realised that they outnumbered the Australians and were far better equipped. They had seen the Australian support planes fly away and knew they would not be back until daylight at the earliest. This gave the Japanese time to strike.

At 2 a.m. the next morning, they opened up with mortar and machine-gun fire on the Australians defending the airfield. The Japanese then made their thrust, resorting to hand-to-hand fighting and overrunning the defenders. The cost was considerable for both sides. Owen was wounded in the chaotic fighting. Watson took charge. He withdrew his troops south to Deniki and was forced to leave Owen, who was close to death.

The Japanese mission was accomplished. They controlled Kokoda's airstrip by the end of 29 July. Believing that the Australians had a force of well over 1000 soldiers rather than just seventy-seven, the Japanese did not pursue them. Instead, they dug in, with the aim of consolidating their hold on their acquisition.[2]

In their post-mortem of events, the Japanese believed that the defenders were poorly equipped and organised. This encouraged their commander to let his superiors in Rabaul know that he thought that the invaders could mount an assault on Port Moresby via the Kokoda Track. In the wake of this optimistic report, the Japanese directed that the short and rotund Major General Tomitaro Horii should transport 10,000 men of the South Seas Force to take that vital port town.

Billy Hughes continued to stir in Canberra. 'There has been a lamentable lack of vision, of initiative, of coordination of control by our military leaders,' he told *Smith's Weekly*.[3]

Curtin claimed that Hughes was wrong. Australia had established a 'satisfactory' defensive position. He was acting on advice from MacArthur. The American had yet to comprehend Papuan terrain, but still he refused to believe that the Japanese would be foolhardy enough to take Moresby via the Kokoda Track.

In private Curtin remained concerned. He had heard this from MacArthur with regard to Burma, Thailand, Malaya, Singapore, the Philippines, Hawaii and everywhere else in the Pacific, including Australia. Yet the relentless enemy military machine kept coming on land and sea, attacking the Allies' shipping, despite the Midway setback.

The US chiefs in Washington wanted to know how this new incursion by the enemy was being handled. MacArthur warded off any criticism of his own inaction by saying that the Australians were to blame: they should have held up the Japanese in Papua but they had retreated. He then cut off any further carping by telling Washington that reinforcements would be sent to Port Moresby.

The Japanese had been in New Guinea for ten days when Blamey arrived in Brisbane. He moved his Land Force headquarters into the unfinished buildings of the University of Queensland at St Lucia.

MacArthur wanted to send his 32nd Division but Blamey talked him out of it. He saw problems in having two separate national forces in the same operational area, especially with MacArthur wanting to control his force from Brisbane. Blamey had experienced such problems in 1918, when Monash negotiated with the British, French, Americans and Canadians in masterminding his big battles.

With this in mind, Blamey proposed to MacArthur that the 7th Division be sent, along with the 1st Australian Corps HQ staff. The 7th was one of the biggest cards Blamey had to play. MacArthur agreed reluctantly but was already planning to cut the Australians out of his plans for retaking Rabaul and – possibly – the Philippines, which still fixated him.

Japanese intelligence maps of Port Moresby were as comprehensive as possible without aerial photography. Laid out were topography; the accessibility of every road; Australian defensive posts; water supply areas; and gun emplacements. Intelligence reports in early August 1942 made the IJA's intentions clear as far as Australia was concerned:

'... the Army directed Army HQ and the Nankai Shitai at Palau and the Yazawa Butai at Davao, to commence preparations and begin the new operation against Australia in East New Guinea area.'[4]

42
39th in Trouble

In a creative display of hypocrisy, MacArthur called for an off-the-record Brisbane press briefing. The thirty journalists stood as he entered the room and he responded with a stiff arm salute. No questions were to be asked. He gave the impression (without saying it) that the 7th Division's move to Papua action was his idea, his directive. He had presented himself as American royalty of sorts, a member of the US's ruling elite. This show of respect demonstrated he had reporters bluffed and where he wanted them in contrast to Blamey, who was respected but not liked by the press. Described by witnesses as 'grave, distinguished and immaculate', MacArthur launched into his well-rehearsed theatrics:

'As Plato once remarked,' he began, 'the scale of human achievement is limited only by the limits of our imagination. For too long now we have been thinking in terms of defending this country along its own shores, but from today we are shifting our frontline forward.'

Having appropriated Blamey's proposal, MacArthur went on:

Australia will be defended in New Guinea and the assault will be led by their own magnificent, battle-scarred 7th Division. They were brought back from the Middle East to challenge the supposedly invincible Japanese. And challenge them they will! We are about to see a turning of the tide. From this point on it is: Attack! Attack! Attack![1]

MacArthur gave a two-hour performance worthy of a true

thespian, a monologue that would never be dared by an Australian general or politician. His clear, unhalting and 'perfectly phrased' speech had all the hallmarks of a stage show, complete with appropriate arm movements, body contortions and lengthy dramatic pauses.

At the close of the performance, the journalists stood in anticipation of the general leaving. MacArthur again held his right arm up in salute. He strode from the conference room with two of his staff following; they bustled ahead of him to open doors before humbly falling back.

Lieutenant General Sydney Rowell, the Commander of I Corps, was sent to Moresby; it was a further declaration by Blamey of his intention to take the initiative wherever possible. In addition, Major General Cyril Clowes was sent to Milne Bay, on the eastern tip of Papua, 320 kilometres from Moresby. Blamey had intelligence from the broken Japanese codes. He moved swiftly to have Milne Bay defended by the air force and army.

Pipe-smoking 'Silent Cyril', as Clowes was called because of his laconic nature, was to command Milne Force, made up of the 7th (Militia) Brigade and the 7th Division's 18th Brigade. He was a Duntroon graduate and professional soldier with a string of decorations from both wars, including CBE, DSO and MC. He started his career as a 'gunner' – an artilleryman – of the highest order, and developed into an accomplished commander despite his reticence to communicate, which was seen as a weakness, especially in a profession that thrived on promotion and self-promotion.

Another 'big gun' of the Australian command, Major General Arthur Allen, heading 7th Division, would set up his headquarters in Port Moresby and take charge of his own 21st Brigade and two militia brigades – the 14th and 30th – that were already in the Moresby region. These hardened warriors of the 7th were expected to stiffen the resolve of the callow militiamen. Nicknamed 'Tubby' because of his fleshy-faced and corpulent appearance, Allen appeared a sensible choice. He was a veteran of World War I, having fought as a captain in Pozières in August 1916 and at Messines in the 45th Battalion in June 1917, when Monash's 3rd Division had won the AIF's first major victory. Allen was awarded the DSO and promoted to major in July 1917. He continued to lead men in combat, at Dernancourt in April 1918 and then as a lieutenant colonel in charge of the 48th Battalion at Monument Wood.

Between the wars Allen combined two careers: accountancy and the militia. In 1939, he took charge of the 16th Brigade in the 2nd AIF's 6th Division. The following year he fought at Bardia and Tobruk, and in the ill-fated Greek campaign in April 1941, which earned him the Greek Military Cross. In the same year Allen took over the 7th Division for the successful campaign against the Vichy French in Syria. In August he was promoted to major general. By the time Allen took over at Port Moresby, he had commanded from platoon to divisional level and had few peers in his service for his country.

All 39th Battalion (militia) reinforcements had reached Deniki by the end of the first week in August, making the force 533 strong. On 8 August 1942 the Kokoda force's uncompromising new commander (following Owen's demise), Lieutenant Colonel Allan Cameron, decided on an offensive. It was in his nature. Cameron had escaped Rabaul with twelve others in a little boat when the Japanese invaded. This was a prudent act, given the enemy's reputation for butchery.

Perhaps paradoxically, Cameron would not tolerate those who retreated from the invaders, calling them 'cowards'. He came across some eighteen-year-olds from the 39th's B Company, led by Corporal Markham, who had fled the fighting after Owen had been killed and Templeton captured. Cameron was a close mate of Owen and was angry. He ordered the youths back into action at Isurava, five kilometres south of Deniki.

Cameron believed his force was strong enough to retake Kokoda. He launched his attack at dawn the next morning, sending three companies from Deniki on the three-hour trek north. But the terrain and the Japanese stopped two of them, leaving just Captain Noel Symington's A Company, whose men succeeded in retaking the lightly held Kokoda.

Templeton and a Private Moffatt were taken by the Japanese to a deserted plantation and interrogated. Templeton was tortured. He was defiant at first but then appeared to give in, saying that there were about 1000 Australian soldiers, led by a colonel, on the Kokoda Track; they had arrived ten days earlier. Judging by the fight the Australians had put up so far, the Japanese were inclined to believe this. With further torture, the Japanese tried to discover the number of Allied soldiers in Port Moresby. Templeton held back and then again pretended to 'crack'.

'Twenty thousand,' he said, 'made up of Americans, Australians and Indians.'

The captors were shocked at the figure. They conferred, then demanded, 'Who is their commanding officer?'

'An Australian, General Morris.'

'But there are Americans!'

'They are on Australian territory. This means someone in General Blamey's command must lead them.'

The Japanese decided that this information was probably correct. A defiant Templeton was later stabbed to death. But his grand misinformation outlived him. The Japanese command believed the figure of 20,000 soldiers. This would dictate their strategy, tactics, actions and attitudes from then on, in their quest to take Port Moresby.[2]

As A Company was taking a tenuous grip on one of the most strategic places in the South-East Asian theatre of the war, about 2000 kilometres to the east the fourteen-year-old heavy cruiser HMAS *Canberra* was ploughing through the South Pacific in an Allied squadron. From 5 to 7 August, the *Canberra* had escorted a US marine force in the opening stages of the campaign to take several islands from the Japanese, including Guadalcanal and Talagi in the Solomon Islands chain.

On the afternoon of 8 August, a Japanese taskforce of five cruisers and a destroyer, commanded by Vice Admiral Gunichi Mikawa, approached the south of Savo Island. His aim was to attack the

Allied naval force supporting the US marine landings. At 1.45 a.m. on 9 August, the destroyer USS *Patterson* detected Mikawa's fleet and alerted the Allied force.

The *Canberra* had been fortunate to miss being hit by torpedoes fired by the midget submarines in Sydney Harbour. Skilful manoeuvring again allowed the ship to avoid being struck by nineteen Japanese torpedoes, but it ran into the range of the enemy cruisers' gunfire. The first salvos killed or wounded several Australian officers, disabled both engine rooms and forced the flooding of her magazines. The *Canberra* was hit twenty-four times in two minutes and the ship was immobilised; it was soon listing to starboard. Fires broke out inside the ship.

During this one-sided engagement, the Australians on board believed they had been hit by 'friendly fire' from the USS *Bagley*. Eighty-four of the *Canberra*'s company of 819 men were killed in the battle, and 109 were wounded. At 3.30 a.m. the USS *Patterson* came alongside and began rescuing the survivors. An hour later, it and the USS *Chicago* became entangled in a fire-fight in the dark, each believing the other ship was an enemy vessel. Vital minutes in the rescue operation were lost in this futile, needless shootout.

At about 5.30 a.m. the rescue of the Australians in the water resumed. At 6.30 a.m. it was decided that the stricken *Canberra* would be abandoned and sunk if its engines could not be repaired. As dawn broke on another day in the clear blue waters of the Pacific, Australian engineers were working frantically. But time ran out. At 8 a.m. the ship was torpedoed by the USS *Ellet*. This would be the only helpful piece of 'friendly fire' in an unfortunate episode for Australian–US naval relations.[3]

Four Allied cruisers went down in the Battle of Savo Island. The losses left Australia almost completely without naval protection.

About the time the *Canberra* was reaching the bottom of the Pacific Ocean, Lieutenant Colonel Cameron, with the 39th's A Company at Kokoda, asked Port Moresby for reinforcements. They would not arrive for a day. Bad weather had set in on the Track, making it impassable. This was enough of an opening for the Japanese to strike back.

Having repulsed the 39th's C and D Companies, Lieutenant Colonel Hatsuo Tsukamoto sent his men to take the airport during the daylight hours of 9 August. It took four attempts, but when darkness fell the Japanese were able to infiltrate through Australian lines. Hand-to-hand fighting ensued until the next morning. Transport planes, for the second time in weeks, could not work out which side held the Kokoda airstrip. They circled low and then departed. By the afternoon of 10 August, the Australians at Kokoda were running out of food and ammunition.

Noel Symington ordered a fighting withdrawal of his A Company west of the Kokoda plateau. They camped through the night. At first light, the struggling, diminished force set out for Deniki. Slowed by the need to carry their wounded, they reached the village of Naro. Symington passed word to Deniki of his force's plight. A small patrol of natives, led by Warrant Officer Wilkinson, took the wounded back through Japanese lines to Isurava, where they joined the rest of the battered 39th Battalion on 13 August.

The five-day mission had failed. Yet the Japanese were hardly in a better position. They had taken back Kokoda but had yet to secure Isurava, just fifteen kilometres south. The terrain and the Australians would make the advance towards Port Moresby the toughest of assignments for the Imperial Army.

Japanese intelligence reports began assessing their opposition. One report, under the heading '*Combat Methods of Australian Troops*', read:

> *Compared to English, American and Filipino troops, the Australian troops have greater fighting spirit, and obey their officers with willing enthusiasm. In close-range combat during the actions at Rabaul, Kokoda and Mt Bellamy, they skilfully used the turns of long forest roads and sniped with automatic rifles at the short range of 30 to 40 metres. They were also skilful in throwing hand grenades from strong points. The native troops sniped from tree*

*tops and then immediately ran. However, against all this, our grenade attack is very strong and the Australian troops cannot make an assault. Although the enemy's precautions are careless, we must exercise vigilance.*⁴

43
Setbacks and Success

In mid-August 1942, reports coming across Curtin's desk from his military advisers maintained the strain on him. He experienced another terrifying nightmare during a train trip to Brisbane, dreaming of torpedoed ships 'burning and sinking in the blackness of the night'. Images of hundreds of men 'jumping into the sea to their deaths' were vivid. He awoke sweating and shaking.

Journalist Alan Reid came across the prime minister in the train's corridor. Curtin spoke of his dream, which related to the information he had just received on the sinking of the *Canberra*. Reports had dwelt on the fires inside the ship, the trapped men, their jumping into the sea and the delay in rounding them up, which caused many more to drown. Reid felt that Curtin believed he was foreseeing a similar disaster for the returning 6th Division, which had been in Ceylon for several months.

'I'm responsible for every life on that ship,' Curtin said in despair, 'and if anything happens like that, it will be because of my decision.'

This sense of huge responsibility was both a weakness and an asset for his prime ministership. Other leaders were less tough on themselves. Men like Churchill and Roosevelt had trained themselves to move on, but Curtin could not. He lived and rode with the weekly, sometimes daily reports of mass deaths. In peacetime, a loss of three or four people in an accident would cause national mourning. Such a small number on any one day in wartime would be a relief.

Curtin's humane side, however, meant that his decisions were made in the best interests of his nation and the lives of every individual fighting for it. His compassion was appreciated by those close to him, and even his political opposition. But friends like Chifley wondered how long Curtin could go on flagellating himself. Curtin had done all he could to ensure the safe passage of the two brigades of Australian troops moving by ship from Ceylon to Fremantle; he had even severed all phone and telegraph communications with Western Australia for a week, to keep the troop movements secret.

The *Canberra*'s sinking led to an uncharacteristic sniping from Curtin. He was also angered by the ease of a recent Japanese air raid on Townsville. He noted in a press briefing how the enemy was striking successfully on weekends – when the civil and military defences were shut down. Curtin was incredulous at the 'Saturday/Sunday slumbering' mentality of Australians, with the war so close. He wanted the journalists to write 'wake-up' editorials highlighting this weakness.

He also blasted his opposition critics. Billy Hughes came in for a special attack over events in the Solomon Islands. Curtin claimed the former Labor prime minister was publicly saying things that could help the Japanese. He used the government censor to stop Hughes' comments going outside the country. Some said Curtin was censuring him on political grounds. But it was true that Japan was using propaganda as a war weapon. Its spies in Australia reported the nuance of every political utterance. Any over-the-top remarks by a powerful figure such as Hughes would be used against the Allies.

These moves caused Warwick Fairfax, the head of Fairfax newspapers, which owned the influential *Sydney Morning Herald*, to resign from the Press Censorship Advisory Committee. Curtin had then to defend the government censor and his own part in this action against Hughes. After spraying invective at Hughes and the opposition, Curtin also berated the press in language termed 'intemperate' by editors. He claimed that the owners of the big papers were 'very afraid' of what a Labor government might do after the war. Reverting to rhetoric more associated with Stalin and the troublesome Australian communists, he said the 'capitalist wolf will not be able to feed on the lambs in the factories and workshops as it has done for 50 years in this country.'[1]

The main reason for Curtin's outburst – the irrepressible Japanese – seemed undeterred by the obstacle of the Kokoda Track, which they and the Allies had underestimated. In fact, the invaders faced more obstacles than they had ever envisaged. Maroubra Force, which comprised AIF and militia units in the Owen Stanley Range, had an unofficial new commander, Brigadier Arnold Potts, who was now moving through with fresh 21st Brigade troops from Port Moresby.

This short, powerfully built 45-year-old British-born grazier from Western Australia looked like a US Marine, with his crew cut, square jaw and confident stride. Officers and the rank and file alike admired Potts. As a teenager, he'd landed at Gallipoli as an original Anzac and distinguished himself in battle. In France, he was promoted to captain. At nineteen, Potts became the youngest company commander in the Australian forces. He won the Military Cross and was twice wounded. When World War II broke out he enlisted again, much to his family's sadness, and left for the Middle East as commanding officer of the 16th Battalion.

At Sidon and Damour Potts earned the Distinguished Service Order (DSO). The citation read: 'Major Potts was outstanding, not only for his personal bravery in going forward under fire, but in his own personal leadership and example.' He was promoted to brigadier and returned to Australia with the 7th Division. Potts was just the sort of commander that Curtin wanted defending the country rather than fighting in Burma. His cheerful courage and calm leadership skills were rare, and vital if the AIF was going to repel any Japanese invasion.

Now Potts found himself in the worst conditions he had ever experienced in war as he pushed his men towards Myola, about forty-five kilometres short of main Japanese positions. One ascent of 3400 steps up Mount Magubi took the strongest soldiers about five hours. Many dropped down on a step and were ill where they lay. Stragglers were urged and sometimes ordered on. Potts was irritated by patrol officers based ahead of his force who seemed oddly indifferent to the in-coming troops.

The force reached the attractive village of Menari, set between two mountain ranges along a less problematic section of the Track. The local Koiari people gave the diggers fruit, vegetables and water. At midday on day five of the trek, they were at a clearing of kunai grass at the base of the 1700-metre Mission Ridge. The soldiers were lifted by the feat of reaching this place; the views alone were a reward. Less inviting was the chilly night, but the men sat around camp fires and sang.

They made Efogi, another twelve kilometres along the Track, by 20 August, and met the first of the 39th Battalion's wounded coming the other way. The experience sobered Potts' troops. The injured soldiers looked battered. Some commented that they were thrilled to be on their way out.

The next destination for the incoming digger troops was the Gap, which lay in an alpine zone. A forest of tall trees blocked the sun, allowing moss to grow up the tree trunks before giving way to glowing slime and light-coloured fungi. Here, the forest floor was made up of tangled vines, roots and odd shrubbery, such as tiny ginger plants. Snakes were spotted here and there, but not enough to alarm. The dank and cold environment was brightened by parrots, huge butterflies and magnificent orchids. The roots of massive pandanus trees protruded from the earth nearly two metres high, and had fronds three metres long. Ancient cycads spread their sharp, symmetrical leaves.

The torrential rain kept coming, with more at night when the temperature plummeted. Potts' men reached another prehistoric landmark: the crater at Myola. They were now twenty-five kilometres away from Isurava, where 400 men of the militia contingents were making a stand. Beyond Isurava, the forward troops of a new enemy invading force were absorbing the original small invading contingent into their ranks.

At Myola Potts expected to find ration and ammunition drops, but discovered less than half of his requirements: only four days' food. The ordnance officer there did not even know they were coming. The last drop had been five days earlier. They were short on Tommy guns and .303 ammunition. This was a miserable supply, given that the force was meant to attack the invading Japanese, whose numbers were unknown.

Potts was incensed. The lack of forward planning endangered his men and the mission. On 23 August he signalled Rowell in Port Moresby in the cryptic language of the war cable. It reflected his angry yet controlled mood far better than any face-to-face meeting could: 'Must have 14 days' reserve of rations by 26 August, also 100,000 rounds small arms ammunitions, 3600 four-second grenades, 1000 seven-second grenades, and 2-inch mortars.'[2]

Potts, who that same day was confirmed as commander of Maroubra Force, could not proceed without these supplies. He dispatched an officer south to make the case further to Port Moresby. Rowell was stunned at the demand for equipment and contacted Blamey. Then he wired Potts, telling him not to continue with his mission unless he had his supplies. Rowell ordered the 7th Division's Tubby Allen to airlift four planes full of supply bales and dump them over the Myola lake-bed crater on 24 August.

Potts had only about 900 native carriers – less than half the number he required to retrieve the bales. Scores of locals, not appreciating being pressed into service, had disappeared, unhappy with their pay and conditions. The brutality of the Japanese towards them had also deterred many. The enemy invaders had been inspired by film of the butchery displayed by Japanese soldiers in their attacks on China five years earlier – most notably, but not exclusively, at Nanking. They had emulated these inhumane acts with their own mutilations, beheadings and general savagery in Malaya and Singapore. Now their depravity had reached new lows in Papua.

Along with the lack of carriers, the scattering of the supply bales from the planes meant that seventy per cent were lost. Potts knew that this monumental logistics failure had irreparably damaged his campaign. There was no way he could 'wipe out' the Japanese with his lack of basic resources. His strategy became a defensive one. Potts would not abandon his mission, but now it had to be a powerful stand here and there rather than an all-out assault.

There would be a week's delay in relieving the militia force of the 39th, 49th and 53rd Battalions, which was dug in at Isurava. Had all the supplies been dropped on time, Potts could have achieved this relief in a couple of days; now he had to recover as much of the supplies as possible and protect the exhausted young militia-men, who were defending against the incessant Japanese patrols high in the mountains, Potts knew his best hope was to acquire enough ammunition and food for a strong fight.

Brigadier Potts was set to begin his modified mission late on 25 August. He pushed his 14th and 16th Battalions up the Kokoda Track, towards the black, forbidding and always drenched Templeton's Crossing, with its ever-present stench of decaying vegetation. The diggers had given it the name in deference to Captain Templeton. The region was dark and murky under a soggy 'roof' of tree branches. They moved on up and down steep hills, reaching the most precipitous of all in the deep gorge of Eora Creek. They rested here before the final crawl to Alola and Isurava.

More wounded militia soldiers limped, shuffled and staggered through. Some were on stretchers. Many were emaciated. Most were ill with at least one of the various tropical diseases. One of Potts' men observed, 'There weren't many laughs in these blokes. They looked more spent than an empty gun cartridge.'[3]

The stretchers were laid out in the mud on the banks of the creek. The wounded diggers' blood-soaked bandages were evidence of deep wounds in desperate need of proper medical attention. Morphine was administered until it ran out. The native carriers, themselves fatigued from their long hauls, sat on logs eating rice on banana leaves.

In those moments, Potts realised that he had little hope of overcoming the Japanese. Some of these bedraggled militia-men would have to be used in support. He could not expect too much from them. They had gone well beyond that expected even from his hardened 21st Brigade. Potts decided on a 'fighting withdrawal'. If this was successful, he might just preserve his forces, and it would give him his best chance of defeating the Japanese. If he kept the enemy coming over a longer time, their supplies would be depleted. Then the Japanese would be vulnerable.

On 25 and 26 August, Major General Horii directed a quarter of his 10,000-strong South Seas Force forward to tackle the 39th Battalion and parts of the 49th and 53rd Battalions. The defending Australian contingent was now down to around 400 men.

Horii was a good friend of General Yamashita, whom he admired for his victories over the British in Malaya and Singapore. Horii knew of the success of Yamashita's jungle fighting, with its full-frontal attacks accompanied by stealthy flanking manoeuvres. But Horii's assignment was tougher than Yamashita's. The jungle around Kokoda was more brutal than that of Malaya. And the Australians were prepared to fight, although they were suffering just as much as the invaders.

The longer the campaign took, the worse it became for the Japanese, who had no emergency rations. Both sides were hit by disease and diminishing food supplies. As the hours and days passed, the invaders attacked with more fury, realising, as Yamashita had in Malaya, that their greater enemy was the conditions and lengthening supply lines. The Japanese had either to retreat or break through to take Port Moresby. Backing down was not an option, especially with Imperial High Command in Tokyo setting them a deadline of mid-September.

The Japanese opted for a two-pronged simultaneous attack. Their push through the Owen Stanley Range now began in earnest.

44
Papua: War on Two Fronts

Milne Bay, on Papua's eastern tip, provided the toughest conditions of the Pacific War. It never seemed to stop raining and the sun was seldom seen, but still it was hot. Diggers who had experienced other places in the Middle East, Pacific and Asia regarded the conditions as dreadful. The permanent steam vapours presented a perfect environment for mosquito infestation. Every soldier who set foot in this hell on earth would contract malaria. Few avoided dysentery, and many would pick up other tropical diseases.

The bay itself, a deep-water harbour, was militarily tempting. But the jungle-covered mountains that rose sharply from close to the coast were uninviting. The only relief from them was the unprepossessing small mangrove swamps and narrow marshy tracks. The odd coconut grove was enticing, yet even they were dangerous: soldiers wore helmets to avoid being hit by falling coconuts.

On the moonlit night of 25 August 1942, the Japanese unleashed 2400 amphibious commandos at Milne Bay. This was a vital mission for the Japanese Navy after its massive setback at Midway, especially with the Japanese Army struggling in the Owen Stanley Range. A victory at Milne Bay giving Nippon the ascendancy in New Guinea would restore the Navy's prestige as the pre-eminent arm of the Imperial Forces.

The Japanese intended to take the two Allies-built, steel-matted runways. This would allow their Zeros to attack Port Moresby in support of their invading soldiers in the Owen Stanley Range. Milne Bay would also be a useful base for a more concentrated attack on northern Australia. This remained the aim of the navy and the army, to prevent Australia from becoming an American base.

The Japanese leadership's orders were even more vehement than usual. They demanded that the landing force 'smash', 'strike' and 'destroy' the 'white soldiers without remorse'. But they were stunned by their early encounters with Australian Kittyhawks that were waiting for them, thanks to the intelligence received by the Allies.

In August, Blamey had sent the crack 18th Brigade to Milne Bay, along with the Kittyhawks. The air squadrons were led by the RAAF's resourceful fearless Group Captain Bill 'Bull' Garing. Fresh from Europe, where he had won the Distinguished Flying Cross for his efforts against the Germans, he was not as gung-ho as his nickname suggested. He was a meticulous planner. Once he was in the clouds he inspired his pilots.

Garing and his squadron attacked the Japanese landing barges at Goodenough Island, killing 350 commandos. The following two mornings, the Kittyhawks continued to strafe the barges, sinking some and disabling others. Supplies of food and ammunition were lost. The surviving commandos were forced to trudge along the boggy coast without their naval support.

Australian hopes and expectations were buoyed by action by the United States some 650 kilometres to the east, across the Solomon Sea. Marines had landed at Guadalcanal, Tulagi and Guvuta a month earlier and were in bloody fights to retake the Solomon Islands. This stressed Japan's resources further. They had to give priority to the fight against the Americans, leaving Horii's operations without the supplies they required for a confident thrust through the Owen Stanley Range.

On 26 August 1942, south of Kokoda, the Japanese engaged the outer positions of Maroubra Force. Its militia soldiers of the 39th, 49th and 53rd Battalions had been reinforced that afternoon by an experienced (Middle East) battle-hardened company from the 14th Battalion of the 7th Division. It had come along the unforgiving Kokoda Track from Myola to Isurava and was to relieve the battling 39th. Other companies from the 14th set up at Alola, a few kilometres south of Isurava, and Templeton's Crossing, about ten kilometres north of Myola. The 39th, exhausted and still fighting against the odds, had to stay in the line, side by side with soldiers from the 7th Division, as the Japanese attempted to break through the perimeter of the Australian zone.

Potts' original mission in Papua – to 'wipe out' the enemy – was much easier said than done. The directive from his commanders back in Port Moresby was still based on their incorrect assumptions about Japan's intentions. Even by late August 1942, no one at the top – including MacArthur and Blamey – could believe the enemy would make a serious attempt to take Port Moresby by trekking across the Owen Stanley Range. But every soldier facing the Japanese in the middle of the godforsaken mountains sensed their determination.

Potts pushed the 14th Battalion to Isurava, using the 39th to protect it. He brought the 16th Battalion up from Myola. In the time it took to deploy the 14th, the Japanese were able to build up their forces in the area to 5000 men – half their original landing contingent. The Japanese, as usual, employed their flanking movement. But despite their superior numbers, they had to contend with the stubborn Australian forces.

At dawn on 27 August, the enemy struck hard on the 39th's 'screen', with heavy mortar and mountain-gun fire, followed by assaults that had penetrated the 39th's defensive line by mid-morning. The 14th came into the line and forced the Japanese back by nightfall, so the perimeter was restored. Yet the Japanese were tenacious. They found a soft spot on the right flank guarded by the 53rd; they burst through and around it, and onto an alternative path to the Kokoda route south. They destroyed the Australian positions, killing several senior officers, including the commander, Lieutenant Colonel Kenneth Ward.

These assaults caused a breakdown in communications between the Australian companies, which led to a collapse of coordinated action. The 53rd Battalion broke down. Its militia-men were forced back to the junction in the Track behind Isurava. Then the Japanese seemed to hesitate, and did not crash through south to Aloha. Potts took the chance to plug the gap by bringing up the 16th Battalion.

While Potts' men defended desperately in the Owen Stanley Range, the Japanese played their ace on the northern shore of Milne Bay. On 27 August they landed their light, high-turreted tanks under the cover of darkness.

Cyril Clowes, unperturbed and smoking his pipe as methodically as ever, was in his headquarters near the village of Gila Gila, on the north-western side of Milne Bay. The village was connected by a boggy four-metre-wide track that ran six kilometres along the north coast to Ahioma, where the Japanese had landed. In the two days since their arrival, Clowes had been inundated with messages from MacArthur, exhorting him to 'clear the enemy' from the bay. Silent Cyril kept his counsel and reputation by not replying, which increased tensions in MacArthur's camp. Clowes, in his own laconic way, was gathering any intelligence he could on the enemy numbers before committing his men.

His silence perturbed everyone, even the Australians on the mainland who knew him well. Rowell and Blamey had confidence in him. MacArthur kept pressing. Those under Blamey began to question how much control he had over the Australian Army. MacArthur's bullying directives revealed his deep concerns about a Japanese breakthrough at Milne Bay, which could lead to the fall of New Guinea. If this happened, his many opponents in Washington would have legitimate reason to end his career in the field.

On day three of the invasion, Clowes acted. He directed one of his battalions into a coconut grove at KB Mission, about halfway to the Japanese base. There they met the enemy in the first horrific night encounter near the edge of cliffs that fell down to swamps and sea below. Japan's tanks gave its men a decided advantage. They ran amok through the Australian lines, their bright lights making it easier for the commandos trotting along behind. The diggers countered by throwing anti-tank grenades packed with nitro-glycerine – 'sticky-bombs' – but these were ineffective in the damp conditions.

Hand-to-hand fighting broke out everywhere along the narrow track. Sensing a massacre, the Australian commanders ordered their men back, west along the bay's shore to the Gama River. There, reserve militia units were able to fend off the Japanese, allowing their more experienced AIF comrades to withdraw to relative, if temporary safety.

45
The Fighting Withdrawal

The bloody, terrible Milne Bay battles continued for three days in the mud and incessant rain. Clowes remained incommunicado through this period, building the frustration of the leadership in Port Moresby and Brisbane.

On 29 August, Clowes took his pipe out of his mouth and mumbled a considered order: a further two battalions of the 18th Brigade were to be sent into the fray. At the same time, Japanese positions on the northern shore were strafed incessantly by RAAF planes. This softened the enemy's resistance and caused confusion; the two fresh battalions of diggers, metre by metre in the mud, began to gain the ascendancy.

Meanwhile, more than 300 kilometres away in the Owen Stanley Range, the fighting became even more intense. The Japanese brought in two reserve battalions, believing they held the ascendancy. Potts' combined militia and regular fighting Maroubra Force was outnumbered but not outpointed; they still held the perimeter.

But on 29 August the Japanese became bolder, attacking with six battalions – more than 4000 soldiers. They took possession of ridges above the Australian positions, which allowed them to rain down mortar and machine-gun fire in support of their ground assaults. The Australians had proved up to the task of defending against superior numbers, but this extra firepower gave the Japanese the edge. The defensive perimeter shrank and many diggers were killed.

At this critical moment, one soldier decided to make a move. The 2/14th Battalion's Private Bruce Kingsbury, one of the few survivors of an overrun platoon, volunteered to join a platoon that had been ordered to counter-attack. In the tradition of Albert Jacka of the 1st AIF's 14th Battalion at Gallipoli and the Western Front, Kingsbury dashed forward, firing his Bren gun from the hip into a wall of Japanese machine guns. Against all odds, he managed to blast a path through the stunned enemy.

Kingsbury kept firing, when perhaps he should have stopped riding his luck. He swept through the enemy positions, killing more than twenty Japanese. No one seemed capable of countering his manic rush. It took a shot from a sniper high on a ridge to bring him down.

Kingsbury's action single-handedly had stopped the Japanese; he would gain a posthumous VC. The enemy were shaken and took time to regroup, but their superior numbers and positioning on the ridges began to give them the initiative once more.

Australian casualties increased as their ammunition ran low. Horii was pushed hard by his superiors in Tokyo to crash through on the alternative track. He deployed four companies on the flanks, and close to the rear of the 14th and 39th Battalions. It seemed the Japanese would surround the Australian positions. But Potts pulled back Maroubra Force before it could be liquidated, and made for positions further south. He sent the spent 39th and 53rd Battalions back to Port Moresby.

This would be mere respite for the 39th, which was brought back into the line when the 7th Division's rearguard action came under pressure. The 53rd Militia Battalion was out of favour with Potts for what he perceived as ill-disciplined fighting. Initially, it was reduced to work duties, but it too had to be used to reinforce Maroubra Force against the ever-pressing Japanese advance.

The further south the Australians edged, the less suitable for defence the terrain became. They mounted delaying actions as they eased away through Alola to Eora Creek on 30 August. It took another three days to slide back the eight kilometres to Templeton's Crossing.

Potts and his men were undertaking an orderly retreat, although he did not use that term. He gathered his officers. Yes, they would withdraw – but they would *withdraw fighting*. The diggers would not turn their backs on the enemy; instead, they would back off over the mountain, fighting the Japanese every step of the way.

Potts was intent on stretching the Japanese to the limit. The longer his men could fight, the more they would stretch the enemy's supply lines. Fatigue, disease and the inhospitable terrain, he hoped, would do the rest.

The Australian patrols were given a truncated course in how to fight during a jungle retreat. They were shown how to set up ambushes, and how to draw the enemy into thick forests. The Japanese flanking manoeuvre would not work as well in such rugged country: it would take days instead of hours to surround the Australians. The Japanese would have to stay on the main Kokoda Track or they would probably perish.

The 'fighting withdrawal' brought quick results. An ambush at Eora Creek saw ten Japanese killed and several more wounded. The Australians' guerrilla tactics frightened the Japanese: using the element of surprise had been their method. Now they were under constant tension as they advanced into the unknown. What awaited them around a bend in the Track? Could the Australians be on that next spur, ready to rain down fire and grenades?

The task of maintaining supplies, which had been the Australians' major problem, now confronted the Japanese. The further they advanced towards Port Moresby, the greater the risk that they would run out of ammunition and food. To make this more likely, the Australians employed a 'tainted track' rather than a 'scorched earth' policy as they edged back. Food in dumps would be contaminated, and ammunition would be blown up.

The opposing forces had now been in action for thirty-eight days. The numbers of their sick and wounded mounted. Tropical diseases, with malaria the most malicious, accounted for ten times the number of those injured in battle.

Despite the experience of the Australian Army in the Middle East in both World Wars, doctors in the militia had not encountered malaria. They did not enforce simple disciplines, such as making sure the men wore more than just shorts and short-sleeved shirts at night. The diggers were not strictly ordered to take the daily quinine – which counteracted the effects of malaria – supplied to them.

By now, the Track was busy with Papuan stretcher-bearers – known as the 'Fuzzy Wuzzy Angels' – who carried and helped wounded diggers south towards Port Moresby. Some had been forced into this work, but it was an essential part of the Anzac ethos that no digger was left behind. Japanese patrols mutilated and executed any wounded Australians they came across. They even placed the bodies of diggers in positions that would lead their mates into traps and ambushes. When their supplies were running out, the Japanese had no compunction about eating Australian corpses.

Potts' slow withdrawal towards Efogi created logistical problems for planes dropping supplies on the dry lakebed at Myola, about eight kilometres south of Templeton's Crossing. The difficulty the planes experienced had changed the nature of the campaign. Now Potts believed Myola could not be held. But he knew that if he eased back beyond it, the 14th and 16th Battalions would not reach food and ammunition. This would affect their capacity to carry out orders for three or four days. The planes had to find other areas to dump supplies.

There were minor compensations this far back down the Track. Now they were closer to home bases in the south, the Australian troops could receive hot food at Myola. There was even a change of clothes, clean dressings for the wounded, and the sheer luxury of a chiropodist – a former Victorian window-dresser, Corporal Clark. A dab hand at flamboyant shopfronts, he proved equally diligent over soldiers' rotting feet. His caring manner was appreciated by the battle – and track-weary – men.

Even more pleasing was the mail. Each soldier cherished the moment he ripped open an envelope from a loved one. It made many emotional but also inspired them. Potts tried to meet his men's demands as much as possible.

Commanders Rowell and Allen in Port Moresby were under increasing pressure from MacArthur and Blamey. They, in turn, bullied Potts in the field, asking him to outline his offensive plans when his force had been resupplied. Allen demanded that Myola be held.

Rowell then wired Blamey: 'I have told ALLEN to order POTTS to hold MYOLA at all costs. Every yard the enemy makes increases his own supply difficulties, which we hope to accentuate by air action . . .'[1]

But Potts shook Allen and Rowell with his response: 'Country utterly unsuitable for defended localities. Regret necessity to abandon MYOLA . . . intend withdrawing [to] EFOGI . . . men full of fight but utterly weary . . . remaining companies 2/27 battalion too late to assist.'[2]

Allen ordered Potts to gather supplies and counter-attack, but again Potts could not comply. The Japanese were threatening to outflank his force, and there was no strong defensive position in front of Myola. Potts found it impossible to explain the problems of the formidable terrain. Instead of responding to orders, he asked for the 27th Battalion to be sent as reinforcement, despite his belief that they still would not hold Myola.

Allen was furious but Potts backed his own judgement. He defied orders and kept withdrawing. He edged his men beyond Myola and directed that the supply base be destroyed.

Potts believed that Maroubra Force could make a stand at Mission Ridge. He gathered his dwindling yet still defiant 39th Battalion and repeated his request for the 27th Battalion. Once the 14th and 16th Battalions settled in at Mission Ridge, the addition of the 27th would give him most of 21st Brigade. This would generate some confidence that he could at least resist the ever-advancing Japanese.

46
Marvels at Milne Bay

The Milne Bay conflict continued to disturb the Americans. MacArthur wanted the hardest response possible, believing the Japanese would reinforce their landing within days. Blamey urged Rowell at Port Moresby to move fast and destroy the Japanese force, but he was confident Clowes would do the job. Instead of hovering in Brisbane or even visiting Port Moresby, Blamey flew to Melbourne to be by his wife's side when her father died.

Something akin to panic seeped into MacArthur's headquarters. His deputy, Sutherland, wrote a curt letter to Blamey, ordering him to instruct Clowes 'at once to clear the north shore of Milne Bay without delay'. In Blamey's absence, his deputy, General Vasey, had no choice but to cable Rowell to this effect. But he also wrote privately to Rowell, explaining the Americans' overreaction. It was their first battle in this theatre since their failed experiences in the Philippines, he said, and they were concerned about any direct engagement with the Japanese. 'They are, therefore, like many others, nervous and dwelling on the receipt of frequent messages.'[1]

Rowell was not impressed by these harrying instructions. He replied that a brigade was, at that moment, 'heavily in action' fifty kilometres to the north of him. He was insulted and embittered by the pressure on him 'from a distance'. 'I think it damned unfair to pillory any commander without any knowledge of the conditions,' Rowell wrote back to Vasey. 'It has rained for ten days at Milne Bay and it keeps on raining. I suppose there will be heresy hunts and bowler hats soon.'[2]

Rowell's anger was justified when, after a week's battle, the invaders were pinned down. Victory was an even-money proposition.

While Rowell raged, Clowes stayed cool on the hot and sodden battlefront. He had total confidence in his man in the field, the corpulent Brigadier George Wootten, who was known for his courage and intelligence. He had deployed the two battalion reinforcements that Clowes had delivered him. The critical moment came when a digger perched high in a coconut tree alerted Wootten that a fresh unit of Japanese commandos was jogging along the track at Gama River. The 18th's machine-gunners were hidden in the jungle. Wootten waited until the enemy was within twenty metres, then gave the order to fire. Within six minutes, ninety-two Japanese were killed and about 200 wounded.

This clinical massacre was an important event in the Battle for Milne Bay and should have led to a complete crushing of the enemy. But on the evening of 1 September, Clowes received word from MacArthur that Japanese reinforcements were being landed at Goodenough Bay. They would soon be coming over the mountains to the north of the Australians. 'Expect attack JAP ground forces on Milne aerodromes from West and North-West supported by destroyer fire,' MacArthur wrote. 'Take immediate stations. MACARTHUR.'

Topography was not proving to be the American's strong suit. It had taken him quite a while to appreciate the terrain of the Owen Stanley Range; considering the incessant rain and mosquito plague of the mountains at Milne Bay, they were, in some ways, an even worse proposition. This communiqué, written in MacArthur's usual dramatic and authoritative tone, had to be taken seriously. Clowes had no choice but to put his offensive on hold and wait for the enemy's attack, although his air reconnaissance did not support the Supreme Commander's astonishing claim.

Clowes, Wootten and the diggers turned their weapons to the north and waited. Just before dawn on 2 September, Clowes decided that MacArthur's message was a dud. No enemy reinforcement was coming. The only effective aid the Japanese had that night was from MacArthur himself. Clowes ordered his force to ignore the mountains behind them and continue the push east.

This distraction had hindered the Australians, but Clowes did not complain, knowing there was little point. He would leave the bunfights to Rowell and Blamey. Clowes resolved to ignore further 'urgent' messages from MacArthur in Brisbane, and instead – being a few kilometres from the action and in constant contact with his commanders on the spot – to rely on his own judgement.

By 3 September, the 18th Brigade had pushed east and taken KB Mission. The sadistic enemy actions – evident in the mutilated bodies of natives and Australians – hardened the diggers as they moved through the village.

There was an added vehemence to the way diggers thrust their bayonets into prone Japanese bodies, just in case some were foxing. They would be unlikely to repeat anything like the acts perpetrated on their mates, but when asked to 'stick' bodies, there was less and less hesitation from the diggers as the battles continued.

The fighting continued east of KB Mission, and the diggers' advance seemed more resolute. They gained confidence as they pushed the enemy back, but they also saw more Japanese atrocities. Now, no officers needed to exhort them to aggression.

Typical was the approach of one 27-year-old veteran of Tobruk, John French, a laconic apprentice barber. His boss back in Crows Nest, Queensland, had wished he was more forthcoming with customers. French never engaged in gossip, just going about his clipping and cutting with a hushed concentration. In his new 'profession' of frontline fighting, he was equally unsociable yet reliable.

On 4 September, just off the Track in the jungle near Goroni, a few kilometres east of KB Mission, French was leading a ten-man section that came across a Japanese machine-gun nest of three separate pits. A quick, whispered conference ensued. The diggers wanted to rush the nest, but French shook his head. His reckoning was ruthlessly simple. If the eleven of them charged in, all might be killed. Instead, he himself would try it alone, to minimise the potential losses. Before anyone could protest, he ordered them all to take cover. Then he made his rush with a Tommy gun.

French struck the left-hand pit with two accurate grenades, killing its three-man crew. A shoot-out followed with the middle machine-gunner, who was also killed, along with his crew. French, by now mortally wounded, swung his weapon right and killed the third enemy crew. Then he stumbled forward and fell dead in front of the third gun pit.

His brave actions allowed the Australian struggle to the east to continue. He was awarded a posthumous VC. He and the Kokoda Track battles' Bruce Kingsbury, who was similarly honoured, were the first Australians to be given this most coveted award on home territory.[3]

47
Austerity Campaign

MacArthur and his camp seemed ecstatic about the Australians' ascendancy at Milne Bay. Blamey, back from Melbourne, visited MacArthur and his Bataan Gang. He observed that they acted as if 'they had just won the Battle of Waterloo'.

MacArthur had felt pressured by the Japanese advance in Papua. He could see his dream of beating the US Navy to the Philippines evaporating. First, he had underestimated the enemy's intentions and determination. Then, with the defence undermanned and under-resourced, he panicked, fearing that Roosevelt would replace him if the Japanese took Port Moresby. Even if he claimed the Australians were at fault, two strikes against him in the Philippines and New Guinea would end his career as a military commander. He had already poured opprobrium on the diggers in his communiqués to Roosevelt and the US chiefs in Washington, just in case New Guinea fell.

Blamey was less moved by the gain at Milne Bay. He had been with Monash at Amiens in August 1918, when the Australians had been the prime force in destroying two German armies within forty-eight hours, swinging World War I the Allies' way. That battle had involved 400 tanks, 800 planes, 102,000 diggers from four of Australia's five divisions (with one in reserve), a Canadian corps and a British corps. After Amiens, every battle was small to Blamey.

In World War II, he had experienced the falls of Greece and Crete in 1941, and had overseen Australia's participation in large battles in North Africa and the Middle East. To Blamey, the contest at Milne Bay was significant in the battle for Australia, but it was not the most vital in the context of the two World Wars.

He wrote to Rowell, congratulating him, but criticised the tactics, in effect saying Clowes had been too slow to react, which had prevented him from achieving a complete victory. Blamey didn't seem to have made allowances for MacArthur's misinformed intelligence, which robbed Clowes of a critical twelve hours.

Despite his hard marking, Blamey's calm attitude exemplified the reason for the faith shown in him by three of the nation's greatest leaders: Monash, Menzies and Curtin. Blamey was a womaniser and cavorted with prostitutes. His drinking was excessive, and he was unpopular with the rank and file and many of his senior officers. But this rugged little man had a steadiness under pressure that was vital in a crisis, and crises were frequent in world wars.

Curtin seemed to be responding to Blamey's mood rather than MacArthur's. He pushed for a further 'austerity campaign', intended to cut 'discretionary spending' by one-third. His image as a Scrooge was re-emerging long before Christmas.

It was irritating to the public that the winter football competitions had been emasculated. In Melbourne, the home of Australian rules football, Victorian Football League (VFL) clubs struggled to field teams and had to resort to second-class players. Attendances dipped by sixty per cent. Before 1942, an average of 112,000 fans watched the six matches of a round. In the 1942 season, that average had fallen to 32,500 people. One team, Geelong, which was based eighty kilometres away from Melbourne, was not in the competition due to travel restrictions. The second-tier competition, the Victorian Football Association (VFA), which often drew crowds that challenged VFL numbers, was disbanded. With many of its better players fighting overseas, the VFL suspended the awarding of the most coveted award of all Australian sport, the Brownlow Medal.[1]

By early September 1942, several sports grounds had been taken over by the military and other 'essential services'. The Melbourne Cricket Ground, along with the St Kilda, South Melbourne and Footscray ovals, had become either service camps or depots.

Curtin was urging restraint very much against his own instincts, but he had the aid of killjoys such as McLaughlin. The prime minister was undergoing a personal realignment. He wanted the nation to follow him into a kind of socialism that denied it capitalist 'goodies', and disdained 'conspicuous' or unnecessary consumption.

McLaughlin and others were trying to make him more spiritual. They had moved him from agnosticism back to a qualified sense of a religious belief. But he vacillated, almost as if he were having an each-way bet on the existence of a supernatural being. He would pray with McLaughlin at moments of extreme crisis. When events seemed to move his way after prayer, it gave him pause. Yet he was a reluctant re-convert.

Curtin would not return to Catholicism, as such. He flirted with the less flamboyant Presbyterianism, which seemed to fit the austerity of the times, but he remained less than convinced. Somehow, real socialism seemed to him to be at odds with the existence of an all-powerful deity. He was happier when aspects of Christianity – such as helping the poor and unemployed, or looking after the aged and infirm – aligned with his political beliefs.

In promoting his 'austerity campaign', Curtin wanted more than simple austerity. He wished to make Australian society more selfless, in line with his socialist ideals. In the rarefied atmosphere of a war that threatened Australia's existence, he did not simply hope to install socialism; he would move to legislate for it.

The two battles for Papua caused Curtin to renew his appeals to Churchill and Roosevelt for additional aircraft, a greater naval presence and even more soldiers. Churchill filibustered, having little or no interest in Australia's plight. He capitulated after a long, hard fight with Evatt in London over the sending of forty-eight Spitfires to Australia, but this was as far as he and his War Cabinet seemed prepared to go. Travelling to Australia by sea, the planes had passed the Cape of Good Hope and were expected by late September. The 700 personnel who would operate them – two-thirds Australian, one-third British – were already in Sydney. The Spitfires could reach a speed of 400 miles per hour. They had cannons and were fitted with special tanks for the tropics.

The Americans were even less forthcoming. President Roosevelt dispensed sympathy but nothing more. He was going all the way with Winston in Europe to defeat the Nazis. Roosevelt reckoned that Australia now had enough military strength to fend off a Japanese army of 200,000 troops.

Curtin realised that he 'could not moan to Roosevelt'.[2] But he felt he could whine, complain and grumble to the mother country and its great chief, Churchill. Curtin told a secret session of parliament that no MPs should criticise any military operation that reflected poorly on MacArthur, the Supreme Commander to whom Curtin had turned over the safety of Australia. Curtin didn't want the American and his staff upset or restricted.

48
Potts' Last Stand

By early September 1942, Potts had fewer than 475 fit men and was about to send the 39th Battalion to join the 53rd back in Port Moresby. More than half of these young militia-men were spent and unfit for battle.

This lack of manpower was justification for Potts disobeying orders and carrying out his battle-by-battle retreat. A stand at Myola would have left the Australians outnumbered more than six to one. Instead, by planning to fall back painstakingly, he was preserving his men and frustrating the enemy's efforts to burst through to Port Moresby.

Major General Tubby Allen was satisfied that the Japanese had been contained at Milne Bay. This allowed him at last to meet Potts' plea for the release of the 27th Battalion from the reserve division at Port Moresby. The 27th joined Maroubra Force at Kagi, three kilometres west of Myola, near Mission Ridge, on 4 September, allowing the 39th finally to withdraw.

These militia youth had given everything in their war initiation, which was as exacting as anything in history, considering the enemy, the conditions and terrain. Their 'gift' to the incoming 27th Battalion was a supply of automatic weapons and a heartfelt wish of good luck. By the next day, the 39th was twelve kilometres south, at Efogi, about seventy-five kilometres from Port Moresby. At the same time, the 14th and 16th Battalions regrouped at Kagi.

As Potts was withdrawing to Efogi to meet the long-awaited 27th Battalion, Major General Horii and more than 3000 Japanese descended on the abandoned Myola. Hungry and undernourished, they gorged on the contaminated rations left by the Australians. Many spent days stricken by diarrhoea.

Allen continued to demand that Potts concede no further ground and counter-attack. Potts threw the cables away. He would fight *his* way and ignore his superiors, who had no real appreciation of the battlefield conditions.

On 6 September, Potts had all three battalions – the 14th, 16th and 27th – at Mission Ridge. They then crept forward to Brigade Hill – a hilltop straddling the Kokoda Track which Potts named for the amalgamation of the three Australian battalions – and waited for the oncoming Japanese.

At the same time, the Japanese landed several thousand more troops, supplies and equipment at Gona, on the northern coast. With their forces bolstered, they set 1000 soldiers for an assault on the Australians' position at Mission Ridge.

Potts and his men observed lights of the advancing Japanese force, which was marching from Myola to Efogi, at 6.30 p.m. on the evening of 6 September. The lights were visible until 2 a.m. on the morning of 7 September.

Potts alerted Port Moresby. He requested that the enemy lines be hit from the air as hard as possible at first light. Eight bombers and four Kittyhawks met the demand at dawn, swooping low over the Track and forcing the Japanese to dive for cover from strafing and falling bombs. The attacks killed about 100 of the invaders, but this was not enough to stop them. They began to move again, under cover of more jungle.

MacArthur was alarmed by the fall of Myola. This was a critical time: Port Moresby seemed likely to be captured. Attempting to pre-empt the blame he would be given by Washington, he cabled

General Marshall: 'The Australians have proved themselves unable to match the enemy in jungle fighting. Aggressive leadership is lacking.'

The pressure on Rowell intensified when Brisbane called for him to 'energise combat action'. Vasey, in charge of Australian command while Blamey was away interstate at a troop inspection, was almost apologetic in his transmission to Rowell. MacArthur, he wrote, disagreed with Potts' tactic of withdrawal. Offensive action was urged.

The weight of all the commanders above him was now on the shoulders of Brigadier Arnold Potts. If things went wrong, he would suffer opprobrium for his common sense, courage and concern for his men. He would be held accountable for the High Command's lack of foresight over Japan's intentions, comprehension of the terrain, and competence.

Potts liked Brigade Hill as a defensive position. However, it would only be of use if he deployed his men with skill. Potts was at the top of Mission Ridge, four kilometres south of Efogi. He perched himself in the 'dress circle', on a knoll at the southern end of the hill.

Looking west, Potts could see a tight forest on a steep cliff, although it was not much more precipitous than the other approaches. He judged that the Japanese would not attack from there, although it was wise not to make assumptions about this relentless and unpredictable enemy, which rarely seemed bothered by the terrain. The Japanese commanders often asked their soldiers to do the near impossible. Potts was more concerned about positions to the north. At a clearing two kilometres away there was a former Christian mission. There was thick jungle to the east, which not even the Japanese could struggle through.

He distributed his limited troops as best he could in the foothills facing Efogi. He had three brigade positions plus his headquarters, which meant there could be communications problems if the Japanese discovered his telephone lines.

Allen sent a liaison officer forward from Port Moresby to report on the fighting conditions faced by Potts, which until now he had not comprehended. Officially, Allen was not allowed to go forward himself to make assessments, because he was responsible for Port Moresby. But he had made no efforts to persuade his superiors that he should go to the front to make his own judgement.

At 4 a.m. on 8 September, the Japanese made their thrust up from the valley, using machetes to cut their way. Their always chilling cries of 'Aussie, you die!' split the night air. The Australians answered with rifle and machine-gun fire. Grenades were hurled but in the dark most were ill-directed.

The rowdy frontal attack was a decoy by Horii. He had also sent ninety men with one Juki machine gun up the unguarded western cliff. They slashed their way forward, with the cacophony of the frontal attack covering them. It took them eleven hours.

The Japanese reached the summit, close to Potts' headquarters, at 5.30 a.m., exposing his failure to guard that approach. The enemy cut the defenders' phone lines. Potts and his staff had no idea they were there until a sentry was shot dead. The bullet may well have been meant for Potts, who was returning from a quick visit to a latrine. He rushed back just as the Japanese swarmed onto the summit.

The solitary Japanese machine-gunner, either by intelligence or luck, was positioned between Potts' headquarters and the rear guard of the 16th Battalion, to the north. There was no time to think: Potts' staff had to act or die. Cooks, batmen, signallers and clerks grabbed rifles, revolvers and grenades and rushed at the enemy, less than a cricket pitch away.

As dawn broke, the machine-gunner could discern human shapes. His weapon spat bullets, killing some Australians and forcing the rest of the staff members to retreat. The Japanese gunner crew, supported by snipers, soon cut off Potts and his staff from the diggers to the north of them, who were fighting the fierce onslaught of the decoy.

The forward Australians rushed back to support their headquarters but could not break through. The defence had been severed in two and the battalions surrounded. Some attacked the machine-gunner but, in the early-morning light, they were easy targets as they rushed from the jungle. About forty Australians were cut down.

Now Maroubra Force had fewer than 350 fit men and was encircled. The diggers could either wait for the inevitable massacre, when the further 5000 Japanese arrived from Efogi, or disband and run for thick forest and jungle east of Mission Ridge. They decided on the latter, although – in the Anzac tradition – they first went to the aid of the wounded, leaving no one who was alive on the Track.

This breakdown of Maroubra Force encouraged the Japanese to attempt to liquidate the diggers. They pursued them into the jungle. But they met with strong resistance from the 27th Battalion's B and D Companies, which had pushed deep into the jungle off the Track. After some close and brutal fighting, the Japanese themselves were running out of supplies. They were forced to back off.

As his men disappeared into the jungle, Potts led what remained of his staff and about forty soldiers back down the Track to Menari. No longer could he claim it was a 'fighting withdrawal'. The Japanese had secured a definite victory at Brigade Hill and Efogi, but at a cost. They had killed seventy-five Australians and wounded about the same number, yet had incurred around 200 killed and 150 wounded.

Early on 9 September, Potts managed to report the rout to Port Moresby. Rowell's immediate reaction was to bemoan his own lack of fortune. But he recovered his composure and maintained, as he always had, that the Japanese would not take Port Moresby. He based this prophecy on the continuing Japanese supply problems. How, he asked, could the enemy keep a sizeable force fed and equipped with weapons and medicine so far from its northern base of Gona? Yet it chilled Rowell to consider that they had reached this far against the odds and without adequate air drops. He knew that making Port Moresby was now at least a possibility.

Rowell belatedly relieved Allen of his responsibility for Port Moresby's defence, allowing Allen to move his headquarters to the village of Uberi on the Kokoda Track. Rowell had the unenviable task of letting MacArthur in Brisbane know of the Brigade Hill/Efogi debacle. He braced himself for the inevitable reaction.

Major General Horii was now more confident than ever about taking Moresby. He still had more than 4000 fit men. They were being fed on victory after a prolonged fight. Many of the commandos had been in China, Thailand and Singapore, but none had faced such a difficult mission. After the Australians' collapse at Efogi and Brigade Hill, however, they had the will to go all the way. Only the supply line problem and events elsewhere would dictate whether or not Horii would attain his goal.

49
Rout of Maroubra Force

Maroubra Force was reduced to little more than a scattered rabble as the fatigued and defeated soldiers, some wounded, struggled to Menari. This village was a relative paradise. There was food, including chocolate and tobacco, along with fresh clothes and new boots. The diggers' spirits lifted as they fed on the supplies that they had needed weeks before.

But the nirvana would be short-lived. Word raced down the Track that the Japanese were coming again. The remnants of Maroubra Force departed in a hurry, some heading into the jungle. Potts' 'fighting withdrawal' was now a full-scale retreat. More than 300 men of the 14th and 16th Battalions, who had scattered at Efogi, had to hack their way wide of the Track and slip into Menari, where they met up with Potts and his staff late on the morning of 9 September. The men were all ill, and had swollen and diseased feet.

Potts still worried about the 27th Battalion, which had yet to appear. He had no choice but to hasten south without it. Ten kilometres on, he reached Nauro and received an abrupt message. He had to report to Rowell post haste.

The 'blame game' – which Alan Reid dubbed the 'Blamey game' – now began. Rowell met Potts late on 9 September and 'relieved' him, insisting that he was not being replaced. The next day, Brigadier Selwyn Porter took over Maroubra Force. Potts was then promised command of 21st Brigade.

Potts had proved himself a fine battle commander under the most adverse conditions. But he'd made 'fatal' errors in the disposition of his troops' defences at Brigade Hill and Efogi. These left him exposed to the culpability for the failure to hold back the Japanese. It was unfortunate for him that, at the most critical of times in the conflict, he had been the last link in the chain of command. Roosevelt was always a tacit threat to MacArthur. Curtin, MacArthur and his staff, who lacked initiative, in turn put pressure on Blamey. Blamey attacked Rowell. Rowell felt compelled to 'score' off someone, and it was Potts. Nevertheless, his 'dismissal' was a soft one, given his shift to command of the 21st Brigade.

Potts was grilled in a tough debrief by Rowell and Allen. He responded with the integrity and tenacity he displayed as a commander, estimating that the Japanese outnumbered his men by five or six to one. Despite this, Maroubra Force, by his reckoning, had killed four times more than the Japanese. Potts conceded that the enemy was better camouflaged and better trained, which had led to the Australians being pushed back along the Track. Rowell agreed. While not discussed at this meeting, it was tacitly understood (and later admitted) that the supply fiasco had been a blunder by headquarters and had nothing to do with Potts.

Allen would later summarise Potts' contribution to the Papua campaign by saying that he had saved Port Moresby from invasion by a numerically superior force. He had, Allen said, 'prevented the catastrophe nearly brought about by the neglect of New Guinea by the authorities . . .'[1]

The term 'authorities' could be usefully broad in meaning, but given that Blamey had not been in charge until six months earlier, this had to indicate the current and previous governments, and the heads of the military. Very soon after his initial service, Potts was judged by his immediate superiors as one of the most important commanders of the Pacific War. Yet his inadequate tactics at Brigade

Hill had left him open to criticism. Whichever way it was viewed or perceived, the withdrawal was a fiasco.

Potts' successor, Selwyn Porter, was told by the Maroubra Force doctor that his men were not yet fit to fight again. Their lack of food and vitamins had weakened them. Porter was sceptical of medical opinion but realised that the reorganised contingent – now combined as one battalion – would be slaughtered by the Japanese, who now outnumbered them by ten to one. Porter ordered them to fall back further south, to Maguli River.

The fight at Milne Bay was over after a fortnight into September. Clowes lost sixty killed and around 300 wounded. The Japanese lost 700 killed and 1000 wounded. The battle was the first in which a Japanese amphibious force had been rebuffed after it had established a beachhead. The downside was the discovery, after the battle, of captured diggers' bodies. They had been 'tortured and obscenely mutilated'.[2] This barbarity showed that the enemy was just as brutal and committed as ever.

By early September 1942, the setbacks Japan had suffered – large and small, from Midway to Milne Bay – as well as the generally stronger resistance of the Allies, had modified attitudes to the Pacific War. The Japanese were still feared and respected as fanatical fighters, but their aura of invincibility – established by their first thrusts into the Pacific and South-East Asia in December 1941 – was not what it had been.

Yet the Japanese kept coming through the Owen Stanley Range. Anger and accusations from MacArthur and Blamey gave way to concern and even panic in Port Moresby, as reports of Japan's persistence continued to arrive. The Australians' latest defensive position was just fifty kilometres from Port Moresby. It seemed nothing could stop the enemy.

News of the withdrawals along the Track upset the politicians in Canberra. Percy Spender and Billy Hughes, members of the Advisory War Council, criticised the conduct of the campaign. Menzies suggested that Blamey should visit Papua.

Curtin called together reporters for one of his confidential briefings and passed on the United States' concerns (from MacArthur and his staff) about the fighting in Papua. MacArthur said that the 'allied' – read 'Australian' – forces had been 'out-generalled and out-manoeuvred'. But he still believed the Japanese could be stopped. MacArthur planned to send an American regiment to Papua. It was claimed that it would cross the mountains east of the Kokoda Track and 'liquidate' the Japanese on the other side.

By passing on this fanciful MacArthurite hyperbole, Curtin showed his own naivety and ignorance about the state of play to his north, and about the standard of the American troops.[3]

Brigadier Porter somehow rallied the depleted 21st Brigade when it reached Ioribaiwa. He organised them into counter units, planning ambushes and guerrilla tactics that might hold the enemy. Their morale was boosted on 11 September, when reinforcements arrived and took up a position on a ridge to their right.

Members of the 39th Militia Battalion, which had briefly been rested, were back in action with the 6th Independent Company, under the command of Lieutenant Colonel Ralph Honner. At thirty-eight, he was a cultured, broadly educated man, similar both to Monash and one of Monash's World War I divisional generals, Charles Rosenthal. Born in Fremantle, Honner was a lawyer and qualified schoolteacher. He loved literature and could quote Shakespeare or the Bible for any occasion, and had played for Claremont in the West Australian Football League. Honner took command of C Company in the 2/11th Battalion and fought at Bardia, Tobruk and Derna, before being sent to Greece. He led his diggers in a series of battles as the Australians withdrew in the face of superior German forces. This earned him a Military Cross.

Honner's mission in the Papuan mountains was to attack Japanese supply lines in a seven-kilometre section of the Kokoda Track between

Menari and Nauro. Patrols were also taking part along the Goldie River, running south-west of the Track towards Port Moresby.

On 12 September the Japanese, having regrouped, rained down a heavy mortar attack on the Australian positions. They also sent out patrols to probe for weak spots in the defensive lines. They were preparing for a mighty assault.

50
Last Razorback Stand

Blamey slipped into Port Moresby on 13 September 1942. He didn't think his presence was warranted. He knew Rowell would be hostile to him, believing his appearance was a vote of no confidence in the way the battles were being run. But everything seemed to proceed amicably when the two visited 7th Division headquarters. Blamey told the press who had accompanied him that Moresby was in no danger: 'I think we shall find that the Japs will be beaten by their own advance with its attendant problems of supply . . . It will be a Japanese advance to disaster; an Australian advance to victory.'[1]

In saying this, Blamey was going on Rowell's assessment and confidence. Rowell still scoffed at talk of capitulation. The reinforcements would stop the enemy, he said. As he was conferring with Blamey, heavy Australian artillery was being winched up the steep wooden staircase to the top of Imita Ridge, about 1.5 kilometres south of Ioribaiwa. Amidst all the private gloom at MacArthur's headquarters, and in Canberra, Blamey's statement maintained Australia's characteristic 'we'll muddle through' mentality.

Blamey's public image was strong, despite his unpopularity among those in the military and Canberra, and most of the press. His attitude to the war in Papua did not help his image with these groups when he ignored Chester Wilmot's suggestion that the diggers were wearing the wrong camouflage – khaki instead of green. Khaki had been designed in India for jungle conditions, and Blamey said he had 'no evidence' that the New Guinea and Papua jungle was any different to that of India. In fact, Blamey had not been in either jungle. Allen privately commented later that Blamey, in this instance, had 'exhibited apathy, ignorance and not the keenness to find out'.[2]

Ralph Honner was pulled off the battlefield to report to Blamey. He too was unimpressed by the Allied Land Forces Commander's attitude. Sydney's *Daily Telegraph* published the conversation, as told to it by Honner.

'Good morning, Honner,' Blamey had said. 'You've just arrived from Australia, haven't you?'

'No, sir,' Honner replied. 'I've been in Papua for some time.'[3]

Honner believed Blamey hadn't known who he was, and hadn't cared about him or his 39th Battalion, whose men were then 'fighting for their lives' at Ioribaiwa.[4] In fact, Blamey did know who he was. Everyone knew of the brave Ralph Honner, one of the inspiring men of Maroubra Force. But Blamey always saved his enthusiasm for people who were important to him and his position, such as Curtin and other key politicians. To others, including diligent reporters such as Wilmot, he often appeared listless and careless.

Blamey had contempt for Arnold Potts and all but ignored the much-respected commander. The feeling was mutual. On one occasion they did speak, Potts found him difficult to communicate with. Blamey pulled rank with 'savage criticism', butting in when Potts voiced a comment or opinion.[5]

On the night of 13 September, the battered rump of the 21st Brigade was replaced by the 3rd Militia Battalion and three fresh battalions from the 25th Brigade, commanded by the resourceful, resilient and strong Brigadier Ken Eather, known to his men as 'Chloroform'. By coincidence rather than design, the men of this contingent were clad in green, demonstrating further how out-of-touch Blamey was with conditions in Papua and New Guinea. Some had dyed their own uniforms, not altogether satisfactorily. The traditional look of the digger – complete with slouch hat – was transforming into that of the American GI, with helmets and knee-length gaiters. This gear was more sensible and safer.

A second important Anzac tradition was dumped just before the replacement force went into battle. Now, if a man was wounded he would have to find his own way back to safety. Too many diggers were being killed in enemy ambushes while going to the aid of injured mates.

This new dictum stripped away the comfort of having such back-up. An important shield, in the digger's mind, had been removed. The Australians grumbled in private about the new directive. Many said they would ignore such an inept doctrine – which would also, in a way, be upholding the Anzac tradition.

On 14 September, Japan's strategy was complicated by its decision to retake Guadalcanal from the Americans. But the attempt was unsuccessful, with Japanese casualties outnumbering those of their American opponents by eight to one. This defeat precipitated an emergency meeting at Imperial General Headquarters in Tokyo. The generals decided that Guadalcanal and its airfield, Henderson Field, were essential to the success of their operations in the South Pacific. They would divert resources from New Guinea to Guadalcanal, at the expense of Major General Horii's campaign.

Orders were sent to him. He had to be ready to withdraw his force north, back to the Buna–Gona beachheads. This shocked Horii. He had driven his men forward by using a mixture of intimidation and inspiration, but it had always been in the name of the Emperor. Now he had to order them to reverse.

He could not simply gather his army and withdraw. Before Horii could carry out this new order successfully he had to counter renewed attacks from a revitalised and reinforced Australian outfit.

The battle at Ioribaiwa began well for the Australians. They set ambushes for the Japanese, whose supplies of food were diminishing by the day. Bully-beef tins were set up on a creek bank, as if they had been abandoned. Forty Japanese, having spotted the food, crept down to the bank. As they reached the tins, the Australian Bren guns spat a wall of bullets at them, killing twenty and causing the rest to flee.

Late on 14 September, a thunderstorm struck, bringing rain so strong that it was impossible to see more than a few metres. When the torrent eased, the Japanese decided it was the moment to take revenge for the creek bank incident. Forty-five enemy soldiers charged up the ridge, their movements visible only in the sporadic lightning bursts. About half the Japanese soldiers were cut down. The rest made it to the top of the ridge in the east, which gave them a vantage point from which to fire on the defending diggers. This allowed another Japanese platoon to fight their way onto the ridge.

Many of the defenders were at breaking point, risking physical and mental breakdown. Brigadier Eather heard the reports and noted the state of his force. Rather than risk being overrun, he moved his 25th Brigade back to Imita Ridge, the last razorback in the Owen Stanley Range before Port Moresby. Eather argued to Allen, his brigade commander, that this gave his contingent a better defensive position; Allen agreed. But Eather wasn't fooling anyone in Moresby, least of all Rowell. He wanted to know why the well-reinforced Australians had been knocked off Ioribaiwa Ridge. Eather said he wanted more time to consolidate and blend his new force.

'There won't be any further withdrawal from the Imita position, Ken,' Rowell informed him. 'You'll die there if necessary. You understand that?'

'Yes,' Eather replied. With firmness, he added, 'I understand that.'[6]

The 25th Brigade and its militia back-up dug in, supported by the 3rd and 21st Pioneer Battalions. Rowell and Allen were now deeply concerned. They sent up the 16th Brigade to further bolster the final fall-back to Imita Ridge.

The Japanese were ecstatic at having taken Ioribaiwa Ridge. They could now see Port Moresby's lights and the moonlit Coral Sea, which was a mere forty kilometres away. No more razorback ridges or mountains blocked their view. It was a big moment for officers and soldiers alike. Their mission had become compulsive. It seemed they would reach the final destination. Some wept with joy; others sang, 'Long live the Emperor!'

General Horii had a quandary. He knew that unless there was a quick breakthrough, he would have to let his loyal troops down and withdraw back over the terrible Owen Stanley Range. He had just 1500 fit men, a quarter of his force. Crucially, he knew that the Australians, although he had pushed them back again, were still being reinforced with fresh supplies and men.

51
'Canberra's Lost It'

The Australians' forced retreat to Imita Ridge was unknown to Blamey as he flew out of Moresby after his time with Rowell. In Brisbane on 14 September 1942, he confirmed that the 6th Division's headquarters would move to Port Moresby – with Vasey as its commander. This was a clear indication that the defence was being shored up for a final stand against the enemy.

The next day, 15 September, Blamey made a national radio broadcast. Late that night he was apprised of the problem at Ioribaiwa, but he still repeated his view of two days earlier – that he was 'fully confident' the Japanese would be defeated. He had 'full confidence' in Rowell.

On 16 September, the day Ioribaiwa was taken over completely by the Japanese, the newspapers reported Blamey's upbeat remarks in full. This sent a propaganda message to the Japanese, putting further pressure on them as they fought tough battles on two fronts – in the Owen Stanleys and on Guadalcanal. It would have appeared to the Japanese that Australia was going to fight to its last soldier.

Given the drawn-out battle in Papua, which had gone on far longer that the Japanese believed it would, Blamey's tough demeanour and strong delivery meant something. He may have been disliked by many in his own force for his unprincipled behaviour and his bullying, but this was what the Japanese expected in their own commanders. His solidity and certitude would have given the Imperial Japanese Army no joy.

But had they been privy to the mindset at the US headquarters in Brisbane, the Japanese may have felt differently. MacArthur's air commander, General George Kenney, reported to him that he thought Moresby would fall if 'something did not happen soon'. He believed Rowell had become defeatist.

Yet Kenny was relying on hearsay. He had never met Rowell, a commander under siege as the Japanese advanced towards him. Rowell was a realist and straight-shooter, not someone to say only what his superiors wished to hear.

MacArthur, in turn, told the US Eighth Army's commander, General Robert L. Eichelberger, that the Australian High Command 'won't fight'.[1]

The Australians and the Americans viewed the Owen Stanley Range conflict through different prisms. Blamey never seemed to panic. MacArthur, in private, was in high anxiety and looking for someone to blame. Yet both men had much to lose if the Japanese reached Port Moresby.

Blamey continued his bolstering in different forums, both publicly and privately. On 17 September he addressed an anxious Advisory War Council and repeated his view that the Japanese would not reach their goal. Billy Hughes and Jack Beasley, the Minister for Supply and Development, were hostile. They peppered Blamey with questions about supply. How had the Japanese supply lines worked? And why hadn't those of the Australians? Why did the enemy seem to be adept tactically when the 'Allies' appeared without a plan for the fighting in the New Guinea and Papua terrain?

Unlike MacArthur, Blamey refused to blame anyone in the field. Instead, he referred to 'Army Headquarters' as the culprit, leaving interpretation to others, but without indicating that MacArthur and the Bataan Gang had shortcomings. He did point out that when he returned to Australia just six months earlier, there had only been untrained militia in New Guinea: the defence had been grossly undermanned. Now that most of the AIF was back home, a stronger, fully trained and equipped force could enter the fray.

John 'Black Jack' McEwen chimed in about his two visits to Port Moresby, suggesting that Rowell only had plans to defend the port. He wanted to know if the defence was still being built up with picks and shovels.

Blamey suggested McEwen was out of touch. Motor transport could now travel sixty-five kilometres from Port Moresby. Mechanical devices were being used to haul artillery to the top of ridges. At the time of the meeting, fifty Australian sappers were using an ingenious pulley system to haul the first artillery piece up to the top of Imita Ridge, via more than 2000 steps – the 'Golden Staircase' – which ran almost perpendicular up the mountainside. The wooden steps were two feet high, and the weapon would take a week to reach the summit.

Curtin had remained quiet during the vigorous, sometimes aggressive questioning of the Land Forces Commander. Blamey could look after himself, yet Curtin detected the pressure on him. He stepped in to placate the council, telling Blamey that he should not feel that he was being made responsible for mistakes and miscalculations of previous commanders. Curtin may have been tempted to say 'politicians' as well, for until now Australia had been left without a proper defence.

Blamey reiterated that his commanders were confident of winning in New Guinea and Papua. Menzies also came to Blamey's defence, saying he had faith in Rowell and the other commanders in Papua.[2]

After the meeting broke up, an angry Beasley approached Curtin. 'Moresby is going to fall,' he said. 'Send Blamey up there and let him fall with it!'[3]

That night, Curtin met his press 'pals' for the usual confidential briefing. Indirectly, he indicated that Beasley and Hughes had been hostile and that there had been a 'bit of a row' between them and Blamey. But while the Australian commanders came in for criticism, MacArthur was left unscathed. The prime minister pointed out to the journalists that Blamey had assured the council that the American must remain above criticism. Curtin's emphasis on protecting MacArthur indicated again how much he was relying on the goodwill of the Americans.

MacArthur's delicate nature was even more apparent later that night during a phone call with Curtin. He was more nervous about the Australian withdrawal than ever.

MacArthur had received the news of the further move from Ioribaiwa to Imita Ridge, which had been put to him as a retreat rather than a move to a more defensible position. MacArthur complained that the Australians were pulling back while the Japanese were not. This was accurate. But had MacArthur himself taken a trip north to see the situation, he may have been less concerned: Imita Ridge was a much better place from which to repulse the enemy. But he hated flying and he had no real desire to visit the front.

Not comprehending the situation fully, MacArthur dwelled on the enemy's problems of supply. Surely, he said to Curtin, these were worse for the Japanese than for the Australians? Curtin put Blamey's more positive attitude to MacArthur, who conceded that the Australian commander might be correct. But still he felt uneasy. He urged Curtin to send Blamey back to Papua for a prolonged period. This was not just to 'energise' the situation but to save himself. If Papua became worse, MacArthur said, it would be tough for Blamey 'to meet his responsibility to the Australian public'.[4]

This was a debatable extension of MacArthur's powers. His urgency, as ever, was caused by his desire to reach the Philippines before his rivals in the US Navy. This put pressure on Blamey, who had no such adversaries in the Australian Navy and whose prime focus was on defending Australia from the Japanese.

MacArthur, perhaps more able as a politician than a military commander, was attributing all possible blame to the Australian command if things were to go wrong. But this further reflected his own insecurity about the fall of Papua and New Guinea. President Roosevelt, in far-off Washington DC, would always see the loss of Port Moresby as MacArthur's failure not Blamey's. Nevertheless, a further visit to Port Moresby by Australia's top soldier might galvanise his officers and the rank and file, even if some hated his presence, at this most critical moment of the war in Papua.

Curtin bowed to MacArthur's expertise. He phoned Blamey and ordered him back to Papua just three days after he'd been there. Blamey did not argue, but he felt it would be seen as a lack of confidence in the field commanders, particularly Rowell. He tried to reassure Curtin that Port Moresby would not fall. But the prime minister was being swayed by others as well. (Later, Curtin would admit that he was wrong to presume that a commander in chief had to be close to the battlefield. He realised that he'd had no idea of the disruption, interference and lack of confidence this would cause competent field commanders such as Rowell and Allen.)

After the War Advisory Council meeting and his phone 'discussion' with Curtin, Blamey was amazed at the panic in the nation's capital. 'Canberra's lost it,' he told a staff officer.[5]

52
Horii's Horrible Dilemma

Anxiety deepened in Canberra and Brisbane, although this was not obvious in Curtin's background press briefings. On 21 September 1942, however, he evinced a heightened alertness. In a general review of Australia's position, he said, 'We have learned to use aircraft as "flying artillery" to be widely dispersed on the ground and concentrated against targets.' Dozens of landing strips and aerodromes had been built in the north to accommodate heavy bombers. Curtin made the point that the defence of Sydney and Port Kembla, south of Wollongong, was really being achieved north of Marlborough, Queensland. This was the reason that £14 million was being spent so quickly there, and to protect the supply routes to Darwin.

'There was a catch,' Curtin told the journalists.

The Japs may discover that they could make an attempt to take Australia from Timor and Java, instead of from New Guinea. That would bring them down the West coast. They might base on the Kimberleys and cross overland. We would need an armoured division. They may bypass Perth and come diagonally across in this direction [towards Canberra]. On the other hand, they might be satisfied to take Western Australia because it is good country. That would make the Indian Ocean as unsafe as the Pacific. That is one reason why Madagascar was important to the Japs. Submarines based there or in Western Australia would allow them to menace all the [Allied] supplies bound for the Middle East, Burma and India. Darwin could be attacked successfully from Port Hedland or Broome.[1]

Curtin's comments demonstrated MacArthur's uncertainty, which he had transmitted to Curtin; he had yet to sway the tough-minded and more experienced Blamey. Curtin rounded up his briefing by telling his audience that he was 'profoundly disturbed'. This explained, in part, his speculation about possible Japanese invasions, which he had not yet mentioned to his loyal confidants in the press.

Blamey was more concerned with the here and now in New Guinea. The fresh soldiers of the 25th Brigade had held firm at Imita Ridge between 17 and 20 September 1942, fighting off a desperate enemy. On 21 September, the 14th Field Regiment struggled forward on the Track with 25-pound mortars. Patrols began to move forward of Imita Ridge – a precursor to the launching of the 25th Brigade's counter-attack.

Horii surprised his troops by ordering them to dig in at Ioribaiwa rather than make further attacks on Imita Ridge. With withdrawal on his mind, the problem lay in his long supply line from Gona. It had broken down, thanks in part to attacks by the diggers between Menari and Nauro, further north on the Track. The Japanese troops would soon be out of food and ammunition.

Horii knew he should be planning to retreat but he was still tempted to take Port Moresby. His men had come so far and achieved so much, and he had sacrificed seventy-five per cent of his hitherto unstoppable army. Very much on his mind was the 'intelligence' extracted from Captain Templeton early in August: that there were

20,000 Americans, Australians and Indians defending Port Morseby. In fact, there were no more than 3000 Australians. Horii feared his army could well be destroyed, but the thought of giving up now was agonising.

Blamey dallied over his return to Port Moresby. He met with MacArthur in Brisbane on 19 September and learnt that the American planned to dispatch the 32nd Division east of the Kokoda Track for an attack on Buna, over the mountains. It was a sign of MacArthur's impatience that Maroubra Force had not managed to defeat the Japanese or drive them back.

On 22 September, Curtin learned that Blamey had still not gone to Papua. 'General Blamey, I thought that you had gone,' Curtin said to him on the phone. 'If you value your position, you will not remain in Brisbane another day!'[2]

Blamey obeyed the prime minister's directive, aware that he had been out-manoeuvred by MacArthur. As well as keeping the focus on Blamey as battle raged just forty kilometres away, the move also removed the only Australian from MacArthur's staff. There was no downside for MacArthur. If the defenders were beaten, Blamey would be blamed. If the Australians were victorious, in conjunction with the new US force, MacArthur would take the accolades.

Now Blamey felt real pressure. As well as MacArthur and his staff, most of the Labor government and caucus now seemed to be hoping he would be toppled. On top of that, the press had further turned against him. Top reporters were confused by Blamey's public optimism and Curtin's private briefings, which reflected MacArthur's fear and pessimism. Consequently, editors were suggesting in print that Blamey was not levelling with the Australian people. Blamey knew that he was on his last chance.

He also faced a confrontation with Lieutenant General Rowell, who would be not simply sensitive to Blamey's intrusion on his territory – he would be hostile. Blamey would have to push Rowell aside or fire him. Their relationship had never been good. In Greece, it had been poor: Rowell had not forgiven Blamey for forcing his army to evacuate. It had also annoyed Rowell that Blamey and his son

(Tom Blamey junior) had taken a sea plane out of Greece during the evacuation.³

Blamey tried to soften the impact of his unwelcome return to Port Moresby by writing to Rowell beforehand and blaming his relocation on the panicky politicians. This was quite a concession and demonstrated Blamey's sensitivity to Rowell's position. But no matter what Blamey said or wrote, Rowell would take his superior's arrival as a vote of no confidence in the way the battles were being fought.

Matters came to a head within a couple of days of Blamey's landing. With Blamey acting 'upbeat', Rowell could not hold his temper and the two had blistering rows.

If the two generals had known what was happening at Ioribaiwa, they might not have been so combative; they may even have celebrated. After four days of entrenching, Horii made the decision to withdraw.

In the end, it had been Templeton's false information that caused him to retreat. Had Horii known the real strength of the Australian force at Moresby, he would have ordered the attack. Templeton's courage in deceiving the Japanese under the threat of torture and death had saved Port Moresby from Japanese attack and probable occupation. It turn, Australia had been spared far greater military pressure from an enemy based in that vital strategic town at a critical time in the Pacific War.

The Japanese withdrawal would be done with as much stealth as possible, with the men moving at night to remain undetected from the air. Horii ordered a barrage of firing across the valley at the Australians on the afternoon of 25 September, aiming to put them on the defensive and making them believe an attack was imminent. At 5 p.m. the first Japanese troops moved out.

Psychologically, at least, this was a watershed moment for the Japanese soldiers. They had come to the end of the road. It was not the Track into Port Moresby, but they had achieved much for the Emperor, who was pleased with their efforts – or so they were told. The fanatics among them would happily have gone on to the ultimate objective, even if it meant obliteration for the depleted force. Now, instead of being certain of one fate – death – they were tantalised by the prospect of making it back to Japan alive. They would surely be feted as heroes of the homeland. The glory of being killed was replaced by the prospect of living.

But the withdrawal towards Buna was anything but easy. The medical issues the underfed and fatigued soldiers had faced on the trek south would triple on the way north. Tropical ulcers on all parts of their bodies would increase. They would move back into a region where the so-called 'New Guinea salute' was continuous, as they waved away clouds of flies and mosquitoes. They would again face biting ants and other insects – not to mention pythons and crocodiles in bogs off the Track. At night, the leeches would return, latching onto men as they slept. Malaria would overtake almost all soldiers, most would experience footrot, and all would have fever. Some would suffer from all three. The worst cases would be shot.

Part Five

Japanese Retreat
OCTOBER–DECEMBER 1942

53
Rowell's Howler

Oblivious to the events just to the north-east of Port Moresby, Blamey laid down the law to Rowell on 26 September 1942, invoking his authority to take over. Blamey intended to use Rowell's staff rather than ship his own people from Brisbane – an exercise in economy. The depressed Rowell took this as a further humiliation and would not accept the terms.

Blamey suggested that if Rowell did not agree to move aside, he would have to take early retirement. At this, Rowell became abusive and insubordinate. He erred more seriously when he did not pass battlefield intelligence on to Blamey. This gave the new commander of New Guinea Force all the ammunition he needed to remove Rowell.

Blamey was conciliatory, however, and sent a senior officer, General Samuel Benson, to counsel Rowell in a genuine attempt to resolve the situation. But Rowell had lost any equilibrium in his thinking. He dealt out intermittent abuse over three days, which ended with an unacceptable tirade when he called Blamey a coward over his actions in Greece. Blamey had no choice now but to dismiss him, which he did on 28 September.

Rowell was furious, and his invective continued in private to his good mates Cyril Clowes and Tubby Allen. 'I am not able to go beyond a certain point in eating dirt,' he wrote to Allen.[1]

Most observers – and, later, Rowell himself – felt that had Rowell complied, he may well have held a position in Papua. But he had pushed Blamey – who was also a good 'hater', according to Curtin – beyond an acceptable limit, and was demoted to colonel. He was prevented from taking overseas posts, although he would much later be in Europe helping to plan D-Day.

Allen let Blamey know he wanted Rowell's job as Corps Commander. But Edmund 'Ned' Herring was selected instead.

Herring's appointment was another imponderable Blamey decision. The two were mates, but with reservations. Herring was a blue-blood, and bright: he had been dux of the prestigious Melbourne Grammar School and a Rhodes Scholar at Oxford. Like Stanley Bruce – also a Melbourne Grammar old boy – he had more affinity with the seat of the Empire than with a dominion outpost. He'd fought for Britain's Royal Field Artillery, serving in France and Macedonia in World War I. Herring earned the Distinguished Service Order and the Military Cross, as did Bruce.

Earlier in 1942, in the 'generals' plot', Herring had tried to prevent the appointment of Blamey as Land Forces Commander. Blamey knew the names of every plotter, but despite this he shrewdly kept Herring close, and Herring became more of a Blamey supporter than ever. This had led to him being appointed commander of Northern Territory Force, and now he was in command of New Guinea Force.

Perhaps Blamey saw the position as a poisoned chalice, especially for someone in his first operational command. Failure was always a strong possibility. The appointment of Herring immediately created friction with Allen, who was now stationed up the Track. The two men had disliked each other since serving together in Palestine in 1941. Apart from anything else, there was a social gap between them: Herring had a born-to-rule mentality, while Allen was a former audit clerk in the New South Wales government. Despite his far more impressive record as a front-line commander in World War I, Allen had been made to battle his way up the military ladder via the militia. Herring expected and was granted promotion.

Now that Herring was in command in New Guinea, his character and capacity to work with his subordinates would be tested as never before. His first handicap was his lack of the 'common touch'. Rowell had it, in his way, as did Allen. While the military was strictly hierarchical, there were commanders who could command and yet still relate to the men throughout the ranks. They could never be 'one of the boys' but they had their respect.

By late September 1942, when Blamey had settled these issues of command, the Japanese supply lines were at breaking point. Soldiers had to take severe ration cuts and scrounge what they could from nearby villages as they eased north. Their morale was also being sapped by rumours of the intensified battle at Guadalcanal, where more US Marines had landed. Then there were the US air attacks on the Track.

These US Air Force squadrons were commanded by the short and stocky General George Churchill Kenney, who was perhaps MacArthur's greatest American asset in the Pacific. The gregarious, extroverted Kenney had the most positive 'can-do' mentality of all the American command. When MacArthur bemoaned that he could not take trucks to New Guinea, Kenney suggested cutting them in half to fit into his transporters, and then welding them together when they were landed. This was lateral thinking on steroids. Yet it reflected Kenney's personality.

Although his intensified air bombardment of Japanese positions in New Guinea was far less successful than the Americans boasted, it depressed enemy soldiers, who felt a sense of siege. Kenney's 43rd Bombardment Group of the Fifth Air Force was more effective in striking Buna's airfield and supply barges.

Horii's force of 1500 fighting men was now isolated by air, sea and communications. Only the land was open to their retreat.

The Australians had sent out patrols to pry around Ioribaiwa, and the Japanese communication lines were cut. There had not been a barrage from them for several days. The relative quiet around Ioribaiwa could have been a trap. Brigadier Eather decided that probing the area was not enough: he would go at the enemy in greater numbers, in the hope of overwhelming them.

Eather sent most of the 25th Brigade on the mission. They eased down to the valley at night, meeting no opposition. They were cautious and slow in crossing the Goldie River. Again, no Japanese attempted to attack them. The Australians, emboldened and not a little surprised that they had no fighting to do, tackled the climb up to Ioribaiwa Ridge with renewed vigour.

Eather ordered a gun barrage on the ridge's summit, before sending the men over the top at dawn on 28 September. Two hundred diggers were assigned to charge into the Japanese camp, but they were able to stroll in unopposed. Eather at first did not believe the report of the Japanese departure. He wondered if his men had their co-ordinates correct. Perhaps they were in the wrong place?

When the retreat was confirmed, the dynamic of the battle for Australian territory changed. The fear that New Guinea and Papua would be another Singapore evaporated.

54
Reversal of Fortune

MacArthur waited several days until certain Port Moresby would not be overrun, then he flew to Papua to take the glory for the sudden Japanese reversal. He had to be centre-stage. Having sent Blamey there when he feared the country would fall, now he feared Blamey would soak up the publicity.

MacArthur arrived with an entourage that would have done an ancient despot proud. He was accompanied by many of his staff, a score of bodyguards, US generals, Blamey, Australian politicians, US war reporters, photographers and publicity people. Blamey joined them and they were driven for ninety minutes in an open jeep up the muddy, potholed road to Owers Corner, the beginning of the Kokoda Track. The neatly pressed MacArthur, wearing his dark sunglasses, posed for half an hour of photos. The man who had fretted in private that Port Moresby would fall 'like Singapore' publicly contradicted the press reports that had secretly reflected his own fears. He was not yet the conqueror of the Japanese, but the image he wished to project was that of a commander who had repelled the invaders.

He and the others mingled with Australia's 3000-strong 16th Brigade, which was just setting off to help pursue the enemy back over the Track. With cameras clicking, he pretended to scan the horizon from a high point, looking across to Imita Ridge. He even allowed Blamey to join him for one shot.

MacArthur pointed to a sign that read *NO TAXIS, ON FOOT.* 'That's the first taxi sign I have seen in New Guinea,' he said to Lieutenant Nick Walsh, whom he questioned on the activity before wandering over to the diggers, some of whom were stripped to the waist and loading supplies. 'He showed great interest,' Walsh later wrote, 'and they were rapt. He made an excellent impression on all of us.'[1]

Some of the retreating Japanese had already reached Myola, more than halfway to Kokoda. The green-clad, steel-helmeted 16th Brigade would provide a huge boost to the Australian troops already hard in pursuit. Most of these diggers were confident, fearless professionals who had fought in North Africa and the Middle East against three different nations – Germany, Italy and the Vichy French – in a six-month period during 1941. They had had good training in jungle warfare after garrisoning Colombo, in Ceylon, on their way back to Australia. They also had a capable commander in Brigadier John Lloyd, who had led the 28th Battalion at Tobruk. Despite his amiability and gracious manner, Lloyd maintained discipline and took a hard line. He had a 'kill or be killed' approach.

There was a sense of invincibility about this brigade. Despite their hardships, they were as cheerful as any digger contingent in any war. Much of their positive disposition was due to their achievements. Every one of these new-look diggers wished to add a fourth nationality to their hitlist. Despite the horror stories about the way the Japanese fought, this new enemy appeared to hold no fears for the 16th as they set off up the Track.

The Japanese retreat and the arrival of MacArthur caused the semantics of war to change almost overnight. The Australians in pursuit took on the language of the aggressors. The Japanese were no longer unbeatable, and they were to be defamed as poor in their military strategy, tactics and methods. The 16th Brigade saw the results of their barbarity on the Track, and Lloyd had no trouble in instilling in them a sense of vengeance.

The turn of the tide in Papua coincided with the first anniversary of Curtin's ascent to the prime ministership. The cautious press reports about the Japanese withdrawal and salvation of Port Moresby showed the leader in a more positive light. He had made the right decisions at critical times, not the least being his determination to bring the 6th and 7th Divisions back to Australia. They had been prominent in the defence in New Guinea, and now some of their best soldiers were taking the fight up to the retreating Japanese.

Curtin had taken the high moral ground in preparing a sometimes diffident nation (depending on the state) for war, and then defence. He told his press 'chooks' on 6 October that he could not fathom the Australian mentality. One day there was panic, the next there was demand for more race meetings. Capricious newspaper leadership, he believed, was a problem here. When things looked bad in New Guinea, the public's morale had weakened. 'Now things are better,' he said in his usual sardonic way, 'they will probably want Christmas off.'[2]

Despite his attitude to the people, they had come to respect him when he was steadfast after the shocks of Pearl Harbor and Singapore, and the horror of Darwin. A Labor Party rally at the Sydney Town Hall celebrated his turbulent year in power. Curtin was given an ecstatic reception, and he took the opportunity to again call for austerity. This time, the major newspapers gave him more support than ever before. They admired his integrity; they liked his honesty of purpose; and they noted his national popularity.

Curtin saw the opportunity for an election win in the next year, 1943, and a chance to follow through on his agenda. His higher approval rating would remain while the nation was on a perpetual war footing, giving him a rare opportunity to reach goals that in other circumstances would have been unattainable. More immediately, Curtin tackled the vexed question of conscription.

Labor's policy prevented conscripted militia from being deployed outside Australian territory. This meant, for instance, that the 39th Battalion, which had distinguished itself in Papua, could not move further north to continue its fight. To all but those of the ruling party, this seemed an absurdity, given the circumstances. The opposition saw a chance to embarrass the government, especially as the Americans were also critical of this anomaly. MacArthur believed it might even prevent Washington from sending more reinforcements.

Curtin defended himself, saying that Australia had 100 per cent 'call up' success. Eligible Australian males had to enlist to serve.

The main issue was whether the AIF – the regular army – and the militia should merge, which the ALP opposed. A major problem in resolving this was the party's history concerning conscription: it had split over the issue during World War I, and Curtin had been at the forefront of the opposition to it. Now he supported conscription and saw the importance of allowing the militia to fight outside Australia.

Curtin's main obstacle was his party's die-hards, such as Victoria's Arthur Calwell, who was in the grip of the far-left and communist elements. In secret, Curtin worked out a plan for the upcoming party conference that would allow him to bypass the minefield of objections. He would propose a compromise. The territories to which conscripts could be sent would be prescribed by the governor-general, who would designate certain areas as 'associated with the defence of Australia'.

There was logic in Curtin's attitude to the issue, especially since the present circumstances were different to those of the last world war: Australia had not then been under direct threat. Now, it made no sense to have militia soldiers fighting in Papua but not in islands around Papua, which also had to be defended. Curtin worked hard, lobbying each state ALP executive.

The ever-troublesome Eddie Ward accused him of 'putting young men into the slaughterhouse, although thirty years ago you wouldn't go into it yourself'. This was on Curtin's conscience, but it took another kind of courage now to do what he saw as the right thing for the nation's defence.

Led by Calwell and Don Cameron, the Victorian ALP Executive met for several hours. Curtin waited outside the conference room, which was humiliating for the nation's prime minister. He smoked a packet of his favourite Capstan cigarettes while sweating over the result, which went against his proposal. Queensland didn't want it either, but the rest of the states were in support.

Curtin could have done without the added pressures of his party. He suffered from neuritis, a medical problem associated with stress that manifested as painful nerve inflammation. He also had a skin disease, psoriasis, again stress-related. The prime minister had debilitating wars on many fronts, just like the diggers whom he was doing his best to support.

Three battalions of the 25th Brigade and the 3rd Militia Battalion were a week further up the Track than the fresh troops of the 16th Brigade, who had been given a grand farewell by MacArthur. As they made their way north, they came across the beheadings, bayonetings and mutilations of Australian troops and locals. Everywhere the Japanese fought in the Pacific and Asia, beginning with the horrors perpetrated in China in 1937, they left a trail of brutality. They exhibited inhumanity on a scale unprecedented in history.

In the pursuit of the enemy, there was more and more evidence of cannibalism, not by the locals, who had practised it as part of their culture, but by the Japanese. They feasted on dead diggers, wrapping meat in banana leaves. The Australians were revolted by the idea of cannibalism, even though they realised that the Japanese were having food supply problems just as they were. The ritual culinary methods, however, endeared the enemy to the pursuing diggers about as much as the decapitations and the other monstrosities carried out on their mates.[3]

Japanese barbarity was a spur for Allied troops – the Australians trudging north along the Track and the Americans and Australians coming from the east. Their attitude hardened as they moved through villages where the enemy had done its worst. The diggers would never be told officially to 'take no prisoners', which in essence meant every enemy soldier should be killed, whether captured or not. But few prisoners would be taken. In Europe, prisoners were incarcerated in huge numbers; but in Papua and New Guinea and other battlegrounds where they fought the Japanese, Allied troops were far less inclined to consider any humane conventions. To avoid ambushes, tricks or booby-traps – such as a Japanese wiring himself for a suicide charge – the Allies now had less compunction about killing prisoners or the wounded.

This attitude created some other advantages. No prisons were required. Fewer stretcher-bearers were needed. There was less need for food and medical supplies for the captured enemy. War and the behaviour of the enemy, in some respects, reduced the Allied soldiers to a level of barbarity not far short of the practices encouraged, inspired and even ordered by sadistic Japanese officers. On top of this, capitulation was not expected. The Allies knew the Japanese would fight to the death, right back to Buna.

55
The Battle for Eora Creek

In the second week of October 1942, Lloyd's men began the phased relief of 25th Brigade, which had been ravaged by disease and mental illness by the time it reached Efogi, thirty kilometres north of Ioribaiwa. The 16th's immediate mission was to tackle Horii's troops, who had dug in fifteen kilometres up the Track, just before Eora Creek and Templeton's Crossing. The pungent smell of grey and white moss made it uninviting but it was one of the most useful ambush points.

The Japanese numbers had swollen with fresh troops from Kokoda. They had set up camouflaged and fortified machine-gun pits, linked by fire trenches. Brigadier Eather, pushed by Blamey and Rowell's more compliant replacement at Port Moresby, Ned Herring, felt compelled to make a breakthrough with some of the 25th before it had been fully replaced by the 16th. He chose 200 men for a two-pronged assault.

Half attacked the fortified machine-gun nests on either side of the Track, south of the creek. Once they pinpointed a nest, they rushed it and lobbed grenades. Tough, close fighting followed. The Japanese fled and were shot. But the Australians could not move further down the Track. The machine-gun fire had alerted the Japanese crews in several other pits. The diggers failed to break through. Eather accepted that his men had to back off for several nights.

The other half of the pincer attack was led by Captain Tim Clowes (Silent Cyril's brother) in a flanking movement, which brought them through thick jungle to a ridge near Templeton's Crossing. They stumbled on the Japanese main camp and had to charge from twenty metres. A hectic fight ensued. Both sides withdrew after inflicting about twenty casualties on each other.

Clowes found a protected area beyond the ridge and set up a position. Seventy metres away, the Japanese did the same. Night fell and each held their position until early on 12 October. The next day Eather decided to send out patrols either side of the Track, attempting to wipe out the troublesome nests that were impeding his men's progress to the all-important log bridge over Eora Creek. He handpicked his toughest men to lead these patrols.

One was Lieutenant Kevin Power, who took with him forty-nine soldiers. It was the kind of assignment that this experienced brigade had been on many times in North Africa and the Middle East. In the deserts, such approaches were easier but exposed. In the jungle, the way forward was more concealed and yet was fraught with dangers not found in the other war theatres. The 'path' to the creek was almost in blackness. Unless machine-gun pits were pinpointed, there was a chance that the diggers could stumble into them. If Japanese crews were ready, they could wipe out the attackers.

Power's contingent worked its way forward of some pits and came across a sizeable enemy camp, which seemed to be protected by the machine-gunners nearby. Japanese soldiers were sitting and eating under a green camouflaged canopy. One was telling a story to a small group. They laughed as he made some animated remarks. The Australians crept close. Power used hand signals to bring up a machine-gunner, Sergeant Jack Elliott, and two Bren gunners. Power motioned for them to fire into the heart of the group. Elliott opened up first, felling six Japanese. The Bren gunners picked out those trying to escape. Power waited a few seconds and led a charge at the camp. After a fight of less than four minutes, many of the Japanese had scattered. Thirty were killed. The Australians lost one man, with four wounded.

This was one of the most decisive actions by either side in the New Guinea/Papua war, and confirmed the reversed positions of the opposing forces. The Japanese, although reinforced, were on the defensive in their intermittent shuffle north. The Australians were making inroads, despite their supply problems. Yet the slow pace had Tubby Allen, who was in Myola, continually having to defend his apparent failure to advance towards Kokoda.

It seemed like inaction to impatient, even hostile Blamey in Port Moresby, and an angry MacArthur in Brisbane. But Allen and his men had seen far more battlefield action than either of these senior commanders or the new man, Ned Herring. Blamey and MacArthur knew this, which is why Allen's spirited defence in cables – he even invited them both up to Myola to do better – was more or less accepted. Had he been so bold face-to-face with either of his superiors, he would have been dumped, as Rowell had been. But seventy kilometres up the Kokoda Track, he could defend his actions with little fear that he would be replaced.

Blamey knew Allen was a good, proven battle commander. MacArthur's continual fuming about the courage of the Australians sounded hollow. Many commanders wished that Blamey would stand up for them instead of letting MacArthur blame them for not 'wiping out' or 'smashing' the enemy. But Blamey seemed preoccupied in keeping his own position rather than supporting others. It was another of his flaws, in the eyes of other officers.

The leadership of Allen, Eather and Tim Clowes, along with the bravery and skill of Kevin Power and many others, cleared the Japanese from around Templeton's Crossing by the morning of 15 October. But the big sweep had only caused the enemy to lodge on a high ridge just north of Eora Creek.

This was at the heart of this steep mountain range with the deepest ravine. The path was under trees that blocked out more light than in any other passage. The thunderous sound of a waterfall crashing from thirty-five metres to rocks made the place feel even more treacherous, especially with the number of dead soldiers from earlier battles strewn around, in various states of decomposition. By 22 October, the 16th Brigade, which by now had replaced the 25th in full, arrived just south of the creek, on an exposed 300-metre rise running sharply to the bank. They halted, waiting for those at the rear to bunch close, while officers conferred on the next move. When the brigade had regrouped, Japanese machine-gunners, artillery and snipers – positioned in bunkers near the top of the northern ridge – opened fire. The Australians were forced to scramble up the greasy slope and away from the shelling and gunfire.

Lloyd met again with his officers. There was no point trying to attack down the ravine, across the creek and up to the spur on the northern side: it could not be 'rushed'. The diggers moving en masse would be exposed for an unacceptable time. Lloyd decided to break up the brigade into smaller entities and try an encircling movement, which was a classic Japanese tactic.

About 300 diggers would creep off to attack from a spur to the west. A smaller group would take the exposed route down into the ravine and across the creek. This was far more dangerous. Some of the officers grumbled at Lloyd's plan, suggesting it was foolhardy and reminiscent of World War I tactics, with soldiers viewed as expendable. The alternative was to take the entire brigade, or at least a battalion of 500 to 600 men, via the stealthy western route around behind the Japanese.

The impetuous, sometimes rash Captain Basil Catterns argued hard. He sensed mental fatigue in Lloyd, who had been under pressure for weeks. But Lloyd refused to consider the jungle tactics that the 7th Division had learnt in Ceylon. There, experienced British commandos, who had fought the Japanese with guerrilla tactics in the mountains of Burma, had hammered home the necessity of easing behind the enemy at all costs. In essence, the British and Australians were learning the Japanese way, used so well by General Yamashita in his victories in Malaya and Singapore. Catterns and others argued that once the diggers were behind and above the Japanese, they would be forced to withdraw.

Lloyd would have none of this. In his state of near-exhaustion, he suggested that anyone who did not cross the log bridge over the Eora was 'gutless'.[1] He stuck to his two-pronged plan.

The attack at first looked likely to be unsuccessful. The western assault units were lost. The exposed direct attack saw soldiers cut down, especially crossing the creek. Many men made their reputations, or enhanced them, as courageous soldiers. Some paid with their lives.

Luck would play a part. The attack took place on a moonlight night, which helped guide some diggers down the slope to the creek. At the critical moment when they wished to cross, a cloud obscured the moon and made their advance invisible to the Japanese gunners. That contingent made it across but others were not so fortunate.

Catterns, never known to take a backward step with his superiors, his men or the Japanese, feared crawling over the log bridge. The diggers had to wriggle past thirteen dead men on the bank; they prayed they would not add to their number as the enemy fire pinged into the bank around them. Climbing the muddy northern wall of the ravine was near impossible under fire, especially with the Japanese lobbing grenades. Lance Corporal John Hunt stalked the grenade-throwers and killed them.

Daring as ever, Catterns could not see a route up to the Japanese on the northern ridge. He decided on an assault with 100 men straight up the ridge. The enemy rained fire down on them. Catterns, leading the way, reached a point thirty metres from the top. He ordered his men to dig in, which was as foolhardy or brave as the full-frontal 'rush' up the mountain. Grenades kept coming down around them.

Catterns and his men were caught in a precarious position. He used handpicked runners to replenish his food and ammunition stocks. These fit men, shouldering injured diggers, faced a four-hour trek to headquarters and back, each time running the gauntlet of Japanese snipers and machine-gunners.

56
Blamey Fires Potts, Allen

On 23 October 1942, Blamey was further frustrated by the delays in retaking Kokoda. To prevent any further criticism from MacArthur, he had to be seen to be doing something. A scapegoat was needed.

Blamey visited Potts' office, knowing that it was going to be confrontational. Potts had a dislike of authority that stemmed from his World War I experiences. Some put it down to a disregard for authority figures after the way he and his fellow diggers were treated. Once at Port Moresby, he had been abrupt and rude with the Minister for the Army, Frank Forde. Witnesses said it was understandable but undiplomatic. Blamey had been informed, Potts was – unofficially, at least – 'on notice'. Now Blamey believed there was reason for disciplinary action. Blamey ordered everyone out of the office, then began an argument with Potts that became acrimonious.

'Kokoda has been a failure,' Blamey shouted, 'it can't be tolerated! The men show that something was lacking . . . [So] it's a change of climate for you, Potts. You go to Darwin tomorrow.'

'Who is running this bloody war?' Potts yelled back. He realised he was being made a patsy and guessed that MacArthur was pulling Blamey's strings.

'I'll see you're finished in the army!' Blamey retorted.

'Good!' Potts replied. 'I can go back and tell the country what a mess you've made of things!'

At that, Blamey stormed out. He would not allow Potts to meet his successor, Ivan Dougherty. The next day, 24 October, Potts was on his way to Darwin.[1] Two days later, Allen became a target for dismissal after Blamey and Herring conferred.

After five days of action, the battle for Eora Creek tightened into a stalemate. The Japanese held firm and Horii called for reinforcements, but the commander at Buna was unhappy about sending his men back along the Track. The soldiers who had made it to the northern coast were suffering from disease. Horii pressed for the men: it was an order. Four hundred Japanese, with just four fit for fighting, had to trudge their way south to Eora Creek.

Meanwhile, Cullen pushed Lloyd to put his brigade together and attack from the west, despite the units which had not made it on the first attempt. Lloyd rejected the request. Cullen challenged Lloyd to have a look at the problem at the creek for himself. Lloyd crept down to the south bank. The Japanese spotted him. Snipers opened fire. He just missed a bullet and retreated with a greater appreciation of Cullen's argument. No longer would he declare that anyone not wanting to risk the dance with death on the log lacked courage.

He decided to link up all the units again and try the western approach. This did not augur well for Catterns and his little force, clinging to its shaky lodgement. It would have to wait several days more for relief.

MacArthur, in Brisbane, became more agitated than ever waiting for news about Kokoda. He fired off a blistering missive to Tubby Allen, who had been sending cryptic cables to headquarters without explaining the delay. Allen could not use the supply problems as an excuse for the time taken to advance.

Blamey once more took the soft option that would please the Americans. He now had 'ammunition' for dealing with Allen, and he fired him on 27 October.

Yet Blamey and MacArthur still seemed reluctant to fly to Myola, although it was a safe distance from any Japanese force. The tall, sharp, efficient 'character' General Vasey, forty-seven, known with more affection than venom as 'Bloody George' – prepared to replace Allen.

Just as Allen was being sacrificed at MacArthur's altar, Lloyd organised a strong attack from the high ground to the west, as his commanders had urged him to do six days earlier. On 28 October the short, nuggetty Major Ian Hutchison commanded a battalion of 600 in three waves down from a spur above the Japanese.

The intensity of the attacks caught the bunkered enemy by surprise. They put up a fight but were caught in a frightening, suffocating dilemma. If they came out of their bunkers, they faced a fierce determined Australian force. If they stayed, they risked being blown up by grenades thrust through narrow fire slits.

The diminutive but dynamic Corporal Lester Pett led the way, using an accurate round-arm throw, like a Test cricketer prowling the covers, to spear through four direct hits. They blew up about twenty Japanese inside the bunkers. (This earned him a Military Medal, posthumously. He would die thirteen days later after a fire-fight.) The assaulting diggers were surprised but not unhappy to see Japanese escaping from the bunkers, dropping their weapons and running into the jungle. They all headed for Kokoda.

This gave the Australians a fine sense of revenge, yet at a cost. About 150 Australians died in this battle. More than 140 were wounded. The terrain had not allowed a skilful, systematic 'win'; the victory owed more to a crude and energetic show of courage. Eora Creek also accomplished something more vital and fundamental, reinforcing that the Australians were turning the tables on their tenacious opposition. The Japanese were now losing the battle of attrition and the actual fighting, just as the Australians had, going in the other direction. And the Japanese had run away – literally – for the first time in the diggers' experience.

Vasey flew into Myola on 28 October to replace Allen, who took the return flight out. This date marked a watershed moment. Hundreds of Japanese, including the impressive, forceful Major General Horii, had for the first time decided that discretion was the better part of valour. The elevated ridge now belonged to the dogged diggers, much to the joy of Catterns and his men, who had clung to their barely defensible positions on the forward slopes. Their liberation registered the end of the battle for Eora Creek, and marked the conclusion of Allen's role in the Papuan war.

In the ghoulish but time-honoured manner of all armies, the Australians looted the depleted Japanese encampment. Most diggers, including officers, grabbed 'trophies' that would later sit in sheds, pool rooms and studies. Swords were most highly prized. Flags were sought, as were knives, wristwatches, books and keepsakes.

As the men jostled for items, intelligence officers sifted through papers with the cold diligence of entomologists dissecting insects. Diaries, logbooks, maps and battle orders, some in Horii's name, were examined. Pioneers and others collected all the ammunition, stacked in neat piles deep in bunkers, along with rifles that hung in and out of trenches. Valuable mortars and machine guns were also commandeered from the rubble of battle.

The medical staff had a more difficult task in the clean-up after Eora Creek. They had to find a way back to Port Moresby for more than a thousand wounded diggers. Due to a lack of organisation, will and air ambulance planes, almost all would have to make the trek on foot or stretchers. It would take some until Christmas, nearly two months away, to reach their destination. This ignoble trek reflected badly on unthinking politicians, particularly the Minister for the Air, Arthur Drakeford, and the careless commanders, headed by Blamey and MacArthur. In particular, the American's self-centred concern for his own reputation as an attacking commander left little thought for those injured at the rear.

Newspaper reports about the turn of events at Eora Creek eased tension in Brisbane. But while the war now seemed unlikely to cross onto the mainland from Papua, locals focused their grievances on the US cultural 'occupation'. There were intermittent scuffles, usually over women who were 'going with Yanks' rather than local lads or diggers.

In altercations, fists were the weapons of choice, but some Americans preferred knives. A combination of inactivity and a dislike of the local culture, no matter how much it was subsumed by their own, was fuelling the GIs' frustration. One American produced a large blade after a verbal spat in Centenary Park, killing an Australian and slashing three others. Another was arrested for cutting an American medical orderly. A third was charged with stabbing three of his fellow Americans and a young Brisbane woman near Central Station.

Guns were sometimes drawn too. An American policeman shot an Australian in Townsville. Not long afterwards, an American corporal in the Brisbane suburb of Inkerman pulled a revolver and started a gun battle with some Australian troops that left one from each side dead. Within a day, twenty drunken diggers fought a group of American sailors and submariners in Brisbane.

Until this one week in October 1942, altercations had been rare. Now they were sporadic. MacArthur and Blamey enforced curfews and attempted further segregation, this time between whites of different nationalities. Canberra and a compliant Queensland government limited reporting on these incidents, which were rumoured in Brisbane and censored in the rest of the country.

Instead, newspapers and radio stations concentrated on the long-awaited positive news emanating from Kokoda. It had become a household name, first as a place of foreboding. Now it was one of heroism and hope.

57
Kokoda Won; Massacre at Gorari

The grand victory at Eora Creek was followed on 1 November 1942 by the 'taking' of Kokoda, unopposed. This was a relief for the tiny patrol that crept in at dawn. The Japanese had left on 30 October; by late on 3 November, the plateau was swarming with Australian troops. Their euphoria was ended by their discovery of the bodies of many more diggers who had fought here three months earlier. Despite the corpses' decomposition, evidence of butchery, decapitation and cannibalism was clear.

After surmounting their initial shock and disgust, the diggers became even more galvanised to inflict terrible revenge on the Japanese. Not since the troopers in Chauvel's World War I Light Horse in the Sinai had come across the Arabs' savagery of British Yeomanry prisoners on 23 April 1916 had Australians been so revolted by a foe. No inspirational talk by a commander could have focused them more fiercely. There would be payback on a grand scale.

Nothing could lighten the sober mood of the diggers, but there was satisfaction that, after about ninety days of foreign occupation, Kokoda was again controlled by the Australians. This was due to the fighting of the frontline men and their previous commander, Major General Allen. Blamey was heaping praise on Vasey to justify his sacking of Allen, but the diggers knew that Vasey had nothing to do with it. The strategy, tactics and battles until the fall of Eora Creek had all been under the old command.

Yet Vasey was a worthy replacement. He insisted on walking the Track from Myola to Eora Creek – its most testing stretch, mentally and physically – and gained a 'hands-on' appreciation of the terrain and what his force had been through. A badly strained and swollen knee was testament to this. Most of his men had carried some form of illness and injury, usually one of each, from Kokoda. Vasey mixed with them and remembered names, which gained him respect among the diggers. Vasey's penchant for profanity, too, went down well with the diggers, although his well-rounded vowels sounded more like those of a British officer.

His intestinal fortitude now took on a more foolhardy nature. He insisted on wearing the red hatband of a general, although it was known that Japanese snipers loved picking off the higher ranks. His officers, too, were ordered to wear their badges when some would have preferred anonymity. Vasey liked to be close to his frontline soldiers. He absorbed the tension, which he believed allowed him to make better decisions under pressure.

Kokoda's airstrip was cleared and ready by early on 4 November for ten Dakota transporters, which lumbered in by mid-morning. By noon they had disgorged American jeeps and a range of new weaponry, including an abundance of machine guns and ammunition. Even more alluring was the food, including fresh meat and vegetables. There was also bread, butter, jam and chocolate. Diggers put aside the boring and tasteless bully beef and biscuits, which had been their staple diet for two wars, and gorged themselves on these luxuries. There were books and magazines.

There was a new spirit among the diggers. They had equipment, a few comforts, decent food and the main mountains of the Owen Stanley Range behind them. Intelligence coming in was informing Vasey and his men where the Japanese were and what they were doing.

Horii had about 1000 fit men in his diminishing army, down another 500 since the withdrawal from Iorabaiwa. He was still confident, especially after being told there were 20,000 Japanese reinforcements coming to assist. The number of new men was significant: exactly the number of Allied troops that Templeton had conned the Japanese into believing were defending Port Moresby. Horii's dream of taking that town was back on the agenda.

But underneath his bravado lurked a realist. He was planning to make even his medical non-combatants take up weapons. Horii would stay with this back-up plan until certain that the first of those 20,000 fresh troops were marching from Buna. Until then, he would dig in on the Kumusi River, forty kilometres west of Kokoda. He also placed about 3000 reinforcements from Buna – not part of the expected 20,000 – at Oivi and Gorari, two villages between the Track and the Kumusi River, at Wairopi, which were roughly parallel.

The quick takeover of Kokoda had Vasey's considerable mind working fast. He saw a chance to push for a complete victory before any Japanese reinforcements arrived. He decided on a big operation. He committed 4000 diggers, in seven battalions, to attack and surround the enemy.

Vasey also had to consider the increasing problem of disease, which was cutting the Australians' numbers nearly as much as the enemy's. Malaria approached epidemic proportions. Dysentery stalked everyone. More than 1000 diggers had become ill since leaving Myola. This confirmed Vasey in his plan: he wanted a knockout blow, aware that a prolonged campaign would destroy his force. His chosen battlefield was five kilometres long and about 1.5 kilometres wide.

MacArthur was putting pressure on too. He was now ensconced with the Bataan Gang at the former governor's bungalow residence at Port Moresby, and doing his job as the region's chief military bully, urger and motivator.

He dictated in his own style. During the day, in full-dress uniform, he would keep secretaries taking notes, while members of his obedient staff ran to and fro, dispensing his directives. He sat at his desk or on a couch, sucking on cigarettes through a gold holder and absorbing intelligence reports. At night, he shed his uniform and put on his exotic black satin dressing-gown that he wore in the Philippines and which kept alive his nostalgia for 'returning'. The cigarettes were replaced by his corncob pipe. He moved to a table and chair on the verandah, where he enjoyed the gentle breeze from the valley below. He scribbled instructions and orders for his commanders, with Vasey and Blamey singled out for the most 'heat'.

Vasey didn't need any reminding of the action to be taken. On 7 November, he called for a mortar bombardment of the Japanese bunkers at Oiva. American bombers pounded them, and their fighters strafed the area. Meanwhile, Cullen and his battalion slipped across open terrain. They met up with the 25th Brigade and prepared to surround the Japanese at Gorari.

On 8 November patrols fought vicious battles in torrential, sheeting rain. The next day, as the diggers edged closer to Gorari, they met stiff resistance and incurred thirty-seven casualties. But they encircled the Japanese, cutting off any retreat to the Kumusi River. Part of the attacking force was now wedged between the Japanese at Oiva and Gorari, whose two contingents were separated.

The Japanese positioned at Oiva tried to smash their way through. But this was not Brigade Hill and they ran into a wall of machine-gun fire. The Gorari force also took desperate measures, dragging a mountain gun into the fray in an effort to blast out the Australians. The gun's range covered the 400 metres to the 33rd Battalion.

The diggers were shelled for more than three hours. The noise was shattering and some ran, but their commanders forced them back. Just when the fire seemed too hot to bear, the gun was silenced by some daring, accurate fire from Australian snipers who had crawled close enough to kill its crew.

The build-up to a final assault had led to forty-eight Australian deaths and 123 wounded, but it was not enough to impede the diggers, who were psyched up for a final close encounter.

58
Blamey's Rabbits

Mid-morning on 9 November 1942, Blamey ordered Maroubra Force on parade at the Koitaka Cricket Ground, ten kilometres from Owers' Corner and the beginning of the Owen Stanley Range. The soldiers were expectant: perhaps decorations would be handed out. Maybe the Australian Commander Land Forces was going to praise them for the fighting withdrawal that had fatigued the Japanese, forcing their reversal up the Track.

But they were not aware of the pressure Blamey felt from MacArthur and his staff, not far away at his relatively luxurious dwelling, not to mention that from Curtin and the federal government, a long distance away in Canberra. He was becoming the whipping boy for the Australians' apparent failure to expel the enemy from New Guinea and Papua. The heat from Brisbane and Canberra, and the humidity in Port Moresby, had stretched Blamey's nerves and he had to vent his anger. He had fired Allen, dismissed the pressman Wilmot and sacked Potts. Now it was time for something else.

Blamey had been given distorted information about the demise of Lieutenant Colonel Bill Owen at Kokoda on 29 July. Owen and his mate, Lieutenant Colonel Allan Cameron, had escaped from Rabaul. When Cameron joined Maroubra Force (30th Brigade), he had been distressed by what he heard about the death of Owen and the disappearance of Templeton, whose fate was still not known to the Australians.

Cameron's arrival at Deniki coincided with the return of Corporal Markham and a small band of soldiers from the 39th Battalion, who had escaped Kokoda on 29 July at the time Owen had been hit. Cameron had berated Markham and his men for not standing their ground. It was an emotional, absurd reaction. Had Markham and his group stayed, they would have been massacred. Later, Cameron had angrily told Blamey that Owen had been abandoned, and added that Templeton had also been 'left for dead' under similar circumstances.

Thus misinformed, Blamey confronted the unsuspecting 39th Battalion. This time, instead of singling out an individual, he decided the entire force needed to be abused.

Blamey looked unprepossessing in his baggy shorts and long khaki coat, which was pushed out by his pot belly. His wide-brimmed hat could not hide his Mephistophelean scowl. He broke out in a cold sweat, which was often attributed to a hangover and resulted in belligerence. He wiped his face with a handkerchief and prepared to speak to the assembled contingent, who had turned out looking their best in slouch hats and pressed uniforms.

'You have been defeated,' he began, without notes. 'I have been defeated. Australia has been defeated.' He paused, his mood aggressive. 'It's not good enough. Every one of you must remember you are worth three Japanese. In future, there will be no withdrawals. There will be advance at all costs.'

A sombre mood fell on the cricket ground. This was the opposite of what the diggers had expected.

'Remember,' Blamey went on, 'it's not the man with the gun that gets shot; it's the rabbit that is running away.'

Blamey's demeanour and words meant only one thing to the assembled diggers, who had just given everything in their country's defence: they were being called cowards. There was rumbling in the ranks, which looked as if it might lead to mutiny. Officers moved among the lines, calming the men. Some diggers called out, 'You fat bastard, Blamey!' The general hesitated, stunned that some had dared to interrupt him in this way.

In the afternoon he ordered a private meeting with the 21st Brigade's officers. Some were so incensed at his performance that morning that they did not attend. Blamey continued his tough line, telling the shocked and disappointed commanders that they were not up to the task of leading the 'magnificent' troops. The description was not said sarcastically, causing some to wonder if Blamey was trying to appease the mood he had incited in the rank and file. If so, it was a blundering way to go about it.

He went on to say that the officers had let the diggers down. 'Some of you have failed,' he said, 'and failed badly. You are not worthy of those good men.'

This was no way to win support among his troops, yet Blamey seemed not to care. His men, it appeared, did not feature in his personal manual for survival at the top. It did not matter that his analysis of Maroubra Force's effort was inaccurate, and confected by him to justify his own decisions and inadequacies. The 21st Brigade's officers and men had been effective in reducing the Japanese to a retreating force that could be defeated, but this was not the way Blamey wished the very recent history to be viewed.[1]

On the same day, 9 November, triple-strangler Edward Leonski read his last letter from an Eltham woman with whom he had corresponded since first being held at the Melbourne city watch-house six months earlier. She had encouraged him to learn Oscar Wilde's 'The Ballad of Reading Gaol', and also to become a communicant of the Catholic Church.

After putting the letter aside, he was led to the gallows and hanged.

On the night of 10 November, at Oivi and Gorari, the Australians were about to reap the full benefit of Maroubra Force's earlier stubborn resistance. Cloud covered the moon and rain belted down, setting a perfect opportunity for the Australians to attack.

They moved silently, all cigarettes extinguished, across flattish, muddy country. Rubber trees, jungle thickets and groves covered their approach to Gorari village from every direction. The Japanese were unsuspecting; many tried to break out, running at the Australians – some with bayonets, others with guns. The diggers had expected this and a bloody battle ensued. Then, just as quickly, those Japanese who had survived now withdrew back towards Gorari. The diggers waited.

The enemy regrouped, and seemed to decide on an 'every man for himself' policy, with smaller units attempting to break through. The blackness caused chaos. Both sides came across each other in the light of flares and tracer fire.

The Australians waited impatiently for first light. They were confident of wiping out all Japanese resistance. The diggers favoured bayonet charges rather than a war of attrition, which might last all day and allow the night to give the enemy protection again.

The Australians fought with unsurpassed fury, bayoneting, shooting, knifing and throwing grenades. There seemed to be an unwritten directive that no prisoners be taken – perhaps the first time that this had been carried out on such a scale by diggers in war. It was against an Anzac tradition but the Japanese brutality had changed their thinking.

Until this moment the Imperial Army believed there would be no consequences for their barbaric behaviour in dealing with the opposition in every country they invaded. The diggers in this battle for Oivi and Gorari were the first judges and executioners of the Japanese after their unchecked and unprecedented rampage through nations of Asia and the Pacific.

Yet the violence was not quite as clinical as it appeared. On most occasions, the diggers had little choice. They could never be sure of the enemy's intentions. Some Japanese feigned death and then sprang up firing. Some charged the Australians' guns, absorbing several bullets before falling. Others sat passively as the diggers charged in. Occasionally, groups of Japanese were discovered devouring food while the battle raged around them. Without exception, it was their last meal.

The battle was over as blackness consumed the battlefield on the night of 11 November, creating a macabre silence to mark the armistice signed twenty-four years earlier on the Western Front. The dawn revealed the extent of the jungle killing fields. Five hundred and eighty Japanese bodies were counted; the diggers lost fewer than twenty dead and wounded.

At Milne Bay, the Australians had inflicted a first land defeat on the Japanese, which had stopped them taking control of New Guinea and Papua. The Australians' massive victory over Horii's best-trained troops at Oivi–Gorari had been the biggest reversal for the enemy anywhere on land in the war to that point. At last, the accolades came to the right commander. Vasey had imposed his character and determination on the diggers. His 'big-picture' gamble on all-out attack with seven battalions was daring and risky, yet decisive.

59
Silence of a Mountain Gun

Horii and his surviving troops retreated through the night to the swollen Kumusi River, which was now 100 metres wide. They had no choice but to make for its northern bank, knowing the Australians would be coming after them. Horii and his depleted force struggled across the treacherous, fast-flowing river in anything they could float.

At this point Horii made an odd move. Instead of staying with his staff after they had crash-landed a makeshift raft on the northern bank, he hopped into a smaller canoe with a staff officer and an orderly. They paddled seventy kilometres with the flowing current to the mouth of the river, where it entered the Solomon Sea. The aim was perhaps to paddle for the Japanese coastal base at Giruwa, fifty kilometres west of Gona. But it is unclear why Horii took this extraordinary action. One plausible explanation is that he came across an Australian patrol and feared capture. Another rumour suggested that he was escaping out to open sea, but this was too befuddling to contemplate.

When a tropical storm struck in the Solomon Sea, Horii and the officer drowned. The orderly made it ashore to tell the sorry tale of his commander's unnecessary demise. The Major General's death was kept secret, so as not to demoralise the troops: he was their symbolic link to the Emperor and important to their state of mind. But such a shock could not be covered up for long, and the men were told that Horii had drowned in the Kumusi. An honourable drowning in the dangerous river water was much more acceptable to Horii's grief-stricken troops.

The Australians pursued the Japanese, arriving on 13 November 1942 at the Kumusi River at Wairopi, about five kilometres upstream of the point where Horii and his troops had crossed. The Wairopi Bridge was now a forlorn collection of pylons; its wire had been stripped away by the wild river. Rubber dinghies and outriggers were strewn on the shore, sabotaged by mother nature.

Australian engineers went to work, gathering 1500 native refugees from Rabaul to collect forked tree trucks, which were shoved into the riverbed. Logs were then fitted into the forks. Steel ropes and pulleys were erected. A crude cable car was slid across the river. This allowed more than 200 men to be swung over the Kumusi every hour.

By 15 November, Vasey's force had assembled on the northern bank, ready to continue their attacks on the Japanese. On 19 November they reached Soputa, sixty kilometres from Wairopi and just thirteen kilometres from Sanananda, the coastal village between Buna and Gona. Vasey had little intelligence on just how many enemy troops were in the coastal region. Aerial reconnaissance estimated between 8000 and 12,000, which included Horii's depleted force, now blended with reinforcements. Enemy units were spread along the coast.

The opposition to the diggers' advance was apparent in the form of a Japanese Type 94 75-mm Mountain Gun, a standard pack artillery piece used by the enemy. Its manoeuvrability and gun-shield made it tough to pinpoint and knock out. This prompted the irrepressible Basil Catterns, who had been so daring at Eora Creek, to volunteer to take it out. He chose a contingent of ninety, including ten platoon commanders who had his own spontaneous nature, which bordered on reckless. Catterns had felt it necessary to charge a steep mountain at Eora Creek manned at the top by an enemy of superior numbers and firepower. Now he considered the route to Sanananda had to be opened up by a brave attack.

Catterns was hoping for a quick strike at the big gun, yet he expected strong opposition as he set out on 20 November. He took his men west for several hours, then east, expecting to come up behind the gun. But his estimation of its placement was out: they had moved too far into enemy-held territory and the weapon was well forward of them.

They were close to a sizeable enemy camp. It was 6 p.m. The unsuspecting Japanese were taking their evening meal. Catterns forgot about the mountain gun. His instinct was to attack. By a fluke, he was in position for a surprise that might just come off. If it did, his raiding party could take control of the main track to the coast inside enemy territory. In circumstances such as Eora Creek, he would consult his commander, Lieutenant Colonel Cullen, before directing his men. In this situation, which could take the lives of many of his charges, he consulted the men themselves. They wanted to attack.

This was due more to desire than bravado. Their inclination was not to back away from any confrontation, especially as they had the useful element of surprise. More importantly, though, the diggers had seen their fellow soldiers' bodies around Kokoda and at Templeton's Crossing. No one expressed it, but all were thinking of swift revenge.

Catterns led a two-man patrol to survey the area, creeping close to the Japanese. One landmark stood out: a massive fig tree, with buttress roots that fanned out a metre above ground. The ninety-man force would set up a defensive base there after the initial attack.

Catterns ordered his men to load up. They carried eighteen Bren guns and thirty-six Tommy guns; the other thirty-six soldiers had rifles and grenades. Catterns spread his men out at five paces, parallel to the main coastal track. They advanced on the camp.

The experience in the Owen Stanley Range now became vital as they edged within ten metres of the unsuspecting enemy force of about 400. A Japanese soldier noticed movement. The Australians attacked, breaking through wire fences and leaping over trenches. Some of the enemy fought back but others panicked; several ran.

Japanese gunners groped for their weapons in bunkers. Some manned machine guns, others were cut down in the chaotic encounter as the Australians destroyed bunkers, dugouts and trenches.

After less than ten minutes of mayhem, some of Catterns' men fought their way to the Sanananda Track and set up a defensive perimeter. Others fell back as planned to the mighty fig tree. The wounded were laid out between its roots. The soldiers dug in all around the tree as darkness enveloped the area. They waited, knowing that the Japanese would settle down, regroup and come after them.

Within hours, Catterns and his men were alert to a Japanese encirclement. The diggers realised they were close to enemy signal lines. Catterns ordered the cables cut. But other Japanese units were alerted by the sudden break in communications and sent patrols to the area. Just before midnight, a sortie of fifty came down the Sanananda Track. The Australians waited until they were within range and then hurled grenades. The Japanese scattered. They made contact with their comrades from the embattled camp and planned a full-on attack of the fig tree area at dawn.

The assault – with rifles and revolvers – came at first light. The Australians, their ammunition holding, fought it off. By late morning, frustration built in the enemy's ranks. One broad-shouldered Japanese had had enough. He charged forward, screaming. Corporal Ralf Albanese grabbed a rifle, climbed out of his dugout, aimed and fired. One bullet to the chest felled the big man.

During the afternoon, the Japanese eased closer, surrounding the fig tree area. They fired at the buttressing roots and trunk, splintering bark and exposing the tree's white sinews. They tried more attacks but were cut down by the Australians, who kept firing their Bren and Tommy guns through the day.

Catterns was cornered. He felt the same sense of siege he had experienced while he and his men had clung to the face of the ridge at Eora Creek. He was concerned about his numbers, especially the officers. Five of the ten commanders he had handpicked for the mission were dead. He counted another twenty-five dead or missing. A further two dozen were lying wounded between the tree's buttressing roots. Some urgently needed medical attention.

At night a thunderstorm struck. Catterns was still unsure how to extricate his men when a runner brought a message from Cullen: Catterns had to report to him. The runner led Catterns through the Japanese lines and back to battalion headquarters. He was ordered to return with a relieving force. Through the rest of that night, in sheeting rain, the wounded were withdrawn, followed by the rest of the soldiers. Only the terrible conditions allowed this fortunate escape.

It had been a costly exercise. Thirty-one men had been killed, and a further twenty-six wounded badly enough to put them out of the war. That left barely a third of Catterns' original ninety-one fit soldiers. But the assault had broken through the outer ring of enemy camps that were protecting the Japanese bases on the northern coast. The mountain gun that had precipitated Catterns' action had been silenced. Vasey's force could advance towards the coast. But they realised the toughness of encounters to come.

Meanwhile, MacArthur and Blamey continued their exhortations to kill every 'Jap' in New Guinea.[1]

The Australians and Americans wasted no time in softening up Buna, Gona and Sanananda. They bombed the three coastal towns from the air and blasted them with artillery on the ground. It devastated an area of about fifteen square kilometres. Father James Benson's little paradise at Gona was flattened, his tropical garden was a cratered pool of mud and his boat had been sunk. The Japanese headquarters at Sanananda was hammered. Soldiers in their bunkers braced themselves; they were not planning surrender.

The Americans, from MacArthur down to the lowliest private in the US 32nd Division, which was moving towards these three towns, crowed with bravado about what they were going to do to the enemy. Their inexperience in these conditions – or any other, in the case of the 32nd Division – led to this cockiness. They were mainly National Guardsmen from the Midwest of the United States who had never expected to leave American shores.

But if commanders such as Rowell, now pruning roses in his Melbourne front garden, were correct, the Japanese would never evacuate New Guinea's north coast, at least not while their brethren were fighting the Americans on Guadalcanal. They would fight to the last man.

This meant that those raw, loud-talking American lads would face everything the marines had encountered, and more. Australians of all ranks had a different attitude, which some of the newer US officers could not quite grasp. The laconic digger and his officers were a different breed; they were hard-nosed soldiers with experience on several fronts – some in both wars, others only in Papua. They had faced this fierce foe; the Americans would learn. When they did, it would be the hard way.

The battleground was a triangle, with its apex at Soputa, eight kilometres in from the coast. Its base of eighteen kilometres ran from Gona in the west, through Sanananda, to Buna in the east. A little way inland from Benson's former Shangri-La, the conditions were not enticing to the new Allied 'invaders'. The wet season had made it a swampland. The torrential rain kept pelting down, feeding the tidal swells that ran into the jungle and drowned many of the kunai patches. Any tracks that existed were mud. The humidity was debilitating. These factors caused a mosquito plague that delivered malaria unceasingly, filling makeshift hospitals with listless diggers.

The Americans – known as Warren Force – were joined by an Australian Independent Company for an assault on Buna from the east. It was the first joint venture on land by these two nations since World War I, when Monash had engineered the association in late September 1918: two US Divisions (50,000 men) had been added to the AIF.[2] Demonstrating amazing prescience, Monash foresaw the importance of Australia's link with the United States as more relevant for the future than its British connection. He had deliberately set the date for the Battle of Hamel on 4 July 1918 – US Independence Day – and managed to weave 1000 American soldiers into his contingent of 10,000 men, against the wishes of General Pershing of the US High Command. The battle had been such a stunning success that when Monash asked for the experienced US 131st Regiment for the far bigger Battle of Amiens on 8 August 1918, Pershing was content to let Monash, a 'foreign' general, again take charge of American soldiers.

Twenty-four years later, the nations' armed land forces were side by side once more, on another terrible battlefield in another hemisphere.

60

US Navy's 'No Show'

The US Navy in the Pacific was not quite the brother in arms that the Australians – particularly Blamey – would have liked. The Americans would not support the sea transport of supplies around New Guinea's northern coast. When heading west from Milne Bay, the soldiers of Warren Force had no choice but to use their just-seaworthy luggers and canvas assault boats, loaded with weapons, ammunition, food and other supplies, without naval protection.

Blamey wanted US battleships to escort them but his demand was refused. There were enough problems, such as craft tipping over when hit by big waves, without the added terror of Zeros zooming in and strafing them. No American carriers meant no US planes to take on the Japanese in the air. The US had gained the ascendancy on the sea and in the air, but still the enemy was able to make quick strikes from secret island bases.

This became rudely apparent on 16 November, when Japanese planes swooped on three luggers and a barge carrying Warren Force troops towards Buna; the small fleet was also carrying the leading American commanders General Edward Harding and Major General Albert Waldron. The Japanese strafed and bombed the boats, forcing everyone to dive overboard. The generals survived but fifty-two other troops, native carriers and media representatives did not. All the supplies were lost.

Blamey thought that the US generals' shock at being forced to swim ashore through rough, shark-infested waters would influence the US Navy to oblige with cover. But he soon learned that the US Navy could be a state unto itself when it came to dealing with other arms of the US military or its allies. On the same day that the Zero attack did as much damage as any of the land battles on the coast, Blamey wrote to MacArthur, saying he was dissatisfied with the US

Brigadier Arnold Potts (right) in full flight.

General Douglas MacArthur and Major General G.S. Allen – possibly at the moment when Allen told MacArthur that American troops would earn his respect when they started to do a bit of pushing themselves. Blamey (centre) looks embarrassed.

Sergeant Thomas 'Diver' Derrick
– one of the true heroes of the
Pacific war.

American General Michael Eichelberger and General Thomas Blamey near a captured Japanese position at Buna.

Seriously ill men waiting outside the 'hospital' hut on the Thai-Burma Railway – the Japanese doctor would see if they were fit for work...

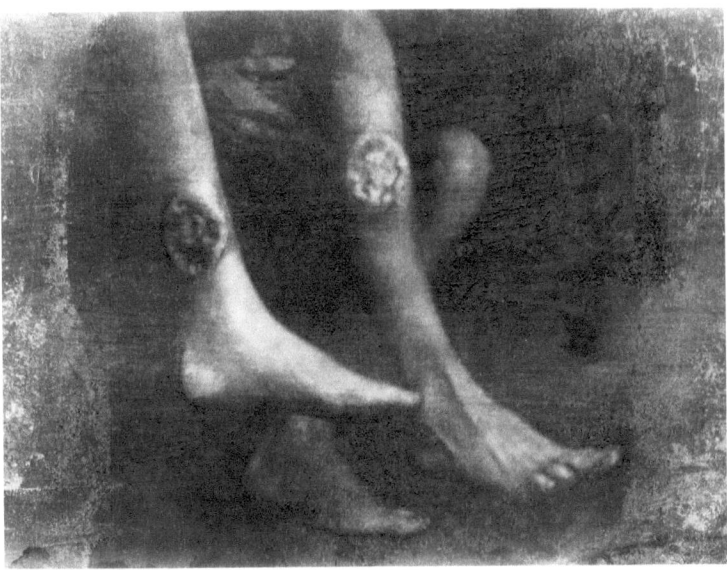

Tropical ulcers on the leg of an Australian POW on the railway – sometimes a leg had to be amputated, without anaesthetic...

Emperor Hirohito.

Admiral Isoroku Yamamoto.

Rex T. Barbour – the American pilot who shot down Admiral Yamamoto's plane over Bougainville 19 April 1943.

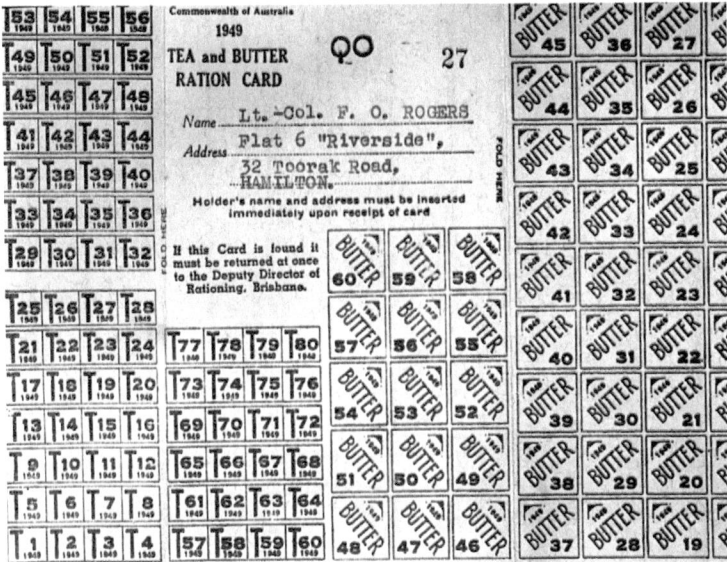

A tea and butter ration card – typical of those used during the war.

The war years saw massive changes on the home front – such as large numbers of women entering the work force.

As well as working in factories, women played a vital part in farming – a section of the Women's Land army at work.

Part of the 'Battle of Brisbane', when Australian and American troops fought each other.

Industrial action didn't stop – a police officer draws his pistol in the *Daily Mirror* office in Sydney, during a dispute.

John Curtin's funeral in Cottesloe, near Perth, in July 1945.

General Thomas Blamey signs the Japanese surrender documents aboard USS *Missouri*.

Peace, at last. One of the iconic images from VJ Day in Sydney.

Navy's refusal to assist. He did not accept the US admirals' excuse that they had to keep their destroyers safe, while merchant boats were taking risks ferrying troops and supplies to Buna.

MacArthur was sympathetic to Blamey but had to remain neutral. He could hardly side with the Australians against the US Navy, however much he loathed the admirals. Their inaction meant that the Allied force would have limited artillery support at Buna, a serious blunder which Blamey had done his best to redress.

Blamey would have been far more concerned had the Allies' intelligence been better and had he known the true strength of the Japanese fortifications. They ran over five kilometres from Cape Endaiadere in the east to the Buna Government Station in the west. The enemy had a surfeit of weapons, ammunition and food – enough to last several months. The battle zone had a wall of concealed machine-gun pits and bunkers. There were also hundreds of snipers, hidden in the swamps, coconut groves and jungle opposite the beach.

There were about 2900 Japanese in the total defence force. The two key Japanese regiments were highly trained and experienced, having fought at Sumatra. 'Resilience' was part of their private motto, and they had lived up to it. Among their ranks were members of the Special Naval Landing Party, who were responsible for the atrocities that had so disgusted the diggers when the Japanese first arrived at Gona and Milne Bay.

The American generals, led by the shaken Harding, nevertheless drew up a plan to take Buna. A pincer movement would aim at squeezing the Japanese into defeat or submission. The United States' Urbana Force would strike at Buna village and the Government Station from the south-west. Warren Force would first hit the two airstrips from the east and then join the other forces in an all-out assault on the village.

The Allies' inadequate number of big guns became clear on 19 November, when the First US Battalion went into battle at Buna and met a wall of machine-gun fire from a score of camouflaged bunkers. The initial troops were butchered by fire strong enough to sever limbs. Some survivors managed to retreat in haste.

This response had not been expected. The overconfident, inexperienced American soldiers were shocked. Hidden Japanese machine-gunners were also devastating at nearby Simemi Creek when the US 128th Regiment's 111th Battalion (in Urbana Force) had to wade through a shoulder-deep swamp to make their assault. They were easy targets for the stream of bullets that caught them, leading to many deaths, some by drowning in the bog.

This awful initiation for the raw American soldiers seemed unlikely to abate.

MacArthur wanted to demonstrate that his Americans were somehow more willing to fight and win than their Australian counterparts in the Owen Stanley Range and at Gona. But he became more frustrated each night on his verandah, sucking on his pipe with increased intensity while contemplating the lights of Port Moresby. He wanted to clear the enemy out of New Guinea and Papua and proceed with his master plan to take back the Philippines.

He could not understand the delays on the northern coast. Why couldn't they smash the Japanese? No one among his obsequious staff had the temerity or courage to remind him that he, too, had failed when confronted by the Japanese in the Philippines. Perhaps they knew he needed no reminding of the humiliation of being forced to run away.

MacArthur was in a fury after learning of the Allies' shocking start at Buna and the failure of the US Navy to aid them. On the morning of 20 November, even before he had consumed his breakfast of a grapefruit and a boiled egg, he bumped his way over in a chauffeured jeep to Blamey's offices. The Australian was not there. MacArthur delivered a blistering missive to the bemused staff anyway: 'All forces must attack the next day, with all columns to drive through to objectives regardless of losses.'

Then he left, with next to no comprehension that the Allies had carried out this instruction, but without managing to break through. Yet all MacArthur really wanted to know was that it had been done and that he could leap towards his 'return' to the Philippines. His anxiety peaked in the early hours of the next day, when he fired off another directive to the hapless Harding at the front: 'Take Buna today at all costs – MacArthur.'[1]

The Australian Independent Company's fifty-man contingent, led by Major Harry Harcourt, looked likely to fulfil this command as it moved on Buna from the east. Their target was one of Buna's two airstrips. Harcourt led the rush at Japanese bunkers, running the gauntlet of machine-gunners and snipers. Several Australians were wounded, including Private Stanley Martin, who took three bullets but kept fighting. He, Harcourt and all but a couple of casualties reached the edge of one tarmac, just fifty metres from its southern end.

Harcourt called for an American contingent to follow up for the main assault. The Americans would have to brave it too, despite Harcourt's men killing at least twenty Japanese defenders on their way to the airstrip. Harcourt repeated his call, sending a runner back to the American commander, who told him his men were refusing to go. Harcourt was forced to withdraw or risk being surrounded and wiped out. After this minor debacle, he and his digger force were scathing about their 'ally'.

The Americans' failure to support the Australians had repercussions. MacArthur, trying to save face after this further humiliation, wanted to send the Brisbane-based US 41st Division to the battle on the northern coast. But Blamey, in his usual manner when dealing with superiors, said he preferred to send in more Australians. Blamey suggested the 21st Brigade, adding with relish, 'I know they will fight.'

MacArthur, Blamey and air force General Kenney met at US headquarters in Port Moresby. The question of additional troops was the focus. Blamey made his case for using the hardened veterans of the Owen Stanley Range campaign. MacArthur had no argument. The 41st was not experienced. The other raw Americans had failed to go into battle in one part of Buna and had been destroyed in another sector. He agreed with reluctance that the diggers should be sent in.

'It was a bitter pill for MacArthur to swallow,' Kenney noted in his memoir, 'but he agreed.'

MacArthur's secretary, Warrant Officer Rodgers, sat at his typing desk in the room where the three were meeting. He observed

MacArthur 'smarting under his own doubt. Blamey had already relieved two Generals. He sat smiling smugly now that the shoe seemed to fit neatly on MacArthur's foot.'[2]

Blamey was quick to let Curtin know about the US troops' failure, and made a point of saying that they were 'definitely not equal to the Australian militia'. He believed the bulk of the fighting should fall to the Australians, despite the far greater size of the US forces, in which he had no faith.[3]

Further west on the northern coast, a skeletal, weakened brigade of the 25th Battalion prepared to charge the Gona bunkers. They were spread over 300 metres, roughly in a semi-circle to the sea, ringing Father Benson's former mission building. Every man in the assault moved out on the command 'Charge!' believing that they would meet little resistance.

The diggers were stunned by machine-gun fire that met them from the front and both flanks. Twenty-four were killed, and forty-two wounded. In one hard, horrible 'lesson', they learned that the Japanese would be just as tough to dislodge here as they had been in the Owen Stanley Range. One problem was that the swamp reduced the Australians' charge to a struggling wade, making them easy targets.

The Australians kept attacking. The Japanese continued to cut them down. It was not that different from the charges diggers had made at the Nek on 7 August 1915, during the Gallipoli campaign. Brigadier Eather, under orders to exterminate the Japanese as fast as possible, found that the opposite was happening. One digger battalion after another was hurled at the enemy, with similar results each time. Eather called a halt.

He knew that the operation needed new tactics. The Japanese had more ammunition than the Allies anticipated. They were surviving by at night netting small amounts of fish and octopus. They scavenged mussels and crabs from the beach. These supplemented their meagre stores of rice, which were down to a few spoons for each soldier a day.

Further, the Australians had to contend with the stoic Japanese attitude to fight to the last breath. Wounded Japanese had to give up their weapons to able soldiers, yet as their numbers whittled down, the wounded were prepared to use bayonets tied to poles, or sticks fashioned into spears.

This resilience, and the Australians' failure to blast the enemy out of the bunkers, caused Eather to wait for reinforcements. Even this had repercussions. The Japanese would emerge out of the night and charge the encamped diggers. The enemy's grit reflected Tokyo's determination to stay in New Guinea and Papua, which kept the Allies' resources diverted away from Guadalcanal for as long as possible.

Tokyo would continue to reinforce the embattled Imperial Army at Gona.

61
The Battle of Brisbane

Americans in Brisbane relaxed in the heat and celebrated Thanksgiving on Thursday 26 November 1942. The most loved day on the US calendar led to locals and Americans drinking more than usual. Alcohol fuelled sentiment, and the visitors became emotional. Some were merry, others were homesick. Still others were angry and itching for a fight, if not against the Japanese then with Australians or even their own countrymen.

The day began badly in the morning hours before tables in American barracks were groaning with turkey and booze. One drunk US soldier, who had started his festivities earlier than most, was staggering about in Albert Street when he was abused, then bashed by an American military policeman (MP). Two diggers intervened and stopped the attack. One of them received several belts himself. Such pummellings for American servicemen were common, but unacceptable to diggers, who would never take such brutal treatment. Several Australians joined in a minor brawl. The incident may have been isolated and forgotten – just one of about twenty each day – but for the occasion.

Most Americans and some Australians took long lunches, and Brisbane shut down from midday to 5 p.m. Americans emerged onto the streets in the late afternoon and mixed with inebriated locals. The US Postal Exchange (PX) on Adelaide Street attracted hundreds, half of them women hoping for some contact with their American friends on their special day. Just fifty metres away, some Australians, hostile after hearing about the American bashing of a digger, gathered at their far less impressive 'canteen'.

Some verbal banter between the servicemen of both nations went on. An American private, who had consumed too much beer over the afternoon, was chatting amiably with three diggers, who had also been drinking. An American MP challenged the private, asking for his leave pass. The American fumbled in his pockets. The MP became impatient. The diggers, mindful of the incident earlier in the day, told the MP to 'take it easy', but he became even more officious.

Some push and shove turned nasty. The MP swung his baton and was joined by others. More Australians leapt in. A brawl developed. Several locals rushed from the canteen where they had been drinking and joined the fray. The Australians chased the MPs towards the sanctity of the PX, flailing them with their webbing belts as they gave chase. The MPs were defended by others. Noticing the building fracas, more Australians hurried out of the nearby Gresham Hotel and joined in, making it a substantial punch-up.

The MP who started it was knocked unconscious. Within minutes a crowd built. The punch-up burgeoned into a riot. About a hundred diggers and locals attacked the PX. Parking signs were ripped out of the ground and used as battering rams against its windows. Diggers hurled rocks and bashed at the door with any available weapon, including cricket bats. Trams, buses and cars came to a standstill in Adelaide Street as hundreds more diggers and Americans rushed to the scene. Many American MPs went down, one with a fractured skull. An ambulance arrived to take him away, causing a lull in the brawling.

By 8 p.m. the hostile crowd had built to more than 2000. An Australian piquet sentry stopped and detained a small truck carrying four diggers. It contained four Owen submachine guns, ammunition and hand grenades. Although the diggers denied it, the piquet was concerned they were about to escalate the riot to a full-scale battle.

An American light weapons carrier arrived from South Brisbane, intent on breaking up the fight. It baulked through traffic and bumped over tram lines. Its occupants were armed with twelve-gauge pump-action shotguns. Australian Private Ed Webster tried to wrestle a gun from American MP Norbert Grant. The gun discharged straight into Webster's chest at point-blank range. He fell dead. Grant fired again, this time spraying and wounding seven other Australians. Grant dashed for the PX, swinging his rifle as he fled and smashing another digger in the head.

After more than hour, Brisbane police and American MPs managed to disperse the combatants. Ambulances ferried the many injured to hospital.

The next day all media were censored. Not even the Brisbane papers and radio stations carried the story. No one outside Brisbane had any clear knowledge of the conflict, although there were rumours. Other sporadic incidents that had occurred in various parts of Brisbane and Queensland in October had been easily covered up, but stories of this bigger, more concentrated brawl spread throughout the city. Rumours of a massacre of diggers reached proportions that threatened to create more trouble.

In the evening, digger gangs roamed Brisbane, seeking revenge. They congregated outside MacArthur's headquarters at the AMP Building, on the corner of Queen and Edward Streets, although the general was still in Papua. Any American serviceman in the area was in danger. Several were bashed during a ninety-minute rampage by angry diggers. Some Americans were 'surfed' – lifted over the heads of the diggers, then dumped and set upon with fists and boots. The marauding locals were severe also on Americans escorting women on Edward Street.

At the end of two hours of disparate fighting along Queen Street, a group of twenty diggers wielding batons taken from MPs confronted US Provost Marshals, who were armed with revolvers. They fired shots into the air, causing the Australians to back away. Australian military and local police stepped in and arrested a couple of diggers. The eruption was quelled and the gangs dissolved and left the area.

One US Army sergeant, Bill Bentson, was shocked to see his fellow

Americans 'flying through the air' during the 'surfing' incidents. He was equally stunned by the reaction of Australians who had joined in the fighting. It was as though they had stepped into a bar-room brawl in a Western movie. Bentson entered a Brisbane pub a couple of days after everything had settled down. He was amazed when an Aussie he did not know came up to him and slapped him on the back. 'Wasn't that a good ruckus the other night, mate?' the Australian said. 'Have a beer on me . . .'[1]

The two days of rioting were also hushed up. The federal and state governments denied it had happened. Brisbane's Chief Censor's Office ordered 'no cabling or broadcasting of details of tonight's Brisbane servicemen's riot'. The Brisbane *Courier-Mail* carried an article on 28 November that simply mentioned a 'disturbance' in which one person was killed and several wounded. There were no other facts; not even the nationalities of those who took part were mentioned.

The units involved were relocated outside Brisbane. The numbers of military police – for both nations – were increased. The Australian canteen was closed. The PX, which had been trashed, was shut down. But with more than 300,000 Americans in Brisbane, another had to be opened elsewhere in the city. Over the next few months, five Australians and Norbert Grant were discreetly prosecuted. The Australians were all convicted. One received a sentence of six months jail. Grant was court-martialled on a charge of manslaughter but was found not guilty on the grounds of self-defence. Other riots occurred in Mount Isa, Rockhampton and Townsville. It was the first of several fights between the two nationalities which continued in Melbourne, Sydney, Perth and Fremantle.

The authorities speculated on the causes. The heavy-handedness of the US MPs was presented as one reason. They had little compunction about belting their own soldiers, but when they used the same methods against Australians, it backfired and created more problems. But a stronger factor was thought to be the attraction the US servicemen had for local women. There were complaints that the Americans were affectionate with the locals in public. They charmed, touched, embraced, kissed and caressed them. The diggers expressed the view that they had become outsiders in their own country. The Americans' manners, style, uniforms, ready cash and 'gift of the gab' combined into a sex appeal with which the diggers could not compete.

This rivalry did nothing for the goodwill between the two forces, and dented the Allies' image as a harmonious army. It was also a disaster in the realm of international propaganda: it was feared that the incidents might even impact on the attitudes of the chiefs in Washington to MacArthur's competence and Australia's need for assistance in the war in the South Pacific.

Japanese propagandists in Tokyo, groping for any advantage as their grip on the Pacific was shaken, made much of the riots, issuing blaring Japanese newspaper headlines and leaflet drops in areas where Australians were fighting. Japanese battle cries now went beyond 'Aussie, you die!' and instead concerned what the Americans were doing to 'your girls'.

The fighting in Brisbane and elsewhere did little, however, to curb the Americans' amorous pursuits. Their appeal to local women wherever they were stationed was undiminished. About 12,000 Australian women would marry Americans during the war. Many had their engagements hastened by pregnancies. More than 1500 women and their children immigrated to the United States, and the rest waited to be reunited with their husbands when hostilities ceased.

62

Escalation

The torpor that had also played a large part in the fighting between the Australians and Americans in Brisbane may never have happened, had the participants been aware of the much more important 'stoush' taking place on New Guinea's northern shoreline. A false sense of security had hit Brisbane after the Japanese had been pushed out of the Owen Stanley Range. This was not helped by premature prophecies of them being swept out of New Guinea and Papua altogether, and the Pacific in general.

But the Japanese were no longer retreating. They were building up their numbers. Nor were they near capitulation on Guadalcanal: their bunkered soldiers were holding out with ferocity. By late November 1942, Vasey was aware that his strategy of attacking the enemy at Gona, Sanananda and Buna was not working. He needed reinforcements to counter the Japanese build-up. He was advised also to concentrate more men on one of the three enemy strongholds.

Vasey called for the 21st Brigade, which spent weeks recovering from the ordeal of their 'fighting withdrawal' down the Track under Potts' command. Its diggers had been stung by Blamey's comparison of them to rabbits. This put the brigade in a vengeful mood when it was flown north from Port Moresby for their second round of engagements with the Japanese.

The pride the diggers had as fighting men after the battles to stop Japanese progress down the Track had been shattered by Blamey's apparent ignorance of their achievement. The diggers were as determined to 'show him' as they were to attack the enemy. Now, the veterans of the Owen Stanley Range battles were coldly determined to take advantage of their superior position as the attacker. The Japanese had withdrawn as far as they could. This would not be the moveable struggle of the mountain range but a battle of fixed positions, tactics and attrition.

The new commander of the 21st Brigade was 35-year-old Brigadier Ivan Dougherty, a veteran of the North African, Greek and Crete campaigns. He persuaded Vasey that he should attack Gona with a larger and more concentrated force.

Dougherty ordered an aerial bombardment of the village. Eight US Flying Fortress bombers lumbered over the coast and dropped eight 500-pounders. Then twelve fighters wheeled in and released a further dozen 300-pounders. These attacks left the beach and village with moon-like craters.

Next it was the infantry's turn. Dougherty, who won a DSO for attacking Tobruk in January 1941, decided on a multi-pronged assault on Gona, with two battalions moving from the east, one from the west, and a fourth from south. He was forced to take his orders direct from MacArthur and Blamey at Port Moresby, who, as always, had little appreciation of the treacherous conditions or the tenacity of the bunkered Japanese. The two commanders briefed him before he left to fly north. They pressured harder than ever for results that would end the resistance.

Coupled with Blamey's stinging assessment of the 21st Brigade, this created a feverish attitude among officers and men, making the strategy more akin to a suicide mission than a clinical method of breaking the Japanese. The waist-deep bog made a cruel mockery of the 14th Battalion's charge from the east. The diggers' forced slow-motion approach made them easy targets for the Japanese machine-gunners, especially those in a well-placed hidden bunker at Small Creek, which had not been noticed by Allied reconnaissance. Thirty-two diggers were cut down in the swamp.[1]

The 27th Battalion, led by Colonel Geoff Cooper, was ordered to charge Gona village from the jungle. Just as they hit the junction of the jungle with the beach, several hidden machine-gunners opened up and cut a swathe through the diggers, who kept on coming. Fifty-five Australians went down and no ground was gained. Cooper repeatedly cabled headquarters, trying to stop the senseless killing. Replies came back urging him to 'push on'. Cooper begged for a battle of attrition rather than these crazy rushes at the enemy but he had to obey orders.

Blamey and MacArthur continued to fire off such missives from the safety of Port Moresby, blind to the scores of Australian bodies littering the fringe of the jungle. If no breakthrough came, they could cable more blistering demands. The chiefs' lives were not at stake, just their jobs.

The 21st Brigade's battalions, spurred by Blamey's goading, were acting as the Japanese had in their waves of suicidal rushes 'for the Emperor', who was safe behind his palace walls in Japan. Eventually Cooper refused to send his men into the dreadful conditions. Other commanders followed suit. These morally brave leaders were removed, their careers finished.

Blamey had been at Gallipoli and the Somme but appeared to have learnt nothing. Occupational self-preservation overrode his humanity.

He and MacArthur deserved to be judged in the same manner as the British commanders Generals Haig, Gough, Godley and Rawlinson, and Australia's own Jack Antill, in World War I. Blamey would dispense plenty of deserved awards, many posthumously, to avoid his name being tarnished for his inhumanity and cruelty. He was also now in competition with MacArthur, after having poured scorn on the Americans' lack of desire for battle; he could not afford to give him another excuse to say the Australians were not up to it.

Vasey spoke up against the loss of men, but by the time he did, it was too late. All he could do was calculate the appalling statistics of the dead.

The killing rates were even worse for the Americans east of Buna. By 1 December, after just nine days of fighting, nearly 500 had been killed or wounded. More artillery had arrived, including two Australian 25-pounders. But this did little to assist the Americans, who had to struggle through swamps before they could obey their orders to charge. Worse still, the mud and rain ruined their rifles and machine guns, and there was still little or no air cover. When it did come, American planes strafed their own troops and did not impact on the Japanese bunkers.

These calamities incapacitated the Americans, diminishing their desire to reach the inconspicuous bunkers. They kept withdrawing from the suicidal situation. General Harding was furious. After surviving the ordeal at sea, he now faced the shock of his forces' failure to break through anywhere at Buna after nearly two weeks of fighting. Along with the fact that most of his supplies had been sunk, this led to the suggestion that a substantial part of his force should be absorbed under Australian command.

One US battalion was directed to come under Vasey's control at Sanananda, but Blamey objected. He rejected the Americans and opted for more Australians – both AIF and militia soldiers. It gave him satisfaction to tell everyone again that at least the Australians would fight.

MacArthur was smarting from all this. He had to act to save face for the Americans in Papua and New Guinea. He must finish the war here, and reignite his floundering plans to retake the Philippines. He chose General Eichelberger to replace Harding and reorganise the US forces on the northern coast.

The new man was a gamble. He had little experience as a commander in battle, but he was bright, likeable, flexible and an outstanding speaker. He knew how to communicate with his troops and would monitor their wellbeing. Despite being a strong motivator, he suffered from bouts of depression, much like Churchill and Curtin.

MacArthur was typically blunt, melodramatic and chilling when he told Eichelberger, 'Take Buna or don't come back alive.'

Eichelberger was appalled by what he discovered at Buna. It offended most things he stood for as a general, including his sense of organisation. For a start, he could not even locate his regiments. The Australians did not know where they were.

Eichelberger searched for the front but couldn't find his force. He was stunned to find his US troops – unkempt in raggy clothes and dilapidated boots – scattered in small groups along the track to Buna. He let MacArthur know there would be no quick fix. He would to go back to basics, clean up his troops, organise them and enforce discipline. He called for a cease-fire and began the transformation.

On 2 December at Buna headquarters, Brigadiers Eather, Dougherty and Porter held a hurried conference. The tactics they were using hadn't worked. Their men had been far more effective and willing than their American counterparts at Buna, but still, all the killing had been for nothing.

Instead of confronting Vasey to demand a more cautious approach, they pleaded for more men for more charges. They all had the same idea: they wanted the 39th Battalion, which Blamey and MacArthur would not recognise for its achievements and collective courage. The best 100 men from the maligned 53rd Battalion would be blended into the 39th.

There was no irony in their request, which was testimony to this unit's guts and brilliance, and that of its outstanding commander,

Lieutenant Colonel Ralph Honner, who had kept his position when Potts had been sacked. As a result, the veterans of the first fight against the Japanese on the Kokoda Track were called up to support the crack AIF brigades of the campaigns in North Africa and the Middle East.

63
Gona: 'Going, Going . . .'

Inspired by their troops' resistance at Gona, the Japanese poured reinforcements into the west of their defensive zone on the north coast. They had well-protected camps at the mouths of the Kumusi and Mambare Rivers. The latter was spotted by an Australian coastline 'watcher', who informed the Allied air force. Planes located a camouflaged set of tents, and five barges anchored at a sheltered inlet. Allied bombers, aided by orange flares that lit up the sea and beaches, swooped low and dumped their loads on the enemy vessels and the camp.

Japanese troops at the Kumusi River were more fortunate. Having landed at night and dispersed into the jungle, they made their way in groups to the bunker area. Learning from the Mambare River fiasco, the Japanese brought in a full combat battalion – led by a fresh commander, Major General Yamagata Tsuyuo – on four destroyers and with plenty of air cover. But it wasn't enough. Allied fighters and bombers strafed the landing craft until all were sunk.

A few days later, on 4 December, the same battalion, now down to 500 men, managed to land in darkness at a different point on the coast. These reinforcements meant that the Japanese had more than 6000 troops in the Gona–Sanananda area. But this landing had been spotted too.

At Gona, the Allies were becoming desperate to break through. An Australian cavalry division – with armoured vehicles rather than horses – decided to use five troop transporters mounted with machine guns as if they were tanks or armoured cars. Americans troops of the 111th Battalion would follow on foot behind the convoy, with the aim of hitting the Japanese bunkers and blasting out their stubborn occupants.

American bombers flew over in a token effort to soften up the enemy, then the twenty 'cavalrymen' drove forward at a snail's pace, with the Americans jogging behind. The transporters were forced to a halt as a fire-fight ensued. Intense machine-gunning caused the Americans to back away, leaving the Australian cavalcade in a most uneven battle. Only four wounded soldiers in the transporters survived the carnage as the Japanese picked off most of the diggers inside twenty-five minutes.

The encounter was a disaster. The Americans' failure to back up this attempt to make inroads at Buna was understandable, but their reputation as being disinclined for battle was maintained. Eichelberger had to instil some vigour and rigour into the demoralised Americans. With MacArthur putting demands on him daily, the reality became clear.

Eichelberger concluded that his men did not have the stomach for action mainly because they had little or no battle experience. He agreed with Herring and the newly introduced Major General Wootten, a veteran of victory at Milne Bay, that only by relying on Australia's hardened troops could the Allies achieve anything beyond a stalemate in Papua. They had to be experienced diggers who knew all about tanks, the weapon most likely to break through Japan's defences. The best brigade for this was the 18th, which had been brilliant at Tobruk and, more recently, Milne Bay.

On 5 December 1942, a small remnant of a special Australian commando unit of diggers, led by Lieutenant Alan Haddy, was entrenched in dugouts under village huts on the beach near Gona Creek. They readied themselves to fight the first contingent of 200 Japanese, who had landed the day before.

Haddy's original unit of 109 men was down to just twenty, and several of them were wounded. Haddy knew that a dozen fit men could not hold out against 200. He decided to move the injured out first and then withdraw the rest, except for himself and one soldier. Haddy saw his role as holding the Japanese off for as long as he could, giving time for his withdrawn men to make it back to headquarters.

He and the digger waited until the Japanese were close by, then fired. The enemy soon realised that fire was coming from a beach hut. They edged towards it, firing and lobbing grenades. One hit Haddy's mate, killing him. About thirty Japanese eased forward, surrounding the hut. Haddy kept firing, bringing down nine enemy soldiers before he too was silenced. The lieutenant had held the enemy up for two hours, allowing his reduced unit to escape.

Ralph Honner and his 39th Battalion arrived amidst greater chaos than he had ever experienced in the Owen Stanley Range, Greece or Crete. The haphazard environment suited his clear-thinking mind. After assessing the situation, he decided on a concentrated assault on Gona on 6 December 1942. Had he witnessed other attacks through the swamp, he may have demurred, but he believed his 'fresh' troops would break through.

But they could not. Fifty-eight men, who had handled the mountains so well, were cut down by the well-fortified enemy machine-gunners. Honner resolved on a drastic change of tactics. His desperate superiors had little choice but to listen to this experienced courageous commander.

Honner asked Dougherty to hold back a further attack of 950 men on Gona from the south. On the present record, he said, it would fail and scores of men would be slaughtered. Honner was against using air support. The bombing and strafing had had little impact on the Japanese bunkers, and too often the Australians had been hit by 'friendly fire'. Honner had been stunned by the pandemonium when the diggers attacked at night: this seemed to cause more mayhem for the Allies than for the enemy. He suggested they go 'over the top' at noon.

The major problem was the strength of the fortified bunkers, from which the enemy could not be shaken. Honner thought long and hard about this and concluded that his artillery men had to make sure their bombs exploded precisely when they reached their underground targets. He hit on the idea of timing and fusing the bombs so that they detonated half a metre underground, which would maximise their impact on the bunkers. This meant that the mortar fire had to have a low trajectory. Advancing diggers would have to keep their heads down. The shock and destruction caused by the greater number of underground explosions would minimise the enemy fire coming at charging diggers.

Honner needed no urging from any commander. On 7 December, with the land battles at Gona at a stalemate, he saw Allied planes bombing and strafing Japanese destroyers carrying 800 reinforcements. Six were sunk and one limped back to Rabaul, but the encounter demonstrated how determined the enemy was to keep a grip on New Guinea's northern coast.

Japanese planes retaliated that afternoon, destroying the US field hospital at Buna – a series of tents marked with large red crosses. The date – 7 December – resonated in the minds of all Americans. Eichelberger, who witnessed the attack, reckoned that it was deliberate. The planes had not hit Allied troops or supply lines; instead, they had swooped over the hospital. He observed that doctors had kept working despite the assault. It stiffened the general's resolve to win at Buna.

There was urgency in Honner's step at Gona after what he had witnessed. Just after noon on 8 December 1942, exactly a year since the Japanese attacks on Thailand, Malaysia and Singapore, he sent his 39th Battalion into battle after fifteen minutes of intense mortar fire. As the men ran forward, the artillery bombs kept skimming and whistling over their heads. After two minutes – the time Honner calculated it would take the diggers to be just short of the bunkers – they ceased.

The commander's calculations were correct. The bombs were devastating, causing blasts in the confined bunkers just as the diggers arrived, yelling and brandishing their bayonets and rifles. The resistance was limited as the diggers wiped out bunkers and their occupants and captured machine guns. The bunkers were then hit by grenades. Any Japanese fleeing along the beach were shot – 'like rabbits', as Herring cabled Blamey.

The 850 Japanese who were not killed cowered in the remaining holes until nightfall. The braver or more desperate made a dash to escape. About fifty crawled to the water's edge; they stood to run away but were spotted by Australian machine-gunners, who fired and felled half of them. The rest dived into the water and began swimming. They, too, were hit by sustained fire. Another one hundred or so Japanese tried to steal away in the dark across a swamp to the cover of the jungle. They too were spotted, as flares illuminated the area. Again, the chilling staccato sound of machine-gun fire split the humid air; every one of the enemy escapees was felled in a bog that had earlier claimed scores of diggers.

The next morning, 9 December, Honner's men invaded Gona at dawn and took control of it. Two battalions of the 21st Brigade prowled the beach from the west. By 8 a.m. the Australians controlled the entire area around Gona and nearly halfway to Sanananda.

At noon, after further minor encounters, the diggers had a moment to observe the results of the fighting. Japanese bodies littered the area around the bunkers. Maggots were already at work on bloated shapes. The Japanese had used their dead fellow soldiers as sandbags in and around the bunkers. A horrific odour hung over Gona; the steady rain, which filled the craters in the village and the swamp, could not wash it away. Australians were already busy burying the dead in mass graves, which soon left a dirt and sand patchwork over the beach. Six hundred and thirty-eight Japanese were buried, and another 300 were interred along the beachfront.

Late in the afternoon, Honner was satisfied that he had all but wiped out the enemy. There were pockets of resistance but he was confident that his victorious 39th would mop them up. He used a field telephone to let 21st Brigade headquarters know of the breakthrough, saying, 'Gona's gone!'[1]

64
Tanks for the Advantage

Honner's words – 'Gona's gone' – were soon phoned through to Herring at Port Moresby. He cabled Blamey. Inside forty-eight hours, Australian newspapers would make a headline of Honner's declaration. Blamey wanted to be the first to let Curtin know. The prime minister congratulated him, unaware that the success owed nothing to him or to MacArthur. Their urging and bullying had in fact been counterproductive, and had cost the lives of hundreds of diggers and Americans.

Honner, whom Blamey had scorned in Port Moresby, was the commander who should have received the accolades. His capacity to harness the courage of his men to his own clever tactics had made the difference. But Curtin was not a hands-on leader. His disdain for the military and loathing of warfare kept him ignorant of what really happened.

There was some merit in leaving the war to the experts. Unlike Churchill, Curtin did not treat his generals like clerks to be hired and fired on a whim. Churchill made his own mistakes by interfering too much, but he was on top of everything and kept tight control over his military commanders. He wanted to know detail so that he could comprehend the 'big picture' and make decisions accordingly. By contrast, Curtin waited for reports and relied on MacArthur first and Blamey second for assessments. This left him vulnerable to their 'spin'. He seemed content to be left in the dark until the chiefs enlightened him.

Despite the massive setback at Gona, the Japanese refused to give up New Guinea and Papua. On 12 December 1942, they landed 500 more soldiers – led by Horii's successor, Major General Oda Kensaku

– at Mambare Bay, where there had previously been aborted landings. The contingent headed east of Gona to the Japanese headquarters at Sanananda.

By mid-December 1942, there was promising news on another front for the Allies. The US division on Guadalcanal had taken the southern part of the island from the enemy, who had lost around 30,000 soldiers. The Americans now had less than twenty-five kilometres to advance in the north to control the entire island.

The diggers mopping up west of Gona came up against resistance from small groups of the remaining 750 Japanese in the jungle near the beach. Most were wounded survivors of Horii's retreat, and many were prepared to fight to the death. Most enemy soldiers of the Gona garrison of more than 1000 were killed in action. Some committed suicide; a handful escaped deeper into the jungle and a few surrendered.

The battles and disease also took their toll on the Australians of the 39th Battalion, which lost 228 of its 350 men over fourteen days of battle. The 2/14th could barely produce twenty-five fit soldiers out of its usual complement of 800.

After analysis, Herring and Blamey expressed satisfaction with the result, considering these losses justified. Ralph Honner would never agree. Nor would he ever forget his failed first attack. He had introduced tactics that won the campaign and reduced Australian losses, but Honner believed the Gona battles were a terrible, unnecessary waste of life.

Ten days after the Allies decided that its lightweight Stuart tank was the answer to flushing out the Japanese, eight were smuggled into the Buna area. The complex operation over two nights involved a freighter, barges and jungle camouflage.

These light tanks of the 18th Brigade's 2/6th Cavalry were the first to be used in New Guinea. On 17 December, at 6.50 p.m. as the sun was setting, mortar fire hit the area of the Japanese bunkers in the coconut grove known as Duropa Plantation, just east of Cape Endaiadere. The whistling, crashing shells drowned out the sound of the tanks squealing their way forward in support. The hideous clanging noise was audible only to the 500 men of the 18th Brigade, who trotted along in the wake of these frightening machines. They gave the diggers extra confidence, as did their new phosphorous grenades, which would destroy enemy soldiers or cause grotesque burns. The Allies had no hesitation now in meeting the enemy's inhumanity with their own.

The forward infantry lit flares to guide the tanks. Diggers with the best throwing arms hurled grenades, landing them close to the bunkers, some of which were made of concrete with steel doors. The tanks crawled up within four metres of them and fired, and the diggers followed. Emboldened, they threw more grenades into the ground slits that marked the bunkers, some of which imploded. Those Japanese soldiers who scrambled from the holes were gunned down.

The main resistance came from sentry snipers in the trees. Every minute they would strike easy targets among the diggers, whose eyes were on the tanks and the bunkers ahead. The order was yelled to spread a little. Still the diggers went down, struck by the unseen assassins above and behind them. Counter-snipers moved to patrol the diggers' flanks. A flash of rifle fire revealed the Japanese positions in the trees, and the counter-snipers would then stalk the Japanese, some climbing into the lower branches to get a better shot. Trees often held two or three snipers, who were sprayed with machine-gun bullets. None surrendered: it was kill or be killed.

A crude pattern developed. Tanks and diggers would destroy one bunker and its men, then the machines would robotically turn towards other bunkers and the carnage would be repeated. But the Australians did not have it all their own way. Some Japanese fulfilled their pledge to the Emperor and went down fighting. One jumped on a tank, jammed his pistol into the vision slit and fired, killing the driver. In seconds, the Japanese was riddled with machine-gun bullets.

Others tried to light fires under the tanks. Many hastily-prepared Molotov cocktails were hurled. One burst on a tank's turret and set fire to it; its driver wheeled left until it was away from the bunkers, and it crashed into a coconut tree. The hatch door was pushed open. The crew scrambled out, protected by gunfire from fellow diggers who had followed the vehicle's plight.

Inside eighty minutes, night fell. The fierce encounter was over. The grove fell silent, but for the odd burst of machine-gun or rifle fire as an escaping enemy soldier was spotted. The entire plantation, riddled with a network of bunkers, had been cleared of the enemy. Up to 500 Japanese had been wiped out, but the Australians lost fifty-four killed and 117 wounded, mostly by the snipers hidden in the trees.

This had been Tobruk in reverse. The Japanese in the bunkers had faced everything from tanks to snipers and artillery. The diggers knew from experience what that was like.

This had been the kind of breakthrough that MacArthur and Blamey had been waiting for. It was significant for its complete destruction of the enemy in the eastern sector of Buna's coastline. Yet there were still Japanese garrisons whose elimination would demand a similar effort.

Nevertheless, MacArthur issued one of his infamous communiqués that would arouse ridicule from Australians and Americans who knew his nature. If truth was the first casualty of war, integrity had now been interred by MacArthur. In this case, he spoke of an 'Allied' victory, when it was exclusively Australian, due to bold planning by the commanders, with Wootten predominant. It was executed by the diggers on foot and in tanks. The US had played a role with artillery, but that was it.

Such propaganda was inexcusable but, coming from MacArthur, understandable. What annoyed everyone, including some American commanders, was that he made it appear as if he had planned the attack and even led the battle charge. MacArthur's overriding concern was his rivalry with the US Navy. He controlled the media, thanks to Curtin's deference to him, and so could ensure that Blamey and the Australian forces received little or no credit for their achievements in Papua.

MacArthur's premature and incorrect announcement about events on the northern coast was unknown to those who were risking and losing their lives at the front. There was still much to do.

The 18th Brigade's tank and infantry juggernaut moved west, with its first obstacle being the coconut grove's western boundary, Simemi Creek. The brigade's objective was to manoeuvre the tanks to occupy an abandoned airfield known as Old Strip. The only bridge over the creek was a forty-metre log structure, which had been destroyed on the far bank.

American engineers tried to repair it but were pushed back by machine-gun fire. Scouts scoured the creek, moving along its westward meander for about 350 metres until they found a place shallow enough for a contingent of twenty diggers to wade over. They moved swiftly back along the west bank and attacked the Japanese defenders, who retreated to the airstrip.

A further two kilometres west, Eichelberger's Urbana Force was having a tough time against the obstinate Japanese in the Government Gardens, which ran up to the Buna Government Station on the coast. Its most difficult obstacle was Entrance Creek, a swift tidal river that formed the western border of the Gardens. The river had a narrow footbridge, which the Japanese protected with machine guns and snipers. Eichelberger's men, in whom he had now engendered courage and will, were braving the bridge and the river, only to be cut down in the rapids.

He moved the assault further north, closer to where the creek created a mote around little Must Island, just 300 metres from the coast. The Americans defeated the small enemy force there. They called for heavy artillery, in preparation for Eichelberger's onslaught, which he had planned for 24 December. This would coincide with the Australian tank and infantry mini blitzkrieg on the airstrips roughly two kilometres away to the east.

The diggers at Simemi Creek held off the Japanese attacks, allowing engineers to repair the log bridge by 24 December. A day of thunderstorms culminated in torrential rain overnight, which provided crude cover as the four tanks rumbled over the creek. They advanced about 300 metres before meeting stiff opposition at Old Strip. The Japanese had set up anti-aircraft guns to fire horizontally.

Two tanks veered south on the airfield to avoid the powerful guns. One ran into a swamp and had to be abandoned. The other slipped into a bomb crater and could not extricate itself. Its crew clambered out and left it before the enemy could reach them.

Two tanks remained. Their crews decided to weave over Old Strip towards the Japanese bunkers. The vehicles' routes were impeded by plane wreckage on the overgrown strip. The obstacles, craters and swamp did not allow the tanks to gain speed as they groped their way forward, making them easier targets. Both were struck and destroyed by the anti-aircraft guns.

The infantry had no choice but to make the running at Old Strip. The Australians moved first, followed by the Americans, who were showing more fight under Eichelberger's tougher command. The Allies were soon entangled in a bitter engagement, fighting their way around the wreckage on the airstrip.

Eichelberger's force at the Buna Government Gardens failed to break through. The Japanese were stubborn at a series of hardened bunkers known as 'the Triangle' at the Gardens' southern boundary. The loss of his troops in these battles brought despair to the strong, yet sensitive general.

Part Six
Battle for Australia
1943

65
Buna Busted

Back in Port Moresby, the fretting and impatient MacArthur took time off for a Christmas Day feast – of duck – for himself, his family and staff. He released a pious communiqué: 'On Christmas Day our activities were limited to routine safety precautions. Divine services were held.'[1]

This was false. No services were held on any of the remaining northern coast battlefronts. All Allied troops were involved in desperate struggles. The Americans were in a precarious position.

A few kilometres away from MacArthur's headquarters, a relaxed, jovial Blamey tucked into a ten-pound turkey with his staff. The occasion was a good excuse for an extra-indulgence in alcohol, especially Scotch. Blamey had invited Herring to fly down from the northern coast to join him, knowing that the general could not leave his post near the front. Both MacArthur and Blamey gave the appearance of having a callous disregard, even an ignorance of events – and certainly of the detail of the horrific battles going on at Buna. They remained interested only in end results, and then only favourable ones.

The coastal front fight at Buna continued to be a slow, brutal grind. It took the diggers at Old Strip through Christmas Day and into 26 December to push the Japanese back 500 metres. But the battle was still on.

The Americans brought their 25-pound field artillery guns to the other airfield – New Strip, on the southern flank of Duropa Plantation. These had a range of almost a kilometre, which meant they did not have to be hauled over the log bridge. Their armour-piercing shells were fired at the Japanese defensive positions on Old Strip. Almost all the bunkers were obliterated. This ended the battle for Buna's airfields, yet there were still hard fights to come. Japan's determination to struggle to the last man made this a bloody, prolonged business.

The 26 and 27 December 1942 brought awful defeats to the Americans in the Government Gardens. They were cut off, trapped and paralysed into inaction. An entire company was wiped out. The tragic episode pushed Eichelberger into a bout of depression. He recalled MacArthur's cruel send-off after their meeting three weeks earlier on the verandah of his bungalow: 'Take Buna or don't come back alive.'

Matters became worse early on 28 December, when Urbano Force attacked from Musito Island. Luck was against them. The only bridge to this tiny isle collapsed, drowning many soldiers and preventing further advances. Eichelberger panicked, believing the Americans would be defeated, which would deliver MacArthur a Philippines-like failure. He became unstable, going into a rage in front of his staff. Some believed he would have to be relieved.

But Eichelberger's sanity and career – as well as American honour and the battle position at Buna – were saved by mid-morning. A contingent of Urbano Force led by Major Ed Schroeder broke through in Government Gardens. In a miraculous turnaround, it took control of the area. Now no supplies could move through to the enemy. Very soon, the Japanese inside the Triangle would run out of food and ammunition.

The Japanese soldiers abandoned their bunkers in the dead of night, slinking off towards their headquarters near the Buna Government Station by the coast. By 29 December their retreat intensified, as Wootten's 18th Brigade from the west and Urbano Force from the south drove the Japanese to the coast. They were soon fleeing east to Giropa Point.

Eichelberger was now on a euphoric high. He wanted American honours at Buna and delivered orders accordingly. But he was too eager. The push ended in disaster for the Americans, who lost many men. They were stopped short of Giropa Point. This allowed Wootten and his diggers to swoop in for the kill.

The Japanese began to evacuate. Those who could not climb aboard boats heading for Rabaul at night instead dived into the sea, using anything that would float them away from the advancing Allies on the beach. Allied machine-gunners parked themselves on the beach and raked the sea with fire, collecting the fleeing enemy soldiers in the choppy waters. Allied planes skimmed the water, searching for escapees. Those spotted were strafed until they disappeared.

By the first week of January 1943, the Battle for Buna was all but over. Wootten's battered but unbowed 18th Brigade lost 267 killed and 557 wounded. The Americans' 32nd Division lost 353 dead and 1508 wounded. The vanquished Japanese fared worse, losing at least 2000 men, although exact figures were never calculated.

Just three Japanese prisoners were taken. Most of their force, from officers down to the last private, had stayed true to their vow of fighting to the death for their unit, their country and the Emperor.

66
Sanananda Sorrow

On 8 January 1943, MacArthur flew out of Port Moresby, taking Kenney with him. Arriving in Brisbane, he told the assembled media, 'The Papuan Campaign is in its final closing stages. The Sanananda position has now been completely enveloped. A remnant of the enemy's forces is entrenched there and face certain destruction . . . This can now be regarded as accomplished.'

No Allied commander at the northern coastal front agreed. Eichelberger was appalled when he learned his chief had said there was only 'mopping up' to do at Sanananda. He believed this misleading pronouncement was just an excuse for MacArthur to leave

Papua. In private letters he told of MacArthur's ignorance. He had exhorted Eichelberger to attack in thousands, not hundreds, a directive demonstrating that he had no comprehension of how the Allied forces were 'divided into many corridors by swamps'.[1]

'The great hero,' Eichelberger wrote sarcastically, 'went home without seeing Buna before, during or after the fight while permitting press articles from his [Brisbane] GHQ to say he was leading his troops in battle.'[2]

Wootten welcomed 1000 fresh Australian troops for the last, gruelling Papua campaign at Sanananda. He planned an attack along both flanks of the swampy track running to the village, and would be supported by an American regiment coming from the west at Tarakena. Wootten had been happy with the impact of tanks at Buna. Although their effectiveness in swampier areas was limited, their capacity to ride right up to the Japanese bunkers, along with their shock value, convinced him to let them lead again.

This time, however, they had further limitations. The tanks had to move in single file; a metre or so either side of the path, the earth was so soft that they would become bogged. The Japanese were better prepared now with anti-tank guns, again including anti-aircraft guns calibrated to fire horizontally.

The enemy unleashed everything they could at the tanks, forcing one off into the jungle and making a destructive direct hit on another. A third was ripped open like a tin of sardines, but its driver wheeled it around and moved back onto the track. This disabling of the diggers' armoured shield left them vulnerable as they approached Killerton Junction, where the Japanese had concentrated their well-camouflaged bunkers. The diggers had gone only a few hundred metres before snipers and machine-gunners blazed into them, felling ninety-nine men within minutes. Wootten called a halt.

A conference was held at Vasey's headquarters. Vasey was aware of the exhausted condition of almost the entire Allied force. He and Eichelberger knew of MacArthur's absurd declaration that there was only 'mopping up' to do at Sanananda. Vasey believed there was a window of opportunity to spare the Allied soldiers and starve out the

Japanese, who were now cornered. Eichelberger, emboldened after the reversal at Buna, wanted to make another full-frontal assault but Vasey disagreed vehemently. 'I won't be party to further bloody murder!' he exclaimed as he departed the meeting.[3]

The Allies' battle tactics remained unresolved for two days. In that time, the Japanese, who had been more shattered by the Allied attack than even the Allied commanders realised, abandoned Killerton Junction. The handful who stayed were defeated easily.

The Japanese commanders had told their men to prepare for evacuation on 25 January 1943: this gave the soldiers about ten days to make their way eighty kilometres west of Sanananda, through Australian-controlled Gona, to the deltas of the Kumusi and Mambare Rivers. They would have to negotiate swollen rivers, swamps and diggers on the lookout for them, in a race against time. Japanese motor-launches from Rabaul would be waiting for the evacuees.

Vasey wasted no time in directing Wootten to push three of his battalions west, past the junction and closer to the coast. The Americans moved in from the south and east, completing the three-pronged sweep; they destroyed any bunker they came across. On 16 January, the conditions conspired to assist Japanese attempts to escape, with the most ferocious thunderstorm yet experienced by the Allies. When it subsided, black clouds descended over the area, reducing visibility to less than a metre. Then the torrents came down in waves, dumping thirty centimetres of rain over an eighty-kilometre stretch of coast. This extraordinary deluge flooded bunkers, forcing out all bodies, alive and dead.

When the storm eased, gales took over, moving water faster than ever, and disgorging bloated, decayed bodies, which floated through the mangroves. Countless coconuts were sometimes indiscernible from bobbing heads, causing diggers to fire at them just to be sure they were not enemy soldiers surging in their direction. On occasions, some of the bodies came alive, as Japanese soldiers, flushed from their bunkers, surfed through the freely flowing swamp. But two companies of the 2/12th Battalion found a small sand island between the angry ocean and the rising swamps, about 100 metres east of Sanananda.

At dawn, the storm subsided just as quickly as it had hit. Daylight revealed the devastating results of the storms. In an hour, the sun baked the area and drew out a sickening, lingering stench. Midmorning, the diggers broke into Sanananda village and overwhelmed the Japanese defending it. Technically, the battle for this third major Japanese stronghold was over. But while commanders may have celebrated, there was still some serious fighting to do.

Wootten's battalions had to tackle an enemy enclave of bunkers and hastily constructed forts, some cobbled together from debris left after the storm. This final island of resistance was a few hundred metres inland from the village and surrounded by a moat of bog, through which the diggers would have to make their way. In places it was above their heads. The Japanese snipers and machine-gunners were able to pick off some of the diggers.

By the end of 17 January 1943, about seventy diggers had been killed or wounded in this final mission. The slow-motion battle continued from 18 to 21 January. Another 150 diggers became casualties in the last drive to kill the remaining hundred Japanese. When they took the mud island, the diggers discovered the remains of the enemy soldiers, their bodies fly-blown and skeletal. There was clear evidence of cannibalism as the starving Japanese struggled to survive. Although this was outlawed by the Imperial Army, there was a secret pact that the dead could be useful to the living in these extreme circumstances.

The enemy was out of this region of Papua after its first land defeat of the war. It was about to be beaten on Gaudalcanal. The Allies had the upper hand but could not become complacent. The Japanese were still well established just 250 kilometres west along the Papuan/New Guinea coast, at Salamaua and Lae, and had no intention to vacate these strongholds.

67
War of Opportunity

Curtin was apprised of the 'success' by MacArthur and Blamey, but was sobered by the statistics that accompanied this first land defeat for the Japanese. About 22,000 Australian troops served in combat or support roles in the Owen Stanley Range, Milne Bay and on the northern coast. Some 2165 were killed, 3500 were wounded and nearly all the rest suffered from diseases, including malaria, tropical ulcers, scrub typhus, dengue fever, dysentery and various other tropical illnesses. Malaria had the greatest impact. Very few Australians left Papua or New Guinea without having had it; some suffered lingering symptoms. Malaria was also the biggest killer.

MacArthur had told Curtin that the threat to Australia was over by mid-1942, but Curtin had not believed this. The struggle in the Owen Stanley Range, at Milne Bay and on the northern coast put it in doubt, even at times in MacArthur's mind.

The Allied casualty rates in Papua were twice those at Guadalcanal, which indicated how determined the Japanese were to hold their positions there. In January 1943, Curtin felt less uncomfortable about the situation but was still guarded. He pushed harder than anyone for military aid from Britain. Churchill, he told journalists, had forgotten about Australia. In the larger scheme of things, with the war in Europe and the Middle East, this was understandable.

Curtin had pushed Churchill for planes to aid MacArthur in taking Rabaul, which the American saw as his first step towards recovering the Philippines. MacArthur's preoccupation with Rabaul had caused him to take his eye off Papua and New Guinea, where he grossly underestimated Japan's intent. Curtin supported his ambitions, which suited his own purposes. The further away the Japanese were pushed, the better for Australia.

To that end, Curtin wished to urge Churchill and Roosevelt to send greater military aid to the Pacific. Curtin sent a message to Washington DC, believing that the two leaders were meeting there, but they were in Casablanca. He need not have bothered: their main aim was still the defeat of Hitler. But because it was clear there would not be an Allied invasion of Europe in 1943, Roosevelt had already decided to pump more defence resources into the Pacific campaign. His factories were producing everything from planes to ammunition.

Curtin made a speech on 26 January 1943, Australia Day, that was broadcast in the United States and the United Kingdom. He put a case for smashing the Japanese as fast as possible, and not indulging in a 'holding war'. Again, he was aiming to win more military hardware and aid for the South-West Pacific. Some British commentators were critical of Curtin's appeal to American public opinion. But MacArthur, who would have had direct input, if not to the speech then certainly to Curtin's mind, told him his speech was magnificent. Better to have the Australian prime minister do the pleading than the Supreme Commander himself.[1]

It was useful for Curtin's image abroad that his Militia Bill, which came before parliament in late January, did not receive much analysis outside Australia. It had been reduced to absurdity. Curtin had been forced by the ALP caucus to set a very narrow boundary in which militia soldiers could fight the Japanese outside Australia. They had to be kept south of the equator. They could not go to New Caledonia or Malaya. Most ridiculously, conscripted troops could not fight in New Zealand. It was an affront to the Anzac tradition.

Australian newspapers attacked Curtin. The federal opposition sneered at the legislation's puniness. In private, Curtin expressed to journalists his disappointment at having to compromise with the Victorian ALP caucus in particular. Arthur Calwell, his main antagonist, pushed to get rid of the bill altogether.

This was galling for Curtin, given what the Australians had been through while fighting the Japanese out of Papua-New Guinea. The Allies, with the Australians prominent in all battles, had to rely more heavily than ever envisaged on their militia troops, especially the 39th Battalion, which acquitted itself so well. To suggest they could sacrifice so much in Papua-New Guinea and then not chase the enemy the short distance to New Britain or Malaya to ensure they could not return to Australian territory defied common sense.

Fortunately for Curtin, the opposition was also divided over the issue. Menzies led a faction that wanted to go further and merge the militia with the AIF. Despite Hughes' attack on Curtin for being 'a man who all his life has bitterly opposed [conscription]', he supported the bill, as did Fadden. This backing helped Curtin's minority government pass the Militia Bill on 19 February 1943.

The opposition's division over this issue and others encouraged Curtin to step up his reform program for the country. He now had more confidence about the next federal election, which he was planning for later in 1943. He wanted a clear mandate from the nation, instead of being dependent on independents and support from members of the opposition, which varied from bill to bill. Curtin was encouraged by his success in transforming Australia's sleepy economy into one adaptable to all the needs of war.

A big factor was excluding the states from collecting income tax. In July 1942, Curtin and Evatt used the High Court and parliament to push through a series of acts to help the states with, among other things, Commonwealth financial assistance, provided they did not collect their own income taxes. These acts would lead to a watershed in federal–state relations, but the immediate impact was to bump up Canberra's power. The federal government now had the resources to consolidate the nation's war footing and continue its commitment to MacArthur to 'take care of the rear' in the Pacific War.

Backed by Chifley and Evatt, Curtin saw the chance to implement social and other reforms. At first, there were grumblings among lower-income workers about increased taxes, but these were offset by Curtin's introduction of a pension for war widows. He then created a 'National Welfare Fund', which would be 'an integral part of the Government's plans for the social security of the people'. If re-elected with a healthy majority, he planned to introduce unemployment, sickness and pharmaceutical benefits. There was also an ambitious plan for hospital and medical benefits, but problems were expected from the strong medical professionals' lobby.[2]

Prime among these was the Statute of Westminster Adoption Act, enacted by the British parliament in 1931. The act declared that 'the imperial parliament would exercise no supervisory powers over the legislation of self-governing dominions'. Since 1931, Australia's governments had let this act lie untouched, asserting that Australia did not need this legal protection for its independence. It was effective without it. The unofficial reasons for the conservative governments' inaction centred on their reliance on British naval power in the Asia-Pacific region. Menzies' Minister for External Affairs, Richard Casey, summed up the view: 'I am against those who say we should have an Australian foreign policy simply for the sake of having it. British foreign policy may be regarded in a very real sense as Australian foreign policy.'[3]

Perhaps in the 1930s it had been acceptable that, in an emergency such as war, the British could enforce their 'supervisory powers'. In other words, they could co-opt Australian forces or even take control of the government. Evatt and Curtin wanted to test this in the federal parliament. In February 1942, Churchill had wanted to push Australian troops to Burma rather than return them home, as Curtin had demanded. Had Churchill been more desperate, he may have been tempted to use his 'supervisory power'.

The Curtin government also reformed the Australian Broadcasting Commission (ABC), and instituted modest regulations for commercial broadcasters, including the setting-up of a parliamentary standing committee to investigate all broadcasting matters. The prime minister wanted to strengthen the ABC as 'an independent source of information' against what he saw as anti-Labor bias by some proprietors, such as Frank Packer in Sydney and Keith Murdoch in Melbourne. In other words, the ABC was to be politicised in the interests of media balance.

These moves did not endear Curtin to the country's newspaper barons, yet his public support was growing. Most papers wished to reflect that, which meant that Curtin received generally positive publicity. He had the support of Canberra's reporters and many other journalists with whom he came into contact; his sensitivity to negative comment, however, caused him to believe that he had more adversaries than he actually did.

Curtin shrewdly broadened Labor's electoral appeal by legislating with women in mind. His Women's Employment Act allowed women to work in areas that had previously been the preserve of men. The government set the terms for pay and conditions. Women were not yet equal with men in the eyes of the law, but Curtin had at least limited their exploitation in the workplace. He also removed the embarrassing rule that young men could be recruited to fight and die for their country but could not vote to say who ran it. Men aged eighteen to twenty-one who had served or were serving could now put their votes in the ballot box. The Australian Soldiers Repatriation Act extended these benefits to young women who had enlisted to serve.

These and other moves demonstrated Curtin was prepared to be proactive throughout the life of his first government, despite its minority disposition. Some accused him of 'socialising' Australia, while the far left of his party urged him to do just that.

68
The Japanese Keep Coming

Curtin's popularity was given another boost when, after months of trying, he managed to extract the 9th Division from the Middle East and return it safely to Australia in February 1943. Both Churchill and Roosevelt had earlier prevented the move, as they had with the 6th and 7th Divisions after Darwin was bombed a year earlier.

Curtin had pushed hard for the 9th in October 1942 when Japanese pressure in Papua was it its height. British Field Marshal Bernard Montgomery needed the division for his second major offensive against the Axis powers in the Middle East's Western Desert. He regarded the 9th as a secret weapon, the strongest of his frontline 'shock' troops. They were in the thick of the fighting around El Alamein over four months, suffering 5827 casualties: 1225 killed, 3638 wounded and 964 captured. This severe attrition was sobering for Curtin and his government, who believed the division should have been back in Australia.

Once more, Churchill had hung on as long as he could, knowing that losing this exceptional force would impact on his war against Hitler. He had managed to keep them for El Alamein, but by mid-December he gave them up reluctantly. This wrangle magnified his grudge against Curtin and the Australian government.

The 9th Division was parked in Gaza in late December 1942. Curtin only relaxed a fraction when told it had embarked for Australia on four troopships on 24 January 1943. There was still considerable enemy activity en route, right through to the Indian Ocean, causing Curtin to worry about the ships until they reached Fremantle on 18 February.

The return of the last of the battle-hardened diggers heartened the nation. The press made much of their achievements. They would support and replace the depleted AIF and militia troops, particularly in Papua, on which the stubborn Japanese still had designs, despite their recent emphatic defeats.

But there was no respite for Curtin, who still faced an internecine battle at home with the extreme elements of his party and the unions. Now that the Japanese threat had receded, coalminers increased strike action in March 1943. Curtin had tremendous political capital, despite his government's minority status, but instead of taking hard action himself, he huffed and puffed about conscripting men to work in the mines and, later, about gaining tough powers to sack miners.

As ever, he faced opposition from Eddie Ward, who would only agree to these measures if the coal industry was nationalised. The press attacked Curtin for his inertia; the affair fatigued him. He set off by train to Perth for some rest, depressed by the thought that his hard-earned popularity had been lost and that his chances at the next election were slipping away.

He was lifted when he saw Australian troops cheering him along the way, which both inspired and humbled him. His decisions meant life or death for them, yet they appeared to support him fully. Curtin would carry on. So would those troops, whom he respected so much and over whom he worried day and night.

There was no respite for the troops, either. The irrepressible Japanese had managed to reinforce their soldiers at Lae, on the coast west of Buna. They raided Wau in January 1943 but were engaged by Kanga Force, which had been strengthened by the addition of part of the 17th Brigade.

By 27 January, Japanese troops were again three kilometres from Wau. By 29 January, they were fighting on the airstrip's perimeter. A further 800 members of the 17th Brigade, who had been held up by bad weather, flew to Wau. They helped repulse the invaders. Battles went on for four weeks, and the Japanese were shoved back to Mubo, between Salamaua and Wau. The enemy lost more than 1200 men but reinforced the beleaguered troops with another 6000 soldiers.

The Australians saw these troop movements as evidence that the Japanese planned to drive the Australian guerrillas out of Timor. The decision was made to evacuate them after their many months of fighting against a sizeable enemy force.

Despite the successes of Australian and US forces on Papua's north coast brawls continued in Australia due to national rivalry. In Melbourne on 14 February 1943 forty locals and Americans had brawled with each other under the clocks of Flinders Street Station. An estimated crowd of a thousand people swirled around the punching, kicking, wrestling servicemen. After about half an hour, police waded in and took several men to the city watch-house. No injuries were recorded and no major charges were laid. Observers believed the hanging of the 'Brownout murderer' Edward Leonski had led to the brawl.

The real war concerning Americans and Australians went on. On a Friday night in mid-February 1943, a Japanese plane flew over Sydney at 15,000 feet. Radio direction finders picked it up. Nine RAAF planes were scrambled to track and intercept it, but it escaped. Curtin linked this plane to the arrival of the 30,000 troops of the 9th Division, whose ship had docked at Fremantle. He believed the Japanese were trying to trace the big carriers arriving on the east coast.

The military and Curtin agreed not to disembark the 9th Division in Western Australia. They would have been stuck there for six months before they could be transported via the primitive and inadequate rail system to the east of the country. Curtin told journalists that he had not slept for three weeks due to his worry about these troops, whom he now considered to be in imminent danger of an enemy attack.

Japan's persistence after the battles of Gona, Buna and Sanananda caused Blamey to believe it was time to begin to remove the Japanese from New Guinea altogether. But it was no easy task: there were still an estimated 8000 enemy soldiers stationed at three bases around Lae and Salamaua. Their reinforcements would bring the number up to about 14,000. It would take an effort similar to that of the Owen Stanley Range and Gona–Buna–Sanananda campaigns to achieve the enemy's elimination.

As Blamey was organising the Australian 3rd Division for this huge and protracted mission beginning in March, General Kenney learned from reconnaissance aircraft of an enemy convoy near Finschhafen, carrying the 6000 reinforcements for the New Guinea coast. On 3 March, RAAF Bostons bombed the airfields at Lae and Salamaua to prevent Japanese Zeros taking off to protect their convoy. This left the Allies free to attack the Japanese ships without retaliation. RAAF Beaufighters, US B-17s and B-25 bombers began a well-coordinated assault.

First the Beaufighters swooped low, strafing the ships' bridges and anti-aircraft guns. The US bombers then thundered in, dropping their loads. The B-25 pilots, for the first time, used 'skip-bombs': released at masthead height, they bounced across the water, penetrated a ship's hull and exploded. This went on, run after run, until all eight merchant ships and four destroyers were sunk. Thirty-two Japanese aircraft were lost in action. Nearly 3000 enemy soldiers became casualties. The Allies lost just thirteen crew-members, with two crash-landings and four planes knocked out.

Hundreds of Japanese survivors were in barges and on rafts, still heading for the New Guinea coast. MacArthur remembered the Japanese convoy that was destroyed heading for Lae almost exactly a year earlier. He delivered chilling orders: no Japanese troops were to make it ashore. In one way, this order was less difficult to issue, given the way enemy troops had behaved in New Guinea. Allied officers and men alike wanted payback. But for the pilots, bombardiers and gunners in the Allied planes, who had not been fighting on the ground, there was some repugnance about carrying out this command. There was something noble about a dogfight. It was challenging to sink a destroyer or aircraft carrier. It was even necessary to blow up merchant ships and troop carriers. But there seemed nothing redeeming in blowing away soldiers on makeshift rafts.

Yet the High Command's directives were carried out, leaving some members of the air crews physically sick. After the cruel battles in Papua and Guadalcanal, the Pacific War reached another level of destruction in what was called the Battle of the Bismarck Sea.[1]

The Japanese realised they were now blocked from reaching the coast by the usual means, but they remained determined. They decided to use submarines and barges from Rabaul at night to deposit reinforcements.

In early March 1943, Curtin announced to the nation that RAF and RAAF Spitfire squadrons were now in Australia. 144 new planes were in the country. A further twenty-seven were on ships coming in. He reckoned that seventy-one squadrons (with twelve to fourteen planes to a squadron) were needed to defend the nation and then launch an offensive. For the first time, the Australian military was gaining confidence that it could win the battle of the air.

Yet there was just too much coastline to defend. The enemy raided Darwin on 11 March, hitting two oil tanks and damaging others. Curtin and some of his chiefs were concerned that Japan's withdrawal from the Solomon Islands would be followed by attacks against Australia, especially since all Australia's air strength had been moved from the west to the north. Despite the new Spitfires, the Australians and their allies did not have enough planes or manpower to defend the north-west and west simultaneously.

Admiral Yamamoto had been the most powerful military figure in Japan since the attacks on Pearl Harbor and Darwin, but a year later, after several defeats culminating in the Battle of the Bismarck Sea, his status had slipped. He needed a success to reassert his prestige.

He and his subordinates developed a campaign – Operation 1-Go – centred on a string of bombing raids on any Allied ships, even hospital vessels, in the South-West Pacific. He put 300 planes into the air from Rabaul, leaving almost none on the ground. Many pilots who were rushed into this operation early in April 1943 had not been in combat or even on bombing runs before. Their inexperience, the weather and the Allied planes conspired to minimise 1-Go's success.

Yamamoto became desperate. He decided to tour all Japanese bases in the South Pacific to inspire better performances. His complete itinerary, including the planes to be used, was signalled to all Japanese bases.

On 14 April, listening posts in Melbourne and Honolulu picked up Japanese Cipher JN-25D signals to Japanese bases. This disclosed Yamamoto's itinerary details, and within minutes the entire Allied force was alerted. For the Americans, Yamamoto, the architect of the Pearl Harbor attacks, was public enemy number one. Every fighter pilot wanted to be the one to blast him out of the sky.

The first leg of his journey was fixed for 18 April 1943, from Rabaul to a new airfield on the island of Ballale near Bougainville, close to New Guinea's eastern tip. Yamamoto would then take a boat to a nearby island. Admiral Nimitz was given the freedom by Washington – presumably by Roosevelt himself – to assassinate Japan's supreme naval commander. Admiral Bill Halsey was given the task. The only problem for the Americans was that if their assassination was successful, the Japanese would change their signals, meaning months of work to decipher them. But the US determination to avenge Pearl Harbor overrode this complication. Nimitz and Halsey were aware, too, that Yamamoto's demise would be a terrific blow against Japan's navy and the nation's morale.

The next question was whether to strike the two bombers, one of which would be carrying Yamamoto, or to hit the subsequent boat convoy. It was decided that it was easier to spot and attack the bombers in the air rather than isolate one boat from the flotilla of up to twenty craft that was expected to accompany Yamamoto.

Major John W. Mitchell of the 339th US Squadron was handed this special assignment, which was named Operation Vengeance. He put eighteen P-38 Lightning fighters into the air before dawn from Henderson Field on Guadalcanal. Mitchell guided his squadron on the 690-kilometre flight at low altitude, with their radios off for the entire journey.

Their timing was perfect. Just as they were over Ballale, at 9.34 a.m., six Zeros were spotted escorting the two Japanese twin-engine planes. One of the US pilots climbed to engage the Zeros, while another, flown by Lieutenant Rex T. Barber, dived after the descending bombers. He tailgated one, which happened to have Yamamoto in it, and attacked it with gunfire. The admiral, clutching his sword, was hit and killed instantly. The bomber crashed into jungle near Buin on Bougainville's southern coast. Barber then evaded pursuing Zeros and joined Lieutenant Besby Holmes in bringing down the second bomber, which crashed in the sea.

It was the longest flight-intercept mission of the war and one of the most successful. As one observer put it, assassinating Yamamoto was the equivalent to winning a major battle.

69
Savige Turn of Events

Blamey's choice to command the front at Wau – the fourth in New Guinea – was Major General Stan Savige. A veteran of Gallipoli and the Western Front, he had one of the most distinguished Australian war records in World War I. He added to this a remarkable yet at times controversial period in North Africa and the Middle East during World War II.

A major point of contention had developed between volunteers and militia soldiers, such as Savige, and the regular, academy-trained army elite. The latter had been taught officer skills but few had actual battle experience. Some disdained the militia soldiers and felt 'superior' to the Anzac breed of World War I soldier. They saw Savige and commanders such as Bennett, Blamey, Leslie Morshead, Herring and Allen as ignorant about modern war methods, tactics and strategies. In response, the veterans argued that what they had learned in their service, in civilian life and as volunteers between the wars outweighed the training of the new breed.

Blamey's patronage of Savige sparked fury among the AIF's top officers. Enemies of both men whispered that Blamey's support was because Savige had provided an alibi for him during the 'badge in the brothel' incident in 1926, which saved his position as commissioner of Victoria's police force.

Savige had commanded 6th Division's 17th Brigade in the thick of action in the initial 2nd AIF engagement in the war, at Bardia, Libya, from 3 to 5 January 1941. The division had been successful, but Savige had trouble reining in his young staff of academy-trained officers, whom he saw as overenthusiastic. The new breed had aimed at a quick and decisive tactical victory, whereas Savige thought that slower, flanking approaches would still see 'wins' but would lose fewer men. He received criticism from above and beneath him.

After the Greek campaign Savige and his brigade were seconded to the 7th Division in Syria to fight the Vichy French. Savige commanded in a five-day battle at Damour (5–9 July 1941), his most successful campaign. By the time he reached New Guinea to lead the 3rd Militia Brigade, which he had trained, he had been on six battle fronts in two wars, fighting and commanding against five enemy nations. No one in 1943 in the AIF or the US forces had his broad experience in frontline and field operations.

Savige disliked using frontal attacks, which he believed futile after his World War I experiences. But the new 'elite' thought differently. Head-on battles were integral to their overall approach. This was a major point of contention between Savige and some of his staff, whom he invariably inherited from the new officer class. Savige later said that 'with more freedom of movement in this war [World War II] I always sought to flank to encircle rather than attack frontally. This was particularly at Derna in the Libyan campaign and at Damour in the Syrian campaign.'[1]

Savige had been scarred by the huge loss of life in the frontal attacks at Gallipoli and on the Western Front. He knew what it was to be wounded during an ill-prepared frontal attack, with hundreds of his fellow diggers dead around him. He looked back on those campaigns as pathetic, inhumane and wasteful. Savige's main principle was the protection of his troops. He cared about every single soldier, which was seen as a weakness by the new officer class. Savige believed in keeping the morale of the force high. He made a point of moving over all the terrain his troops did, and in visiting them at every opportunity. This was scorned by MacArthur and his staff, the new officers, and even Blamey, who were rarely in touch with the frontline soldier, except for photo opportunities.

Yet Blamey did not underestimate Savige's strengths. He had a high regard for him that stretched back to August 1915, when Savige, one of the most accurate rifle shots in the 1st AIF, had been sent onto Gallipoli's Sniper's Ridge. It was the first assignment for this Sunday school teacher and scoutmaster. He was ordered to take on the Turkish hill snipers, who had wreaked havoc on Anzacs in the valley below. After just a nine-day stint, Savige had made thirty kills.

Blamey warned Savige that the operational areas between Wau and Salamaua were in 'the foulest country' and that this command was 'a poisonous job'[2]. But Savige was not deterred. He had seen some officers such as Allen, Rowell and Herring in key roles in New Guinea. Savige wanted to end his career with a fighting command. He soon acquainted himself with the terrain, which was as bad as anything in the Owen Stanley Range or the northern coast. He wrote: 'Such conditions of rain, mud, rottenness, stench, gloom, and above all, the feeling of being shut in by everlasting jungle and ever-ascending mountains, are sufficient to fray the strongest nerves.' He noted 'the tension of the constant expectancy of death from behind the impenetrable screen of green'.

Apart from nerves of steel, commanders and soldiers had to have 'morale of the highest to live down these conditions'. They had to be accepted 'as a matter of course'. The men had to 'maintain a cheerful yet fighting spirit'.[3]

Savige felt he was the man for the job, even if only Blamey was supporting him with any enthusiasm. The tactics of jungle warfare suited him. By instinct, he turned to the Japanese way of furtive, flanking attacks. There would be great reliance on air support, which, over the past months, had become a big factor in winning this protracted war. Most importantly, Savige generated the strongest team spirit possible. In his eyes, those with the best *esprit de corps* would beat the conditions and their enemy. From his first day, he moved among his troops. He knew the importance of getting mail to his 'boys'. There would always be a hot meal for them, even in the 'hottest' war spots. He would go to the front, feign an apology for interfering, and talk on the phone to commanders he knew.

Apart from being liked as a 'good bloke' who looked after his men, Savige was known as a 'winner' across two wars and several generations. His inspiration and his insistence on the welfare of his troops brought greater efforts in surprise attacks and more determination in hand-to-hand fighting.[4]

Savige's force included his former AIF 17th Brigade, commanded by Brigadier Murray Moten, which had seen off the Japanese when they first hit Wau in January a few months earlier. There was also the 2/3rd Independent Company, which had arrived soon after that battle. The remnants of Kanga Force, which had skirmished with the Japanese for some time in the area, were relieved by Savige's raw 3rd Militia Brigade. The link to the hard nuts in 17th Brigade was inspired, especially with Savige astride the entire new combination.

He had his plans for the defeat of the Japanese ready by the end of his first week at his initial headquarters at Bulolo, 100 kilometres from the coast and Salamaua. They called for the landing of US troops at Nassau Bay, sixty kilometres south of Salamaua. Savige was ready by 1 May 1943, which was just in time.[5] On 9 May the Japanese moved out of Mubo, where Moten had pushed them three months earlier, and attacked Australian contingents at Lababia Ridge, about thirty kilometres inland from the Huon Gulf.

The conflict and skirmishes of the past few months between the two opposing forces had stepped up. The fourth battle for Papua and New Guinea had begun.

70

Red Herring

The increased fighting meant more casualties, and traffic of hospital ships ferrying the wounded from New Guinea increased. One such Australian vessel was the *Centaur*. It was sailing in calm waters south-east of Cape Moreton on Queensland's coast on the night of 14 May 1943, on a return trip to New Guinea from Sydney. On board were doctors, nurses, field ambulance staff and crew. The ship was illuminated and marked with bright green stripes and three large crosses along the hull. There were also red neon crosses on each side of its funnel.

At 4.10 a.m. the ship was struck in a fuel tank on the port side by a Japanese submarine's torpedo. Most on board were thrown from their bunks. The ship caught fire. The crew scrambled to loosen life rafts, but even as they did so the *Centaur*'s nose was going under. About 150 people jumped into the sea. The ship went down in less than three minutes. More than 200 were trapped below decks engulfed by flames, then water. In all, 268 were killed. Just sixty-four survived. Although injured, Ellen Savage, a nurse, carried on working in the water, attending to others who were burned or hurt by the explosion. These heroic acts would later earn her the George Medal. Survivors were picked up thirty-six hours later by an American destroyer, the USS *Mugford*.

Curtin was stunned by Japan's blatant breaking of the Geneva Convention. It left him with a feeling of impotence, then depression. But as before, he summoned the strength to carry on in the pre-election months of mid-1943.

Curtin still had to deal with the more troublesome elements of Labor's broad church, most notably Eddie Ward. As the election loomed, Ward had been stepping up attacks on the conservatives about the so-called 'Brisbane Line'. He claimed that the opposition, if in government, would have abandoned the rest of the nation to the Japanese. In reality, the Labor government had more or less followed this approach since it had taken office, on advice from the military chiefs. But Ward was making it seem as if the conservatives cared less about the defence of the nation.

The opposition attacked Curtin over the accusation, calling on him to rebuke Ward. But Curtin would not. There was good political mileage in the issue, and Curtin did not wish to split the party, as he had over the Militia Bill. The prime minister filibustered at the dispatch box and a party conference to defuse the issue. He somehow united the necessary support for his position – which, in this case, was to do nothing. He had mastered the art of making clichés sound original and inspiring in a speech.

With conflict looming in the Wau–Salamaua area, Savige received further instructions. First, he had to drive the Japanese north of the Francisco River, sixty kilometres from his headquarters, as soon as possible. Second, he had to establish a beachhead for a proposed US force at Nassau Bay, ninety kilometres west. Once that was done, he was to develop a communications link with a battalion combat team from the US 41st Division, and then continue to push the Japanese north of the Francisco. In effect, the Americans would be under his command.

But Savige was not informed of the greater plan, which was to distract Japan's forces inland of Salamaua with 'raids' rather than battles. Blamey did not want Savige to take Salamaua. He planned to use two of his best battle commanders, Wootten and Vasey, to make an amphibious attack on Lae, sixty kilometres north of Salamaua.

Blamey wanted Savige and his diggers to draw the enemy from Lae, which would make it an easier target for the main assault.

Because of secrecy over the master plan, Herring himself was confused. He had been urging other officers, including Major General Frank Berryman, that Salamaua should be taken *before* Lae, yet he was concerned about Savige's intentions. Herring could have flown to Wau to speak with his commander, but neither he nor any member of his staff made the trip. This major error caused resentment towards the Port Moresby headquarters from all in the Wau–Salamaua operation.[1]

Herring had to coordinate and blend Australian and US forces. An added complication was that MacArthur and his Bataan Gang had disproportionate influence. Their opinions were often contradictory, ignorant of conditions or superfluous. On top of all this, Herring was not a good communicator. His instructions were unclear.

He ordered Savige to 'threaten' Salamaua, but was he to isolate it? Was he to secure it? Absorbing all the incoming commands, communiqués and intelligence, Savige understood that he was not to go 'too hard' at the enemy in the drive to shove them over the river. He directed his officers to avoid frontal attacks. Savige reined in his commanders who were keen to move with too much force, which, to the more adventurous among them, seemed an odd order. But with Herring's hesitant instructions, Savige was firm. If officers were too gung-ho and lives were lost unnecessarily, they would be shipped out.

MacArthur met with Curtin in Sydney on 10 June 1943 in front of a huge US and Australian media contingent. After the photo opportunity, MacArthur informed him that the Pacific War had begun a new stanza. The so-called 'holding war' was over. From now on there would be an offensive against Japan, with Australia still a key base.

Curtin then told the media that Japan would not be able to invade Australia. Yet he cautioned that the nation might still experience damaging raids. He was not specific about this, but bombings of targets on the mainland were ongoing. Darwin and surrounding areas had been hit about sixty times by air raids (until June 1943). Other towns and cities to be attacked and strafed included Queensland's

Horn Island, Townsville and Mossman. Western Australian targets included Exmouth, Broome, Wyndham, Port Hedland, Kalumburu, Onslow, Exmouth Gulf, Derby and Drysdale Mission. Apart from these raids, Sydney, Newcastle and Port Gregory (near Geraldton, Western Australia) were either bombed from the air or torpedoed by Japanese submarines. Scores of ships, large and small, were also being hit by them and sunk around Australia's coast-line.

In an off-the-record chat eight days after this public display, Curtin told his small corps of press confidants that Australia's entire armoured (tank) division was now in Western Australia. The state's flat terrain made it suitable for this force. He informed the journalists that, earlier in the war, there had been plans to build a road from the state's north-west to its more populated areas. This had been abandoned. 'Military authorities' believed an invading force might use it to attack the unprotected state. Now, with the danger of invasion over, the road was being built.

'It will not be so much a road as a trafficable artery,' Curtin said. The terrain's natural advantages were being utilised. He added that 'the engineers were merely filling in the soft spots.'[2]

Curtin faced a no-confidence motion from the opposition, which was an attempt to take government before an election was called. Arthur Fadden was banking on the two independents switching sides. He used Ward's allegations about the Brisbane Line, Curtin's weak handling of coal strikes, and his failure to support a national government as reasons for the no-confidence motion.

The subsequent parliamentary debate lasted two days. Curtin parried criticism and concentrated on his 'success' in handling the war. He informed the House that his government's policies had won the 'battle for Australia'. He spoke of Evatt securing aircraft from Roosevelt to boost the RAAF, and of the economy and its revival. The no-confidence motion was defeated.

Curtin appeared confident, on top of his job and in command. On 25 June, he called an election for 21 August 1943. The polls pointed to a Labor victory.

Savige continued his role, with its murky constraints, reading all patrol reports, requesting further details and watching every move in the forward areas. He offered suggestions to his commanders and sometimes even gave orders, which he admitted would have been interference in 'ordinary' warfare. Yet Savige knew the team spirit he had engendered allowed him such liberties.

He attacked the important Japanese stronghold of Mubo on 7 July 1943. This was followed by heavy RAAF air strikes on surrounding enemy positions. The 2/6th Battalion captured the western side of Observation Hill and, with the 2/5th Battalion's support, snared all but a few enemy posts. On 10 July, the encirclement of Mubo, fifty kilometres short of Salamaua, was completed by the US 162nd Regiment, linked with the 2/6th Battalion. By the next day the battle for this important enemy position was over.

Savige was summoned to Port Moresby for a conference with Herring on 19 July. Again, Herring was vague about Salamaua. MacArthur was interfering again, directing that Salamaua should be taken before Lae, which was what everyone but Blamey seemed to want. Herring had neither the will nor the ability to clear up the plan. He did not know how to handle Savige, or how to relate to the rank and file.

After their meeting, Savige went back to the front none the wiser, but he was determined to continue his overall directive of pushing the Japanese back over the Francisco River. He struck at the enemy's strongest defensive positions and repulsed counter-attacks. It was non-stop warfare, made even more dangerous by the jungle terrain. Savige drew on his long experience. He preserved his men with sound decisions that limited losses and fatigue.

71
Curtin's Electoral Appeal

While the experienced Savige turned the fourth Papua/New Guinea battlefront Australia's way, Curtin was fighting his own battle for political victory. And like the military veteran of two world wars, the Labor doyen of politics was a model of thoroughness. There would be no surprises in his own seat of Fremantle, which he nearly lost in the 1940 election.

In looking ahead to postwar Australia, Curtin spoke about the 1930s depression. 'Our energy, ingenuity and power will be devoted to ensuring that the manhood of this country will not rot in unemployment as it did after the last war,' he vowed. 'This government's policy of full development of resources, full employment of manpower . . . is a basis not only for Australian reconstruction, but for a stable and peaceful commonwealth of nations.'[1]

When Curtin flew the 2260 kilometres from Adelaide to Perth in a four-engine British Lancaster bomber, the message was obvious: he was a leader in touch with the armed forces. This was a media opportunity not available to Billy Hughes, leader of the opposition United Australia Party.

The war was good politics for Curtin. The nation had been consumed by the conflict in the Pacific since the last election. Curtin pointed out that since he had come to office, the number of people in the armed services or war industries had more than doubled to 1,172,000. He had successfully put a nation with mixed views about the war – some cynical and careless, yet most of it supportive – on a war footing. It pleased Curtin's socialist disposition to talk of pouring £82 million into 'taking care of the rear' for MacArthur, via the Allied Works Council, which had built roads and airfields across the neglected northern reaches of Australia's vast continent.

Curtin was a touch disingenuous in saying that the previous

governments had left the country unprepared and therefore undefended. His record in opposition was not notable for pronouncements warning of dangers from foreign predators, as Churchill's was in Britain. In fact, it was the British who urged Australia's governments to build up their defences. As early as 1919, the British naval mission to Australia, headed by Admiral of the Fleet Lord Jellicoe, recommended building key fleet bases at Darwin and Singapore. A decade later the world faced economic depression and James Scullin's Labor government opted for savage defence cuts. With Curtin front and centre, the ALP had been strongly pacifist until it took office under Curtin in October 1941.

Had Menzies stayed in power, his government would doubtless have scrambled to build the nation's defences, as Curtin had. It would have taken conscription further. No matter who was in power, there could have been no choice in the matter. Curtin's claims about his work to prevent 'this great country from being doomed' were credible not so much for their general attitude as for the integrity he had shown. Curtin had argued and pleaded with Churchill and Roosevelt over the return of the 6th, 7th and 9th Divisions to Australia, and, in the end, he had defied them.

All the opposition leaders and the government's envoys abroad tried to stop him. With support only from Evatt and Chifley, Curtin had wrenched the 6th and 7th from the war against Hitler and put them into the Pacific War for the direct defence of Australia. He had also returned the 9th from the Middle East. These divisions had been vital in holding New Guinea. They were still doing it.

As Curtin moved around the nation, mostly by train, Savige was overcoming the Japanese. His battle-hardened warriors were fighting alongside the raw recruits of 3rd Brigade, whom Savige, with his unmatched experience and intelligence, had trained from scratch. If Curtin had not been so determined to bring these Australian forces to New Guinea, the inexperienced Americans would have been spread too thin. Without the Australian 6th and 7th (and later the 9th) Divisions, along with the militia soldiers, fighting above their weight, the Japanese would have had a far less difficult road to Port Moresby.

They would most likely have taken that strategically vital town. The mighty US Air Force and the RAAF had an impact, but without the men on the ground the Allies would not be turning the war.

Curtin's mates and confidants among Australia's political journalists were aware of his achievements in standing up to Churchill and Roosevelt. Even if the Murdoch and Packer papers were editorialising against him and supporting Hughes in the election, journalists and editors were reporting in favour of Curtin, almost in defiance of their owners.

The experienced Edgar Holt, in Frank Packer's *Daily Telegraph*, acknowledged Curtin's brilliant handling of the opposition in parliament, suggesting he could send its members into an opium trance with his deft speeches. He fell back on a trusted description of Curtin as someone who had missed his calling as an accomplished thespian.

Yet Holt felt compelled – no doubt mindful of Packer's political sentiments – to balance this opinion with some less than flattering remarks about the prime minister. Curtin was ill a lot of the time with stress-related problems, which could mean he was a 'worry wart' over illness. Holt called him a hypochondriac. He also said Curtin lacked friends, which was wrong, and had a weak handshake, which was unlikely.

The Fairfax-owned *Sydney Morning Herald* was kinder. It was backing Curtin and Labor for the first time. Likening him to a stern headmaster when irritated, its political commentator, Ross Gollan, nevertheless spoke about the prime minister in almost obsequious terms. The journalist said Curtin was possessed of a 'cool and quiet manner' – this was his persona only for those close to him. Gollan also claimed that, regardless of his veneer of uncertainty and nervousness, Curtin had strength, with which no one who knew him well would disagree.[2]

The pressmen generally agreed that Curtin deserved a new mandate from the nation. Public polling, in its infancy but still a fair indicator, was consistent in its stronger support for Curtin and Labor than for the opposition. The ALP slogan reflected a confidence in Curtin that was unprecedented in Australian politics: 'You can't have Curtin if you don't vote Labor.'

72

Savige Sets Up Fourth Victory in Papua, New Guinea

The most important moment for the Wau–Salamaua operation came on 16 August, when the 2/6th Battalion moved to take Komiatum Spur, just thirteen kilometres from Tambu Bay on the New Guinea coast. Almost its full strength moved along a track made by patrols two days earlier. The diggers communicated in whispers to avoid detection. It took ten arduous hours to reach the foot of a ridge 400 metres from the Japanese position. The diggers then settled down to wait until 5.45 a.m. the next morning, when they would attack.

At about 5 a.m. one soldier forgot the rules and struck a match to light a cigarette. 'The noise of the striking match could be likened to an express train; the flare of the match to a searchlight,' a member of 6th Battalion later said. 'I wonder how many years we aged during the following hour or so before Zero Hour.'[1]

Allied artillery from the coast opened up on the spur right on time and with unerring accuracy. The diggers crept off, the shells whistling in and providing cover as they scrambled up the side of the ridge almost unopposed.

The Australians took and held the spur, pushing back counter-attacks over the next three days.[2]

'We found solutions to win through at Mount Tambu, Komiatum and Bobdubi Ridge,' Savige noted. He mentioned the 'heroism' of his charges. He also praised 'the supporting fire given by the 42nd Militia Battalion, elements of the 2/5th Battalion, and the artillery'. Savige forgot no one. 'The guts displayed by the men of other companies of 2/6 Battalion, who manhandled five tons of stores to the two companies forward, across rough country, defies description.'[3]

After taking over the main ridges and spurs, the next objective was the junction of the Bobdubi and Komiatum Tracks to Salamaua on the southern bank of the Francisco River. The heavily laden diggers strained, sweated and swore their way up the final slopes to the rough Komiatum Track.

The main threat to the Australian thrust was Japanese planes based at Wewak, further along the coast, where the enemy army had moved from Rabaul and Ambon to counter the Allies' progress. General Kenney established an airstrip in the Markham Valley, 100 kilometres west of Lae. On the night of 17 August 1943, Kenney ordered an air strike on Wewak and 175 Japanese planes were destroyed on the ground.

On 19 August the Japanese began to abandon the Bobdubi, Komiatum, Mount Tambu and Goodview positions.

'We were "mates" in a team,' Savige later said. 'Plans to obtain victory were the outcome of discussions on the level of Company Commander to Divisional Command, rather than on a plan formulated only at the headquarters of any one.'

Savige's approach differed from that of the staff college officers – and it was working. Mubo had been taken. Bobdubi Ridge was only a few kilometres from the river and about twenty kilometres south-west of Salamaua. No matter what the Japanese attempted, Savige's men countered and defeated them. If they couldn't see a way over the razorback ridges, they encircled the area, cutting the Japanese off. On the coast at Nassau Bay, the enemy moved to destroy Australian and US artillery. Savige sent a patrol to defend the weaponry before the enemy could lay their demolition charges. It was not his role to protect artillery but he did so anyway, despite some rebuke.[4]

Savige was close to his objective of the Francisco River. He moved fast to capitalise on his men's success, directing the 15th Brigade to patrol across the river for the first time. The diggers were ordered to pursue the Japanese, who fought hard in their retreat. Savige made sure that the high ground across the river was occupied by the diggers. The Japanese would not be coming back. Soon the Australians would be within 1.5 kilometres of Salamaua's aerodrome.

Although the Japanese were still active throughout the battlefield area, Savige had them under control. He was confident that he could take Salamaua and Lae from the hinterland, if it was ordered. He and his commanders were keen, even though they and their men had been through hardship for up to four months, some longer.

Salamaua remained the prize that Savige wanted and deserved, but would never take. Once his mission of reaching the Francisco River was accomplished, he was replaced. He had predicted this but still it disappointed him. He 'celebrated' the fact that the operation was over by visiting the front at Laver's Knoll, where the 6th Battalion's D Company was making a counter-attack. Its commander, Major H.L. Laver, was not pleased to see Savige in such a hot area. He didn't want a dead major general on his hands.

'To hell with you!' Savige replied with good humour. 'Get on with your battle and forget us. We won't interfere. You are the boss.'[5] It was a typical and fitting last gesture.

Savige returned to Port Moresby, having contracted malaria and hookworm. Blamey tried to bully him about pressing Salamaua too hard, which, he said, endangered his plans for taking Lae. Savige pulled out the files and orders to refute the chief, who lost the argument. Blamey told Savige that he had overridden MacArthur's decision: Lae was still the first main target, with a fresh force directed to take it from the Huon Gulf.

Savige left Papua and New Guinea satisfied with his impact on the fourth major battle over its territory. He had won the 'hard yards' that would make a final assault more than likely to succeed.

While militia soldiers and those of the 6th, 7th and 9th Divisions were in action on several fronts, the men of the 8th Division continued to be used by the Japanese as slave labour throughout the Pacific and South-East Asia. In the eighteen months after the fall of

Singapore, more than 2400 POWs (three-quarters of them Australian, and one-quarter British) were forced to build a camp and military airstrip at Sandakan, North Borneo. Conditions were similar to those experienced on the Thai–Burma railway. The men were often beaten. The food rations were pitifully small. Medical attention was scant.

In August 1943 the Japanese decided to break the men's spirits further by separating them from their officers and commanders, who were sent to a camp at Kuching. The POWs then had no say at all in how they were treated. Rations were reduced even further. Sick prisoners were forced to work on the airstrip. The rate of deaths and illnesses was already higher than at the Thai–Burma railway, where one in every two POWs would die. This new level of cruelty meant these rates would increase.

73
Post-Election Spoils

The 1943 election drew out fresh political divisions in both parties. Menzies undermined Hughes and Fadden by announcing that he disagreed with a central opposition policy. This signalled his intention to regain control of the nation's conservative forces. Similarly, Evatt hindered Curtin by saying he would join a national government if Labor lost.

When he learnt of Evatt's public pronouncement, Curtin was bitter. 'It's a great world, isn't it?' he remarked to journalists.[1] They had become used to Curtin's banter about Evatt, who had never shown finesse when handling the press. Curtin had high standards. He rarely praised ministers or other key performers at his off-the-record conferences. He would not allow criticism of MacArthur but hardly mentioned him, which suggested his support for the general was primarily political.

Curtin continually defended Blamey, and much defence was needed. But as long as MacArthur was happy – and also supported

Blamey – Curtin would not move against his Australian commander. He attacked the troublesome Ward, whose allegiance to the communists seemed stronger than that for his country. Curtin avoided criticising Calwell, although he never praised him. Journalists had the impression that Curtin regarded his deputy, Forde, as a ditherer who lacked confidence when acting leader. Curtin supported two of his 'personality-free' ministers, Arthur Drakeford and John Dedman, whether or not he agreed with journalists' criticism of them.

He had consistent praise for Ben Chifley only. They were great mates, but in any case there was little to attack him on. Curtin recognised Chifley's stature and had already anointed him as his successor.

Evatt's pronouncement about national government exposed his naivety and ambitions. He had never been as politically savvy as Curtin or Chifley. He was not friendly with the media and seemed out of touch with the electorate. He made some in his party nervous over his support for Stalin and the Soviets: Evatt always wanted increased ties, both overt and covert, with Moscow. He had grudgingly agreed to seek US and UK assistance in the Australian war effort. His general hostility to the US and Churchill was well-known in Whitehall and Washington, and had been counter-productive for Curtin.

Evatt's long trip to the United States and the United Kingdom seeking extra war planes may have left him oblivious to the Australian people's mood, which was pro-Curtin. It didn't help that his mission had failed. He had been demanding – he was not the type to beg, cajole or even bargain – heavy bombers for the war in New Guinea and the Pacific islands, and to keep the peace after the war. But Roosevelt and Churchill gave him nothing, claiming they needed the bigger beasts of the air for the fight against Hitler.

A more skilled diplomat than Evatt may have done better. Churchill had said he would consider sending three Spitfire squadrons but delayed giving his decision, thus denying Evatt even the appearance of success. All Evatt could do was speak in platitudes about Churchill's intentions, which in press terms was nothing. Evatt then disappeared for the rest of the election campaign, allegedly ill with bronchopneumonia. Curtin didn't believe he was sick and let his mates in the press gallery know it.

Curtin was more than nervous in Perth on election night, 21 August 1943. He was exhausted and feared the worse, despite the opinion polls predicting a clear win for Labor. He had his personal secretary bring a whiteboard to a room at his hotel, which would register the results from the eastern states as they came in. The whiteboard had only been in place for fifteen minutes when it became clear that Curtin and Labor had won a huge victory.

Nevertheless, he fretted over the result in his own seat, where counting had gone on for days after the last election before he had scraped in by 600 votes. Now each booth was giving him a lead of well over that number. By the end of the night, he had a majority of 20,000.

Labor won forty-nine seats, having endured for nearly two years with a minority government that held just thirty-two seats. The opposition now had just nineteen, slipping from thirty-six. The two independent MPs who had allowed Curtin to govern were re-elected. Curtin had won the mandate he craved. After a term of crafty government, in which 208 acts of parliament were passed, it was a relief for him to have such a clear 'green light' from a formerly sceptical electorate. He had endured internal party criticism over the pace of reform and his preoccupation with the war. Now he could govern with less fear. There was still a war to be won, but he could now turn to the agenda about which he had spoken modestly, for fear of riling anti-socialist forces.

In the early hours of 22 August 1943, Curtin relaxed and had his best sleep for years.

74
More than 'Mopping Up'

Blamey's plan for Lae worked. Around 8000 of the 11,000 Japanese soldiers there were drawn towards Salamaua to take on Savige's men. Now it was the turn now of the 7th and 9th Divisions to hit the beaches at Lae.

Blamey had been at Gallipoli. He had long hoped to make another amphibious landing, but this time with better planning, more knowledge of the terrain, and the advantage of air support.

At dawn on 4 September 1943, five destroyers began shelling two beaches east of Lae. The men of Brigadier Victor Windeyer's 20th Brigade climbed into sixteen landing craft and motored towards the beach. Their machine guns began firing long before they reached the sand, further softening up the defending Japanese. The craft slid up the beaches. The ramps lowered and the Australians dashed across the short beach to the jungle.

The 26th Brigade's landing boats slammed into the second beach but were attacked by Japanese planes from Rabaul, which killed seven and wounded twenty-eight. Australian and US planes swooped in to tackle the enemy fighters, which were shot down or fled. Six further Allied craft slid up the sand, disgorging tractors, graders, vehicles, weaponry and diggers. Within four hours, 7800 soldiers were moving into the jungle.

Despite Allied air cover, Japanese fighters returned for sporadic hit-and-run attacks, until three squadrons of P-38 Lightnings flew into the Japanese raiders, shooting down about thirty. By now, the Japanese realised they had been duped. Six thousand of their soldiers were rushed back to Lae in barges.

On 5 September the Allies made an airborne assault. Eighty-seven Dakotas lumbered over the jungle and dropped three battalions of US paratroopers and machine-gunners. It took less than a day for a makeshift airstrip to be constructed, which allowed big transport carriers to rumble in, carrying diggers from the 7th Division. On 7 September General Vasey's headquarters and an infantry company arrived. The following morning, Vasey sent Eather's 25th Brigade down the Markham Valley, towards Lae.

On 11 September the 5th Division militiamen attacked Salamaua. 13 September saw the opposing forces engage. The Australians used artillery before the diggers went onto the battlefield of Heath's Plantation. Japanese machine-gunners ambushed them, killing five and wounding three, including the popular platoon leader, Corporal Billy Richards, who suffered bullet wounds to his arm, back and stomach.

Richards managed to crawl behind a tree, unable to move further. 'Nips at two o'clock!' he yelled to his men. 'Aim there!'

Losing blood, Richards was vulnerable, and the enemy did not want him directing fire at them. One of his men, an Irishman, Private Richard Kelliher, was sitting in a shallow gully. He could see Richards. 'I'd better go and get him,' Kelliher said to his mate, Private J. H. Bickle. Pointing to Bickle's last grenade, he said, 'Give me that.' Bickle obliged.

Kelliher ran seventy metres down a hill. He hurled his grenade, disrupting the Japanese machine-gunners but killing no one. Realising he would be mowed down if he went further, he sprinted back up the hill and grabbed a Bren gun. Without hesitation, he dashed down the slope again, firing. Japanese machine-gunners responded but Kelliher kept coming. He killed nine Japanese in an enemy gunpit. Others ran for cover.

Kelliher lifted Richards and dragged him to safety, supported by diggers who kept the enemy snipers occupied. Kelliher bustled past two other wounded men, calling out that he would return for them. True to his word, he hustled back to them. With sniper bullets whistling close, he managed to pull them to safety.

This selfless act of bravery earned Kelliher the Victoria Cross. Corporal Richards recovered and was decorated with the Military Medal for bravery in the field.[1]

With efforts such as this, Heath's Plantation was cleared by 14 September, after heavy engagements. The next morning, the 25th Battalion of the 7th Division entered what was left of the almost obliterated Lae. They were just three hours ahead of the 9th Division, which began shelling the city. This 'friendly fire' caused Eather's 25th Battalion to withdraw, but he managed to inform the 9th that the 7th Division was already in occupation. There was always competition between divisions. As Eather later commented, the 9th Division's artillery had been 'over-exuberant'.

Once more, this fourth battle for New Guinea and Papua was proving to be far more than 'mopping up'. It took the full force, experience and skill of the Australians' 7th and 9th Divisions to defeat the Japanese. The Allied air force and navy played a large part, but once the Japanese were pulverised from the air, the soldiers still had to go in and fight.

MacArthur tried to take all the glory for himself first, and for the US forces second. As Eichelberger later observed in his memoirs:

> *In New Guinea the fighting into the autumn [southern spring of 1943] was largely an Aussie show. Our Air Force made it possible, our Amphibs did much of the fetch-and-carry, elements of our 162nd Infantry Regiment handled themselves gallantly, but the main responsibility was borne by the 7th and 9th Australian Divisions. Because of the term 'Allied Forces,' which the censors then employed, many Americans still believe erroneously that our own troops carried the burden of that back-busting advance against the Salamaua–Lae–Finschhafen sector.*[2]

Nearly 1600 Japanese died in battles around Lae, with at least that many wounded. The 9th Division had 547 casualties: seventy-seven dead, 397 wounded and a further seventy-seven missing, such were the grotesque conditions in those encounters. The 7th Division had thirty-eight killed and 104 wounded.

Around 7800 Japanese scattered. Some attempted the exacting 120-kilometre trek north over the mountains to Sio, on the coast of the Huon Peninsula. Others staggered to Finschhafen, 100 kilometres due east, aiming to reach the coast, be picked up by a Japanese ship and be taken the eighty-five kilometres to the relative safety of New Britain.

Many seemed to lose their way, stumbling towards the coast but ending up in the Markham or Ramu Valleys, south of the fierce Finisterre Range, the northern slopes of which ran to the coast. The Australians pursued them into the mountains. More than 2000 Japanese were hunted down to Shaggy Ridge, a quaint euphemism for a hideous razorback mountain pock-marked with steep ravines. They enemy dug in for a siege.

Meanwhile, another 5000 retreating Japanese soldiers passed by a Lutheran mission building at the jungle-covered Sattelberg Ridge as they headed for the coast. It afforded good vision of the countryside to the coast, eight kilometres away; it was also the last stop for several Japanese battalions en route to Finschhafen.

MacArthur and his staff were hampering the Australian efforts to tackle the enemy by refusing to believe the numbers of enemy soldiers involved. Again, had members of the Bataan Gang bothered to visit the front, they would have made a different assessment. But they were taking their cue from MacArthur, whose energies were focused on pursuing the Japanese to the Philippines. His obsession with 'returning' had again caused him to take his eyes off the challenge of driving the Japanese from New Guinea.

Brigadier Windeyer's men landed at night at the moonlit Scarlet Beach, ten kilometres north of Finschhafen. The Japanese in the area attacked the Australians as they advanced towards the town. Windeyer asked Wootten for an extra battalion to guard the beachhead so he could continue on with his 20th Brigade towards its objective. In Brisbane, MacArthur's staff haggled over this for three days before acceding to the request. But they would not allow Windeyer to have tanks, which would have settled any fight over Finschhafen quicker.

Under siege in New Guinea, the Japanese planned to counter-attack in the north of Western Australia. The Drysdale Mission buildings and airfield were on flat country near the King Edward River. The mission had been the subject of at least six Japanese reconnaissance operations between March and November 1942, and for good reason:

the airfield was a refuelling and ammunition depot for the RAAF anti-submarine aircraft that operated between Darwin and Fremantle.

The RAAF's Beaufighters had been damaging Japanese submarines, curtailing Japan's destruction of Allied shipping. The Japanese now decided the Drysdale airstrip had to be destroyed. The grass airstrip was cut into the side of a hill and ended on the edge of a cliff, with a sheer 100-metre drop down to the King Edward River. Planes landed on the hill and took off over the cliff, regardless of the wind's direction or strength. This was a tricky operation for Clyde Fenton's Flying Doctor Service, which used DH Dragons, let alone for the Beaufighters. Any damage to the Drysdale airfield would render it inoperable for some time.

Just before 10 a.m. on 27 September 1943, twenty-one IJAAF Kawasaki Ki-48 bombers, escorted by a dozen Zeros, bombed and machine-gunned the Drysdale airfield. A bomb struck the ammunition hut, exploding it, while a direct hit on a slit trench at the mission building killed Father Thomas and five Aboriginals. It would take some time for the strip to be rebuilt. Work began the day after the destruction.

The Bataan Gang's dithering over the extra Australian battalion for Windeyer motivated the Japanese to send another 2400 soldiers from New Britain to Finschhafen, building their forces in the region to around 7400; it was as though MacArthur's intransigence was picked up by Japanese intelligence. Japan seemed unable to countenance giving up New Guinea despite having lost four major encounters.

The Allies realised the extent of the build-up. The rest of the 24th Brigade soon reached the coast near Finschhafen and headed for Wootten's 9th Division headquarters at Langemak Bay, a few kilometres south. Equipment and tanks arrived too.

Wootten gathered all the intelligence he could. In early October 1943, he decided that the Australians had to take Sattelberg Ridge to cut the flow of Japanese, before then attacking Finschhafen. Wootten reckoned the operation would take weeks. He and his division were in for a fight equal to, if not tougher than any they'd had in North Africa.

75
Menzies Thwarted; Finschhafen Sorted

After the 1943 election, Curtin moved to cut off Menzies, the new UAP leader, from influential efforts to redirect Australian foreign policy back towards Britain. Curtin would get in first. Although the two men derided each other to their respective parties, there was no doubting their mutual respect. Each confided in the other, Curtin the more so because of his insecurities and poor health. Menzies always felt superior to his political opposite, but Curtin was proving to be the more accomplished wartime prime minister. He was far more popular with the electorate.

Menzies tried to explain this as good image management by press secretary Don Rodgers, but this was superficial. The tough press corps had access to Curtin. They accepted the usual spin but he took them into his confidence over major issues. He never misled them but would give them nothing if it was in the national interest. They reported the prime minister's public image and knew the integrity of his hidden reality.

There was a sense that Curtin had done well. The general consensus among the electorate seemed to be that everything, including the war, had turned out okay with John Curtin in charge. This irked Menzies. His move against Hughes after the election had, in part, been out of frustration over the driven opposition leader. Curtin was calling for Australia to be a 'second Britannia in the Antipodes'. He called for more British immigration. The White Australia Policy should be kept in place, with British factory workers brought to the country to work in the secondary industries that had been established since 1940. There was no more mention of the United States as Australia's number-one partner.

The moment of truth regarding Australia's primary allegiance came at the War Conference of 1 June 1942, when MacArthur made it clear that Australia was nothing but a base for the Americans. From that moment on, Curtin rarely mentioned MacArthur and the US link to his confidants in the press. In fact, he began to disparage the US war leaders and their policies. Instead of showing 'gratitude for a great and powerful friend', Curtin exhibited 'a sort of wearied resignation about what must be'.[1]

If anything, Curtin demonstrated that he was cynical about, even contemptuous of American motivations and what they expected to gain from the Pacific after the war. Many of Curtin's moves now were conciliatory gestures towards London. At the ALP Conference at the end of 1943, Curtin again pushed to consolidate Australia's 'Empire' connections by calling for the creation of a permanent 'imperial secretariat'.

This was not a breathtaking about-face but a simple political expediency. The United States had served its purpose. Curtin had excessively praised MacArthur to Eichelberger, telling him that no Australian could have done more for the country than he had. Ever the diplomat, Eichelberger would have winced at this. Given how MacArthur had presented himself as Australia's saviour, Curtin may have believed this, even if it did not stand up to analysis. Yet he was also preparing the United States for Australia's shift back to the British, now that the direct threat from Japan was receding.

In any case, MacArthur was not giving much thought to the prime minister's views by then. He was looking north to a fresh battle area. MacArthur wouldn't tell Curtin whether he planned to include Australian troops in his push for the Philippines. The American was hedging his bets: he did not wish to share the glory of the retaking of his former domain. He knew that Blamey and the experienced Australian divisions – and now the militia as well – would have to be prominent in any invasion of the Philippines, if given the chance.

MacArthur's prevarication was problematic for Curtin, who faced manpower problems within Australia, especially in farming and food production. His government couldn't assess its needs and prepare its budgets without knowing for how long the armed forces would remain active. The Australian commitment to the South-West Pacific was far greater than that of the United States. MacArthur's army consisted of about 500,000 Australians and 200,000 Americans.

There were 136,000 Australians in the RAAF, compared to 55,000 in the US air force in the region.

Curtin had once again been kept out of the Churchill–Roosevelt loop. They met in Cairo in November 1943. Chiang Kai-shek, the leader of the Chinese Nationalists, was included in discussions, thanks to the US State Department's preoccupation with China.

Curtin's affection for the United States and Roosevelt was souring. His feeling for MacArthur, on the other hand, was genuine. By an odd quirk of fate, the two had found their personalities complementary and compatible. But in general Curtin reverted to an old-style socialist mentality when dealing with the Americans. He detested their 'dollar-chasing souls'. He had never really tried to comprehend the capitalist way, and had never wanted to. At nearly fifty-nine, Curtin was unlikely to become a convert.

Yet Curtin loved the Capstan cigarettes MacArthur 'smuggled' to him. He adored the books – US history and westerns – that the general gave him. He read Stuart N. Lake's *Wyatt Earp, Frontier Marshal* and enjoyed anything about Doc Holliday. One of Curtin's favourite books was James Fenimore Cooper's *The Last of the Mohicans*.

But smokes and popular literature were the extent of Curtin's American 'taint'. He had not forgiven the United States for not letting Australia have transport aircraft to keep its civil aviation system operating. He had been incensed by the Americans' insistence that, in exchange for providing planes for the region's defence, they would control the postwar transport and passenger services. The US diplomatic representatives were far more hard-nosed than the British, and they treated Australia as a backwater to be dominated.

Curtin was uncomfortable about what the Americans might do with their bases across the Pacific. He realised that US postwar colonisation would be more economic than territorial. Then there were all those airfields and bases across northern Australia. What 'payback' – in the form of control or influence – would the United States demand?

While grumbling about these issues in private, the realities of the present took precedence. Australia, Curtin told his press 'chooks', had become 'a hewer of wood and carrier of water'. The nation would now concentrate on its role as a supplier, particularly of food, while the Americans would do the fighting at the front.

Despite this shift in the nation's role, there was still some serious fighting to be done by Australia's soldiers. A case in point was the battle about to break on New Guinea's northern coast as the Japanese hung on stubbornly.

76
Sattelberg Breakthrough

It took Major-General Wootten a month to be in a position to attack Sattelberg Ridge. The 48th Battalion had fought its way to a point just to north of the stronghold, and Wootten sent artillery and nine tanks in support. The 23rd Battalion had cut its way through rough forest to a point just south of the ridge. This left the west as an escape route for the Japanese but they were unlikely to take it: it would leave them back in the rugged jungle hinterland.

On 18 November, the 48th made its move. The Japanese had entrenched at the northern approach, near the top of Steeple Tree Hill. They looked down the sharp slope as the 48th scrambled up, hurling grenades and firing from any cover they could find, including the slow-moving tanks, which were hampered by the incline and loose surface. They struggled towards the top on 22 November 1943, just before the 23rd Battalion reached the 650-metre slope to the summit. The 48th were blocked by heavy fire from the well-positioned enemy, then a landslide caused by Japanese detonations stopped the Australian tanks well short of the summit. The battalion's assignment was even tougher now. The diggers decided to proceed in small units, fighting spur by spur from various points north.

Japanese resistance held. The 48th battled on another two days, until its commander called a halt. He ordered a withdrawal.

Although exhausted, some diggers were disgruntled at having come so far for no result. Among them was Adelaide's Sergeant Thomas Derrick. This cheerful larrikin believed that no position was hopeless. At Tobruk in Libya, his aggressive patrolling of enemy positions had seen him promoted to corporal and recommended for a Military Medal. An officer described him as a brave, resourceful and selfless individual who looked after his men.

A year later, on 10 July 1942, at Tel el Eisa, Egypt, he braved a wall of grenades to destroy three German machine-gun posts and capture 110 enemy soldiers. The next day, the enemy had counter-attacked. Derrick ran forward. Like a cricketer fielding close to the wicket, he whipped grenades at two approaching tanks, destroying them. This brought a roar of approval from the other diggers, who were inspired to fight and hold on. Derrick was promoted to sergeant. A Distinguished Conduct Medal was added to his growing collection of awards for freakish feats of bravery.

At El Alamein in late October 1942, he led his men fiercely, but with awareness and control, in a week of violent battle. This time, he again single-handedly destroyed three machine-gun nests, but he was wounded slightly for his trouble. Those among the forty-one left in his company who witnessed this act swore that he had to earn a Victoria Cross. All had shown courage but they watched Derrick's fearless effort in awe.

By the time Derrick left the Middle East, he was a legend of 9th Division and was being compared to Tasmania's 'Mad' Harry Morgan, the most highly decorated soldier of World War I, and Victoria's Albert Jacka. It was an honour for other diggers to fight with or under Tom Derrick.

Derrick lingered when ordered to withdraw at Sattelberg. He looked up at the almost vertical slope of thick jungle, which hid about ten Japanese machine-gun posts. Beyond that was a less demanding incline of about 100 metres, which ran up to the crest. His company commander noticed him contemplating the summit. Knowing Derrick's mentality, he told him not to even think about it. Derrick believed he could make it to the crest, if he had enough covering fire. His commander pointed out that the slope would be near-impossible even if the enemy wasn't there. But Derrick wasn't listening.

'The CO has given the order!' the commander said.

'Bugger the CO!' Derrick snapped back. 'Just give me twenty minutes and we'll have this place.'[1]

Others urged the commander to let him 'have a go'. There was very little choice. Once Derrick set his mind on something, no one, not even this well-entrenched enemy, could stop him from attempting it. The commander relented.

Derrick collected a dozen grenades in a haversack. His company comrades positioned themselves and began firing to cover him. Derrick slung his rifle and haversack over his back, and began his almost vertical climb. After twenty metres, he grabbed a root by one hand and hurled a grenade into a Japanese dugout. Judging from the screams, his throw was accurate. His men, their adrenaline pumping too, urged him on, yelling directions for his throws.

Derrick hurled grenade after grenade. His company gave him even more intense fire cover as he edged his way up. His mates eased closer to the foot of the slope, distracting the Japanese. Derrick reached a ledge that allowed him to stand upright. He pulled his .303 rifle around, took aim and fired at an enemy dugout, killing a gunner. Then he hurled a grenade, destroying the nest.

He repeated this feat a second, third and fourth time, obliterating four machine-gun nests before he was spotted. Even then, his almost vertical ascent made it difficult to hit him. After attacking, he would hold his body flat against the cliff face. When the firing abated, he would grip a sapling and continue his slow haul up.

The diggers below could hardly believe what they were witnessing. With every few metres gained, and each machine-gun post he knocked out, the odds about him achieving his outrageous objective shortened.

Derrick was aided by the fading light as he approached the crest of the ridge. His company, emboldened, began to follow him up. Near the top, he hit four posts in quick succession. Four explosions and six shots later, Sattelberg Ridge fell silent for several minutes. Derrick could see and hear his diggers moving up. The Japanese began firing down again, but in fewer numbers and with less force.

The 48th Battalion had a part-hold on the ridge by nightfall. Derrick and his company settled in for the night, determined to finish the job at dawn.

As the first shafts of light reached Sattelberg, the 48th made its move. Derrick led his platoon with his usual verve, charging at the mission station building. There was no opposition. The Japanese had slipped away during the night, abandoning this most important stronghold. The platoon sat around smoking and having breakfast as the sun began to bake the area by 7.30 a.m. They checked all the machine-gun posts below the crest and found fifteen enemy dead. An estimated twelve more had been wounded, judging from the blood trails and abandoned equipment around the posts.

Derrick had managed to sleep well during the night while his soldiers kept watch. Now he smoked, chatted and joked as he clambered about, examining his destruction of the enemy posts. He expressed astonishment at the sharp drop from the summit: it was like being on the highest diving board. Diving had been Derrick's sport of choice – so much so that he was nicknamed 'Diver'. He did not boast or gloat, but remarked more than once how lucky he had been to survive the ascent.

But observers felt that luck had played a small part, when compared to the determination, courage, will and military skill Derrick had displayed. He was later awarded the Victoria Cross.[2]

Derrick's action cleared the way for the 9th Division to take control of Finschhafen, which it did just over a week later, in early December 1943. More than 5500 Japanese soldiers were killed in these actions, leaving a few thousand more holed up at Shaggy Ridge. These enemy survivors still had to be cleared. Judging from the way the Japanese had fought over the last three months, the Australians would have to brace themselves for these final fierce assaults.

77
The PM's Many War Fronts

By December 1943 Curtin was receiving intelligence from the UK concerning Churchill's plans to defeat Hitler. Just as the Japanese were being turned, 1944 promised major breakthroughs against the Nazis in Europe. The Allies were expected to invade France, probably in the first half of the year, and attempt to take it back from Hitler.

Curtin and his ministers were interested in what military intelligence services were saying about the mighty Battle of Kursk on the Eastern Front. In July 1943 the Soviet military had thrown two million men into the fray, along with 20,000 artillery pieces, 3444 tanks and 2172 planes. This massive force had taken on fifty German divisions – nearly a million men – supported by 10,000 artillery pieces, 2700 tanks and 2000 aircraft.

In World War I, Field Marshal Douglas Haig had been nicknamed 'Kill More Germans': his philosophy had been that if the Allies killed more of the enemy than they killed of the Allies, then the Allies would have won. That hideous sobriquet had now fallen to Stalin. During the Kursk battle, the biggest in history, Hitler had been forced to throw in an extra nine divisions – about 250,000 soldiers – in the middle of the fight to ensure he did not lose. In the end, the Germans did not take any ground; this effectively meant victory for the Soviets.[1]

Six months later, analysts were beginning to see this battle as the turning point in the European war. It was all painfully slow, yet still promising for the Allies, and it had to augur well for Australia.

Although Curtin could now enjoy at least fitful sleep, other major issues were sapping his energy. These included the recalcitrant members of the Labor Party, Calwell and Ward, and the incorrigible New South Wales miners. Curtin had attempted to neutralise the two politicians with moves that revealed him to be tougher and shrewder than he often appeared.

Calwell was made Minister for Information, which must have brought wry smiles to others, such as Chifley and Forde. Calwell had always railed against the 'capitalist press'. He loved to insult the media owners, calling them 'business crooks'. Their editors were 'mental harlots', which was a reference more to their intellectual proclivities than their sanity.[2] The media barons, in turn, would have to deal with a man they regarded as an unmanageable socialist propagandist, even a communist apologist.

The prime minister dealt with Eddie Ward similarly, putting him in charge of the Departments of Transport and Territories. Transport, which was mainly concerned with the railways, was controlled by the army; Ward would make no headway there. Australia's 'territories' – such as Papua – were still being retaken by the armed forces, so there would be little for him to do in this field until after the war.

Curtin turned his mind to his new political agenda. He no longer needed the support of the two independent MPs to push through his long-awaited legislation. The Japanese could no longer invade Australia, while Guadalcanal was controlled by the United States. Reports from New Guinea, from both MacArthur and Blamey, were positive, and Washington appeared to support this view.

Roosevelt invited Curtin to the White House for two days of discussions about the future 'military, naval and air protection of Australia'. He also wanted to speak about all the Japanese-controlled islands, and the 'future policing of the whole Pacific or Asiatic area'. The Americans may have been contemplating a 'deputy sheriff' role for Australia, if Curtin were amenable. His 'back to Empire' utterances during and after the election campaign seemed to make this unlikely, however.

Evatt had been busy since the election stitching up the so-called 'Anzac Agreement'. In it, Australia and New Zealand declared that they had the final say over the sovereignty of Pacific territories, and that this could not be changed without their approval.

The agreement was as cheeky as it was worthless, and the US leadership was annoyed. It would have a major say on the issue, arguing that its men had fought for certain islands, and that the cost in lives and money made these territories theirs to deal with as they wished. The UK found it irritating too, given their history in Pacific islands such as Fiji, and in South-East Asia.

Even more debatable was the Anzac assertion that the United States could not retain control over bases it had built on British Commonwealth territories, including Australia and New Zealand. Evatt's overly ambitious initiative promised to set back Australia's relationship with both the United States and the United Kingdom.

The Australians pursued the remaining units of Japanese soldiers through the Ramu Valley to the six-kilometre Shaggy Ridge, the last enemy stronghold before their escape route through Madang, on the coast 200 kilometres north-west of Lae.

Early on 27 December 1943, the Australians began a terrific artillery barrage of 'the Pimple', one of three strongly defended rocky outcrops on Shaggy Ridge. At the same time, dive-bombers descended to further soften up the Japanese. Then the 16th Battalion of the 21st Brigade began the awkward climb up the southern slopes, sixty kilometres from Madang. They surprised the shaken Japanese with the intensity of their assault, and by night had secured this fort.

The enemy retreated along the ridge and regrouped with the other forts, and within days began counter-attacking. The Australians entrenched at 'the Pimple' and repulsed almost daily attempts by the Japanese to retake the position.

Early in the new year, Vasey brought in 48-year-old Brigadier Frederick Chilton and his 18th Brigade. Chilton was another lawyer from Sydney. He had been prominent in the 6th Division's battle at Bardia, earning a Distinguished Service Order, and in the taking of Tobruk.[3] He and Vasey decided that the 10th Battalion would feint an attack while the 12th moved with stealth up the sharp cliff face towards the second enemy stronghold, and the 9th edged along a smaller sharp ridge towards the third.

After continual fighting along the entire Shaggy Ridge until the end of January 1944, the three forts had been destroyed. The remaining Japanese had made for the narrow track to Madang. On 10 February 1944, the Australians, who once more had done the tough fighting and clearing, linked up on the coast at Saidor with the relieving American troops, who would take over the patrolling of the region. The Australians took their leave of New Guinea, pleased to a man to be done with the place.

After five months of fierce encounters, the Huon Peninsula campaign, begun by Savige and ended by Vasey, was finally over. It had been as demanding as the other three major Papua/New Guinea battles: on the Kokoda Track, at Milne Bay, and at Gona, Buna and Sanananda. General Kenney's airpower, along with the RAAF's operations, had made a considerable impact. But in the final analysis, the Australian ground troops – the militia and the three divisions that Curtin fought so hard to bring to the region – made the difference. They held, repulsed and defeated the Japanese in the nearly two-year war for control of Papua and New Guinea.

If the diggers had not been successful, Port Moresby would have fallen to the Japanese. This would have caused massive problems for the Australian mainland's northern regions. More cities than just Darwin and other selected bases would have been targeted for intense bombing. The big US and Australian bases in Brisbane and other Queensland centres would have been pinpointed. Indeed, the Japanese may well have revived the idea of an invasion of the Australian mainland.

Curtin never had time for reflection or diary scribbling. But if he had taken a moment to ruminate in February 1944 on his decisions as prime minister, he would surely have judged the moment on the weekend of 21–22 February 1942 when he stood up to Churchill and Roosevelt over the return of the Australian divisions as the most important. It saved Australia from a fate far worse than the one it endured over those two dark years, the most challenging in the nation's short history since federation.

Part Seven

Battle for Japan
1944

78
Reluctant Voyager

Menzies attempted to disrupt Curtin's leadership by walking out of the War Council in February 1944. His excuse was the fact that Eddie Ward had not been sacked from the government. Menzies had always wanted a 'national' government, like that of the British, but Curtin had refused in opposition and when he became prime minister. Menzies told Curtin that since there was no national government, the UAP felt it could do more for the war and reconstruction effort by freely expressing its views in parliament.

Menzies' deputy, Hughes, went with him, but Fadden and his Country Party refused, thus splitting the conservative coalition. Then the UAP's highly respected Percy Spender, a former Minister for the Army, decided to stay in the War Council. Curtin congratulated Spender on putting his nation ahead of his party. Hughes later changed his mind and returned to the council.

Curtin had such a comfortable majority that he could afford to take an overseas trip to see Roosevelt and Churchill. He was a reluctant traveller but realised that he had to make the effort, especially since the two powerful Allied leaders had invited him several times to Washington and London. Yet before he sailed off, he had to oversee war strategies in his country's north. On 6 March 1944, Cabinet approved expenditure for the development of air facilities at Darwin. Concrete runways were to be built for heavy bombers, costing £1.5 million. These would take eight months to complete, and it was expected that the work would be targeted by the Japanese. Because of this construction, Curtin told his reporter friends, 'all the dive bombers we can muster are being sent to strips along the northern coast of Australia'.[1]

Days before his trip, another worry emerged. A massive shift of Japanese naval vessels was detected between Singapore and Sumatra.

Perth went on air-raid alert but the threat subsided. 'We got everything in readiness for an attack,' Curtin told reporters, 'but the Japanese ships turned back.'[2] He might have been forced to abandon his trip had the Japanese been more offensive in their efforts to protect their oil supplies coming from the Netherlands East Indies.

On 17 March 1944 the government threw a formal dinner at Parliament House to mark the second anniversary of MacArthur's arrival in Australia. He was invested by the Governor-General with a knighthood, organised by Curtin, for services rendered in saving Australia. Curtin remained naive and perhaps happily ignorant of the Australian forces' attitude to MacArthur and his role, and to the notion that a foreign general controlled them.

Curtin did not wish to concern himself with this. In his eyes, MacArthur was the nation's saviour, and a gentleman with whom he could deal. They had forged a strong bond, even chatting at the Lodge about a holiday they would take together with their wives after the war.

MacArthur spoke to Curtin about Roosevelt. 'Roosevelt is quite unscrupulous in getting away from his own expressions of agreement,' he said, with Shedden in earshot, 'and repudiating his word if it suits him.'[3] It was another way of saying the US president could not be trusted.

MacArthur's comment would have tallied with Curtin's own assessment of Roosevelt. He seemed to have been so much in Churchill's thrall on most issues that he lacked credibility, at least in their cable communications. Curtin's main aim abroad would be to heal Australia's fractured bonds with the United Kingdom.

Hughes had warned Curtin that Churchill had no time for 'colonials'. Curtin had experienced Churchill's aloofness, wrath and vindictiveness over the return of the Australian divisions and airmen, and other issues. From Casey's reports, Curtin knew Churchill was hostile towards the Australian government: he had reminded Casey that he 'wasn't kickable'. But Curtin wondered if he were malleable, given the state of the war on all fronts. Was the Allies' great leader a man to carry heavy grudges? Hughes said he was.

Curtin remained optimistic about making a new approach to the government of the Empire. In his eyes, it was no longer sufficient for Britain to manage Commonwealth affairs with its London-based ministers. Curtin wanted a permanent imperial secretariat or Empire Council. He hoped this would lead to a new era in Imperial affairs after the war.

Curtin was seeking new machinery that would 'provide for full and continuous consultation' between Britain and her overseas dominions, including India, Australia, Canada, New Zealand and South Africa. He wanted the council conferences to move between the capitals of all the dominions, not just London. Such a setup, Curtin believed, would better protect Australia's interests.

Blamey surprised the military hierarchy by promoting Stan Savige to lieutenant general and making him commander of II Corps, responsible for all Australian activities in New Guinea. He relieved Major-General Frank Berryman, who took over I Corps, the army's strike force of AIF divisions.

Many observers believed Savige had been promoted beyond his capacity, although this charge had been unfairly levelled at him before. There was some merit in his promotion, but it appeared to be Blamey's most transparently political appointment. He would not promote powerful contenders to commands from which they could threaten his position. Worthy generals such as Morshead, Vasey, Lavarack, Bennett and Robertson were ignored. Savige was not ambitious for further advancement, and certainly not for Blamey's job. He was a loyal friend and could be trusted.

This controversial appointment occurred when Australian military operations were being wound down in New Guinea. Little fighting was expected in the coming months. Curtin was advised that there was no impediment now to his lengthy overseas trip.

Curtin refused to fly over the Pacific Ocean. On 5 April 1944, he and Elsie boarded a crowded American naval transporter, the SS *Lurline*, at Sydney. Travelling with him were Blamey, Shedden, Rodgers, McLaughlin, 400 wounded US military personnel and fifty Australian war brides.

Curtin went into a depressive funk on day one. He hated the idea of being away from the nation, his family and friends for the several months the tour required. There were also dangers to consider. The US navy was gaining control over the Pacific Ocean, but Japanese submarines still lurked. If they picked up that the Australian prime minister and his Armed Forces chief were on board, they would take risks to torpedo the ship. The voyage brought back the nightmares Curtin had about Australian ships going down in flames after enemy attacks. Now he was in the position of the diggers and sailors over whom he fretted.

Curtin was anxious also about his meetings with President Roosevelt and his chiefs. Their relationship had not been cordial during the worst months of 1942, but Curtin had not realised the Americans' respect for him as a man who stood up to them when others were compliant. They were inviting him to meet them. This in itself gained him some leverage, as did mainly favourable reports from the United States' representatives in Australia. The worst thing that was reported to the US chiefs was that Curtin was a stubborn individual and soft in dealing with the far left.

Curtin had proved himself as a wartime leader and had succeeded with the domestic economy. His last challenge was to be seen as a statesman; at least, this was how the media portrayed it. The trip's significance for Curtin was evident in a remark he made at a parliamentary farewell: 'It seems like a dream that the lad who ran only the streets of Creswick, Ballarat and Brunswick is about to represent his country overseas.'[4]

The conservative British High Commissioner to Australia, Sir Ronald Cross, pandered to Churchill's prejudices against Labor politicians and 'colonials' in general when he delivered his view of Curtin's mission. 'Curtin found himself in the midst of events that dwarfed the little realm of his life's thought, knowledge, experience and undertakings,' he said in a cable to the British Foreign Office. It was a jaundiced, out-of-touch remark, given Curtin's obvious growth and success in office and in the war. However, it demonstrated the angst generated by Curtin's stand against Churchill and Roosevelt early in 1942, and by his ongoing independent actions.[5]

The Australian newspapers wished to crown Curtin as a statesman, but his objective was to remind the British and the Americans of Australia's war effort. He wanted them to agree that Australia should be involved in the next stage of the Pacific War, and in deciding who got what in the postwar carve-up of the region.

79
Meeting Roosevelt

The fourteen-day voyage to San Francisco was not pleasant for Curtin. Elsie was ill for a few days. Blamey worried him by smuggling on board a case of whisky, despite the US Navy's no-alcohol policy. Blamey proceeded to work his way into the two dozen bottles, much to the annoyance of others. He organised a party in the spacious cabin of the ship's doctor, to which some of the war brides were invited. It began as convivial and ended 'boisterous' – so much so that the *Lurline*'s commander protested to Curtin, who was most disapproving, especially now that he had been abstemious for three and a half years.

Curtin had not spent this amount of time with Blamey before, and he was not enamoured with the commander of Australia's forces. The hedonist Blamey had a habit of letting loose on his overseas ventures, away from the press, especially after his lust for prostitutes had nearly ruined his career twice. He underestimated Curtin's reaction to his boozing, believing that a man with his drinking inclinations would understand. If anything, Blamey's excesses persuaded Curtin he would side with MacArthur if any choice had to be made between the two.

They arrived on 19 April 1944 and took a train to Washington, via Chicago. The Australian party was forced to travel in a crammed carriage because of a mix-up. A saving moment for the Curtins was the celebration of their twenty-seventh wedding anniversary. At a stop in Cheyenne, Wyoming, they were presented with a bunch of flowers to mark the occasion. The train ride took four days. Although he could have flown the distance in hours, Curtin had wanted to see the American west. MacArthur had endorsed this arrangement, knowing it would leave Curtin far less time for discussions with Roosevelt and the chiefs. It snowed most of the way, which was a novel experience for Curtin, who reread his favourite 'wild west' books en route. He arrived in the US capital early on Sunday 23 April, feeling nervous yet prepared.

The Americans turned on the diplomacy and meetings. The secretary of state, Cordell Hull, met them at the train station and escorted them to Blair House, the huge four-storey townhouse at 1651 Pennsylvania Avenue reserved for visiting guests of the president. On 24 April Curtin had a tiring round of engagements, including meetings with James Byrnes, the director of war mobilisation, Admiral Ernest King, the chief of the US Navy, and Cordell Hull.

Hull wanted to discuss the Anzac Agreement. He claimed the United States took it as an attack on its interests in the Pacific. But Hull did not blame Curtin, aware that Evatt had made this issue his own. The State Department was upset by Evatt's imprudent reference in a cable to statements by Roosevelt that had been made in confidence and informally at a Pacific War Council meeting in Washington in 1943. After Evatt's 'bad manners' – so characterised by Hull – Roosevelt had abandoned the council meetings.

At 5 p.m. Curtin hosted a cocktail party at the Australian Legation for the US vice president, Henry Wallace, and the chief of the US Army, General Marshall. The eccentric, introspective Wallace spoke to him about a trip he was making to China in a few weeks' time, enhancing Curtin's appreciation of the Americans' obsession with their relationship with China. Wallace would be investigating whether the Nationalists, led by Chiang Kai-shek, deserved a $1 billion loan to fight the Japanese. He was concerned that the loan might be used to fight Mao Zedong and the communists.[1]

Later on 24 April, the British military's representative, Field Marshal Sir John Dill, hosted a dinner in Curtin's honour. The combined chiefs of staff were present. Elsie, meanwhile, had a quiet meal with the president's wife, Eleanor, at the White House.

The next day, Tuesday 25 April, Curtin flew with Elsie and Eleanor to have lunch with Roosevelt in South Carolina. Roosevelt and Curtin had three hours of discussions, but nothing substantive came from them. Roosevelt seemed too fatigued for detail, and Curtin did not wish to commit to anything regarding the postwar Pacific. Their meeting over lunch was cordial after the acrimony of the cables twenty-five months earlier, when Roosevelt had acquiesced in Churchill's failed attempt to intimidate Curtin. Both nations' successes in the war against the Japanese had tempered issues and reduced tensions.

After lunch, Roosevelt raised the issue of the Anzac Agreement. Curtin suggested that Australian and New Zealand officials may have been over-enthusiastic in drawing up the agreement, which the president took to mean that Curtin was backing away from it. They agreed that the issue should not be brought up again.

Curtin was unhappy. The directness of Roosevelt's approach was like the attempted intimidation Curtin had felt over the 'hot' cables he had received when he wanted the 6th and 7th Divisions back in Australia. He felt isolated and depressed after this first meeting with the second-most important Allied leader. This was not the comradely experience he had with MacArthur. The breathless, pale-skinned, wheelchair-bound polio victim Roosevelt was at the real fulcrum of Western power.

After this mild but surprising admonition, Roosevelt became solicitous. Leaning forward and half-pointing, he commented on Curtin's wall eye. Roosevelt said he could arrange for it to be corrected by surgeons at the US naval hospital. This was the first time someone had raised the quirk in Curtin's appearance that irked him every time he looked in a mirror. But he had learned to live with it. He chuckled, embarrassed by the president's comment. 'Thank you, but no,' he said.[2]

The Curtins and the First Lady flew back to Washington later that day and stayed the night at the White House. Curtin had a difficult night and fell ill early in the morning. The travel by boat, train and plane, along with the compressed round of engagements, had fatigued him. The criticism of him, first by Hull then Roosevelt, also weighed heavily. It made him comprehend first-hand that Australians had far more in common with the British than the Americans. It confirmed MacArthur's analysis that the United States could not care less about Australia or its people, and justified Curtin's decision to revert to Australia's connection to the British Empire.

Curtin cancelled his demanding itinerary of 26 April, which had included General Marshall. A doctor was called. The prime minister's blood pressure had rocketed. He had head, back and stomach pains. Reports spilled out that he had 'neuritis', the unspecified problem associated with nerve inflammation that, for Curtin, always seemed to follow highly stressful moments.

The prime minister rested during the day and felt well enough in the evening to make a radio broadcast speech to the US people. He spent 27 April recuperating further. His three days of 'work' had been a disappointment and essentially a waste of time, considering how long he had taken to arrive. Curtin did not enjoy the stay but looked forward to reaching the United Kingdom.

On 28 April he steeled himself to take a Boeing flying boat across the Atlantic. Elsie had stayed behind in Washington, where she would wait until he returned in a month. There was no one to comfort the nervous traveller when they skimmed over the ocean towards Ireland.

Blamey lay on a bed and snored his way across. Rodgers read. Curtin sat rigidly for most of the journey, his hat and jacket on, before his fatigue gave way to sleep.

80
Rendezvous with the Bulldog

Curtin woke up at dawn on Saturday 29 April 1944, as the flying boat made its descent onto the River Shannon, near Foynes on Ireland's west coast. It was close to his parents' birthplace but he had no time to see it. The party continued on its way to London, this time in a twin-engine Dakota.

No sooner had Curtin touched down at Croydon, in southern London, than he was into his first speech, which ramped up his 'return to Empire' theme, begun ten months earlier. He expressed his admiration for the British for having 'stood alone as the rampart of civilisation'. Curtin wanted it understood that he spoke for 'seven million Britishers'. His words thwarted any questions about his past squabbles with Churchill or his turning to America late in 1941.

The next day he awoke at the Savoy, which was impressive even in wartime, although sandbags, blacked-out windows and reinforced scaffolding changed its visage. Helmets, gasmasks, fire drills and evacuation routines were all part of daily life. Curtin partook in everything he was asked to. He was told about the 'Flying Bombs' – the German V-1 guided missiles. An air-raid siren would sound, which would be followed by the low engine buzz or whine of a missile. Curtin was told that if a missile was passing overhead and the noise stopped, he was to duck for cover: the silence meant the missile was going into a terminal dive and would explode on impact.

Perhaps to drive home the message about the need to take precautions, he and the party were taken one morning on a tour of bomb-damaged London, including St Paul's Cathedral and Buckingham Palace. He lunched with Stanley Bruce, Blamey and Shedden. In the afternoon, a special cavalcade was laid on for sightseeing at Windsor and Burnham Beeches, the ancient woodland tract on the southern Buckinghamshire border.

Next, by special request Curtin was taken to the churchyard at Stoke Poges, where the poet Thomas Gray composed his famous 'Elegy Written in a Country Churchyard'. Curtin sought out Gray's own grave, stood before it and recited the first few verses of the poem, which he had learnt as a child and had never forgotten. In recent weeks he had an enhanced sense of his own mortality. The words never seemed more poignant to him. He was touched by its dwelling on the solemn meaning and the levelling impact of death:

The boast of heraldry, the pomp of power,
And all that beauty, all that wealth e'er gave,
Awaits alike th'inevitable hour:
The paths of glory lead but to the grave . . .

Curtin was the most grounded of individuals. He rarely embraced ceremony, except for special occasions such as the Parliament House dinner for MacArthur the previous month. He had felt particularly mortal over the past two years, wondering if he would live through it all. Yet this visit was a reminder, too, that he still had projects to complete for Australia while he remained in power. Time might be running out; he had a job to do.

Curtin's itinerary was demanding, especially for a man whose health was so much on the decline that, in reality, retirement would have been better for him. Yet he was not about to fade out of office. This was his moment.

He had a formidable month in front of him. He would walk as much as he could, eat well and get plenty of rest. He knew that his meetings with Churchill would be difficult; they required a deal of preparation, concentration and effort. Curtin wished to engage the seat of Empire with its outposts in a more formal way so that it remained intact, and it could protect itself against conflicts in the future.

The Empire prime ministers' conference began on Tuesday 1 May 1944, the day after Curtin's visit to Stoke Poges. He was refreshed and ready. He began by disagreeing with Churchill's proposal that the meetings should include prime ministers only, like a cabinet meeting. Churchill planned to chair them. Even some of his own closest confidants acknowledged this meant that he would dominate them.

Curtin wanted Blamey and Shedden, his two heavyweight officials, with him. Shedden comprehended the detail, while Blamey would not miss anything, especially to do with the disposition of Australian forces. Just as important was Blamey's reputation with the British military chiefs. He was rugged and uncompromising, and had grand experience of the war in both hemispheres, which no one at the conference could match. Curtin made the self-deprecatory remark that these two would 'keep him on the rails', but he would still be the driver.

Churchill and his chiefs were consoled that Shedden and Blamey were both Empire men who would prefer the British over the American link. Knowing this, Churchill relented, adding the caveat that on some occasions the advisers would have to leave the meeting. This was simply about saving some face; the advisers were never asked to leave any discussion.

On Thursday 3 May, Curtin had the floor for the first time. He got straight to the point, criticising Britain's lack of policy direction in the Pacific War. This was Curtin's way of expressing his distaste for the manner in which he had been treated when, time after time, he asked for support of troops, planes and equipment. Churchill had been neglectful before Singapore's fall and worse afterwards.

Curtin then turned to the present, saying that Australia could not make decisions about manpower unless it knew Britain's plans for its forces against the Japanese. If the British were going to step up their troop numbers in the Pacific, Australia had to know if it would be expected to provide supplies. This meant Australia might have to take men out of active service and place them in, for instance, the food and munitions production areas.[1] Curtin said he welcomed the prospect of British forces in Australia, despite the strains this would place on resources. He reminded everyone, especially the British, that Australia was inside the United States' sphere of responsibility in the South-West Pacific. Any changes to the command in Australia would have to be approved by Washington. Without saying it, he was supporting his good friend MacArthur's role.

Churchill listened without interrupting. He paid attention to Blamey, who backed up Curtin's presentation with an account of how close Australia had come to invasion. Blamey graphically described the protracted war in New Guinea and Papua, mentioning the tough conditions and the Australian losses. Judging from the silence when he spoke, none of the British or other dominions had been fully briefed on the major battles for 'Australian mandated territory'.

When Blamey had finished, Churchill discussed a so-called 'middle strategy' that was short on specifics, demonstrating Churchill's lack of engagement with the Pacific theatre of war. It proposed a British-Australian force would move north from Australia and 'aid' MacArthur's liberation of Borneo. No one objected. Blamey was quick to interject and say that MacArthur had yet to outline such a plan, but he, Blamey, had. He said it was vital to retake the small but oil-rich island of Tarakan, off Borneo's north-east, and to seize its airfields. Blamey said also that Brunei, the oil-rich British possession in the northern half of Borneo, should be regained.

Pleased that he and Blamey were thinking the same way, Churchill agreed that, after Borneo, this force should either strike at Malaya and Singapore, or at Hong Kong and the Chinese coast. Again, the US commander had not been consulted. Churchill's 'middle strategy' covered everything but was specific about nothing.

81
Churchill's Big Distraction

Churchill was distracted by another military plan that meant much more to him. The amphibious Allied invasion of France was set for 6 June 1944 – D-Day – little more than a month away. All his energies and vested interests were in it. He had not been ready until now for the big launch of 'Operation Overlord', as the attack was called.

Churchill did not discuss it with the other prime ministers. The Germans were being led to believe that an attack would come along the Pas de Calais, while the beaches of Normandy, east of the Cherbourg Peninsula, were the real target. Churchill's preoccupation with D-Day meant he was vague on any Pacific plan, which was, to a large extent, out of his control. But where a plan was non-existent, there was room for some Churchillian mischief.

Churchill was well aware of the jockeying for power within the services of all military machines, not just his. He was shrewd in handling egos that were driven primarily by power, about which he could write volumes. He knew Blamey was taking a back seat to MacArthur, and this caused him to offer that he liked the idea of a joint British-Australian force, under an Australian commander. This last comment was aimed at Blamey, who loved the idea.

Curtin sensed that Churchill's intent was to undermine MacArthur's role. He repeated that this proposed joint force was in the United States' sphere of influence, as agreed by Churchill and Roosevelt. Churchill was then forced to concede that MacArthur would have to be in charge. Brooke, Churchill's foremost military adviser – and the only one to stand up to him – noted in his diary that Curtin was 'entirely in MacArthur's pocket'. This was a gratuitous appraisal given that, after World War II, Brooke himself ranked MacArthur alongside Churchill, Stalin and Field Marshal John Dill as those he admired most in the conflict.

Churchill floated the further idea that the land and air components of the proposed new force in the South-West Pacific might be entirely Australian, while the navy component could be predominantly British; this would cut MacArthur and the United States out of the new force altogether. Blamey, having served as number two to a general to whom he felt superior, was delighted by this idea.[1]

When discussion turned to MacArthur's plans, Blamey remarked that Australia should not be too eager to use its own forces. The comment hung in the air without clarification. Shedden drew the conclusion that Blamey now thought, based on what Churchill was saying, that he should withhold the AIF from MacArthur's use for his push to the Philippines.[2] Curtin, however, would not be swayed against MacArthur.

Curtin liked having lines of demarcation in life, politics and the war. In opposition, he refused to be part of a bipartisan national war cabinet, and in government he had refused to have one. He saw it as divisive and leading to indecision. Likewise, he believed that his policy of having MacArthur in charge had worked, no matter what the faults and drawbacks. He was not going to change something that he did not think needed changing. Curtin was also being true to his word with MacArthur and the United States.[3]

Even Brooke was surprised at how easily agreement was reached over Curtin's proposal to set the Australian army at six divisions, and to increase its RAAF squadrons from forty-eight to fifty-three. This meant that the men in action or reserve would be halved over the next year. In turn, Australia's production of food, munitions and other essentials would be boosted. Churchill remained in a good frame of mind at the conference, which augured well for future days.

On 4 May, Curtin went to Buckingham Palace for the first time and was sworn in as a Privy Councillor. Until the seventeenth century, the Privy Council was England's supreme legislative body, operating on the monarch's behalf. With the advent of parliamentary democracy, it dispensed economic and political advice to the monarch. As the power of the monarchy declined over the centuries, it became mainly symbolic.

In the evening, Curtin received a sealed letter from Churchill, who asked that Curtin not discuss the United Kingdom's views – that is, Churchill's – on the proposed new Anglo-Australian force under Australian command when he returned to Washington. Churchill emphasised that Blamey had no authority to mention the matter to MacArthur.

The next day, Saturday 5 May, Curtin returned to Buckingham Palace to have lunch with King George VI and Queen Elizabeth. Every day was a new, stimulating experience for Curtin. On 6 May he travelled with New Zealand's prime minister, Peter Fraser, to Cambridge University to receive an honorary degree. The two chatted about Curtin's pet topic for the trip – full employment. Curtin planned to discuss it with as many 'experts' as possible, especially in the British

Labour Party, which had similar postwar reconstruction aims if it won power.

With Don Rodgers, Curtin took time also with Rodgers to compose a long press statement to be published in London and Washington. It outlined the sacrifices Australia had made over the past two years, and emphasised that no nation had faced greater danger after the fall of Singapore. This was meant to justify Curtin's redirection of resources away from the military and into food production, both for the British public and the American forces in the Pacific. Curtin maintained that Australia's combat forces would remain as they were; only garrison forces would be reduced.

The press release was issued after a radio broadcast on 6 May, in which Curtin restated that Australia was a bastion of British institutions, the British way of life and democracy. Curtin intended to continue hammering these themes throughout the month in his many meetings. He did not vary the speech much, which made the strenuous round of engagements a fraction easier.

On Tuesday 8 May, Curtin dined with the British Labour politician A. V. Alexander, the First Lord of the Admiralty. Always looking ahead, he was grateful for Alexander's comments on full employment. They agreed it was a huge topic. The discussion prompted Curtin to consider a 'white paper' to investigate the issue and come up with proposals. He decided to act on it as soon as he returned to Australia.

On 10 May he received the keys to the City of London, and again delivered his speech about Australia being a land of seven million Britishers. He was cheered by the distinguished guests, especially after he again explained how close the Japanese had come to invasion of the mainland.

82
Checkmate at Chequers

The weekend of 12–13 May 1944 was spent at the British prime minister's official country residence, 'Chequers', in Buckinghamshire. There was not much time for Curtin to meet privately with Churchill, who was often tucked away with key military personnel. D-Day, still top-secret, was approaching. Curtin met West Australian feminist Bessie Rischbieth on the 14th, and in the evening went with her to a London performance of the Moral Rearmament Revue, which his government had sponsored in Canberra.

On 15 May, instead of attending the prime minister's conference, Churchill took King George VI to a final briefing by Field Marshal Bernard Montgomery and General Eisenhower on the Allied invasion of France. In his absence, the conference addressed the issue of greater cohesion of the Empire through a Council of Imperial Ministers. Like Alfred Deakin before him, Curtin got nowhere with the proposal. He had hoped the Canadian prime minister would back him, but Mackenzie King was on Churchill's side and Churchill was not interested. King bargained the disappointed Curtin down.[1]

The conference was wrapped up on Wednesday 16 May. Magnanimously, Curtin thanked Churchill at the formal closing for chairing the talks 'successfully'. Now playing to two audiences – in the United Kingdom and in Australia – Curtin claimed that the war had broadened the brotherhood of the Empire. He offered homage to King George VI. Menzies would have been happy with such sentiments.

On 17 May Curtin repeated his mantra, which by now he could deliver without notes, at a meeting of the Empire Parliamentary Association at the House of Commons, chaired by the Labour Party's opposition leader, Clement Attlee. Curtin's delivery was improving and he enjoyed the thunderous applause. The next day there was an Australian Club luncheon, chaired by the King's brother, Prince Henry, the Duke of Gloucester. He sat on Curtin's left, and Churchill was on his right. Without Churchill hearing, Curtin asked the Duke if he were interested in becoming Australia's next governor-general; the Duke was enthusiastic.

Churchill made a speech and played to the audience as only he could, touching on the difficulties of 1942. He made it seem that he at last appreciated what Curtin and Australia had been through. Churchill was aware that everyone in the room knew of the conflict he'd had with Curtin in that critical year.

'Now, Prime Minister Curtin and I had not met before this month,' he said, pausing for effect and glancing at Curtin, 'except in correspondence.' The audience's laughter turned to applause. Churchill went on. 'I have now joined the right hand of friendship to that most commanding, competent, whole-hearted leader of the Australian people.'[2] A standing ovation followed.

Curtin acknowledged Churchill with a nod and smile. He then rose to the occasion, performing at his best. He mentioned his decision in 1941 not to form a national government. He was too polite to say that it had not been any of the British leader's business. Instead he attempted to put the concept on a higher level, speaking of the 'supremacy of persuasion' and 'the triumph of reason', which could be given freer rein if both a government and an opposition remained. Churchill remained unconvinced, as did much of the audience, but this was not the time for a debate on the subject.

Curtin turned to his main theme: 'We [Australia] are now in an American sphere of responsibility, but that this does not mean any reallocation of relationships.'[3] This brought a further standing ovation.

Churchill's anger about Curtin's 'turning to America' seemed now to have been quelled. But at Chequers the next day, Churchill, primed by several brandies, took the time after dinner to confront Curtin over the issue that had upset him so much. Over port (refused by Curtin) and cigars (accepted), Churchill attempted to play on Curtin's professed desire for closer Imperial ties and consultation.

Curtin, sober yet fatigued, was not in a mood to be conciliatory. He replied, 'If the British Commonwealth had been at war with

Japan, and war with Germany arose later, what would you have done? Would you have appealed to the United States?'

'Yes, most certainly,' Churchill said.

'Well, that is just what I did when you were at war with Germany and Japan came in.'[4]

This was a simple, clear enunciation of the 'reason' of which Curtin had spoken at the Australian Club the day before. Churchill, however, could not forgive or forget. He would touch on the issue in his published history of World War II, but he never again mentioned it to Curtin.

On Sunday of Curtin's second weekend at Chequers, Churchill explained that he had been called away urgently from the conference at the last minute when Curtin's motion for imperial governance came up. The secret Operation Overlord took precedence. Churchill gave the appearance of being amenable to Curtin's proposal. He agreed that British prime ministers should meet once a month with their dominions' high commissioners. But then he undercut Curtin by saying that such an arrangement would mean it was unnecessary for Stanley Bruce to attend Britain's War Council meetings. This would reduce Australia's access and consultation at the top level.

As Hughes had predicted to Curtin, Churchill was attempting to concede as little as possible. Nevertheless, the diplomatic charade continued, with Churchill promising to invite his daughters to meet Curtin over afternoon tea. At the appointed time, Curtin found Churchill discussing Pacific strategy with his ministers and military chiefs. He cancelled the afternoon tea and joined the discussions, which centred on MacArthur.

Late in the day, discussion turned to who Australia's next governor-general would be. Churchill favoured his friend Field Marshal Wavell. Curtin knew that Blamey did not like Wavell, or the way he had tried to use Australian troops in North Africa and the Middle East. The feeling was mutual. Blamey had also spoken to Harry Chauvel, who had dealt with Wavell in the Middle East in World War I and who was similarly unimpressed.

Curtin took quiet delight in telling Churchill that he had already sounded out the Duke of Gloucester, who was keen to take the job. As Graham Freudenberg wrote in his book *Churchill and Australia*, 'A Royal Duke trumped a Field Marshal.'[5]

Curtin refused Churchill's invitation for all prime ministers to tour the preparations for Operation Overlord and the unveiling of the secret D-Day operation. Instead, Curtin visited two air bases in Lincolnshire, where Australian airmen, seconded to the RAF, were already bombing France to distract the Germans and destroy their fortifications. He met one crew, watched them take off and sent them a 'good-luck' message as the bombers flew over the French coastline.

Churchill would have taken Curtin's decision not to tour the Overlord preparations as a snub, which it may have been. Curtin may have been disinclined to show Churchill's plans any special consideration, since Churchill had never shown interest in Australia's battles with the Japanese. Curtin further ignored Churchill's big moment by continuing with his plans to leave the United Kingdom before the D-Day invasions.

But Churchill was not alone in being irritated. Blamey, too, wanted to stay to witness the historic event. Instead, he was compelled to leave with his prime minister's party.

On Tuesday 22 May, Curtin was driven to Badminton for lunch with Queen Mary, mother of George VI. The next day, he called on the King at Buckingham Palace for the third and final time. The whirlwind round of lunches and dinners with the elite of British society led the weary Curtin to remark to Rodgers on 24 May, a rare free night, 'Let's go out and find some bloody Australians.'[6]

On the evening of Friday 25 May, Curtin dined with the Welsh-born Hugh Dalton, a prominent Labour Party leader and the current president of the British Board of Trade. The subject, once again, was postwar reconstruction.

Dalton was a graduate of the London School of Economics, where

Marxist theory had flourished since the 1920s, making it Britain's most radical university between the wars. He encouraged Curtin to take governmental control of the economy's levers as far as possible. He endorsed the concept of full employment, which he said would be a strong plank of the Labour Party at the next UK election.

The men discussed Keynesian theory and how it should work in practice. Both were believers in a 'welfare' state. The state had to look after the less fortunate and provide a 'safety net'. Some Australian government planners, such as H. C. 'Nugget' Coombs, had strong Keynesian views. Curtin decided to involve Coombs, who knew and admired Dalton, and others in the development of his white paper.

After the inspiring dinner, Curtin travelled to Chequers the same night for the final time. Churchill invited him for a one-on-one chat late the next afternoon, a Saturday, but by now Curtin had had enough of his monologues. He politely declined, saying he had to return to London on the Saturday night. His excuse was legitimate enough: the following day, Sunday 27 May, he wanted to watch a one-day cricket match between servicemen at Lord's: Australia versus 'the Rest'.

Despite this, Curtin expressed his admiration for the British leader in an off-the-record briefing of his press contacts:

He is the most important person arrayed against our enemies. He is indispensable because I do not know of any other equal who can replace him. He is an inspiration, a driver. He has the complete faith of the British people. He is the master of the House of Commons. And no man has yet been its master.[7]

By all accounts, the two had gotten along well. Curtin believed Churchill had 'a great tiredness about him', which he thought was anxiety over the second front he was setting up in France. 'Mr Churchill fires every shot and suffers every wound,' Curtin said.[8]

Observers thought Curtin was never happier on the entire trip than when in the MCC Members' Long Room, watching the team of Australian servicemen play some of England's greatest cricketers. Lord's was packed with a crowd of 26,500. Curtin was moved by the fact that a match could go on in front of a sell-out crowd despite the prospect of German missiles. The atmosphere was a festive reminder of stoic resistance, British-style. It helped that the batsmen played attacking cricket.

Curtin met the two teams at lunch. He was delighted to shake the hands of some England Test cricketers he admired, such as Walter Hammond, Len Hutton, Walter Robins and Denis Compton. The Australians won by one wicket, which gave Curtin even more satisfaction, especially as a West Australian RAAF pilot, Keith Carmody, smashed a brilliant eighty-six. Ten days later, Carmody would be shot down off the Dutch coast and spend the rest of the war in a POW camp near Berlin.[9]

Curtin likened the stress of his US and UK trips to an election campaign. But the pressure was not over when he left England on 29 May. His flying boat took him to Canada, where he spent three days meeting with the Canadian government. Elsie joined him and together they returned to Washington, where Curtin briefed the combined chiefs on his agreement with Churchill to scale down Australia's military and beef up its food production.

He then addressed the National Press Club. Most of the questions after his speech concerned MacArthur. Curtin spoke glowingly of what the Supreme Commander had done for Australia's 'preservation'.

He met for a second and final time with Roosevelt, this time at the Oval Office. They discussed his meetings in the United Kingdom and Curtin left him with a succinct written brief. He was in New York when the Allies launched Operation Overlord, which promised to be a major turning point in the war against Hitler.

After four days, the Australian party prepared for their boat voyage to Australia. Blamey asked Curtin if he might return by air; his excuse was that he needed to visit Honolulu and New Caledonia for 'military purposes'. Curtin was happy to let him go. He had become estranged from his top commander during the trip.

MacArthur later told Shedden that Blamey had said, 'I couldn't bear the journey back with the prime minister's crowd. I trumped up reasons to return by air.' MacArthur characterised this as 'disloyalty to the prime minister', and Shedden passed his comments to Curtin.[10]

In Brisbane on 24 June 1944, Blamey told MacArthur of Churchill's plans for a new South-West Pacific Area Force made up of Australian and British forces. MacArthur was stunned. Blamey said he thought MacArthur had been informed.

'General Marshall had only informed me about the proposed [reduction of] strengths of the Australia Forces,' MacArthur said, annoyed that he seemed to have been cut out of the loop, and perhaps even unofficially demoted. Blamey did not wish to talk about the matter further.

'You knew about my program,' MacArthur said accusingly, referring to his plan to move north to attack the Japanese forces and to retake the Philippines.[11]

Blamey said he had not known of the plans. MacArthur claimed that he had given them to him before Blamey left Australia with Curtin. For his part, Shedden recalled that Blamey had often referred to a MacArthur timetable for retaking the Philippines during the trip.

'But you criticised my plans,' MacArthur continued. 'You said you didn't think Australian troops would be ready. You claimed they would take a long time to get up to strength. I even remember you saying that some of them had been out of action for a prolonged period. But you did say the 7th would be ready by September.'

'It won't be ready by then.'

MacArthur was furious.

Blamey diverted the conversation. 'I won't be directly commanding the new force,' he said, 'I have instructed Berryman to do it.'

MacArthur was speechless. It seemed to him that Blamey saw the new force as a *fait accompli*.[12]

'There is another matter,' Blamey said. 'I believe it would be better if I was given command of the RAAF.'

'Why?' MacArthur asked, still recovering.

'There are drawbacks in the lines of communication between [Air Vice Marshal] Jones and [Air Vice Marshal] Bostock,' Blamey said, referring to the chiefs of the United States' and Australia's air forces.

When Blamey left, MacArthur said to his deputy, Sutherland,

'That bastard has been disloyal to me in London. He wants command of everything!'[13]

Sutherland remained silent. He knew it was best to let the issue simmer.

But his boss wasn't finished yet. He added, with some vehemence, 'I want you to prepare a plan with American Forces only.'[14]

83
MacArthur Dumps the Diggers

MacArthur met Curtin and Shedden at the Brisbane docks on 26 June 1944, concerned after his acrimonious meeting with Blamey two days earlier. Curtin was angry. Churchill had specifically said that Blamey was not to discuss these developments with MacArthur.

'I'm convinced he supports the proposals for this new Command,' MacArthur remarked. 'His personal ambition is to become the Commander.'[1]

Shedden agreed with MacArthur's assessment, later writing that

It fitted with his enthusiasm for the British proposal that the land air forces would be all Dominion [Australian], and the naval forces would be predominantly British. Furthermore Blamey's personal assistant had flown the kite with my assistant regarding the deserving case of General Blamey for promotion to Field Marshal.[2]

MacArthur was incensed. 'He wants to become the commander of the entire Australian defence forces,' he said, 'in the same way I command all the naval, military and air forces in the area.'[3] After a few moments' reflection, MacArthur said he was willing to 'make any change that might be desired to accommodate the wishes of the Australian Government in regard to General Blamey and his position'.

This comment was a far cry from MacArthur's attitude two years earlier, when US Lend-Lease operative William Wasserman attacked

Blamey and MacArthur defended him. MacArthur's about-face put pressure on Curtin to act against Blamey.

'The set-up remains the same,' Curtin told MacArthur. 'Just as before, Australians troops are under your command for your assault on the Philippines. There is no change Douglas, none at all. These ideas were just being floated at the Prime Ministers' Conference. I made it very clear that you were in charge. Full stop.'[4]

Shedden backed up Curtin's version of events.

'Then it seems,' MacArthur said, 'that General Blamey has been disloyal to you, John.' He then told Curtin of Blamey's excuse for not returning by boat from the United States with Curtin and his party. He relayed Blamey's remark about not being able to stand 'the prime minister's crowd'. Shedden told MacArthur how Blamey had played up by partying on the SS *Lurline* on the way over.[5]

MacArthur complained further. 'The position of Commander of the Allied Land Forces is now a fiction,' he said. 'Unlike the commanders of the Navy and Air Forces, General Blamey refuses to associate closely with me . . . I shall take personal command of the operations against the Philippines.' He added that if 'the position of Commander, Allied Land Forces, fell vacant, I wouldn't continue the appointment.'[6]

This was another hint for Curtin to fire Blamey, but the prime minister demurred.

'I receive larger [negative] fan-mail about General Blamey than about anything else,' MacArthur said, piling on the pressure. 'It comes from members of the Australian Forces, with whom he could not be considered a popular commander. He is intensely disliked by most of the senior staff officers, except the few who had benefited by promotions and awards.'[7]

Curtin continued to listen without committing himself. He had always been a reluctant firer, whether in a union, in his party or in government. Perhaps the most outstanding instance of this was his decision to keep Eddie Ward as a minister when there was a big push to oust him. Curtin always sought harmony, which, as ever in his life, was both a strength and weakness.

Curtin's inclinations were to dismiss Blamey. But there was still no Australian with the power and personality to stand up to the British

– and indeed to the Americans, including MacArthur. Vasey might have been capable if given the opportunity, but Curtin considered it a late stage to be blooding a new chief of the Australian military.

MacArthur kept trying to sway Curtin, whom he had always found accommodating and malleable. 'John, you should keep a very close watch on whom he recommends for promotions and awards,' he added. 'He surrounds himself with his own special selections. For instance, the promotion of Lieutenant General Savige over Major General Vasey is outrageous.'

Curtin and Shedden both said that this issue had already been discussed by the government. Curtin had asked for a judgement from his deputy, Frank Forde, the Minister for the Army. Forde had agreed with Savige's appointment. 'That's where the matter finished,' Curtin said.[8]

MacArthur was displeased by what he saw as Curtin's inaction over Blamey. He said that, in view of his discussion with Blamey two days earlier, he had asked Sutherland to rewrite the program for his advance north, taking into consideration the possibility that by then he might not be commanding Australia's forces.

Curtin was disappointed. Leaving the AIF out of the fighting would lessen Australia's influence in the postwar discussions over the Pacific territories.

Seeing his reaction, MacArthur said, 'I have to do this, John. I can't afford a disaster. I can't afford a disruption of the program.'

Curtin reiterated that MacArthur was in charge as before.

'As Commander-in-Chief,' MacArthur said, 'I have to be certain of just what forces I have to carry out plans.'[9]

Curtin attempted to reassure him that he would have command over all Australian forces. But MacArthur seemed to have made up his mind. As further evidence of Blamey's intentions, he cited an instruction sent by Blamey from London to Australian Lieutenant-General John Northcott to 'hold up the advance of Australian troops on the northern coast of New Guinea'.

'Northcott protested to me that Blamey did not understand the position,' MacArthur said. 'But this was not the case at all. Since my interview with him, he was apparently holding back the Australian troops for the new [Ango-Australian] command.'

Shedden recalled Blamey saying at the London conference that 'we should not be too eager to use Australian forces concerning MacArthur's plans'. MacArthur waited to see if Curtin would take action against Blamey, but still he would not.

MacArthur then tried another tack, which bordered on intimidation. 'I can't see Admiral King and General Marshall agreeing to the proposed change in the South-West Pacific area,' he said. 'King has a free hand as a member of the joint Chiefs of Staff. He would be unlikely to agree to adding to his masters if the area came under the control of the Combined [UK and US] Chiefs of Staff. The same applies to Marshall.'[10] In other words, the American military chiefs would be most unhappy if the British poked their noses into their area of control in the South-West Pacific, or if they tried to take it over.

Curtin remained impassive. MacArthur may not have been aware that it was impossible to bully him. He may not have known how Roosevelt and Churchill had failed when they ganged up on him after the bombing of Darwin.

MacArthur then tried another approach, wondering whether Curtin might be vulnerable to public opinion. 'Any change will evoke a strong reaction by Marshall,' he said. 'I'm certain there would be a similar reaction by the American and Australian people.'[11]

But Curtin was not concerned. He had won a strong mandate to rule at the elections. He tried to placate MacArthur, but the American was set on his new course, without the AIF. Curtin knew the importance of Australia being in the action to overcome Japan. The Australian High Command wanted it. War was their business, and there was nothing bigger than this conflict. To opt out of the final stages, if they were to be the final stages, would be unacceptable. Politically, too, it was important for Australia to be at the postwar settlement table.

Yet the pacifist side of Curtin was not unhappy about MacArthur's petulant decision to dump the difficult Blamey and his digger army. Curtin knew that the lives of thousands of Australians could be spared by this decision. The nation had already sacrificed much, and the fighting would continue on the islands close to home. Curtin lost sleep over many things, but this decision by MacArthur would not be one of them. This was a major reason why Curtin allowed

Blamey to hold his position. A more bellicose prime minister would have sacked him for the disgrace of causing the Australians to be left behind. Inadvertently, Blamey had done Curtin a favour.

MacArthur moved to make sure the British were kept out of the grand finale in the Pacific. He wrote to Admiral Ernest King, who reserved much of his almost perpetual rage for the United Kingdom:

> *The British have contributed nothing to this campaign, and, in fact, opposed the Australian proposal to make available Australian troops for the defence of their own country. They now propose to enter this theatre at the moment when victory lies clearly before us in order to reap the benefits of our success.*[12]

This intercession promised to keep the British out of the action to come.

As soon as Curtin returned to Canberra, Evatt wanted him to launch a referendum campaign that would give the government the power to protect the nation from inflation and unemployment, the two evils that had arisen fifteen years earlier with the onset of the Depression. Curtin, too, was keen for postwar prosperity but he was half-hearted about the campaign. After the election in 1943 and his arduous overseas journey, he was irked by the thought of a third campaign inside a year, with endless speeches, radio broadcasts and press conferences.

Curtin launched it on 25 July 1944, but he let his Canberra journalists know that he would be putting more effort into war business than the referendum. Other advisers and critics pointed out that Curtin already had the power to implement any policy he wished – the referendum was redundant. Not surprisingly, it failed.

Curtin told close friends that he was overworked, often distressed and maudlin. He could not concentrate the way he used to. Fatigue came quickly when he was at work. Elsie had returned to Perth and seemed more supportive of her family there than of her husband. She had little time for Canberra life, not feeling up to the task of being the nation's First Lady.

Curtin was urged to retire by some close to him. Menzies was sparing him nothing in parliament, finding excuses to put him under pressures that, two years earlier, he would have surmounted easily enough. But Curtin's energy levels were sinking, and along with them his willingness for the political fight.

Yet he kept going. Among other things, he wanted to develop his full employment white paper into a blueprint for postwar development. He directed the Department of Postwar Reconstruction, established nearly two years earlier with Ben Chifley as its minister, to produce the white paper. According to 'Nugget' Coombs, the director of the project, Curtin saw the paper as a political manifesto. It would assert policies designed to rally community support for the war, and would inspire the nation to continue accepting hardships. In return, the government would ensure that there would not be another depression. The gains already achieved in social welfare and security would be retained and developed.

When Curtin received the white paper, the ever meticulous and thoughtful 'editor' made substantial changes and sent it back to the department for further work.[13]

84
The Forgotten POWs

Although the Australian forces had now been dropped from MacArthur's plans, tens of thousands were still in action in the army, air force and navy all over the Pacific. Many others were trapped in terrible Japanese labour camps in Burma, Thailand, Singapore, French Indo-China (Vietnam), Japan and other places.

On 4 September 1944, at a former camp of the French Foreign Legion, a group of 900 Australian and British prisoners who had survived the horrific building of the Thai–Burma railway were roused from their sleep.

'All go Nippon!' a guard screamed: 'All men go Nippon.'[1]

These POWs had first been imprisoned at Changi after the fall of Singapore. In March 1944, after a year of slave work on the railway, they had been taken by rail to Bangkok and Cambodia's Phnom Penh, then by boat down the Mekong River to Saigon and their current camp. After four months there, in conditions that had only just allowed them to survive, they were sent back to Changi. They then slipped back to the levels of malnutrition and disease experienced in Thailand.

Now they were on the move again, to Japan, the home of the enemy. At the docks the men groaned when they saw the two freighters, which were carrying blocks of raw rubber bound for Tokyo. The *Rakuyo Maru* would carry the Australians, while the American-built *Kachidoki Maru* was to transport the British.

The POWs' officers protested. The ships had no Red Cross markings and therefore would be targets for Allied air, submarine and battleship attacks. Korean guards with sharp bamboo sticks prodded them below decks, where the air was fetid and stifling. The POWs protested. The guards prodded harder, yelling, 'Speedo! Speedo!' This was the prisoners' most hated word, which they had heard every day while building roads, railways and bridges in Thailand and Burma.

The ships sailed north, joining other Japanese vessels from Manila. They entered an area swarming with American submarines. At 5.12 a.m. on 12 September 1944, the still unmarked *Rakuyo Maru* was hit by two US torpedoes. The explosions were muffled. The blast was absorbed by the packed rubber, but water gushed into the hold. Some POWs rushed the ladders. They were held back by their officers, who had realised that the rubber would keep them afloat longer than in other circumstances. This gave the POWs precious minutes to make an orderly evacuation.

On deck, the guards would not allow the POWs into the life rafts. During the commotion, explosions lit the still dark skies, signalling that US torpedoes were striking an accompanying Japanese tanker. In the confusion, some of the POWs took revenge on their more sadistic guards. Several were killed.

Groups of the POWs managed to secure several lifeboats. The *Rakuyo* seemed buoyant enough. While many wished to abandon ship, some of the Australians stayed on board and fashioned a life raft out of hatch covers. They worked fast. The ship was making hideous splitting and tearing noises. The rubber would not keep it afloat for much longer. The men scavenged for food and water for their 'voyage'. The raft was lowered into the ocean at 5.15 p.m. – twelve hours after the first torpedo hit the *Rakuyo*. The men paddled away. They had gone just 100 metres when the ship keeled and sank to the bottom of the South China Sea.

The ocean seemed empty except for the lifeboats and rafts. Within minutes, two Japanese frigates and a merchant ship loomed. The frigates circled like cautious sharks, while the merchant slowed to see if there were any useful pickings amongst the debris. The men on the raft paddled close to the merchant. Its engines stopped. Those on the raft grabbed rope ladders and began to haul themselves up. But the crew pushed them off. The merchant's propellers whirred. The ship pulled away, leaving the POWs yelling abuse.

An hour later, darkness was falling. The men cried 'Cooee!' to distant shapes. Their calls were answered. Just as blackness enveloped them, the men manoeuvred their raft towards a dozen lifeboats manned by other Australians. Brigadier Arthur Varley was on board one, while ship's electrician Val Duncan had taken command of another.[2] Duncan had survived the sinking of the HMAS *Perth*, and this, in the absence of officers, gave him authority. Both commanders believed their chances would be better if they made for the coast of China, 350 kilometres away. Others reckoned they should remain where they were and hope to be picked up by returning Japanese ships. The men took a vote on what they would do.

Three boats stayed put. Ten set off for the Chinese coast. The six in Varley's squadron carried 200 POWs, while Duncan's squadron of four boats held 136.

After three days' rowing, in which the two squadrons drifted about ten kilometres apart, smoke was observed on the horizon. Three Japanese corvettes materialised. Two headed straight for Varley's six lifeboats. The Japanese machine guns opened up, destroying the boats and killing those who did not jump clear. The third corvette moved towards Duncan's little flotilla, its guns manned. It slowed as it came close to them.

'If you believe in God,' Duncan called to his men, 'start praying now.'

A Japanese officer leaned over the side of the corvette.

'Are you American?' he yelled.

'No!' the POWs yelled.

'Are you British?'

'No, Australians!' the men bellowed back. 'We are bloody Australians!'[3]

The Japanese officer gave an order to his crew. The POWs watched the machine-gunners, whose weapons were pointing down at them. But the officer was signalling for something else. A rope ladder tumbled down the side of the corvette. The POWs could not believe their fortune as the climbed onto the deck.

The 136 survivors were taken to Sangai Harbour on the island of Hainan, and then transferred to a Japanese whaler, which took them to Japan. They were sent to the Karasaki POW camp. Coalmines and shipyards were locations for further labouring work. It was tough. The food rations were meagre, but all agreed that the conditions were better than those experienced on the Thai–Burma Railway.

Val Duncan and those lucky enough to go with him had survived. But their fates, and the deaths of more than 1100 British and Australian POWs in the sinking of the *Rakuyo Maru*, were unknown anywhere outside Japan in mid-1944.[4]

Early on the morning of 5 August 1944, more than 1100 Japanese attempted to break out of a POW camp at Cowra, a country town in western New South Wales. It took an army and police posse nine days to round them all up. 231 Japanese were killed and 108 wounded. Four Australian soldiers perished during the breakout and the biggest manhunt in Australian history. Curtin told his press contacts on 21 August that all Cowra POWs had been accounted for but told them that no official statement would be made. He was worried about reprisals against Australian prisoners in Japanese hands.

85

MacArthur's Farewell; Savige's Way of War

By September 1944, MacArthur was at last ready to fulfil his theatrically outlined plan to 'return' to the Philippines. He seemed to have won the argument – put personally to Roosevelt on 26 July – that the Philippines should be the first stage of the counter-thrust to defeat the Japanese in the Pacific. The US chiefs would have the final say, but MacArthur was implementing his plans in anticipation of them being accepted.

The alternative concept, proposed by Admirals Nimitz and King, was to secure the island of Formosa (Taiwan) off China's southeast coast. They then planned to set up airbases for their new B-29 Superfortress bombers on the Chinese mainland. These were the biggest planes the US had produced. Nearly 4000 were coming off production lines across America. Both admirals reckoned they would finish the war in the Pacific. They could bomb the Japanese into submission. But MacArthur argued that the war would still have to be won on the ground, island by island, all the way to Honshu. The Japanese would never surrender, he said.

Roosevelt would prefer to back the admirals but MacArthur's submission was compelling. The president realised he had erred in not appointing an overall Pacific supremo. With the massive egos of his experienced admirals and generals roaming the Pacific, cohesion might become a problem. MacArthur's knowledge of the area and his determination to take back the Philippines gave him the most sway.

MacArthur flew from Brisbane to Canberra to see Curtin, armed with the usual carton of Capstan cigarettes and two more westerns. Curtin was pleased that his friend, with his great assistance, was in a position to do what he set out to do from the moment he fled the

Philippines and landed in Australia. MacArthur was sad to see the deterioration in Curtin's appearance. His face was ashen; his body slightly stooped. He was far from shambolic, but he was less lively than at their last meeting, two months earlier.

The two men spoke again about 'that trip' they would take together with their wives, once the war was over. Both may now have felt that it would never happen.

Curtin began a two-week trip to Perth, commencing on 2 October. He addressed students at a state school in his electorate and spoke at a town hall meeting in support of the flagging 'Second Victory Loan' campaign. He wanted Australians to keep a measure of austerity, despite the obvious turning of events in the war. It was more prudent to invest in the loan than to waste money on consumer goods, he argued. Raw materials were scarce; better to leave them for war production, rather than have them used up on items that people could do without.

This may have sounded like a plaintive cry in a nation that was beginning to acquire a taste for material goods such as ovens, cars and fridges, if they could be bought. But Curtin's campaign for the war effort continued to have an impact. The loan was boosted towards full subscription.

MacArthur's Philippines push saw him remove his US troops from the small island of Bougainville. It and Buka Island, just to the north, were Australian territory, although geographically they were part of the Solomon Islands. Because they were Australian mandated areas, there was no problem with militia troops fighting there.

The Americans on Bougainville had fought off a major Japanese counter-attack in March 1944, killing 5000 enemy soldiers. After that, they had done little except develop the base, protect their perimeter and build outposts on the major tracks leading to Torokina, a village on the coast.

Now the Americans were replaced by Lieutenant General Savige and his II Corps, made up of militia contingents: the Australian 3rd

Division and 11th Brigade, reinforced by a Fijian Infantry Regiment. Savige also used the 23rd Brigade to garrison neighbouring islands. In all, with the Americans' departure north, two-thirds of the Australian Army was fighting or containing Japanese garrisons, some of which were huge.

Blamey ordered offensive campaigns on Bougainville. This was approved by Curtin and his cabinet and endorsed by the bipartisan Advisory War Council. Yet there were caveats. Savige could not commit 'major forces'. Nevertheless, Blamey added that it might be possible for II Corps to 'undertake the elimination of the Japanese forces in the area'.

The directive was based on the Americans' estimate that there were as few as 13,400 Japanese on the island. In fact, there were 40,000, and so any effort to destroy the enemy would need major force.

Savige would have been happy to carry out the order, but he was aware that he would have to undertake his 'tasks' within limits. There could be no massive battles that would lead to thousands of his men being killed.

By fluke or good management, Blamey's appointment of Savige, who had such thoroughness and care for his troops, looked to be an inspired choice for the tricky assignment. Adventurism and reckless attacks had to be curbed. Yet the Japanese, mainly garrisoned in the island's south, had still to be countered and eventually eliminated.

Savige ascertained that about 8000 Japanese were in posts well forward of their southern base. He decided on three separate drives. First, he planned to push the Japanese into the narrow Bonis Peninsula in the north, where he could contain them. Second, he aimed to seize Earl Ridge, at the centre. This would give the Australians control of the east–west thoroughfares and protect his forces against counter-attacks. Taking the centre would also open the passage for a drive to the east coast. Third, Savige would push, with his usual caution, towards the bulk of the Japanese at the town of Buin, in the south.

The campaign would have handicaps. Savige wanted to make an amphibious attack on the south. But the army's General Sturdee put this ambition in perspective: 'GHQ controls all shipping,' he said, referring to MacArthur and his staff. 'I doubt whether they are the least bit interested in what goes on in Bougainville now that the US troops are out of it.'[1]

No shipping meant no artillery and no replacement equipment, which would hamper Savige's campaign. He would have to develop land supply routes for his trip south. Sturdee was concerned that some of Savige's commanders would be spoiling for an all-out fight that would lead to a wholesale loss of soldiers. Savige understood and began to 'micro-manage' to make sure no unnecessary risks were taken. This upset some of his brigadiers.

'Bill Bridgeford,' Major-General Frank Berryman wrote, 'finds Stan Savige's interference in detail most trying.' Arnold Potts, too, complained 'bitterly' about the restrictions on his brigade. Seeking redemption following his sacking by Blamey, Potts was more enthusiastic than any other commander about charging ahead and engaging the Japanese in major battles.[2]

Savige had to stop him undertaking 'unnecessary adventures' on three occasions. After the last, Savige wrote to Sturdee: 'Potts feels he must redeem his name after the events on Kokoda Track by the full employment of his Brigade in one area.' Savige believed this would have led to big losses and refused to endorse it.

Sturdee replied:

Potts must be strongly restrained from embarking on wild cat schemes in either the Northern or Central Sectors in order to redeem his reputation. We are not interested in personal reputations at the expense of unnecessary loss of Australian lives in operations that do not contribute to the attainment of the main objective.[3]

Potts must have been more than peeved. He had been pilloried by Blamey for not being more offensive against the Japanese in the Owen Stanley Range; now he was being held back for thinking too offensively. In this case, he was at odds with how the 'main objective' should be attained. A corps commander such as Savige might have ruined any other campaign by reaching down so far into his subordinates' responsibilities. But Bougainville was different and

Savige had to keep casualties low. Discretion and caution were just as important as valour.

The conditions on the island helped his aims. The thick jungle ensured that battles would be intermittent affairs fought under dense foliage canopies. Equipment shortages, especially in artillery, would limit advances and breakthroughs. On top of that, Savige did not believe the Japanese would capitulate. Progress south to Buin and ultimate victory would be slow.

86
The Comeback

The island of Leyte in the Philippines was found to be lightly manned by the Japanese. This caused Nimitz to recommend that MacArthur and his US South-West Pacific Force attack there and Mindanao first. MacArthur decided to land 120,000 soldiers – four divisions of the US Sixth Army – with another 57,000 in two reserve divisions. A further 70,000 armoured, amphibian and artillery troops would hit Leyte from the east. MacArthur believed in overkill; he would later want to finish the Korean War with an atomic bomb.

Roosevelt's dithering over appointing a US supremo for the Pacific began to cause problems. No one quite knew what naval force should be committed. MacArthur requested and received Admiral Kinkaid's mighty Seventh Fleet, which had more than 700 ships. Battleships, cruisers, transporters, escort carriers, destroyers and specialist support craft of all types descended on the Philippines. There was also a covering force – the Third Fleet – commanded by Admiral Halsey, who was answerable to Nimitz.

Kinkaid did not care for MacArthur's decision to leave the Australians out of the attack. As far as he was concerned, MacArthur controlled the infantry and he controlled the navy in this coming battle. Kinkaid knew and liked the Australian naval commanders, particularly Commodore John Collins and Captain Emile Dechaineux, with their heavy cruisers, HMAS *Australia* and HMAS *Shropshire* respectively. He wanted them and their ships in his fleet. Kinkaid also included two Australian destroyers, HMAS *Arunta* and HMAS *Warramunga*.

MacArthur left Australia on 15 October for Hollandia, then boarded the SS *Nashville* bound for Leyte Gulf. On 18 October 1944, US naval intelligence passed radio information (supplied by Filipino guerrillas) to the US Bombardment Force, which was ploughing through the ocean less than 100 kilometres from the island of Leyte. This squadron had a strong motivation. It included five of the battleships sunk or damaged at Pearl Harbor. At 6.55 a.m. on 20 October, part of the force opened up its guns on certain Leyte beaches designated by the guerrillas. Two hours later, the Australian fleet, along with the *Phoenix*, cruised through the line of US battleships and opened up their guns on more Japanese targets. At 10 a.m. MacArthur sent infantry attack forces ashore, one in the island's north, the other in the south.

MacArthur called a press conference on the *Nashville*'s bridge at 11 a.m. Using as much stagecraft as a Broadway director, he lit his corncob pipe and addressed four American correspondents. No photographs were allowed.

'Exactly forty-one years ago, on 20 October 1903, I was a second lieutenant arriving at Tacloban,' he said, peering at the Filipino city in the distance. 'I was joining the United States Army Corps of Engineers.'

The correspondents scribbled then paused, waiting for MacArthur's 'I have returned'. But he was not going to deliver the finest line of his life so far without a bigger media contingent. Besides, he was not yet on the beach. His statement did, however, ensure that he garnered all the early publicity and upstaged the admirals.

At noon, a landing barge slipped alongside the *Nashville*. MacArthur and his party, including General Kenney, the Bataan Gang, the four correspondents and now their four photographers, climbed in. They chugged over to a troopship. The president of the Philippines, Sergio Osmena, and other Filipino military chiefs also boarded; Osmena had recently replaced MacArthur's friend and patron Manuel Quezon, who had died on 1 August, as president. The barge weaved its way through the boats that were pounding towards the beaches carrying US soldiers.

MacArthur, his sunglasses on and his pipe poking from a jacket pocket, directed his vessel to pull alongside another barge. With reporters close and scribbling, he waved to a helmsman. 'Son, where is the hardest fighting going on?' he called out. The astonished helmsman pointed to a beach, which the Filipino generals confirmed to be Red Beach, a known hotspot. 'Then head for Red Beach,' MacArthur commanded.[1]

The barge scraped onto a sandbank thirty metres short of the beach. MacArthur was disgruntled. He wanted to land directly on the beach. Instead, he was forced to get his shoes, socks and trouser legs wet as he waded through the mild surf. Photographers scrambled ahead, all wanting the definitive shot of MacArthur striding towards his goal. It had taken almost three years.

MacArthur still held back his big moment, waiting for an Australian Signals Corps to organise a transmitter for a broadcast from a nearby weapons carrier. While waiting, he moved about the beachhead, chatting to the startled unit commanders, who seemed unsure whether to pause and salute or go on with their jobs. MacArthur caused a mild disruption as he moved about the sand dunes, inspecting a machine-gun nest here, an artillery position there. Some GIs, overwhelmed by the sight of the man himself, left their posts to watch.

A CBS radio reporter, Bill Dunn, tested the transmitter's microphone by telling the US soldiers now moving through the coconut groves and coastal villages that MacArthur and President Osmena would soon be speaking on the 'Voice of Freedom' wavelength. An hour later, MacArthur climbed onto the weapons carrier. The reporters and photographers assembled, along with a handful of soldiers.

'People of the Philippines,' he called, 'I have returned. By the grace of almighty God, our forces now stand again on Philippine soil – soil consecrated by the blood of our people.' He mentioned that 'your President Sergio Osmena' was with him. But he asked the population to 'rally to me'. Like a union leader, he invoked the slogan 'Rise and strike!' MacArthur was mindful of the Catholic influence in the islands. He mentioned God many times, consecration twice, and pledged to 'follow in His name to the Holy Grail of righteous victory'.

This performance left the country's actual leader with very little to say. As it began to rain, MacArthur handed him the microphone.

The next morning, 21 October, a Japanese Ki-51 light bomber approached the *Shropshire* and the *Australia*, which were without air cover. It flew low. The *Shropshire*'s gunners opened up, striking the plane's fuselage. It dipped and wobbled. The plane's low trajectory caused it to skim off the water and bounce like a flat stone up the *Australia*'s port side. It crashed into the ship's bridge. Wreckage and fuel were sprayed in all directions, killing twenty-five Australians, including Captain Dechaineux. Commodore Collins received severe burns, and another sixty-three others were wounded.

The first Japanese suicide attack was successful. They planned to introduce this new shock weapon in all future naval battles.

Curtin was in his Perth office when he heard the news. He was devastated and began crying. An official walked in and found him slumped, his head on the desk.

'What's wrong, John?' the worried official asked.

Curtin sat up and handed him the cable telling of the *kamikaze* attack, and the Australian deaths.[2]

The *Australia* was crippled and needed repairs. The massive US fleet pulled off a huge victory against a Japanese fleet, losing one light cruiser and two escort carriers, two destroyers and a destroyer escort – just six ships in its 78-vessel armada. The Japanese lost thirty ships – three battleships, four aircraft carriers, ten cruisers and thirteen destroyers – in its biggest defeat since the Battle of Midway.

The encounter at Leyte made it difficult for the Japanese navy to recover. It had thrown all it could at the Americans. The only positive to come out of the battle was the success of its suicide pilots. But the

Japanese and the Allies knew this was a development that signalled desperation from the Imperial Force.

Having landed safely at Leyte, the US forces ran into a powerful Japanese army that had been rushed to the area. It was commanded by the brutal but brilliant General Yamashita, who had disposed of the British in Malaya and Singapore. Prime Minister Tojo was sacked in July 1944, and Yamashita was back in favour after more than two years in the wilderness. He had been granted a belated audience with the Emperor. The general now commanded the 14th Area Army in the Philippines, with ten infantry divisions and one armoured division. The Tiger of Malaya was not prepared to be the pussycat of the Philippines.

87
Curtin Down;
MacArthur Makes Running

Curtin was depressed for days after the news of the *kamikaze* attack. The pressure of his responsibility for all fighting servicemen and women was the greatest stress factor in his life. He had refused a drink for years now. Cigarettes provided a minor tension release. The ritual of finding a place to smoke alone, reaching for one, lighting it and drawing in the smoke brought temporary relief from the terrible tension of office.

He'd had the habit since he was a boy in inner Melbourne. It was like barracking for his beloved Fitzroy, and he often enjoyed doing both simultaneously. A pack in his pocket had been part of his life for nearly half a century. In office, he spoke of it as his last 'vice'. As prime minister, he was smoking more than ever before.

Fighting men, too, craved cigarettes. A smoke in the jungle, on the high seas, in the trenches or in a bomber was normal. Soldiers had them before and after battle. There was always time for a 'fag'. Even as life slipped away from a wounded digger, his last request was often for a final few drags of a cigarette.

Curtin's habit caught up with him on the train ride from Perth to Melbourne in late October 1944. He felt ill, had trouble breathing and experienced nagging but sharp chest pains. He did not wish to see doctors, believing that several days in his hotel room in Melbourne would help him recover.

He kept smoking and working. He couldn't sleep and didn't even want to go for a walk. The pain increased. A doctor was called on 3 November 1944. His diagnosis was that the prime minister had had had a heart attack, and he sent him by ambulance to the Mercy Hospital. Tests confirmed that Curtin had a 'coronary occlusion' – an obstruction of blood flow in the artery to the heart. Complete rest was advised.

Doctors suggested that Curtin 'cut back' on his cigarettes but not that he give them up altogether. He dropped down to twenty a day. On 6 November, the press was informed that he was ill but there was no mention of a heart attack. Instead, the public was told that his condition was due to 'overstrain'. He would be off work for a few weeks, reports said.

In that time, the government slowed down to a crawl. Chifley was recovering from a minor operation. John Beasley, Minister for Supply and Shipping, was also ill, suffering from high blood pressure. Drakeford was in the United States. A meeting of the War Cabinet was cancelled due to a lack of a quorum.

After a week Curtin's doctors were not happy with his progress. They argued with him over his cigarette consumption. He agreed to reduce to twelve a day. From a peak of forty to fifty cigarettes a day – or on average one every twenty minutes he was awake – Curtin was now down to fewer than one an hour. Curtin went through mental agony watching the clock until he could have another.

Frank Forde was in charge of the country. On 11 November, he announced that Curtin would rest for the remaining weeks of 1944 and would resume full duties in January. On 15 November, Curtin wrote to Elsie in Perth, telling her in confidence that he had heart problems. Doing his best not to alarm her, he said he was beginning to recover. Yet she would have realised that he was putting on a brave face when he told her to remember the joys they'd had together, just in case anything happened.

On 16 November, thirteen days after his heart attack, Curtin could not stand the strain of watching the clock for his next smoke. Of his own volition, he gave up cigarettes altogether. He found the first week of withdrawal painful. On 23 November, he felt he had beaten the addiction. He wrote a brighter letter to Elsie, telling her about it.

'I did smoke far too many,' he wrote, 'anyhow in here [hospital] I came to the conclusion I should give the treatment the field to itself without the adverse influence of nicotine.'[1]

Curtin was still bedridden by the end of November. In December, he began to receive family and friends, and then colleagues who wished to pay their respects. Archbishop Daniel Mannix came and said a prayer for him. Scullin visited and spoke only about sport, particularly cricket, ignoring political issues or even tittle-tattle. Blamey, as ever, was relaxed and jolly. He assured Curtin that the *kamikaze* 'weapon' would not impact on the course of the war. The Australians at the front, he told Curtin, were safer than ever before. What they did not discuss was the fact that diggers were not involved in the current fight for the Philippines, where Yamashita and his Japanese army were challenging MacArthur's troops. Blamey may not have cared. Curtin would have been relieved that there were fewer chances for Australian deaths in battle.

Curtin's political 'enemies', too, came to see him. Calwell was sympathetic. He had opposed Curtin on several issues and caused him aggravation often. But they respected each other. Curtin appreciated the gesture. Although he'd developed a thick skin, he still preferred to be liked rather than hated.

He received a letter from another nemesis, Billy Hughes, who said all the right things, even though they were to the point, in the writer's style. Hughes assured Curtin that everything in Canberra was running smoothly. Yes, the War Council meeting had been cancelled, but it could wait until the new year. Hughes advised him to take life calmly. 'Even the most glorious epitaphs and the most glorious of tombstones,' Hughes wrote, 'are poor substitutes for life.' He believed

Curtin might do 'much to guide Australia into harbour' if he allowed himself to recover fully. Continuing the memorial metaphors, Hughes warned that if he returned to work too soon, he would simply 'add one more of the statues that flank the King's Hall.'[2]

None of the doctors had been this direct. Curtin agreed with Hughes. He was too ill to do otherwise. Daughter Elsie arrived from Perth, boosting his spirits more than anyone.

MacArthur was dependent on carrier aircraft for cover on Leyte as his force battled inland. He would have loved to have had Kenney's support, which he had in New Guinea with mixed success. But the general's planes were now out of range. Emboldened by the US air paucity, the Japanese increased their raids on the fleet offshore and on Tacloban, where MacArthur had his headquarters – if he was not on the *Nashville*, which was also coming under attack.

In the weeks after the landing, Yamashita's force not only held ground, it counter-attacked. MacArthur began to find excuses, referring especially to the divide in command between himself and Nimitz. But the elements were also playing a major part in retarding the American effort. It was the monsoon season. Torrential rain and floods disrupted troop movements, pilot visibility, airbase construction and the work of logistical support units. MacArthur hated asking Nimitz to recall carriers to support the Sixth Army, but he had no choice. Still, they weren't an adequate substitute for land-based planes, and the Japanese took advantage of this, pouring more troops onto the island. Intense fighting followed.

By mid-December 1944, the US forces were gaining control. On 18 December Roosevelt appeased his two most powerful operatives in the Pacific. He promoted MacArthur to become a five-star general of the US Army. Then he promoted Nimitz to Fleet Admiral, also a five-star rank. MacArthur wasted no time in commissioning a Filipino silversmith to craft his new badges from American, Australian, Dutch and Filipino coins. Impatient as ever, he issued a communiqué on 26 December, saying that 'the campaign [for Leyte] can now be regarded as closed except for minor mopping up'.

Again, this was premature: there were still more than 30,000 enemy soldiers on the island. But the US controlled more territory than the Japanese, and this was enough for MacArthur. Yamashita had withdrawn to Luzon with 287,000 troops, but MacArthur refused to believe enemy estimates even of 234,000. This time he travelled to Luzon on the USS *Boise*, which came under attack from submarines and planes. MacArthur pronounced this operation as the 'decisive battle for the liberation of the Philippines and the control of the South West Pacific'. Most of the US media focus was on him. He appeared to be making the running.

Part Eight

Japan Defeated
1945

88

Curtin Recovers

Curtin recovered. He took his time to return to Canberra, chauffeured by his driver, Ray Tracey, just before the new year. He celebrated his sixtieth birthday on 8 January 1945 at an informal dinner at the Lodge attended by a few cabinet colleagues and friends.

It suited the prime minister that the nation's capital, somnolent at the best of times, was comatose in January. It aided his decision to battle on instead of retiring, as many advised him to do. Curtin felt compelled to continue in office. Politics was his life. He had much work to do, and in January he was free of the interruptions from visitors, friends and journalists.

Curtin was still 'taking care of the rear' for MacArthur, who was more preoccupied than ever with his front as he swept towards Manila. But now Curtin focused on issues at home, particularly those concerning his full employment white paper, the centrepiece of his Keynesian-based planning for the postwar economy. He again edited a fresh draft himself, scribbling changes in the margin. Curtin baulked at an incomes policy and was stubborn about a figure for unemployment. His experience of the Depression influenced his desire to see it at zero. Most advisers reckoned four per cent was acceptable.

Curtin pandered to unions more than most advisers thought he should. But he was compelled to do so. The unions were his party's base. They had given him his start in politics. The white paper had already been diluted since its first draft, becoming a less than powerful document. Yet it could be the catalyst for Australian's postwar reconstruction, by retraining soldiers and spending on public works.

Another issue that took Curtin's attention was his wish to nationalise Australia's civil aviation – namely, the interstate airlines. During the war, the Americans had manoeuvred to secure the local airline system, treating its ally as just another Pacific island, which it was, and the Australians as beholden to them, which they were. The United States' aim was to run Australia's airways after the war; Curtin was determined that, in any future conflict, no foreign power would be able to stop civil aviation. He knew that Menzies and co. would fight to stop the airlines being nationalised.

The conservatives had also cried 'socialist' when Chifley announced a banking bill. This would give the Commonwealth Bank the functions of a central bank, controlling interest rates and the volume of credit. Again, Curtin and Chifley believed that the government should hold the levers that would help prevent another depression. The bank's governor would be answerable to the cabinet, not the parliament. A new charter would keep a tighter rein on the bank. Curtin and Chifley had bitter memories of the way the independent Commonwealth Bank behaved during the Depression. At that time, Prime Minister Scullin was defied at every turn, and Curtin held the bank to be at least partly responsible for the economic mess into which the nation descended.

Many on the left of the ALP wanted the entire banking system nationalised, but the new bill fell well short of that. Once more, the past dictated the present. Curtin in 1931 had campaigned to nationalise the banks and lost. He knew the Australian electorate was pragmatic. It accepted some moves towards central power and control during war, but it was not ready for full-blown socialism, especially with the opposition arguing against it so convincingly, supported by most of the press.

Curtin expected less opposition to his plan to nationalise the airlines. At his first press conference after his illness, he remarked, 'I am not going to permit American interests to get a grasp on companies professing to be Australian; companies, which recently were within an ace of not being Australian.'

He referred to a recent proposed merger between US and Australian companies in which shareholders would have been offered a ten per cent return on their capital. 'You can be quite sure,' Curtin said, 'big business is behind that. And it was not Australian business.'[1]

A moment of 'official' pleasure for Curtin came in January 1945, when he welcomed the Duke of Gloucester to his new role as governor-general. The prime minister looked forward to another good relationship with the British monarch's Australian representative.

MacArthur's bold plan to let the infantry bypass islands such as Borneo had repercussions for the hapless POWs there. MacArthur believed that softening up the enemy with aerial bombing would be enough, before he implemented invasion plans. MacArthur wanted the Battle of the Philippines under control before Borneo was taken.

In January 1945, Allied planes bombed and destroyed north Borneo's Sandakan airfield, which had been so painfully built by Australian and British POWs. Only about 500 men had survived, out of the 2400 sent from Changi to slave on the project. The bombing caused the sadistic Sandakan camp commander, Captain Hosijimi Susumu, to fear that an Allied invasion was imminent. Knowing that he would suffer for his brutality, Susumu decided to evacuate his Japanese battalions 260 kilometres west, to Ranau in the mountains.

Four hundred and seventy of the POWs were forced to carry the Japanese bags, equipment and supplies. They were given four days' rations for the nine-day trek. The deteriorated condition of the POWs meant that many did not survive the march through vast marshlands and dense jungle, with a final push up the steep eastern slope of Mount Kinabalu. By the halfway mark, prisoners began to collapse from exhaustion. They were either left to die or were shot, depending on the whim of the Japanese guards.

When they reached Ranau, near the west coast, the survivors were forced to build a temporary camp, and were herded into insanitary and crowded huts. Dysentery was soon rife and caused many more deaths. If there were any intelligence on the whereabouts of these wretched men, MacArthur sent no missions to liberate them. Borneo, when he retook it, would be his base for the attack on Java. Any freeing of Australian and British POWs would be incidental.

Australian ships – the repaired *Australia*, the *Shropshire*, the *Arunta* and the *Warramunga* – were prominent in the growing armada that supported MacArthur's drive towards Manila. The closer the fleet came to Luzon, the greater the number of *kamikaze* planes that tried to disrupt it. The *Australia* received six hits. Leading war correspondent Denis Warner was on board an Allied ship when it was attacked by suicide pilots. He wrote that:

> ... *repeated Kamakaze attacks demolished her too few gun crews and left her a sitting target. In the final attack Lieutenant David Hamer, in the exposed and dangerous defence position above the bridge, had been broadcasting a running commentary and directing the anti-aircraft fire as a Kamakaze approached. The crew could see that the plane was heading straight for Hamer . . . To their astonishment, they saw Hamer stand up and shake his fist at the approaching plane.*

The *kamikaze* plane passed a metre above Hamer's head. It dived under the foreyard, tipped a masthead and fell over the side. Warner noted that it was 'the first recorded plane to be brought down by a clenched fist. This was the end of the *Australia*'s battles with the Kamakazes, which was just as well. Morale was at breaking point when she was pulled out of action.'[2]

On 30 January 1945 MacArthur was nearly 'home'. He ordered the US First Cavalry Division to make an advance raid on Manila, and on 3 February it reached the city's northern outskirts. Around 3700 internees were liberated from the campus of Santo Tomas University. But once more MacArthur would have to wait. The Japanese planned to defend Manila to the death, and a battle raged for three weeks.

MacArthur prohibited air strikes, for fear of destroying the local population. Yet he could not stop thousands dying in the crossfire or in massacres by the Japanese. He refused to restrict the flow of Filipinos fleeing the battle zone, although it meant civilians were clogging the roads out of Manila.

By 24 February the city was back under US control. MacArthur had more than fulfilled his promise to return. But he was far from ridding the islands of the stubborn Japanese, who would refuse to surrender unless the Emperor decreed it.

Observers, including reporters in Curtin's favoured Canberra group, noticed deterioration in the prime minister as the weeks of 1945 slipped by. He was pallid and his energies were limited. He blew up at press conferences, which he had never done before. In the ALP caucus he found his detractors harder to dismiss. He was defensive, although Chifley, Forde and others didn't think he needed to make his cases so painstakingly.

In parliament, Curtin felt the pressure from Menzies, who had reinvented the conservative side as the Liberal Party, at the expense of the failed UAP. The new party was said to be the champion of free enterprise. Menzies had done his homework during his days in opposition. He developed simple themes aimed at what he called the 'forgotten' middle class of small-businesspeople, professionals and salaried people, and all those who fell outside the main unions. Menzies emphasised the importance of a strong private sector, as opposed to Labor's push for a more muscular state system. He stressed Australia's connections with the British Empire, although Curtin by now was also in favour of this.

Menzies knew Curtin was waning, but the prime minister still had control of the House of Representatives. He delivered a speech there on 28 February 1945 that held the nation's attention. He spoke of Australia's identification with the US and UK war policies as battles raged all over the Pacific to the nation's north. His 'austerity campaign' continued. The people still accepted this, even if they didn't always adhere to it. Four years of restrictions, along with Australia's growing distance from the action against the Japanese, were beginning to make some less concerned about frugality.

Curtin spoke of his hopes for the League of Nations' successor, a new world organisation – the United Nations – that would soon be the subject of a conference in San Francisco. He hoped it would help drive the postwar world and guarantee a more peaceful co-existence between all nations. Curtin delineated his support for Australia's White Australia Policy. There were few arguments against this, given the identity of the aggressor that had caused Australia so much grief in the present war.

Yet Curtin was more reticent about using the term 'white Australia' than earlier in the war. He had asked his press contacts not to play up the term because of its effect on 'coloured people, particularly the Chinese, who are on our side in the war'.[3] Yet some newspapers still protested any attempt to interfere with the policy.

More broadly, Curtin railed against 'race ambition', by which he meant the attempts by Germany and Japan to assert their superiority over other peoples, no matter what their colour or creed. He threw 'nationalism' into the mix, which, in excess, he saw as dangerous. It was an idealistic comment, yet also insightful, given the war's causes.

On the night of 8 March, the US Air Force attacked Tokyo. The bombs and resultant firestorm killed 80,000 people and injured another 44,000. The country was traumatised yet remained stoic. The Emperor was terrorised but said nothing. Japan's chiefs of the armed forces knew their nation was in big trouble, but there was no real discussion of surrender. They were prepared to tough it out, even though an invasion by the Allies, led by the United States, would kill millions.

Curtin had a throat infection on 18 March that prevented him from answering questions in parliament. The press pounced on this, noting that there seemed to be as much of a manpower shortage in cabinet as there was everywhere else.

On 12 April 1945 President Roosevelt died. This was a great blow to the Allied cause and to Curtin's own morale. He told parliament on 18 April that the president's death had 'lessened to some degree mankind's hopes for a better day'.[4]

Nine days later, Curtin was forced into hospital with lung congestion. His wife, Elsie, who had replaced his loving daughter as the family member in Canberra, was advised by doctors not to return to Perth as she had planned. Still Curtin would not retire. Ben Chifley, his preferred successor, took over as acting prime minister.

89
Borneo Blunders

Curtin's commitment to MacArthur left Australia at this time with a military power vacuum, which Blamey attempted to fill. MacArthur left broad instructions. The Australian Army was to relieve Americans in New Guinea, New Britain (primarily around Rabaul), and the Solomon Islands, where Bougainville was heavily garrisoned by the Japanese. Along with Borneo, these were the main Pacific islands that MacArthur had decided to bypass in his rush to retake the Philippines, thus avoiding wasteful and time-consuming fighting.

Despite the enmity between Blamey and MacArthur, Blamey had kept the 7th and 9th Divisions together as I Corps, just in case the Americans relented and asked for his assistance in the Philippines. It was apparent in the early months of 1945, however, that there would be no use for the Australians there. Logic dictated that, under such circumstances, the Australian government should have reasserted its control over its own army. But Curtin's loyalty to MacArthur transcended other national interests, and his illness, along with his general disinclination to immerse himself in military matters, caused him to retain the status quo.

A critical conflict caused by this unwieldy situation occurred over the Anglo-Dutch island of Borneo. MacArthur had drawn up plans for it six months earlier, before deciding to go island-hopping. At that time, in late 1944, retaking Borneo was an obvious military target and was still part of MacArthur's overall strategy. The Japanese had taken it in the first place because of its enormous oil reserves, but its airfields and harbours would be useful bases for the Allies' reconquest of Java.

MacArthur put it to the US joint chiefs that the Borneo campaign should go ahead. They were lukewarm, and not as savvy as him concerning the rapid turn of events transpiring in the South-West Pacific. When they hesitated in giving him the go-ahead, MacArthur played on their ignorance and bluffed them. 'Failure to carry it out,' he told them, referring to the taking of Borneo, 'would produce grave repercussions with the Australian Government and people.'[1]

Borneo had hardly been mentioned in cabinet or at War Council meetings, let alone by Australians at the pub, in 1945 or at any other time. The US joint chiefs gave MacArthur the go-ahead. He bypassed Blamey and General Sturdee and delivered orders to Lieutenant General Sir Leslie Morshead, a veteran of North Africa and the Middle East who now commanded I Corps. Morshead was to undertake a three-pronged operation. First, he had to take the small island of Tarakan and its airfield, just north-east of Borneo. Second, he would capture Brunei, the oil-rich British possession in the northern half of Borneo. Third, he had to secure Balikpapan, the site of 700 wells and oil refineries in Borneo's southern half, which was owned by Royal Dutch Shell (whose biggest shareholder was Queen Wilhelmina of the Netherlands).

This was the Australian–UK combined force plan that Blamey had put to Churchill at the prime ministers' conference in London in May 1944, except for the third leg of the attack. Blamey now complained to Acting Prime Minister Chifley (since Forde was overseas) that the third prong was an unnecessary stretch of I Corps' resources. Chifley communicated with MacArthur, telling him it should be dropped. MacArthur, however, now said that he was under orders from the US joint chiefs to implement all aspects of the three-pronged attack.

If MacArthur had been dealing with Churchill, he would never have gotten away with such brazen behaviour. But he knew Curtin and the Labor cabinet were not closely engaged with decisions about what was happening on each front. They would not query his assertions. Thus, MacArthur duped both his ignorant superiors in the United States and his out-of-touch supporters in Australia.

Morshead's troops sailed from the small island of Morotai in the Molucca group in the Netherlands East Indies on 27 April 1945. They reached the shores of Tarakan and moved into the mangrove swamps on 1 May. The diggers confronted blazing oil tanks that had been bombed by Australian and US planes and ships. The 9th Division's 26th Brigade moved further inland, looking for the airfield, and were followed by Dutch oil engineers aiming to right their wells and restart oil production. The diggers reached the airfield's outskirts and set up their gun positions in the night.

The main road to the airfield was flanked by impassable swamps. The Japanese had set up a huge concrete machine-gun bunker on a rise on the road. Approaching midnight, two intrepid diggers carrying flame-throwers crawled onto the bunker's top. They waited until dawn, when they could discern slits in the solid facade, then fired their flame-throwers. The Japanese unit of twenty-six men was incinerated.

When the 26th Brigade took the airstrip on 6 May, news reached them that another enemy had been incinerated in a bunker – but this time in Berlin. Hitler had committed suicide on 30 April. It was not a complete surprise to those in the Pacific when Germany capitulated on 8 May 1945.

The war in Europe was over. There was joy everywhere, especially in the United States and Europe. Churchill, in arguably the most complex, single-minded effort in history, had achieved his aim. He had been the most important instrument in defeating a powerful force for evil. The Allies everywhere celebrated.

But Australia could not yet afford to be too excited. Japan was still fighting in the Pacific. Leslie Morshead's diggers, who had fought the Germans in North Africa, were now finding the Japanese a ferocious foe. Their stand on Tarakan, along with the continued *kamikaze* attacks in various naval battles, suggested Japan was more desperate than ever. The nation's attachment to its Emperor meant it was unlikely ever to capitulate.

Morshead's 9th Division pressed on from the airfield, knowing there was still considerable Japanese resistance to be overcome. One bunker high on a ridge harboured three machine-gun nests. Twenty-two-year-old Corporal John Mackey took his section of thirty-two men up to one end of the ridge, which left them no room to manoeuvre. He made a quick decision. He would charge the nests.

Like Private Kingsbury at Isurava, Mackey believed that going it alone was the best course of action. Fewer lives – perhaps none – would be lost if he made a solo attack.

Mackey sprinted at the first enemy position, climbed a small rampart and dropped on top of a gunner. They wrestled and Mackey shot him. He pushed him aside then rushed the second position, where a two-man heavy machine-gun crew was swinging their weapon around to face him. They were not quick enough. Mackey jumped on the bunker's one-metre wall. He propped, aimed and fired, killing the two men. The final pair of gunners, in the third bunker, swung their weapon around and fired. Mackey was hit but kept coming, shooting and killing the Japanese. Then he stumbled and fell dead. Like Kingsbury, John Mackey would be awarded a posthumous VC.

90
Beyond the Call

All through the Pacific theatre on any given day, Australians were going beyond the normal brave limits of soldiering to give their units, battalions, brigades, divisions and corps the edge. And they would die doing it, often in acts of sacrifice that would save scores of diggers' lives and liberate many others. They played the odds with as much fervour and endeavour as they would when betting on a horse at the races. More often than not, they were ordinary, laconic diggers, not blustering bruisers. They liked a bet, a beer and a smoke, and to look after their mates or subordinates. Invariably, the comment describing each one, even before they produced these acts of controlled madness, was: 'You'd like to be in the trenches with him.'

Tom Derrick VC was one such man serving with the 9th Division at Tarakan. He was a born leader. His superiors recognised his individual acts of courage, which were both reckless and inspirational. After his acts at Tel el Eisa, El Alamein and Sattelberg Ridge, he was cajoled into attending Officers' Training School. He did this on condition that he would be returned to the 48th Battalion, which he saw as his second family. He was promoted to lieutenant and expected not to do any more fighting. But stopping Derrick from rejoining his men was like trying to prevent him from having a bet or a laugh. He was a frontline dynamo, always encouraging, urging and leading his men.

Derrick heard about the heroics at Wewak, on New Guinea, of Private Ted Kenna, a Victorian. On 15 May 1945, Kenna had been pinned down under heavy machine-gun fire with his company, from the 2/4th Battalion. In the tradition of Jacka, Murray, Kingsbury, Mackey, Derrick and many others, some of whom did not win VCs but who were just as courageous, Kenna dashed at a Japanese machine-gun crew. He destroyed it, allowing his company to counter-attack and succeed. It earned him a VC.

A week later, at Tarakan, Derrick led a small contingent through a defended position close to the enemy. They were surrounded by Japanese in the early hours of the next day, 23 May. Derrick called for support. By the time it arrived, he and his little band had been nearly massacred. Derrick received bullet wounds but was still able to calmly tell the soldiers carrying him back to the Australian sector what had happened.

Tom 'Diver' Derrick died on 24 May. He had ridden his luck, just as he had liked to do at the horseraces, until it ran out. It was his way. No promotion, enticement or situation – short of the war ending – could stop his addiction to daredevil acts at the front. A fortnight later, Ted Kenna was shot in the mouth at Wewak. The copious bleeding made medics believe that his number was up, but, unlike Derrick, he survived.[1]

The Japanese were pushed into the mountains at the centre of Tarakan Island. The Australian attack forewarned the new Japanese commandant at Sandakan, on Borneo's north-eastern tip, Captain Takakuwa Takuo. The diggers of the 9th Division had heard that there were POWs in northern Borneo. Intelligence services confirmed it. They wondered why they had wasted time attacking Tarakan when they could have invaded northern Borneo and liberated their Australian and British comrades. Every member of the AIF would have made that the priority.

Instead, three units of Australia's finest frontline soldiers, who had few peers in World War II for experience and fighting ability, were busy all around the remote area of Borneo's northern tip. Many observers considered this mismanagement of resources as one of the biggest failures of the Pacific War. But MacArthur had little time for POWs. He had his strategy and always seemed pressed for time.

While the 9th Division was taking Tarakan, Captain Takuo was demonstrating that he lacked nothing in inhumanity when compared to his predecessor. Fearing discovery of his camp, he ordered a second set of marches to Ranau for a further 536 POWs, who would move in groups of about fifty, with guards accompanying them.

These prisoners were far weaker now than those who had set out for Ranau in January. All had some illness and the march took far longer: twenty-six days. There were so few rations that the men were forced to forage for food en route. Two Australians, Gunner Owen Campbell and Bombardier Richard Braithwaite, reckoned that even if they reached Ranau, their chances of surviving the war were next to zero. They decided to escape into the jungle. They struggled for a day before finding a village, where locals, hostile to the Japanese, hid and fed them. Another four men managed the same feat.

The Sandakan camp was destroyed in a desperate attempt by the Japanese to obliterate evidence of their brutality. They were tormented now by the unthinkable: that the Allies might defeat them in battle and take them prisoner. Captain Takuo was considering exterminating all POWs to erase any clues to how they had been treated. He did not care if men dropped on the second march: they were going to be slaughtered anyway.

Realising this, gunner Private Neil Cleary, who had survived the first march in January, and a mate, gunner Corporal Wally Crease, escaped from the camp at Ranau. Cleary was recaptured and thrown into an empty area known as the Guard House. He was tied up by two Japanese guards, who then punched and kicked him on all parts of his body, including his neck. Rifle butts and sticks were used freely on him. This brutality was carried out in view of the other POWs, who were reminded by guards that if they escaped, this would be their fate.

Crease was then recaptured. Both men were bashed through the night. Crease managed to escape again the next morning; he was recaptured and shot. Cleary was tortured for another twelve days, then left, still tied up, to wallow in his own vomit and excrement. POW Private Keith Botterill witnessed the grotesque episode. He helped clean Cleary up when the guards accepted that he was dying. Botterill and others looked after Cleary over the next few days, until his death.

On 9 June, Takuo decided to send another seventy-five of the remaining 250 or so POWs on a third march. The men were too weak. All were walking skeletons, weighing little more than thirty to forty kilograms. Within a few kilometres of Sandakan, they began to drop from exhaustion. When this happened, the Japanese would shoot them in the head. After covering twenty-five kilometres in four days, twenty-five men had been slaughtered in this manner. At fifty kilometres, the Japanese had killed all seventy-five POWs. Almost all the men left at Sandakan either were shot or died from malnutrition or disease.

While this inhumanity was being perpetrated 300 kilometres away, the attack on Brunei, on Borneo's north-west coast, by the second of the 9th Division's forces began on 10 June 1945. The aim was to set up an advance naval base for MacArthur's planned Java operation. Within two weeks, the 10th and 23rd Brigades appeared to have destroyed the enemy's main positions, but there were still some pockets of resistance.

The town of Beaufort, in northern Borneo, became the last Japanese stronghold. They placed four machine-gun posts in front of the town, on the only viable access track, along a thickly wooded spur. The enemy gunners blocked the diggers' attack.

Private Leslie Thomas ('Tom') Starcevich, a 26-year-old Western

Australian, was in a unit that came under heavy fire from these posts. The casualties mounted. He volunteered to go forward. Before his commander gave him the go-ahead, Starcevich carried his Bren gun into action, surprising the Japanese with his daring. He ran from post to post, firing into each one and killing five gunners. The Japanese fled and Starcevich's unit advanced.

When they were held up by two more posts, Starcevich again wanted to attack. He rushed one post, which held several of the gunners who had fled during his first attack; this time he killed another seven Japanese. His solo effort earned him a Victoria Cross, opened the track to Beaufort and marked the end of the resistance in northern Borneo.[2]

Meanwhile, all Japanese resistance on Tarakan was overcome by 21 June. Some 1500 enemy soldiers had been killed, while the Australian brigade lost 249.

Back at the top of northern Borneo, only 183 of the 536 POWs herded on the second set of marches from Sandakan to Ranau reached their destination on 24 and 25 June. They found that just five Australians and one Briton were still alive out of the contingent of 470 who had made the first march, arriving in January. These treks were aptly named 'death marches'. They and the camps provided the worst conditions ever experienced by Australian and British POWs, claiming nearly 2500 lives.

MacArthur's plan for Balikpapan, the oil port in south-eastern Borneo, was considered overkill by Blamey. The area had been hit hard from the air by RAAF Liberators and the Far East Air Force, then by the US Seventh Fleet, which included several Australian ships, among them *Shropshire*, which had survived many *kamikaze* attacks. The port's buildings were pulverised by the time units from the Australian 7th Division came ashore on 1 July.

91
Last Call

Curtin resigned himself to the fact that he would not see the end of the war in the Pacific, which he expected would continue into 1946. But he was satisfied that he had done his best. The last military news he had absorbed was that the 9th Division was taking Tarakan. Borneo was now a target for two of the three divisions he had fought so hard to bring 'home' to defend Australia. This was the finest of Curtin's many legacies, and he knew it. He believed Japan would be defeated.

In the early days of July 1945, friends began to visit the prime minister at the Lodge, aware that he was near the end. Forde hustled back from the United States and was taken to see him by Chifley. Forde had not seen Curtin for several weeks and was shocked by his condition. He believed it was time to inform the public that their prime minister did not have long to live.

On 4 July Curtin's family and friends gathered. Curtin was losing his lucidity. His hands were ice-cold. His friend and driver, Ray Tracey, arrived at the Lodge at 10 p.m. to say goodbye. Tracey found him sitting up in bed looking very ill.

'Ray,' Curtin said, 'who won the match?'

It was midweek; there was no football that day. Tracey had the presence of mind to humour rather than correct him. 'Fitzroy won it, sir,' he replied.

'Well, that's good, isn't it?' Curtin said. 'That's good.'[1]

Elsie Curtin had tea with her husband just before midnight. He took his nightly sedative and told her, 'I'm ready to go now.'

Curtin died at around 4 a.m. on 5 July 1945.

Curtin had planned his funeral. There was a service at Parliament House on 6 July, then a short period when his body lay in state in King's Hall. A friend, the Presbyterian minister Hector Harrison, broadcast a brief service to the nation. Harrison represented Curtin's compromise between his Catholicism and his religious uncertainty: his broadcast was Low Church and low-key, without frills. It was Curtin's way.

Curtin's casket, draped in an Australian flag, was then flown to Perth in a Dakota, with an escort of six Kittyhawk and six Boomerang fighters. The city shut down for his funeral, which was led by a vanguard of 500 unionists. The gun carriage bearing his casket set off from Cottesloe in bright sunshine. The procession was watched by 20,000 people lining the streets of the route. It stopped for a minute outside his Jarrad Street home before proceeding to the cemetery at Karrakatta.

Curtin's pall bearers, whom he had personally chosen, included Frank Forde and Robert Menzies. The latter's role demonstrated that Curtin and Menzies were far closer than some observers cared to acknowledge. Wishing to appear egalitarian rather than elitist, Curtin had included Percy Trainer, an old drinking buddy from his Perth Trades Hall days.

Only Chifley among his closest friends was not present. He had been overcome with emotion when Curtin lay in state in Canberra. Chifley, it was said, had to stay behind to 'mind the fort' in the capital, but in reality he was too upset to attend. He had lost his closest friend. The nation had lost one of its finest sons.[2] His gravestone inscription summed him up well enough:

His country was his pride
His brother man his cause.

Postscript

92
Japan Capitulates

Curtin died knowing nothing about the Allies' 'Manhattan Project' that developed nuclear weapons. Churchill had told Stalin about it – although the Soviet leader had known from his British spies anyway – but he had not informed Curtin or any other of the Empire's leaders.

US military chiefs, in consultation with the new US president, Harry Truman, decided to use an atomic bomb on a Japanese city. Truman's reasoning was typical of this common-sense leader. The Japanese were refusing to surrender, even after the attacks on Tokyo. They would fight to their last citizen.

Truman and Churchill estimated that a million Americans and 250,000 British forces would be killed if the war continued. These figures would include up to 50,000 Australian soldiers, sailors and airmen, assuming MacArthur included Australian troops in his massive assault on the islands of Japan. Then there were the Japanese themselves: it was estimated that their spirited defence would see another two million slaughtered.

These calculations meant a cold but easy choice for Truman: one million Americans dead, as opposed to none if the bomb pushed the enemy into submission. The president could also have argued that although the bomb would destroy around 250,000 inhabitants of one or possibly two Japanese cities, ten times that number would likely be killed in an Allied invasion. Truman was not the deeply introspective or reflective type; he was a political pragmatist.

On 4 August 1945, US aircraft dropped leaflets on Hiroshima, the headquarters of Japan's 2nd General Army, warning its citizens to expect terrible destruction if Japan did not surrender. This was ignored. The first atomic bomb – codenamed 'Little Boy' – was dropped by the Americans on Hiroshima on 6 August.

The Emperor and the Japanese military chiefs remained mute, although any sign of surrender would have stopped the United States from again using this most terrible weapon. The next target was the city of Kokura, the base for a huge army arsenal. On 9 August, thick clouds over that city caused the B-29 carrying the second nuclear weapon – 'Fat Man' – to be diverted to Nagasaki, a port with naval installations.

More than 210,000 Japanese were killed by the two weapons. Many more would die later from 'radiation sickness', as it was known. Gunner Russell Savage of 2/10 Field Artillery 8th Division was in a POW camp in Japan. He recalled discussing the rumour that a massive bomb had hit Hiroshima, which one of the guards confirmed. 'Oh, very bad!' he said. 'One American plane, 40,000 dead.'

Thinking this was just another exaggeration by the Japanese, Savage said, 'You mean 40,000 American planes, one Japanese dead?'

'No, one plane, 40,000 dead.'

Russell discussed this with mates in the camp. One commented, 'They must have split the atom.' Then he corrected himself: 'But they can't have. The chain reaction would have killed all of us.'[1]

On 14 August, more than 800 US bombers struck military targets on Japan's main island, Honshu. A badly shaken Emperor Hirohito met his government in a bunker at the Imperial Palace. There were reports that the Red Army was pressing Japan's northern borders. His subjects were restless over the competence of the Japanese cabinet, the prime minister and the Imperial chiefs. The people were hardly rebellious, but they were complaining enough for the Emperor to take notice.

Hirohito told his government that 'the unendurable must be endured'. This meant that he would surrender. The government contacted the Allies to accept the terms of the Potsdam Declaration. The Emperor recorded a capitulation speech that was broadcast to the nation the next day, 15 August. His voice trembled, high-pitched and weak. It was a most uninspiring moment for his listeners, even though it was the first time his nation had heard him.

Hirohito, speaking in the language of the Royal Court, which was barely understood by his subjects, named the atomic weapons as the reason for his surrender. His voice quivered as he tried hard to mask a stutter, building towards the point of his message: 'The enemy has now begun to employ a new and most cruel bomb, the power of which to do damage is incalculable, taking the toll of many innocent lives.'

When the Japanese people comprehended his words, they wept. They felt a mixture of shock, relief and humiliation, and not a little fear about what the conquerors might do to them. The Pacific War was over.

The end was a huge surprise and massive relief for all Allied forces. The war ground to a halt over the next few weeks all over South-East Asia and the Pacific. Fighting ceased in China, Burma, Thailand, Indo-China (Vietnam), Malaya and Sumatra, and in Okinawa, Formosa, the Philippines, Leyte, Mindanao, Moratai, Borneo, Java, the Celebes, Timor, New Guinea, New Britain, Bougainville, Guadalcanal, the Solomon Islands, Yap, Guam, Saipan, Tinian, Iwo Jima, Bonin Island, Truk and many other islands further east through the Pacific.

Hundreds of thousands of POWs and enslaved people were liberated, although many still suffered during this period. In northern Borneo, the last thirty-eight of the POWs marching to Ranau were murdered by the Japanese, two weeks after the official end of hostilities.

On Bougainville, Lieutenant General Savige cancelled his plans for a final push south to Buin with his considerable force of 32,000 soldiers, which was set to attempt one of the biggest operations the Australian army had undertaken. Many would have been killed in the final clash with the larger force of Japanese. As it was, 516 Australian lost their lives in the campaign, and a further 1500 were wounded. Savige's restrained mission remained that way, thanks to torrential rain and flooding in July and the end of the war in August. The Japanese lost 8500 killed in action after the Australians occupied the island. Another 9800 died through illness, while 23,571 survived to surrender.

At Changi, on Singapore, one-third of the more than 70,000 POWs died before Allied troops could free them. Those who had survived the coalmines of Japan were stunned rather than elated by the news. When a Japanese lieutenant delivered news of the surrender at Russell Savage's Sakata camp, a hush fell over the assembled POWs. 'No one cheered, moved, said anything . . .' he recalled. 'A few shook hands, a gesture that seems so inadequate, so inappropriate, in the enormity of this moment.'[2]

The POWs had been told they would never survive the war. Their captors swore they would execute them before the Allied armies arrived. Now that the Japanese were the vanquished, the mentality of the guards and officers changed. The slaughter of any POW could no longer be covered up.

Savage had survived the fighting in Malaya and Singapore, the slavery on the Thai–Burma railway, the sinking of a Japanese ship taking him to Sakata, a small port on Honshu, and then the work there in freezing conditions. He had a further explanation for the POWs' reaction. 'For three and a half years we had been burying our emotions, afraid to give full rein to our feelings,' he noted. 'Mood swings – highs and lows – were luxuries we could not afford.'

The POWs had coped with the horrors by keeping an almost surreal detachment. The British officers in the camp began drills on the parade ground. But the Australians revolted. 'We weren't having any of that,' Savage noted. 'We were wartime volunteers. The war was over!'[3]

The ex-POWs wanted to move on. They were taken to Sendai for the train trip across Honshu to Tokyo. Unarmed guards from the camp went with the POWs to guide them and interpret with railway officials. Savage bumped into an old Brisbane friend, Geoff Gourlay, who was with the HMAS *Bataan*. Observing the guards, Gourlay asked, 'Which one of these bastards do you want shot?'

'No,' Savage said, shaking his head, 'forget it.' He had no time for the Japanese, whom he described as 'barbaric', yet he was beyond caring about revenge. Like most POWs, he just looked forward to getting home.[4] Some of the Japanese guards had been sadistic, but Savage and other POWs recognised that they had terrible jobs and were under unbearable pressures from their superiors. The diggers would neither forgive nor forget, but they would move on.

MacArthur, with both eyes on history, planned a staged entrance to Japan. President Truman had chosen him to receive Japan's surrender, and then to 'govern' and reform it. At 2 p.m. on 30 August 1945, he swooped into Atsugi airbase, forty-eight kilometres from Tokyo, on board a silver C-54 plane. The khaki-clad MacArthur appeared at the plane's doorway, took a few steps down the ladder, then paused.

The crowd, which included around a thousand Japanese, half-expected something dramatic to happen. There had been rumours of a sniper. Atsugi was the *kamikaze* base. Would one or more of them swoop from the skies in the ultimate act of defiance, to kill the American conqueror?

But there would be no suicide attack. The day before, propellers had been taken from the scores of planes on the tarmac. MacArthur's pause on the ladder was not due to fear of assassination. He merely adjusted his dark glasses, tugged at his five-star general's cap and sucked on his corncob pipe, giving the swarm of movie-camera operators, photographers and reporters the chance to capture him in his moment of triumph. He had famously 'returned' to the Philippines; now he became an American emperor, arriving at the seat of the enemy empire. Not only was he a conqueror, he would also be a dictator, benevolent but strict.

MacArthur stepped onto the tarmac and strolled with intent towards the military cavalcade that would drive him thirty-two kilometres to the port city of Yokohama, south of Tokyo. The truckloads of helmeted, armed US marines guarding him were not there for ceremony but remained alert to any maverick attack.

As the Americans were aware, not long after the Emperor's speech of surrender there had been an attempted coup, which had fizzled out. But there was no certainty, just a few weeks after the national disgrace, that some other radical group would not attempt to disrupt MacArthur's procession. In a daring extra piece of stagecraft, Japanese soldiers lined the cavalcade's hilly route. But they turned their backs, as they would with the Emperor, in deference to their new commander.

On 2 September 1945, MacArthur was master of ceremonies as the Japanese surrendered aboard the USS *Missouri* in Tokyo Bay. All Allied nations were represented, with Blamey heading the Australian delegation.

An armada of victorious Allied ships lined Tokyo Bay. The battered but proudly afloat *Shropshire* was among them, its Australian flag full out in a breeze. A day later, Blamey flew from Tokyo to Morotai, the island of the Dutch East Indies between the Celebes and New Guinea, to accept the surrender of the Japanese Second Army's commander, Lieutenant General Teshima.

A formal ceremony was held in the open. Teshima stood on one side of a table and handed his sword to Blamey. Teshima was directed to sit and sign the instruments of surrender. Blamey at first refused to sit in front of him, but instead stood behind his chair, staring down at his opposite number. The Australian waited until his counterpart had finished, then sat and signed too. Once this was done, Blamey moved to a microphone and delivered a scathing speech, with the directness and invective that made him a commander to be reckoned with at the highest level in two world wars.

'In receiving your surrender,' he said, with the scowl that had withered tougher men than Teshima, 'I do not recognise you as an honourable foe.' This was the ultimate insult to the Japanese military and its traditions. Blamey went on. 'You will be treated with due but severe courtesy in all matters.' Then, hardly glancing down at his script, he eyeballed the commander, his words being translated by an interpreter, and added with typical vehemence:

I recall the treacherous attack upon our ally China . . . I recall the treacherous attack made upon the British Empire and the United States of America . . . I recall the atrocities inflicted upon the persons of our nations as prisoners of war and internees, designed to reduce them by punishment and starvation to slavery.

His tone was at odds with MacArthur's more formal, dignified approach. But Blamey did not have to govern the Japanese. He hoped that as many of the military hierarchy as possible – from the Emperor down – would be executed or given long prison sentences.

'In the light of these evils,' Blamey concluded, 'I will enforce most rigorously all orders I issued to you, so let there be no delay or hesitation in their fulfilment – ' he paused and then added, with emphasis – 'at your peril.'[5]

Blamey pushed MacArthur hard for Hirohito to be prosecuted for 'crimes against humanity'. But the American would have none of it. He believed that having the Emperor in the dock for a long, drawn-out trial would be catastrophic for his aims. It would humiliate the Japanese so greatly that it would invite rebellion, especially if the Emperor denied all charges.

Blamey disputed this, pointing out that the Pacific War had been waged in the Emperor's name, and likewise enslavement, torture and murder had been perpetrated. Hirohito was complicit at every turn, which would be easy to prove, Blamey believed.

MacArthur was forced again to carry out a round of mendacious bluffing – his specialty – to get his way and save Hirohito for his own purposes. He told Truman and the chiefs that there was no evidence that Hirohito had been involved in any decision-making concerning war operations. Blamey claimed that this was demonstrably untrue. MacArthur then put to the US War Department that if Hirohito were put in the dock, up to a million US soldiers would be needed to restore order. The bean-counters at the department thought this would be too costly and sided with the American general.

MacArthur also played the 'communist' card. Soon after the end of the war, the Soviet Union became the main enemy of the West. MacArthur planned a new Japanese constitution, which would make Japan a stronghold against communism. MacArthur was nothing if not visionary. Like Churchill, he could already see the emergence of the two postwar superpowers – the United States and the Soviet Union – which would oppose each other in the so-called 'Cold War'.

Blamey was no match for this high-level politicking and Hirohito was spared. Others would not be so fortunate. The Japanese had surrendered unconditionally. Under the Potsdam Declaration of 26 July 1945 (between the United States, the United Kingdom and the Soviet Union), all war criminals were to be 'severely' punished. The vehicle was the Tokyo War Crimes Trials.

MacArthur set up a panel of eleven judges, nine from the nations that signed the instruments of surrender. Australia's Sir William Webb, Justice of the High Court of Australia, was appointed president of the tribunal. Harry Truman appointed American Joseph B. Keenan as chief prosecutor. Mr Justice Alan Mansfield, Senior Judge of the Supreme Court of Australia, was one of eleven prosecutors. Twenty-eight Japanese leaders, including four former prime ministers, were prosecuted as Class A War Criminals. Seven defendants, including Prime Minister Tojo, were found guilty and executed. Another sixteen were sentenced to life imprisonment.

The trials went on throughout the Pacific and South-East Asia. Around 5600 Japanese, Taiwanese and Koreans were prosecuted for lesser war crimes. More than 4400 were convicted and 1000 were sentenced to death, among whom were Generals Yamashita and Nishimura, for atrocities committed by them and their soldiers. Specific mention was made of the massacre at Parit Sulong, when Yamashita had directed that 110 wounded Australians and thirty-five wounded Indians be murdered.

The devastation and inhumanity forced on the Pacific region by the marauding Japanese army began to be revealed. More than thirty million Asian and European civilians and service-people had lost their lives. The worst mass crimes committed by the Japanese were in China, where fifteen million people died. In assaults on many towns and villages no human beings were spared.

Early in the war the Japanese had spoken of the 'liberation' of nations from the yoke of European empires. But in very short time they proved to be immeasurably worse than the British, Dutch, French or Germans. The Japanese trumpeted their move into Indo-China, where they took over from the French, but then proceeded to force the mainly agrarian workforce to produce food for the Imperial Army. Farmers were forced to plant their rice fields with fibre crops. By 1944–45, this had produced a famine in which a million Vietnamese died. Another million in the Philippines and more than two million in the Dutch East Indies starved to death for similar reasons.

Australia lost 39,800 servicemen in World War II. The nation lost officially 700 civilians, although unofficial estimates put this figure closer to 2000. More than 1.1 million Australians were in service, from the population of around seven million people. Every family was touched by the Pacific War. Many military men and women went back into peacetime life wounded or mentally scarred for life. Their individual and collective efforts should be remembered and honoured.

A memorial inscription at the Thanbyuzayat War Cemetery, in Burma, best sums up their sacrifice:

When you go home, tell them of us and say,
for your tomorrow, we gave our today.

Epilogue

93
At the Centre

John Curtin's uncompromising determination to bring Australian troops home from the Middle East brought on his mental depression. The cumulative impact of his many tough decisions – and their consequences – took their toll. His strong, assertive and inspirational leadership was all the more admirable for his overcoming self-doubt, loneliness, alcoholism and depression. The bouts of physical and mental illness, coupled with the strains of high office, killed Curtin.

His accession to the Australian prime ministership coincided almost entirely with Australia's involvement in the Pacific War, which ran from December 1941 to August 1945. It was the most calamitous and crucial four years in the nation's history. The serious threat to Australia's survival caused unparalleled disruption. This reluctant wartime leader grappled with everything from the threat of takeover by a powerful foreign predator to the drastic alterations to Australia's economy that prepared it for war. He succeeded in both endeavours.

His finest achievement was the return of Australia's three crack divisions, the 6th, 7th and 9th, against the express wishes of the two most important Allied leaders, Churchill and Roosevelt. Against all senior diplomatic and political advice, except that from two or three senior Labor ministers, Curtin stood firm when Churchill and Roosevelt tried to intimidate him into changing his mind.

When the Japanese struck Pearl Harbor in December 1941, Australia's only major defence had been its 8th Division, which was positioned north of Australia, only to be captured and incarcerated in Singapore. This left the nation without any serious defence. Curtin's responsibility was to defend it. He acted with a stubborn single-mindedness that defined him and his period in office. He believed Australia faced the real possibility of invasion and take-over by Japan. He called it the 'Battle of Australia', and likened it to the Battle of Britain.

This proved to be an accurate analogy, although there were differences. UK territory was bombed incessantly but never invaded. Australian territory – in Papua – was bombed and invaded incessantly. Britain's major cities were bombed. Australian cities and towns were bombed, particularly Darwin, but the country's major population centres, except for Sydney, were not hit. Most Australians at home did not experience the immediate trauma that struck Britain, but Australian military personnel – the diggers – most definitely did. The Japanese army made four determined attacks – in the Owen Stanley Range, at Milne Bay, at Buna, Gona and Sanananda, and at Lae. More than 200,000 Japanese were in Papua and New Guinea during the war.

Every one of the frontline troops in the 2nd AIF, along with Australia's remarkable militia forces – most notably the 39th Battalion – was needed to repel the Japanese. The Imperial High Command made its biggest blunder by not taking Australia when General Yamashita wanted to march on it after smashing the British in Malaya and Singapore in early 1942. Some top admirals in the Japanese Navy were keen also to launch an attack on the Australian mainland in mid-1942. They may have persuaded the Japanese leadership to approve it, had they won the Battle of Midway. After the United States won that major naval encounter, the Imperial Navy never fully recovered.

Yamashita and some of the admirals believed that once Australia and New Guinea/Papua were under Japanese control, the United States would be cut off from its biggest troop and aircraft carrier – Australia itself. Had they acted in early 1942, MacArthur would never have been able to head for Australia. The one US commander in the Pacific who comprehended the region and had the motivation to fight back against the Japanese would have been thwarted.

By the time Prime Minister Tojo approved a plan to take Australian territory – Papua – it was mid-1942. The United States already had more than 150,000 troops in Australia, making it a near perfect springboard from which to launch the US counter-attack. Because Curtin was 'taking care of the rear' so well with food, munitions and other supplies, one million Americans would ease into a land and culture that could accommodate them. No other country in the region was remotely suitable for such an operation. Curtin's dedicated, unwavering support allowed the Americans to prepare to fight their way back to the Philippines and then on towards Japan.

The 2nd AIF thwarted the persistent Japanese efforts to disrupt the US bases in Australia. Curtin went to great pains to bring back the big Australian divisions from the war in the northern hemisphere. While the Australians parried, halted and then smashed the Japanese army, MacArthur turned his mind to returning to the Philippines, with the considerable force of all arms of the US military moving west across the Pacific to assist him.

Tojo's two major blunders paralleled Hitler's. The Fuhrer's much-vaunted image as a military genius took a huge blow when he decided to take Russia in the winter of 1942. Had he turned to history, he would have learned that Napoleon destroyed his own army by attempting the same thing. Both prolonged campaigns were failures and led to defeat.

Hitler, like Tojo, underestimated the might of the United States. Had Hitler invaded Britain straight after taking France in mid-1940, he would have controlled the small but important aircraft carrier (the UK itself), and denied it to the US military. With Churchill disposed of, there would have been no inspiring British leadership. The United States would have become more isolationist. It would not have entered the war in Europe. Similarly, Tojo and the Japanese admirals made their greatest strategic blunder by attacking Pearl Harbor, which ensured the United States entered the war in the Pacific. Australia should have been the target for occupation *before* Pearl Harbor was hit.

Being thrown centre-stage in the Pacific War was anathema to Curtin. But he surprised many with his clear-headed decision-making, flexibility and pragmatism. On occasions, he was forced to decide between his ideals and Australia's survival. He was against conscription — an issue that split his party — during World War I, but backed it with certain caveats in World War II. He regarded the United States as the epitome of capitalist evil but embraced MacArthur and the American military machine for Australia's sake.

So complete was Curtin's accommodation of US support that he effectively passed sovereignty to a foreign military governor — MacArthur. This shocked many in the Labor Party, especially those on the left and far-left, who regarded it as a sell-out, and one that went too far. But the oddly compatible liaison between Curtin and MacArthur, which was forged from necessity and mutual benefit, became one of the most powerful and important bonds of the entire war. Curtin would allow no one to say a bad word about MacArthur, whom he viewed as Australia's saviour. MacArthur could not believe his luck in finding such a pliable, hard-working politician who seemed to understand and support him. No American politician, including the president, afforded him such belief.

MacArthur wrote:

[Curtin and I] promptly came to a sense of mutual trust, cooperation, and regard that was never once breached by word, thought or deed. He was the kind of man the Australians called "fair dinkum." As I rose to leave [after their first major meeting], I put my arm about his strong shoulder. "Mr. Prime Minister," I said, "we two, you and I, will see this thing through together. We can do it and we will do it. You take care of the rear and I will handle the front." He shook me by both my hands and said: "I knew I was not wrong in selecting you as Supreme Commander."

MacArthur saw Curtin as the 'heart and soul of Australia'.[1]

Curtin jettisoned the British link when it was clear Churchill had abandoned Australia to concentrate on defeating Hitler. Then, when it suited Curtin, he embraced the British again, once more much to the chagrin of many in his party who wished to distance themselves from the nation's former imperial masters. They felt the war had offered Australia greater independence from its dominion past. Curtin not only restored these links, he even suggested tightening them, through closer consultation with the seat of Empire.

Yet Australia's link with America would have greater ramifications for the nation after the war. Successive governments – except for Gough Whitlam's, from 1972 to 1975 – felt compelled to go 'all the way' with the nation that had saved it from the Japanese in World War II, even if it had been by default rather than intent. Australian forces would fight alongside the Americans in Korea, Vietnam, Iraq and Afghanistan.

Australia's World War II experience demonstrated that it could be far more independent, militarily, than it ever believed. Two developments in particular indicated this. First was the impact of Australia's army when fighting in New Guinea. The four major battles there were dominated by the Australian regular army and militia; on most occasions the Americans were little more than garrison troops. This does not mean that Australia could have coped with the Japanese without the Americans in the Pacific. Its army's battles beyond New Guinea, its navy and its mighty air force, were vital factors in defeating the Japanese. Yet the battle skills of Australia's three military arms showed – as they had in World War I, under General Sir John Monash – that they could fight against any foe and win.

Second, Australia's production of equipment and munitions, thanks to the powerful industrialist, Essington Lewis, surprised even Curtin. He had no real sense that Australia could produce everything from tanks and machine guns to planes and bullets, all of an equal if not superior quality to anything produced in Britain or the United States. Perhaps Curtin's socialist and pacifist inclinations had blinded him to the potential of men such as Lewis to produce such materials, but he was happily surprised to see what could be made in short time and with high quality.

Despite this evidence that Australia could manage well in these two vital areas – fighting capacity and war production – there was still not the will in Australia to become a truly independent state. There was no need, if it was supported by the United States. It was easier and economically more prudent just to tag along with the world's foremost military power. In the seven decades after World War II, Australia's defence policy was based on the American alliance.

In recent years, the United States has strengthened its bases in Australia as part of a 'containment' policy regarding China. President

Barack Obama confirmed this when he visited Darwin in mid-2011. Marines were stationed in Australia's north-west. The US link is again an insurance policy for Australia, against any expansionist aims the Chinese or any other Asian neighbour may have for the future. In this regard, Australia's foreign policy has come full circle since the Japanese threat of 1941–1945, relying once again on the United States to support it against any challenge from another power in the region.

Curtin's speeches were always compelling, well-written and impressively delivered, which helped make him sound sincere in his various about-faces on certain issues. The media, the parliament and the public marvelled at his performances, which were so impressive that they often overrode any criticism or analysis. Some, such as Sir Paul Hasluck and certain blinkered historians, suggested the federal opposition and the press harried Curtin into sickness and an early grave. But the opposite was more likely the case. Curtin enjoyed nothing more than to beat his parliamentary foes, outdo the media barons and manipulate enemies in his own party. He freely criticised his Australian enemies – such as some in the media or the communists – at his off-the-record press briefings.

The nation's most important reporters knew Curtin as a driven, occasionally vindictive and manipulative prime minister, who thrived on political battles. He and his press secretary, Don Rodgers, saw his tenure in office as a permanent campaign, and seized every opportunity to capture the media's – and the nation's – attention. The more the public saw of Curtin, the more it was reassured that he was the right leader for the times. By the 1943 election, Curtin had turned the opposition, who felt they were born to rule, into parties that seemed to be carping and irrelevant. Curtin's political skills allowed his initial minority government to introduce modest reforms. Once elected a second time and with a sizeable majority, he initiated greater reforms – in banking, economics, education and welfare – that went partway towards his long-term socialist aims.

At the most critical times of the Pacific War, and therefore Australian history, Curtin made decisions that proved, in time, to be the right ones for his country. His steadfast refusal to form an all-party war government allowed him to make his decisions without hindrance, for better or for worse. Curtin's offering of his nation and its military to MacArthur, rather than to Australia's military chiefs, caused problems. But it allowed MacArthur to command without hindrance of any kind, at least from within Australia. Curtin wrote MacArthur a blank cheque for the war against Japan. Allowing the American's ego to run unfettered led him to believe his own publicity, but it worked. MacArthur used his Australian connections to bluff and deceive Washington into giving him the men and equipment he needed for his push back against the enemy.

Curtin and MacArthur complemented each other. MacArthur was a supreme narcissist who wanted to conquer all enemies and win sole credit for it. Curtin was ego-free, although well-rooted in who he was. He did not wish to conquer anyone except his political opponents. MacArthur became Japan's governor and reconstructed it in the American image after the war; Curtin simply wished to repel the Japanese so comprehensively that they would never threaten his country again. MacArthur was an American conservative. Curtin was an Australian socialist. It's a fair bet they never bothered each other with political philosophy, but they did discuss Australia's freedom and Japan's defeat, and achieved both.

Curtin was tested like no other Australian prime minister. He came through the trials. Australia played its part in defeating the enemy, while the economy was kept strong. Curtin presented a vision for his nation based on a preoccupation, even an obsession, with preventing a repeat of the economic Depression through which many of his compatriots suffered. Andrew Fisher and Billy Hughes had their trials during World War I. Robert Menzies appeared up to the task while Australia's war was in the Middle East, North Africa and Europe. But only Curtin faced the massive pressures of invasion of Australian territory by a fierce enemy. He took on this responsibility and came through.

In so doing, he caused Australia to see itself as it was at the time: an outpost of an Empire, dependent on greater powers to help it defend its territory in crises, but capable of standing alone. For these reasons, there is a strong case for judging John Curtin as Australia's greatest prime minister.

Notes

CHAPTER 1: CURTIN UP
1. Sir Arthur Fadden, *They Called Me Artie*, Jacaranda Press, Queensland, 1969, pp. 80–81.

CHAPTER 2: SAME PEAS; DIFFERENT PODS
1. David Day, *John Curtin: A Life*, Harper Perennial, Australia, 2006, p. 534.
2. Lloyd Ross, *John Curtin: A Biography*, Sun Books, Melbourne, 1983, p. 44.
3. It is no coincidence that the pub across the road from Melbourne's Trades Hall building was later to be named the John Curtin Hotel. It was so-called perhaps as much for Curtin's drinking as for his leadership in the labour movement. Certainly, it would not have been named after him had he been a non-drinker. Bob Hawke, before he became a successful prime minister, also had a major problem with alcohol; he haunted the John Curtin Hotel. Drinking in the union movement was an important characteristic of worker machismo.
4. Lloyd Ross, Draft biography of John Curtin (MS 3939), Box 27, Lloyd Ross Papers, National Library of Australia, p. 240.
5. Letter from J. A. J. Hunter to Lloyd Ross, 6 June 1959, MS 3939, Lloyd Ross Papers, National Library of Australia.
6. *John Curtin: Portrait of a Prime Minister*, by producer/writer John Thompson, ABC radio tape, Battye Library, Perth. See also notes for a speech by Curtin's publicity officer, Don Rodgers, MS 1536, Box 5, 1926–1978 Folder, Don Rodgers papers, National Library of Australia.

CHAPTER 4: TUGS OF WAR
1. Cable from Curtin to Churchill, 8 October 1941. A 467/7, from R4/1/2, NAA.
2. Sir Robert Menzies' 1941 diary, NAA, A5054, 2340, p. 84.
3. Advisory War Council Minute 533, 16 October 1941, DAFP, Vol 5, p 141.
4. Advisory War Council, Minutes, 16 October 1941, CRS A 2682/XR, NAA, page 2.
5. Advisory War Cabinet Minute 60, 7 November 1941, DAFP, Vol V, Document No. 104.

CHAPTER 5: THE SINKING OF INNOCENCE
1. The loss of the HMAS *Sydney* remains Australia's worst naval disaster. Its wreck was discovered in 2008.
2. Roger Bell, *Unequal Allies: Australian–American Relations and the Pacific War*, MUP, Melbourne, 1977, pp. 69–70.
3. I. A. Cumpstun, *Lord Bruce of Melbourne*, Longman Cheshire, Melbourne, 1989, p. 177.

CHAPTER 6: MASS ATTACK
1. Lloyd Ross, *John Curtin: A Biography*, Macmillan, Australia, 1977, p. 240.
2. Paul Hasluck, *Diplomatic Witness: Australian Foreign Affairs, 1941–1947*, Melbourne University Press, Melbourne, 1980, p. 126.
3. *Smith's Weekly*, 13 December 1941, page 4.

CHAPTER 7: BLOW TO THE ADMIRALTY
1. www.john.curtin.edu.au
2. Not everyone put their bats and balls into storage. Limited forms of park cricket went on, while beach cricket games became more common. Backyard matches still prevailed in the summer, despite some irritating trenches on a good length.
3. Michael McKernan, *All In!*, Nelson, Melbourne, 1983, p. 106.
4. www.john.curtin.edu.au
5. ibid.
6. John Curtin, press statement, 11 December 1941, A 5954/69, item 54, NAA.

CHAPTER 8: NO HOLIDAY FOR NIPPON
1. Gordon Bennett, *Why Singapore Fell*, Angus and Robertson, Sydney, 1944, pp. 64–65.
2. Bennett, *Why Singapore Fell*, p. 74.
3. Alan Reed to the author, 4 April 1974.
4. D. M. Horner, *High Command: Australian and Allied Strategy 1939–1945*, AWM, Canberra and Allen & Unwin, Sydney, 1982, p. 143.
5. Sir Frederick Shedden, manuscript, Book 4, Box 1, Chapter 8, pp. 1–3. Shedden file, NAA.
6. Lloyd Ross, *John Curtin: A Biography*, Macmillan, 1977, pp. 242–244.

CHAPTER 9: PUSH TO INVADE AUSTRALIA
1. *The Age*, Melbourne, 23 December 1941, p. 3.
2. Goldstein and Dillon (eds), *The Pacific War Papers, Japanese Documents of WW2*, Potomac, Washington DC, 2004, p. 311.
3. Sir Alan Brooke, *War Diaries 1939–1945*, Orion Books, London, 2002.

CHAPTER 10: EVATT AND CURTIN BLUNDER; CHURCHILL'S WRATH
1. Cable from Churchill to Curtin, 25 December 1941, *Documents in Australian Foreign Policy* (DAFP) Vol. 5, p. 371.
2. Cable from Curtin to Churchill, 30 December 1941, DAFP, Vol. 5, p. 391.
3. Cable from Casey to Curtin, 22 December 1941, DAFP, Vol. 5, Document No. 213.
4. Cable from Curtin to Roosevelt and Churchill, 23 December 1941, DAFP, Vol. 5, Document No. 214.
5. Richard Casey, *Personal Experience 1939–1946*, Constable, London, 1962, p. 81.
6. William Manchester, *American Caesar*, p. 214.

CHAPTER 11: ARTICLE OF INTENT
1. *The Melbourne Herald*, 27 December 1941.
2. R. M. Younger, *Keith Murdoch*, HarperCollins, Sydney, 2003, p. 253.

CHAPTER 12: AMERICA'S CHINA CARD
1. Cable from Casey to Evatt, (footnote); 3 January 1942, DAFP, Vol. 5, page 405.
2. Ross, *John Curtin*, p. 247.

3. John Morton Blum, *The Price of Vision, The Diary of Henry A. Wallace, 1942–1946*, Boston, Houghton Mifflin, 1973, pp. 347–348; Roland Perry, *Last of the Cold War Spies*, Da Capo, US, 2005, pp. 153, 154.
4. Ross, *John Curtin*, pp. 253–254.
5. Ross, *John Curtin*, pp. 253–254.
6. Ross, *John Curtin*, p. 254.

CHAPTER 13: CABLE BICKERING; JAPAN'S FIRST SETBACK

1. Cable from Churchill to Curtin, 8 January 1942; DAFP, Vol. V, Document No. 262.
2. Cable from Curtin to Churchill, 11 January 1942, DAFP, Vol. V. Document No. 266.
3. Cable from Churchill to Curtin, 12 January, 1942, DAFP, Vol. V, Document No. 271.
4. *Nichi Nichi*, 13 January 1942.
5. *Japan Times*, 15 January 1942.
6. Charles Kappe, *The Malayan Campaign*, AWM, www.awm.gov.au/Mica_documents_catalogue/research_centre/RC00789_1.pdf.

CHAPTER 14: MALAYA FALLING

1. Various newspaper comment and editorials (*The Age*, *The Sydney Morning Herald*), 6–10 January 1942.
2. Frank Legg, *The Gordon Bennett Story*, Angus & Robertson, Sydney, 1965, p. 198.
3. Cable from Churchill to Wavell, 15 January 1942; cable from Wavell to Churchill, 16 January 1942; Winston Churchill, *Hinge of Fate*, pp. 43, 44.
4. Churchill, *Hinge of Fate*, p. 44.

CHAPTER 15: ANDERSON'S LAST STAND

1. Cable from Churchill to Curtin, 18 January 1942, DAFP, Vol. V, Document No. 281.
2. Despite the massacre, five men escaped into the jungle.

CHAPTER 16: CHURCHILL'S ABOUT FACE; THE FALL OF RABAUL

1. Cable from the Australian government to Churchill, 23 January 1942, DAFP, Vol. V, Document 294.
2. Henry Frei, official Japanese War History: Senshi Sosho [English translation].
3. Cable from the Australian government to Churchill, 23 January 1942, DAFP, Vol. V, Document 294.
4. Winston Churchill, *Hinge of Fate*, pp. 52, 53.

CHAPTER 17: THE LULL BEFORE

1. Horner, *High Command*, p. 152.
2. Horner, *High Command*, p. 152.
3. Japanese war history series, South Pacific Area Army Operations (1) Port Moresby—Guadalcanal first campaigns, Vol. 1, p 355. In action reports produced by the Imperial Naval Units during WW2; in the National Institute for Defense Studies, Tokyo.
4. Herbert P. Bix, *Hirohito and the Making of Modern Japan*, HarperCollins, New York, 2000, pp. 445–6.
5. Legg, *Gordon Bennett Story*, p. 237.
6. Bennett, *Fall*, p. 163.

CHAPTER 18: SINGAPORE'S SEIGE
1. Brett Lodge, *Lavarack: Rival General*, Australian Military History Series, Allen & Unwin, 1998, pp. 204–207; cable from Curtin to Wavell, 12 February 1942, DAFP, Vol V, Document 239.
2. Article, Charlton, 'Humiliating Fall of an Impregnable Fortress', *The Australian*, 15 February 1992.
3. Legg, pp. 241, 242.

CHAPTER 20: OPERATION AUSTRALIA
1. John Deane Potter, *A Soldier Must Hang*, pp. 11–15; Bergamini, *Japan's Imperial Conspiracy*, pp. 897–902; *The Complete History of the Great East Asia War*, Vol. 1, pp. 356–359.
2. Toland, *The Rising Sun*, pp. 300–303.

CHAPTER 21: AFTERSHOCK
1. Cable from Curtin to Churchill, 17 February 1942; Documents on Australian Foreign Policy (DAFP), Vol. V, p. 527.
2. *The Age*, 16 February 1942.
3. Norman E. Lee, *John Curtin: Saviour of Australia*, Longman Cheshire, Melbourne, 1983.
4. Speech by Curtin, 17 February 1942, NAA A5954/69, item 2205/1.
5. Cable from Bruce to Curtin, 18 February 1942; DAFP, Vol V, Document No. 344.
6. Cable from Page to Curtin, 19 February, DAFP, Vol V, Document No. 347.
7. Advisory War Council Minutes Meeting, Series A5954, Vol 4, Nos 597–869; Meeting 19 February 1942, Sydney.

CHAPTER 22: ATTACK ON DARWIN
1. Peter Grose, *An Awkward Truth*, Allen & Unwin, Sydney, 2009, p. 115, 116.
2. Grose, *An Awkward Truth*, p. 115, 116.
3. Grose, *An Awkward Truth*, p. 134.
4. Grose, *An Awkward Truth*, p. 188.
5. Mitsuo Fuchido & Masatake Okumiya, *Midway: The Battle That Doomed Japan*, Hutchinson, UK, 1957, p. 198.
6. Report of the Lowe Commission, Darwin Attack of 19 February – 9 April 1942, NAA.
7. John Hammond Moore, *Over-sexed, Over-paid and Over Here: Americans in Australia 1941–1945*, UQP, Brisbane, 1981, p. 32.
8. National Archives of Australia, Fact Sheet 195 – The Bombing of Darwin. www.naa.gov.au/about-us/publications/fact-sheets/fs195.aspx.

CHAPTER 23: A SENSE OF ISOLATION
1. Hasluck, *Diplomatic Witness*, pp. 43–44.
2. *The Age*, 20 February 1942.
3. Cable from Churchill to Curtin, 20 February 1942, DAFP, Vol. V, Document No. 352, NAA.
4. Cable from Roosevelt to Churchill, 20 February 1942, cited in Warren F. Kimball (ed.), *Churchill & Roosevelt – The Complete Correspondence*, Vol 1, R-107, Collins, London, 1984, p. 365.
5. Transcript of interview with Curtin's daughter, Elsie Macleod, Battye Library, p. 31.
6. Kimball (ed.), p. 366.

CHAPTER 24: THE PRIME MINISTER GOES MISSING
1. This was an era when issues were seen in terms of race, and Australian leaders' speeches were peppered with reference to 'yellow hordes'. The Japanese, for their part, were no less racist, seeing their role to defeat and subjugate all white races – except, of course, the more acceptable ones of their fellow fascists in countries such as Germany and Italy.
2. Cable from Curtin to Churchill, 22 February 1942, DAFP, Vol. V, Document 357.

CHAPTER 25: JAPAN'S ARMY V NAVY
1. Frei, *Japan's Southward Advance and Australia*, p. 162.
2. The diamonds, which would be worth around $50 million today, were lost; investigators believed they had been rifled from the plane's wreckage.
3. Of the 158 on board, 138 were either killed in action or died on the life rafts. The lucky survivors were picked up five days later by the Dutch submarine KIL.

CHAPTER 26: JAPANESE BASE AT LAE
1. The Gulf of Exmouth would be used as a base for the US Navy Auxiliary and the US submarine *Stingray*, which serviced southbound US subs.

CHAPTER 27: MACARTHUR PARKS IN AUSTRALIA
1. William Manchester, *American Caesar*, Little Brown, Boston, 1978, p. 266.
2. Manchester, *American Caesar*, p. 275. [address to the United Services Instutute by Major-General Gordon Maitland, 31 May 2005].
3. Manchester, *American Caesar*, p. 275.

CHAPTER 28: MEETING THE AUSTRALIANS
1. Interview with Pamela Myer Warrender (see also Pamela Myer Warrender, *In Her Own Right*, Hardie Grant Books, Melbourne, 2007).
2. Sources for the characters and descriptions of Curtin and MacArthur:
Meacham, Jon, *Franklin and Winston*, Random House, New York, 2003, pp. 259–261.
Manchester, William, *American Caesar*, Little Brown, Boston, 1978, p. 778.
Horner, David, *Blamey*, Allen & Unwin, Sydney, 1998, pp. 93–98; pp 274–276.
Gallaway, Jack, *The Odd Couple*, University of Queensland Press, Brisbane, 2000, p 263; p. 267.
Freudenberg, Graham, *Churchill and Australia*, Pan Macmillan Australia, Sydney, 2008, p. 603.
Day David, *John Curtin*, Harper Perennial, Sydney, 1999, pp. 133–134.

CHAPTER 29: BLAMEY IN THE MIX
1. Manchester, *American Caesar*, p. 276.
2. Manchester, *American Caesar*, 276.

CHAPTER 30: BLAMEY V MACARTHUR – THE RECORD
1. There would be ramifications for this new link with the United States, but they would come in the postwar era, beginning with the Korean War, when Australia was compelled to support the Americans.
2. Manchester, *American Caesar*, p. 94.
3. Roland Perry, *Monash: The Outsider Who Won a War*, Random House, Sydney, 2004, pp. 435–437.

4. John Hetherington, *Blamey: Controversial Soldier*, AWM, Canberra, 1973, p. 42.

CHAPTER 31: OF DOUBTFUL CHARACTER
1. David Horner, 'Blamey, Sir Thomas Albert (1884–1951)', Australian Dictionary of Biography, National Centre of Biography, Australian National University, http://adb.anu.edu.au/biography/blamey-sir-thomas-albert-9523/text16767.
2. Ibid.
3. Stewart Rintoul, article in *The Australian*: 'Blamey quit after back-seat sex romp', 25 July 2005.
4. Gavin Keating, *The Right Man for the Right Job*, Oxford University Press, 2006, p. 138.

CHAPTER 32: TAKING CARE OF THE REAR
1. Letter from Shedden to MacArthur, MS 3939, Box 30, folder (ii) Lloyd Ross Papers NLA.
2. Broadcast by Curtin on BBC Radio, A461/7, Item R4/1/12, NAA.
3. Day, *Curtin*, p. 597.

CHAPTER 33: SECOND ENEMY SURGE
1. Diary of Joseph Alexander, senior correspondent in Canberra for the Melbourne *Herald*, MS 2389, NLA.
2. Admiral Tomioka made clear his views about taking Australia to Gordon W. Prange, who, with a staff of 200, carried out extensive interviews with all the key Japanese figures still alive in Tokyo straight after the war (from 1945 to 1951). Prange directed the huge historical staff in Tokyo when General MacArthur was its postwar governor. Prange ran the official archive of the war from the Japanese point of view. His papers are at the University of Maryland Library.
3. War Conference, 23 April 1942: NAA Series no: A 5954 1/1.
4. *The Age*, 27 February 2002.
5. *The Age*, 27 February 2002.
6. Interview with Diana Gollar, 23 July 2011.
7. Interview with Diana Gollar, 23 July 2011.

CHAPTER 34: BATTLE OF THE CORAL SEA
1. john.curtin.edu.au/sport/innings.html.
2. National broadcast by Curtin, 8 May 1942, A461/7, item R4/1/12, NAA.
3. PM's War Conference, 11 May 1942; NAA A5954, 1/1 and ½.

CHAPTER 35: MIDGET RAMPAGE
1. Interview with Diana Gollar, 27 July 2011.
2. Horner, *Inside the Cabinet*, p. 120.

CHAPTER 36: MACARTHUR'S BLUNT MESSAGE
1. Horner, *Inside the Cabinet*, p. 120.
2. Minutes of the Prime Minister's War Conference, 1 June 1942, Digital: NAA A5954, 1/1.
3. Minutes of the Prime Minister's War Conference, 1 June 1942. A5954 1/1. Also see Peter Edwards' speech at 2002 History Conference – Remembering 1942; 'Another look at Curtin and MacArthur'.
4. Digital NAA, A5954 1/1 (1 June 1942).

CHAPTER 37: MIDWAY
1. MacArthur was given the 'South West Pacific Area' (SWPA), and a third command was set up for the 'South East Pacific Area'.
2. Horner, *Crisis of Command*, pp. 95–96.
3. Horner, *Crisis of Command*, pp. 95–96.

CHAPTER 38: 'AUSTRALIA IS SECURE'
1. In the end, Blamey was proved correct: the Japanese were not removed from Rabaul until the end of the war.
2. Diary of Joe Alexander, 8 June 1942, NLA MS2389.
3. Statement by Curtin, 11 June 1942, in DDA no. 37, 5 to 24 June 1942; JCPML00110/37.
4. National broadcast by Curtin, 17 June 1942, JCPML. 00652/2/9.
5. ABC News Stateline, Northern Territory, 13 August 2010; Cleary, Paul, *The Men Who Came Out of the Ground*, Hachette, Sydney, 2010.

CHAPTER 39: OVERSEXED AND OVER HERE
1. This novel, first published in 1928 in Florence, Italy, and concerning a working-class man having a relationship with an aristocratic woman in England, was considered taboo in the United Kingdom and Australia. It was not officially published in Britain until 1960, and later in Australia.
2. Interviews with Shirley and Grace Barnbaum, December 2010.

CHAPTER 40: ESSENTIAL ESSINGTON
1. Clem Lloyd and Richard Hill, *Backroom Briefings*, National Library of Australia, Canberra, 1997, p. 49.
2. Digital NAA A 5954, 1/1 (War Conference, 19 July 1942.)
3. Lloyd and Hill, *Backroom Briefings*, p. 49.
4. The Boomerang did not prove to be the equal of the Zero. It was never used as a frontline fighter, although it was deployed in army support later in the war.
5. Lloyd and Hill, *Backroom Briefings*, p. 76
6. Fifty-eight tanks in all were produced, and the project was cancelled in July 1943.
7. Digital NAA A 5954, 1/1 (War Conference, 19 July 1942.).
8. IJA Intelligence report, OKI Group Staff report No. 37, 14 July 1942; AWM.

CHAPTER 41: JAPAN'S SECOND THRUST
1. The separate states of Papua and New Guinea would combine in 1975 to become the independent nation of Papua New Guinea.
2. Interview with Carl Johnson, historian, Melbourne, 13 August 2010.
3. *Smith's Weekly*, 27 July 1942.
4. Japanese Intelligence report Western Garrison HQ March to August 1942, p. 51; AWM.

CHAPTER 42: THE 39TH IN TROUBLE
1. Manchester, *American Caesar*, p. 272.
2. Japanese intelligence report [Australian War Memorial: Enemy Intelligence report no. 28; page 39, point 39, number 3.] File supplied by Carl Johnson and Sarah Wells.
3. The *Canberra* was one of several ships sunk in the area around the Solomon Islands that was eventually named 'Ironbottom Sound'. The ship's wreck was discovered in

July 1992, half a century after her scuttling. She lies upright on the ocean floor, about 760 metres below the surface.
4. Japanese intelligence report [Australian War Memorial: Enemy Intelligence report no. 28; page 39, point 39, number 3.] File supplied by Carl Johnson and Sarah Wells.

CHAPTER 43: SETBACKS AND SUCCESS
1. *Sydney Morning Herald*, 19 August 1942.
2. Messages concerning 7th Division involvement in Maroubra Force, August, 1942, AWM 54 577/6/4.
3. Letter from Private Martin Crest to his father, August 1942. (Crest private collection, Carl Johnson Museum.)

CHAPTER 45: THE FIGHTING WITHDRAWAL
1. Cable from Rowell to Blamey, 3 September 1942, Blamey papers, AWM.
2. Rowell Papers, AWM, 3DRL6673.

CHAPTER 46: MARVELS AT MILNE BAY
1. Letter from Vasey to Rowell, 28 August 1942; Rowell Papers AWM; Sir Arthur ('Tubby') Allen Papers, 3DRL No 2381 AWM File 419, AWM.
2. Letter from Rowell to Vasey, 30 August 1942; AWM 54, 225/2/5.
3. John French and Bruce Kingsbury are buried at Bomana Cemetery in Port Moresby.

CHAPTER 47: AUSTERITY CAMPAIGN
1. Some of the VFL's best were being held at the Changi POW camp. Under the watchful eye of Japanese machine-gunners, the prisoners there organised a six-team competition, made up of 200 inmates. It had its own unofficial 'Changi Brownlow', which was won by a former St Kilda player, Peter Chitty.
2. *Backroom Briefings*, p. 81.

CHAPTER 49: ROUT OF MAROUBRA FORCE
1. McCarthy, *South-West Pacific Area – First Year, Kokoda to Wau*, p. 225.
2. Manchester, p. 296.
3. *Smith's Weekly*, 11 September 1942.

CHAPTER 50: LAST RAZORBACK STAND
1. Blamey to press, 11 September 1942, US National Records Center, RG 407; G-3 Journal; Horner, p. 323.
2. Horner, p. 324.
3. *Daily Telegraph*, 23 September 1942.
4. *Daily Telegraph*, 23 September 1942.
5. Bill Edgar, *Warrior of Kokoda: A Biography of Brigadier Arnold Potts*, Allen & Unwin, Sydney, 1999, p. 196.
6. Sydney Rowell, *Full Circle*, Melbourne University Press, Melbourne, 1974, pp. 121–122.

CHAPTER 51: 'CANBERRA'S LOST IT'
1. Horner, p. 325.
2. Minutes of the Advisory War Council Meeting, Canberra, 17 September 1942; CRS A5954, 814/1.
3. Hetherington, *Blamey*, p. 240.

4. Hetherington, *Blamey*, p. 240.
5. Hetherington, *Blamey*, pp. 239–242.

CHAPTER 52: HORII'S HORRIBLE DILEMMA
1. *Backroom Briefings*, p. 92.
2. Horner, *Blamey*, p. 328.
3. In this, Blamey may well have felt compelled to pull rank for his son. His other son, Charles, had died in an aircraft accident at Richmond, New South Wales, in December 1932. The thought of losing two sons may have been too much for him to bear.

CHAPTER 53: ROWELL'S HOWLER
1. Letter from Rowell to Allen, 11 October 1942, Allen Papers, 3DRL, no 2381, AWM 419/3/1.

CHAPTER 54: REVERSAL OF FORTUNE
1. Lieutenant Nick Walsh, 'Kokoda Track 1942', via the Rats of Tobruk Association, Albert Park, Victoria, Australia.
2. Curtin briefing to press, 6 October 1942.
3. During the New Guinea/Papua campaign, a handful of Australian troops who were lost or starving are also believed to have resorted to eating their dead mates on rare occasions after pre-arranged 'pacts'. The jungle terrain and atmosphere led to desperate measures. Extreme hunger and the will to survive did the rest. Yet there was no evidence that the flesh of Japanese soldiers had been consumed by diggers.

CHAPTER 55: THE BATTLE FOR EORA CREEK
1. Paul Ham, *Kokoda*, ABC Books, Sydney, 2004, p. 370.

CHAPTER 56: BLAMEY FIRES POTTS, ALLEN
1. B. Edgar, *Warrior of Kokoda*, Allen & Unwin, Sydney, 1999, pp. 190–196; Blamey Papers, AWM.

CHAPTER 58: BLAMEY'S RABBITS
1. N. D. Carlyon, *I Remember Blamey*, Macmillan, Melbourne, 1980.

CHAPTER 59: SILENCE OF A MOUNTAIN GUN
1. D. McCarthy, *South-West Pacific Area – First Year, Kokoda to Wau*, AWM, Canberra, 1959, pp. 385–393. E. C. Givney, *The First Year at War: The Story of the 2/1st Australian Infantry Battalion 1939–1945*, Association of the First Infantry Battalions, Earlwood, Sydney, 1987, pp. 316–321.
2. Roland Perry, *Monash: The Outsider Who Won a War*, Random House, Sydney, 2004, p. 421; letter from Monash to his wife, Victoria, 29 September 1918. NLA. S4.

CHAPTER 60: US NAVY'S 'NO SHOW'
1. Horner, *Blamey*, p. 360.
2. Horner, *Blamey*, p. 360; see also Paul P. Rodgers, *The Good Years: MacArthur and Sutherland*, Praeger, New York, 1990, p. 336.
3. Blamey Papers, AWM, 3DRL/6643; Blamey cable to Shedden, 4 December 1942, NAA 5954, Box 532; 30 November 1942, NAA A5954, Box 532.

CHAPTER 61: THE BATTLE OF BRISBANE
1. Peter Dunn, 'The Battle of Brisbane', Australians @ War, www.diggerhistory.info/pages-battles/ww2/battle/battle-brisbane.htm; Peter A. Thompson; Robert Macklin, *The Battle of Brisbane: Australians and the Yanks at War*, ABC Books, Sydney, 2000.

CHAPTER 62: ESCALATION
1. This was reminiscent of the Battle of Passchendaele in World War I, when General Monash had been the only Allied commander to state directly to Field Marshal Douglas Haig that a charge at a heavily fortified small ridge across a bog in torrential rain would fail. In response, Haig had given the Anzacs one day's respite but continuous rain kept the conditions swampy. Five thousand Australians and New Zealanders were casualties as a result of that folly.

CHAPTER 63: GONA: 'GOING, GOING . . .'
1. Carl Johnson, *Mud Over Blood*, History House, Melbourne, 2006, p. 144.

CHAPTER 65: BUNA BUSTED
1. Manchester, *American Caesar*, p. 326.

CHAPTER 66: SANANANDA SORROW
1. Robert L. Eichelberger, *Our Jungle Road to Tokyo*, Viking, New York, 1950.
2. Jay Luvaas (editor), *Dear Miss Em: General Eichelberger's War in the Pacific, 1942–1945*, USA, 1972.
3. D. Horner, *General Vasey's War*, Melbourne University Press, Melbourne, 1992, p. 233.

CHAPTER 67: WAR OF OPPORTUNITY
1. *Sydney Morning Herald*, 27 January 1943.
2. National Archives of Australia – guide to archives of Australian prime ministers by David Black and Lesley Wallace, p. 23.
3. Speech by Paul Keating, at the Fifth John Curtin Prime Ministerial Library Anniversary Lecture, 5 July 2002. http://john.curtin.edu.au/events/speeches/keating.html

CHAPTER 68: THE JAPANESE KEEP COMING
1. It was misnamed, as the battle had actually taken place in the Solomon Sea.

CHAPTER 69: SAVIGE TURN OF EVENTS
1. W. B. Russell, *There Goes a Man: The Biography of Sir Stanley G. Savige*, Longmans, Melbourne, 1959, pp. 260, 261.
2. Russell, *There Goes a Man*, p. 266.
3. Ibid.
4. Russell, *There Goes a Man*, p. 288,.
5. Gavin Keating, *The Right Man for the Right Job*, Oxford University Press, 2006, p. 129.

CHAPTER 70: RED HERRING
1. *Backroom Briefings*, p. 158.
2. D. Black, *In His Own Words: John Curtin's Speeches and Writings*, Paradigm Books, Perth, 1995, p. 223.

CHAPTER 71: CURTIN'S ELECTORAL APPEAL
1. *The Age*, 16 August 1943.
2. Edgar Holt, *The Daily Telegraph*, 16, 17, 19 and 20 August 1943; Ross Gollan, *The Sydney Morning Herald*, 19 and 20 August 1943.

CHAPTER 72: SAVIGE SETS UP FOURTH VICTORY IN PAPUA, NEW GUINEA
1. Russell, *There Goes a Man*, p. 279.
2. Russell, *There Goes a Man*, p. 279.
3. Russell, *There Goes a Man*, p. 279.
4. Russell, *There Goes a Man*, p. 268.
5. Russell, *There Goes a Man*, p. 280.

CHAPTER 73: POST-ELECTION SPOILS
1. *Backroom Briefings*, p. 26.

CHAPTER 74: MORE THAN 'MOPPING UP'
1. Presentation by military historian Brad Manera on 12 September AWM; www.awm.gov.au/atwar/remembering1942/kelliher/index.asp; Thompson, *Pacific Fury*, p. 378.
2. Eichelberger, *Our Jungle Road to Tokyo*, p. 107.

CHAPTER 75: MENZIES THWARTED; FINSCHHAFEN SORTED
1. Lloyd and Hall (editors), *Backroom Briefings*, pp. 13–14, 31–35.

CHAPTER 76: SATTELBERG BREAKTHROUGH
1. John Coates, *Bravery Above Blunder: The 9th Australian Division at Finschhafen, Sattelberg and Sio*, Oxford University Press, Melbourne, 1999, p. 226; Australian Dictionary of Biography – online edition. Derrick, Thomas Currie (Tom) (1914–1945.)
2. Ibid.

CHAPTER 77: THE PM'S MANY WAR FRONTS
1. Roland Perry, *The Fifth Man*, Sidgwick & Jackson, London, 1994, pp. 5–13.
2. Day, *Curtin*, p. 572.
3. Brigadier Sir Frederick Chilton died on 1 October 2007, aged 102.

CHAPTER 78: RELUCTANT VOYAGER
1. *Backroom Briefings*, p. 203.
2. *Backroom Briefings*, p. 203.
3. *Backroom Briefings*, p. 203; Day, *Curtin*, p. 572.
4. *Daily Telegraph*, Sydney, 25 August 1943.
5. David Horner, *High Command: Australia's Struggle for an Independent War Strategy, 1939–1945*. Allen & Unwin, Sydney, 1992, p. 313.

CHAPTER 79: MEETING WITH ROOSEVELT
1. Roland Perry, *Last of the Cold War Spies*, 2005.
2. Don Rodgers' observation. Radio tape produced by John Thompson: *John Curtin: Portrait of a Prime Minister*; ABC Archive, Sydney; NAA and John Curtin Prime Ministerial Library, Canberra.

CHAPTER 80: RENDEZVOUS WITH THE BULLDOG

1. Horner, *Defence Supremo: Sir Frederick Shedden and the Making of Australian Defence Policy*, Allen & Unwin, Sydney, 2000, p. 196.

CHAPTER 81: CHURCHILL'S BIG DISTRACTION

1. Soon after this meeting, Blamey's personal assistant suggested to Shedden's assistant that Blamey be made a field marshal, which would complete his trumping of MacArthur. It was obvious from this indirect request that Blamey anticipated that the command would change in his favour, with British support. Shedden mentioned the idea of Blamey's promotion to Curtin, who rejected it, reminding Shedden that Monash had only been made a full general twelve years after World War I, by Scullin in 1930. There was no way Blamey would be elevated higher by a Labor government. In the end, Menzies made Blamey a field marshal in 1949.
2. DFAT, Vol. V11, Document no 206; Note by Shedden of discussions with MacArthur, Brisbane 27 June 1944; NAA.
3. Lord Alanbrooke, *War Diaries 1939–1945*, Orion Books, London, 2002, pp. 512–513, 544, 550.

CHAPTER 82: CHECKMATE AT CHEQUERS

1. Horner, *Defence Supremo*, p. 201.
2. *The Times*, 19 May 1944.
3. Horner, *Defence Supremo*, p. 201.
4. Ibid.
5. Graham Freudenberg, *Churchill and Australia*, Pan Macmillan Australia, Sydney, p. 484.
6. Horner, *Defence Supremo*, p. 197.
7. *Backroom Briefings*, p. 210.
8. Ibid.
9. Ian Woodward, *Cricket, Not War*, SMK Enterprises, Melbourne, 1994, p. 35.
10. Sir Frederick Shedden, DAFT, 206: 'Note by Shedden on discussion with MacArthur', Brisbane, 27 June 1944. NAA.
11. Sir Frederick Shedden, DAFT, 206: 'Note by Shedden on discussion with MacArthur', Brisbane, 27 June 1944. NAA.
12. Sir Frederick Shedden, DAFT, 206: 'Note by Shedden on discussion with MacArthur', Brisbane, 27 June 1944. NAA.
13. Sir Frederick Shedden, DAFT, 206: 'Note by Shedden on discussion with MacArthur', Brisbane, 27 June 1944. NAA.
14. Sir Frederick Shedden, DAFT, 206: 'Note by Shedden on discussion with MacArthur', Brisbane, 27 June 1944. NAA.

CHAPTER 83: MACARTHUR DUMPS THE DIGGERS

1. Sir Frederick Shedden, DAFT, 206: 'Note by Shedden on discussion with MacArthur', Brisbane 27 June 1944. NAA.
2. Sir Frederick Shedden, DAFT, 206: 'Note by Shedden on discussion with MacArthur', Brisbane 27 June 1944. NAA.
3. Sir Frederick Shedden, DAFT, 206: 'Note by Shedden on discussion with MacArthur', Brisbane 27 June 1944. NAA.

4. Sir Frederick Shedden, DAFT, 206: 'Note by Shedden on discussion with MacArthur', Brisbane 27 June 1944. NAA.
5. Sir Frederick Shedden, DAFT, 206: 'Note by Shedden on discussion with MacArthur', Brisbane 27 June 1944. NAA.
6. Sir Frederick Shedden, DAFT, 206: 'Note by Shedden on discussion with MacArthur', Brisbane 27 June 1944. NAA.
7. Sir Frederick Shedden, DAFT, 206: 'Note by Shedden on discussion with MacArthur', Brisbane 27 June 1944. NAA.
8. Sir Frederick Shedden, DAFT, 206: 'Note by Shedden on discussion with MacArthur', Brisbane 27 June 1944. NAA.
9. Sir Frederick Shedden, DAFT, 206: 'Note by Shedden on discussion with MacArthur', Brisbane 27 June 1944. NAA.
10. Sir Frederick Shedden, DAFT, 206: 'Note by Shedden on discussion with MacArthur', Brisbane 27 June 1944. NAA.
11. Sir Frederick Shedden, DAFT, 206: 'Note by Shedden on discussion with MacArthur', Brisbane 27 June 1944. NAA.
12. Horner, *High Command*, p. 330.
13. David Black, *In His Own Words: John Curtin's Speeches and Writings*, Paradigm Books, Perth, 2005, p. 223; Natalie Thomas, 'Reconstructing Australia: John Curtin's Legacy', research essay, Curtin University of Technology, 2005.

CHAPTER 84: THE FORGOTTEN POWS

1. K. Wheeler, *War Under the Pacific*, World War II Series, Time Life Books, US, 1980, p. 129.
2. Wheeler, *War Under the Pacific*, p. 129.
3. Quotations from an extract of 'Just Soldiers – Stories about Ordinary Australians Doing Extraordinary Things in Time of War'. Anzac Day Commemoration Committee (Qld). Inc. 2004.
4. These POWs were liberated by American Occupation Forces in September 1945.

CHAPTER 85: MACARTHUR'S FAREWELL; SAVIGE'S WAY OF WAR

1. Diary of Frank Berryman, 24 March 1945, AWM PR84/370 Item 5.
2. Diary of Frank Berryman, 26 March 1945, AWM PR84/370 Item 5.
3. Communication between Sturdee and Savige; 15 July 1945, 18 July 1945; AWM 3DRL2529, Item 84.

CHAPTER 86: THE COMEBACK

1. William Dunn, *Pacific Microphones*, Texas A & M University Press, Austin, Texas, 1998, p. 5–6.
2. Day, *Curtin*, p. 612.

CHAPTER 87: CURTIN DOWN; MACARTHUR MAKES RUNNING

1. Ross, *John Curtin*, p. 370.
2. Ross, *John Curtin*, p. 370.

CHAPTER 88: CURTIN RECOVERS

1. *Backroom Briefings*, p. 236.
2. Denis Warner, *Wake Me if There Is Trouble*, Penguin, Melbourne, 1995, p. 6.

3. *Backroom Briefings*, p. 236.
4. Hansard, *Curtin speech*, 18 April 1945.

CHAPTER: 89: BORNEO BLUNDERS
1. *American Caesar*, p. 431.

CHAPTER 90: BEYOND THE CALL
1. Ted Kenna spent fifteen months recovering at Heidelberg Military Hospital. In 1947 he married Marjorie Rushberry, who had nursed him there.
2. The track to Beaufort was later renamed Victoria Cross Road, in honour of Starcevich.

CHAPTER 91: LAST CALL
1. John Thompson, *On the Lips of Living Men*, Lansdowne Press, Melbourne, 1962, p. 75.
2. *The Sun*, 6 July 1945; *The Age*, 7 July 1945; *The West Australian*, 8 and 9 July; see also Crisp, *Curtin*, p. 221.

CHAPTER 92: JAPAN CAPITULATES
1. Russell Savage, *A Guest of the Emperor*, Boolarong Press, Queensland, 1995, p. 118.
2. Savage, *A Guest of the Emperor*, p. 119.
3. Savage, *A Guest of the Emperor*, p. 119.
4. Savage, *A Guest of the Emperor*, pp. 119, 122.
5. Blamey Papers, AWM 3DRl6643; PR85/355.

CHAPTER 93: EPILOGUE: AT THE CENTRE
1. Douglas MacArthur, *Reminiscences*, MacGraw Hill, USA, 1964, p. 151.

Bibliography

BOOKS

Agawa, Hiroyuki, *The Reluctant Admiral, Yamamoto and the Imperial Navy*, Kodanshi International, Tokyo, 1982.
Alanbrooke, Lord, *War Diaries 1939–1945*, Orion Books, London, 2002.
Ambrose, Hugh, *The Pacific*, Text, Melbourne, 2010.
Barker, Anthony J. and Jackson, Lisa, *Fleeting Attraction*, University of Western Australia, Perth, 1996.
Bassett, Jan, *As We Wave Them Goodbye – Australian Women and War*, Oxford University Press, Melbourne, 1998.
Bean, C.E.W., *Official History of Australia in the War of 1914–1918*, Vol V, 'The AIF in France', Angus & Robertson, Sydney, 1997.
Bell, Roger, *Unequal Allies: Australian-American Relations and the Pacific War*, MUP, Melbourne, 1977.
Bennett, Gordon, *Why Singapore Fell*, Angus & Robertson, Sydney, 1944.
Bergamini, David, *Japan's Imperial Conspiracy*, Heinemann, London, 1971.
Bix, Herbert P., *Hirohito and the Making of Modern Japan*, HarperCollins, New York, 2000.
Black, D., *In His Own Words: John Curtin's Speeches and Writings*, Paradigm Books, Perth, 1995.
Blum, John Morton, *The Price of Vision: The Diary of Henry A.Wallace, 1942–1946*, Houghton Mifflin, Boston, 1973.
Boei-cho Kenshujo Senshishitsu (ed.), *Senshi Sosho*, Military History Department of Asagumo Shinbunsha (National Institute for Defense Studies), Tokyo,1968.
Bolt, Andrew, *Our Home Front 1939–1945*, Wilkinson Books, Melbourne, 1995.
Braddon, Russell, *The Naked Island*, Pan Books, London, 1963.
Bridgland, R. J. and Jacobs, J. W., *Through: the Story of the Signals 8 Australian Division and Signals A.I.F Malaya*, 8 Division Signals Association, 1995.
Brooke, Sir Alan, *War Diaries 1939–1945*, Orion Books, London, 2002.
Caulfield, Michael, *War Behind the Wire*, Hachette Australia, Sydney, 2008.
Bullard, Steven, *Japanese Army Operations in the South Pacific Area: New Britain and Papua Campaigns, 1942–43*, Australian War Memorial, Canberra, 2007.
Carlyon, Norman D., *I Remember Blamey*, Macmillan, Sydney, 1980.
Casey, Richard, *Personal Experience 1939–1946*, Constable, London, 1962.
Churchill, Winston, *Hinge of Fate*, Penguin Classics, UK, 2005.
Cleary, Paul, *The Men Who Came Out of the Ground*, Hachette Australia, Sydney, 2010.

Clifford, Alexander, *Three Against Rommel*, George G. Harrap, London, 1943.
Cody, Les, *Ghosts in Khaki*, Hesperian Press, Perth, 1997.
Coates, John, *Bravery Above Blunder: The 9th Australian Division at Finschhafen, Sattelberg and Sio*, Oxford University Press, Melbourne, 1999.
Cook, Haruko Taya, and Cook, Theodore F., *Japan at War: An Oral History*, New Press, New York, 1992.
Day, David, *John Curtin*, Harper Perennial, 1999.
Dunn, William, *Pacific Microphones*, Texas A & M University Press, Austin, Texas, 1998.
Eade, Charles, *Churchill by his Contemporaries*, Hutchinson, London, 1953.
Eichelberger, Robert L., *Our Jungle Road to Tokyo*, Viking, New York, 1950.
Fitzsimons, Peter, *Kokoda*, Hodder, Sydney, 2004.
Frei, Henry P., *Japan's Southward Advance and Australia*, Melbourne University Press, Melbourne, 1991.
——*Official Japanese War History: Senshi Sosho* [English translation].
Freudenberg, Graham, *Churchill and Australia*, Pan Macmillan, 2008.
Fuchido, Mitsuo and Okumiya, Masatake, *Midway: The Battle that Doomed Japan*, Hutchinson, UK, 1957.
Gallaway, Jack, *The Odd Couple*, UQP, Brisbane, 2000.
Gilbert, Martin, *Road to Victory: Winston S. Churchill 1941–1945*, Heinemann-Minerva, Britain, 1989.
Grose, Peter, *An Awkward Truth: The Bombing of Darwin, February 1942*, Allen & Unwin, Sydney, 2009.
Ham, Paul, *Kokoda*, ABC Books, Sydney, 2004.
Hasluck, Paul, *Diplomatic Witness: Australian Foreign Affairs, 1941–1947*, Melbourne University Press, Melbourne, 1980.
Heatherington, John, *Blamey, Controversial Soldier*, Australian War Memorial, Canberra, 1973.
Horner, David, *High Command: Australia and Allied Strategy 1939–1945*, Allen & Unwin, Sydney, 1982.
——*Blamey*, Allen & Unwin, Sydney, 1998.
——*Crisis of Command: Australian Generalship and the Japanese Thrust, 1941–1943*, Australian National University Press, Canberra, 1978.
——*General Vasey's War*, Melbourne University Press, Melbourne, 1992.
——*High Command: Australia's Struggle for an Independent War Strategy, 1939–1945*, Allen & Unwin, Sydney, 1992.
——*Defence Supremo: Sir Frederick Shedden and the Making of Australian Defence Policy*, Allen & Unwin, Sydney, 2000.
Jess, Lieutenant-General Sir Carl, Report on the Activities of the Australian Military Forces 1929–1939, historical document, Department of Defence.
Johnson, Carl, *Mud Over Blood: The 39th Infantry Battalion 1941–43, Kokoda to Gona*, History House, Melbourne, 2006.
Keating, Gavin, *The Right Man for the Right Job*, Oxford University Press, Melbourne, 2006.
Knightley, P., *Australia: A Biography of a Nation*, Jonathon Cape, London, 2000.
Laird, John, *The Australian Experience of War*, Mead & Beckett, Sydney, 1988.

Leary, W. M., *We Shall Return! MacArthur's Commanders and the Defeat of Japan 1942–1945*, The University of Kentucky, Lexington, US.
Lee, Norman E., *John Curtin: Saviour of Australia*, Longman Cheshire, Melbourne, 1983.
Legg, Frank, *The Gordon Bennett Story*, Angus & Robertson, Sydney, 1965.
Lindsay, P., *The Spirit of Kokoda: Then and Now*, Hardie Grant Books, Melbourne, 2002.
Lloyd, Clem and Hall, Richard, *Backroom Briefings: John Curtin's War*, National Library of Australia, Canberra, 1997.
Lodge, Brett, *Lavarack: Rival General*, Australian Military History Series, Allen & Unwin, Sydney, 1998
Long, G., *MacArthur as Military Commander*, Angus & Robertson, Sydney, 1969.
Luvaas, Jay, (Ed), *Dear Miss Em: General Eichelberger's War in the Pacific, 1942–1945*, Greenwood Publishing, USA, 1972.
Lynes, E. T., *Supply Column at War: A History of the 7th Division Supply Column, Australian Army Services Corps 1940–45*; Goodenia Rise Publishers, Melbourne, 1996.
Macklin, Robert, *The Battle of Brisbane: Australians and the Yanks at War*, ABC Books, Sydney, 2000.
Manchester, William, *American Caesar: Douglas MacArthur, 1880–1964*, Little, Brown and Company, Boston, USA, 1978.
Manning, P., *Hirohito: The War Years*, Dodd Mead, New York, 1986.
McKernan, Michael, *All In!* Nelson, Melbourne, 1983.
Meacham, Jon, *Franklin and Winston*, Random House, New York, 2003.
Meaher, Augustine, *The Road to Singapore: The Myth of British Betrayal*, Australian Scholarly Publishing, Melbourne, 2010.
Monash, General Sir John, *The Australian Victories in France in 1918*, Lothian, Melbourne, 1923.
Moorehead, Alan, *African Trilogy*, Text, Melbourne, 1997.
Moore, J .H., *Morshead: A biography of Lieutenant General Sir Leslie Morshead*, Haldene, Sydney, 1976.
——*Over-sexed, Over-paid and Over Here: Americans in Australia 1941–1945*, QUP, Brisbane, 1981.
Morgan, Kevin, *Gun Alley*, Simon & Schuster, Sydney, 2005.
Norwich, John Julius, *The Duff Cooper Diaries*, Weidenfeld & Nicolson, London, 2005.
Perry, Roland, *Monash: The Outsider Who Won a War*, Random House Australia, Sydney, 2004.
——*The Australian Light Horse*, Hachette Australia, Sydney, 2009.
——*Changi Brownlow*, Hachette Australia, Sydney, 2010.
Persico, Jospeh E., *Franklin and Lucy*, Random House, New York, 2008.
Potter, John Deane, *A Soldier Must Hang: The Biography of an Oriental General*, Four Square, London, 1963.
Ross, Lloyd, *John Curtin: A Biography*, Sun Books, Melbourne 1983.
Rowell, Sydney, *Full Circle*, Melbourne University Press, Melbourne, 1974.
Russell, W. B., *There Goes a Man: The Biography of Sir Stanley Savige*, Longmans, Melbourne, 1959.
Savage, Russell, *A Guest of the Emperor*, Boolarong Press, Queensland, 1995.
Schmidt, Karl M., *Henry Wallace*, Syracuse University Press, USA, 1960.

Sledge, E. B., *With the Old Breed—At Pelelui and Okinawa*, Ballantine USA, 2007.
Storr, Anthony, *Churchill's Black Dog*, Fontana/Collins UK, 1990.
Thompson, John, *On Lips of Living Men*, Lansdowne Press, Melbourne, 1962.
Thompson, Peter, *Pacific Fury*, William Heinemann Australia, Sydney, 2008.
Toland, John, *The Rising Sun: The Decline and Fall of the Japanese Empire 1936–1945*, Penguin, London, 2001.
Warner, Denis, *Wake Me if There is Trouble*, Penguin, Sydney, 1995.
Warrender, Pamela Myer, *Pamela: In Her Own Right*, Hardie Grant Books, Melbourne, 2007.
Wheeler, K., *War Under the Pacific*, World War II Series, Time Life Books, US, 1980.
Williamson, Kristin, *The Last Bastion*, Lansdowne, Sydney, 1984.
Wilson, Keith, *You'll Never Get Off the Island*, A Susan Haynes Book, Allen & Unwin, Sydney, 1989.
Wurth, Bob, *1942: Australia's Greatest Peril*, Macmillan, Sydney, 2008.
Younger, R. M., *Keith Murdoch – Founder of a Media Empire*, HarperCollins, Sydney, 2003.

ARTICLES, BOOKLETS, SPEECHES, MANUSCRIPTS, MEMOIRS, OTHER

Adams, K.W. and Barnes, L. T., 'History of Brunswick', Moreland City Library, 1988.
Beazley, K.M., 'John Curtin: An Atypical Labor Leader', Australian National University Press, Canberra, 1972.
Black, David and Wallace, Lesley, 'John Curtin: Guide to Archives of Australia's Prime Ministers', National Archives of Australia and John Curtin Prime Ministerial Library.
——(ed) *In His Own Words: John Curtin's Speeches and Writings*. Paradigm Books, Perth, 1995.
Cavalier, Rodney, 'Hung parliament in wartime was one of our best', *The Australian*, 2 September 2010.
Charlton, Peter, 'Humiliating fall of an impregnable fortress', *The Australian*, 15–16 February 1992.
——'Bloody Retreat from Malaya', *The Australian*, 15–16 February 1992.
Chen, C. Peter, World War II database: Douglas MacArthur.
Coombs, H.C. *Trial Balance*, Macmillan, Melbourne, 1981.
Coulthart, Ross, 'Kokoda Mystery Solved', *The Australian*, 24–25 April 2010.
Curran, James, 'Empire Champion', *Australian Literary Review*, vol. 6, issue 2, March 2011.
Day, David, 'Final crack in empire of eggshell', *The Australian*, 15–16 February 1992.
Edwards, P., *Australia Through American Eyes, 1935–1945: Observations by American Diplomats*, University of Queensland Press, Brisbane, 1979.
——'Another look at Curtin and MacArthur', Remembering 2002, Australian War Memorial.
Evans, Raymond and Donegan, Jacqui, The Battle of Brisbane, 2 October 2009.
Fanous, Samuel, (ed), 'Instructions for American Servicemen in Australia 1942', Bodleian Library, University of Oxford, 2006.
Grattan, Michelle, *The Australian Prime Minister and the Press: A Study in Intimacy*,
Harper, Norman, *Australia and the United States*, Thomas Nelson, Melbourne 1971, pp 135–139.

Horner, David, 'Blame for disaster has to be shared', The Australian, 15–16 February 1992.
Hudson, W. J. and Stokes H.J.W. (eds), *Documents in Australian Foreign Policy 1937–49* (DAFP), Vol.V, AGPS, Canberra, 1982.
John Curtin Ministerial Library Occasional Paper, Perth, 1998.
Keating, Paul, 'John Curtin's World and Ours' (speech), John Curtin Prime Ministerial Library, 5 July 2002.
——remarks at the launch of *Churchill and Australia* by Graham Freudenberg, 30 October 2008.
Leece, David, Brigadier Sir Frederick Chilton, United Services 59 (1) March 2008.
Maitland, Major-General Gordon, 'Field-Marshal Sir Thomas Blamey: Australia's most promoted, but least appreciated soldier', address to the United Services Institute, 31 May 2005.
Masters, Elizabeth, 'The Sinking of the Australian Hospital Ship Centaur', *Memento*, Issue 39, 2010.
Morrison, James, 'Tiger's bluff led to quick capitulation', *The Australian*, 15–16 February 1992.
——'Bennett's ambition the Achilles heel', *The Australian*, 15–16 February 1992.
Munro, Ian, 'Overpaid, oversexed and over here', *The Age*, 27 February 2002.
O'Leary, Dennis, The Battle for Australia, 2009.
Nelson, Hank, 'Gallipoli, Kokoda and the making of national identity' (seminar), Humanities Research Centre, Australian National University, February 1996.
Nicholson, Brendan, 'Hero of both world wars among VCs in hall of valour', *The Australian*, 11 February 2011.
Pyvis, David, 'When the AIR BEER CEER pushed the Aussie twang', School of Social Sciences, Curtin University of Technology, 1993.
Rintoul, Stuart, 'Blamey Quit after Backseat Sex-Romp', *The Australian*, 25 July 2005.
Ross, Lloyd, *John Curtin for Labor and for Australia*, Australian National University Press, Canberra, 1971.
Tracey, Rowan, 'Conflict in Command during the Kokoda Campaign of 1942: did General Blamey deserve the blame?' *United Services* 61, June 2010.
The Royal Australian College of Physicians, 'The Long Days of Slavery', 1996.
Vernon, P. V., 'Notes for Platoon & Section leaders, Jungle Warfare, Allied Land Forces in the South-West Pacific Area', F J Hilton & Co, Melbourne 1943.
Walsh, Nick, (ed Miles, Stephen), Kokoda Track 1942, Bookaburra Printing.
'While you were away: a digest of happenings in Australia 1940–1945' (booklet); The Argus, Melbourne, 1946.

Documentaries and broadcast interviews

ABC News Stateline, Friday 13 August 2010, interview with author Paul Cleary.
Manera, Brad, The Battle of Timor, 20–23 February 1942, Australian War Memorial, PASU0171.

Acknowledgements

Many thanks to Hachette publisher Matthew Kelly and then sales and marketing director Matt Hoy. Initially, I had in mind writing about Australia's involvement in World War II in the Pacific, North Africa, the Middle East and Greece. They suggested confining the story to the Pacific, which proved a more manageable book and better narrative. Their input and suggestions were greatly appreciated. This is my fourth book with Hachette. Kelly reminds me very much of England's (late) outstanding publisher at Sidgwick & Jackson, William Armstrong. Both have an 'old-style' feel and approach to writing and publishing, with an eye for a neat balance between a story with 'meat' and a respectful regard for the market. Both understand that, in writing about history, narrative and character are everything. Kelly and Armstrong also possess a love of books, from the use of the language to the finished product.

The most important sources for the book were Canberra's National Archives of Australia, Perth's John Curtin Prime Ministerial Library, Tokyo's Military History Department of the National Institute for Defense Studies (which is the main policy arm of Japan's Ministry of Defense), and the Australian War Memorial. Historian Carl Johnson passed on hitherto unpublished and untranslated Japanese intelligence reports, and other material that was most useful. Locational research was carried out in Western Australia, the Northern Territory, Queensland, New South Wales, Victoria, South Australia, Indonesia (including Java, West Papua, Ambon and Borneo), Papua New Guinea, Guam, Singapore, Thailand, Malaysia and Burma.

Thanks also to the following for interviews and/or information: Grace Barnbaum, Shirley Barnbaum, Major-General James Barry, Kim Beazley, Rod Beattie, Graham Brooke, Jim Cardinal, Albert Champion, Don Clarke, Dr Mickey Dewar, Tim Fischer, Diana

Gollar, Neil Graham, Jack Grossman, Thos Hodgson, Phillip Knightley, Carl Johnson, Richard Joslin, Natalie Lees, Leon Levin, Tony Maylam, Nate Gluck, Brian O'Shaughnessy, Dennis O'Leary, Bob Owen, Trevor Perry, Richard Peterson, Professor John Radcliffe, A. Sumner Reed, Joseph Salfas, Fred Seiker, Peter Singer, Russell Savage, Rolly Tasker, Greg Thomas, Nick Walsh, Pamela Warrender, Sarah Wells.

Roland Perry

Photo credits

Images on pp 1 (top and bottom), 2 (bottom), 3 (top and bottom), 6 (top), and 7 (top and bottom) of the first photo section; and pp 4 (both top photos), 5 (top), 6 (top and bottom) and 7 (top and bottom) of the second photo section are courtesy of Newspix/News Ltd. The image on p 5 (bottom) of the second photo section courtesy of the Australian War Memorial (negative no P00784.199); and the image on p 8 (bottom) of the second photo section courtesy Fairfax Photo Library. All other images are from private collections.

The map on p (x) is based on the map in *Volume V – South–West Pacific Area – First Year: Kokoda to Wau*, of the Official History (Army).

Index

Abukuma 122
Adelaide 85–6, 112, 151, 360
Advisory War Council 12–16, 38, 119–21, 127, 134, 159, 163, 190, 260, 266, 269, 374, 387, 428
Afghanistan 463
Africa
  North *see* North Africa
Akagi 122, 203
Albanese, Corporal Ralf 305
Alexander, A. V. 401
Allen, Major General Arthur 225–6, 234, 244, 252–5, 256, 258, 262, 264, 269, 277, 278, 287, 290, 291, 292, 294, 298, 353
Alola 235, 238, 239, 242
Ambon 44, 364
Amiens 5, 167, 170, 249, 307
Anderson, Lieutenant-Colonel Charles 80–5
Andrews, Major H. H. Irvine 47
Anking 140
Anstey, Frank 11
Anzac Agreement 382–3, 392–3
Argyle, Sir Stanley 173
armaments and ammunition 214, 463
  Papua, in 233–4
Attlee, Clement 402
Auckinleck, General Sir Claude 165–6
Austerity Loan 189
austerity measures 40, 63, 114, 177, 189–90, 206–7, 212, 248–51, 360, 419, 437
Australia
  Britain, ties to 61–4, 164, 176–7, 198–9, 343–4, 375, 389, 395, 401, 402–4, 462
  defence of 4, 13, 21–2, 30, 33–5, 39, 41, 47–8, 70, 74, 106–7, 115–16, 118, 121, 128, 139, 177–8, 191, 192, 205, 269, 283, 356, 358, 361, 460, 463–4
  Japanese plans for 50–2, 72–3, 94, 102, 110–14, 138–9, 180, 215
  US military forces in 143–5, 156–8, 162–3, 183, 184–6, 198–200, 211–12, 293–4, 347, 461
Australian Army
  AIF and militia, merger of 283, 342
  1st Division 27
  3rd Brigade 361
  3rd Division 348, 420
  5th Battalion 363
  6th Battalion 363, 365
  6th Division 5, 34–5, 66, 101, 106, 116, 119, 121, 128, 129, 132, 136, 145, 165, 226, 230, 265, 282, 345, 352, 361, 365, 383, 393, 459
  7th Brigade 225
  7th Division 34–5, 66, 101, 106, 116, 119–21, 128, 129–30, 132, 136, 142, 145, 205, 220, 223, 224, 225, 232, 234, 238, 242, 261, 282, 288, 345, 352, 361, 365, 369–70, 393, 439, 446, 459
  8th Division 14, 22, 30, 34, 57, 73, 80, 82, 85, 91, 109, 129, 136, 142, 365–6, 450, 460
  9th Division 3, 17, 34–5, 106, 116, 119, 129, 145, 165, 174, 200, 345–8, 361, 365, 369, 371, 373, 378, 380, 439, 441, 443, 445, 447, 459
  10th Battalion 383

Australian Army (*continued*)
  12th Battalion 383
  14th Battalion 239, 241–2, 244, 245, 252, 253, 319, 328
  14th Brigade 225
  15th Brigade 364
  16th Battalion 239, 244, 245, 252, 253, 255, 383
  16th Brigade 226, 264, 280, 281, 284, 287
  17th Brigade 347, 352, 354
  18th Battalion 103
  18th Brigade 225, 237, 240, 245, 247, 323, 328–9, 331, 336, 337, 383
  19th Battalion 77, 78, 80, 81
  20th Battalion 103
  20th Brigade 369, 372
  21st Brigade 225, 232, 235, 258, 260, 262, 299–300, 311, 318–19, 326, 383
  22nd Battalion 88
  22nd Brigade 98, 105
  23rd Battalion 377
  23rd Brigade 420, 441
  24th Brigade 373
  25th Battalion 312, 370, 371
  25th Brigade 262, 264, 270, 279, 284, 285, 297, 370
  26th Battalion 98
  26th Brigade 369, 440
  27th Battalion 244–5, 252, 253, 256, 257, 319
  27th Brigade 98, 104–5
  28th Battalion 281
  29th Battalion 77, 78, 81
  30th Battalion 75, 98
  30th Brigade 225, 298
  33rd Battalion 297
  39th Battalion 209, 221, 224–30, 233, 235, 238–9, 242, 252, 260, 262, 282, 298–9, 321, 324–6, 328, 342, 460
  48th Battalion 377, 380, 443
  53rd Battalion 239, 242, 252, 321
  combined force 101–2
  counter-attack 208, 281, 291, 357
Australian Broadcasting Commission (ABC) 344

Australian Labor Party (ALP) 3, 7, 12, 16, 32, 63, 164, 176, 282, 356, 358, 361–2, 366–8, 375, 434, 437, 462
Australian Workers' Union (AWU) 13
aviation, civil 433–4

Balikpapan 440, 446
banking reforms 434
Barber, Lieutenant Rex T. 351
Bardia 226, 352
Barnbaum, Grace and Shirley 212
Barnett, Bernard 185
Bataan 43, 71
Bataan Gang 161, 162, 170, 248, 266, 297, 357, 372, 373, 423
Beasley, Jack 266, 267
Beaufort 445–6
Bedell, Flying Officer 28
Bellamy, Edward 11
Bennett, Major General Gordon 14, 28, 44, 45, 72, 73, 82, 83, 86, 389
  escape from Singapore 105–6
  Singapore, defence of 30, 34, 46, 73–6, 90, 95–6, 97, 103
Benson, Father James 219, 306, 307
Bentson, Sergeant Bill 315–16
Berryman, Major General Frank 357, 389, 408, 421
Bickle, Private J. H. 370
Birdwood, General William 165
Bismarck Archipelago 68
Bismarck Sea, Battle of the 349–50
Bix, Herbert P. 102
Blamey, General Thomas 4, 22, 34–5, 46, 83, 101–2, 110, 128–9, 142, 156, 178, 187, 189, 191–2, 206, 208, 209, 293, 351–2, 366, 389, 404, 420, 439–40, 446
  character 162, 166–9, 170–4, 213, 249, 265–6
  Commissioner for Police 171–4
  Curtin's visit to the US and UK 390, 391, 395, 397–8, 399, 405, 407
  Japan, in 454
  MacArthur and 161–3, 164, 170, 175, 176, 213–14, 248, 266,

271, 280, 298, 308–9, 311–12, 408–9, 409–13
media and 172, 224, 261–2, 280
military record 165–9, 174, 175
Papua and New Guinea 220, 223, 238, 239–40, 244, 245, 247, 258, 259, 261–2, 265–8, 270–2, 277–8, 280, 287, 289–91, 294, 298–300, 318–21, 327, 348, 353, 356–7, 369
prostitutes, and 171–4
Bobdubi 363–4
Bonis Peninsula 420
Bonus Expeditionary Force (BEF) 35–6
Borneo 46, 71, 85, 207, 366, 398, 435, 439–46, 447, 451
Botterill, Private Keith 445
Bougainville 419–20, 439, 451
Braithewaite, Richard 444
Brett, Major-General George H. 59, 64, 151
Bridges, Colonel William 27
Brigade Hill 253–4, 256–9, 297
Brisbane 110–12, 115–16, 156–7, 292, 293, 384, 384
  American forces in 211–12, 220, 223, 293–4, 313–17
  riots 314–16
Brisbane Line 356, 358
Britain
  Australian ties to 61–4, 164, 176–7, 198–9, 343–4, 375, 389, 395, 401, 402–4, 462
British Army
  18th Division 53, 73, 87–8, 90, 101, 130
Brooke, Sir Alan 52, 399
Brooke-Popham, Air Chief Marshal Sir Robert 19–22, 29, 30
Broome 140, 358
Brophy, John 173
Brownout Strangler 186, 193–4, 347
Bruce, Stanley 27, 31, 54, 58, 119–20, 135, 150, 278, 395, 404
Bruche, Sir Julius 172
Brunei 398, 440, 445
Buin 420, 422, 451

Bukit Timah 94, 95, 104, 108
Bulgaria 26
Bulolo 354
Buna 209, 210, 219, 263, 271, 273, 279, 285, 290, 296, 303, 306–11, 318, 320, 321, 323, 325, 328, 330, 335–7, 348, 384, 460
  Government Gardens 331–2, 336
Burma 20, 45–6, 68, 72, 82, 87, 90, 98, 106, 109, 110, 116, 119–20, 128–36, 142, 164, 207, 223, 232, 270, 288, 344, 451, 457
  Japanese invasion 102–3, 136, 160
Burnett, Joseph 22–3
Button, Reverend Dr C. N. 178
Byrnes, James 392

Cairo 22, 200, 376
Callinan 208
Calwell, Arthur 283, 342, 367, 381–2
Cambodia 43
Cameron, Don 283
Cameron, Lieutenant Colonel Allan 226, 228, 298
Camp Pell 184–6
Camp Robinson 184
Campbell, Gunner Owen 444
cannibalism 284, 294, 340
Carew, Squadron Leader John 89
Carmody, Keith 407
Carolina Islands 26
Casey, Richard 'Dick' 27, 54–5, 57, 58, 66, 73, 87, 150, 344, 388
casualties 456–7
  Borneo 446, 452
  Broome 140
  Darwin 125–6
  Malaya 81, 83
  Middle East 345
  naval 25, 138, 181, 190, 196, 204, 228, 355, 425
  Papau and New Guinea 241, 255, 259, 286, 292, 297, 301, 305–6, 312, 319–20, 323, 324, 328, 337, 340, 341, 348, 369, 371, 380
  Singapore 104
Catterns, Captain Basil 288–9, 291, 303–6

Centaur 355
Ceylon 180–1, 230, 231, 281, 288
Chalk, Lieutenant John 220
Changi 110, 142, 207, 415, 435, 452
Chauvel, General Sir Harry 47, 172, 294, 404
Chequers 402–5, 406
Chifley, Ben 29, 32, 87, 89, 101, 133, 179, 231, 343, 361, 367, 382, 434, 437, 438, 440, 447, 448
Chikuma 122
Childs 144
Chilton, Brigadier Frederick 383
China 20, 62, 120, 129–30, 257, 284, 376, 392, 398, 438, 451, 455, 463
   Japanese invasion 4, 13, 14, 15–16, 26, 31, 43, 50, 66–8, 93, 109, 116, 138, 234, 456
Churchill, Clementine 10
Churchill, Winston 3–4, 15, 21, 27, 33, 46, 91, 116, 119–21, 150, 199, 367, 381, 387, 390, 412, 441, 459
   alcohol 6, 70
   atomic bomb 449
   attitude to war 9–10, 69
   Burma, and 119–20, 128–35
   character 5, 6–7, 19, 91, 129–30, 175, 230, 327
   Curtin, relationship with 16–18, 31, 41, 43, 52, 54–6, 58, 65–6, 68, 70, 81–2, 129–30, 181–2, 251, 341–2, 361–2, 384, 388, 403
   Curtin's Christmas 1941 article 65
   Curtin's visit to the UK 395–407
   destiny 10–11, 128
   Florida, in 70, 73
   Japanese attack on the Pacific 41–2
   manic depression 8
   Pacific War, on the 42–3, 46, 397–8, 404
   Roosevelt and 42–3, 46, 52, 54–7, 66, 70, 131–2, 376
   Singapore, and 87–8, 110
   writer, as 10–11
Clark, Corporal 244
Cleary, Paul 207
Cleary, Private Neil 444–5

Clowes, Captain Tim 285–6, 287
Clowes, Major General Cyril 225, 239–40, 245–7, 248, 259
Cold War 456
Coles, Arthur 3
Collins, Commodore John 423, 425
communications 97–8, 103, 279, 305, 356, 408
communism 9, 15, 17, 26, 30, 53, 54, 60–2, 67, 76, 79, 115, 177, 190, 231, 283, 392, 455–6
Compton, Denis 407
conscription 9, 33, 282
   industrial 176, 346
Coombs, H. C. 'Nugget' 406, 414
Cooper, Colonel Geoff 319
Cooper, Duff 19, 21–2
Coral Sea, Battle of the 186–93, 198, 201, 204, 215, 219
Corregidor 43, 82, 91, 149, 152, 191
Country Party 7, 13, 387
Crace, Admiral Sir John 187–8
Crease, Corporal Wally 444–5
Crete 5, 56, 73, 87, 116, 134, 248, 324
cricket 39, 92, 188, 406–7
Cross, Sir Ronald 390
Cullen, Lieutenant Colonel 304, 305
Curtin, Elsie 8, 24, 68, 85, 117, 134, 179, 390, 391, 393, 394, 407, 413, 427–8, 438, 447
Curtin, Elsie (daughter) 8, 101, 131, 179, 429
Curtin, John 3–5, 21, 29, 91, 116, 127–8, 168, 189, 281–3, 327, 433, 459–65
   affairs 156
   alcohol 6–8, 85, 156, 459
   attitude to war 9–10, 31–2, 38–40, 41, 462
   Blamey, relationship with 175, 248, 267, 366–7
   Britain, breaking ties with 60–5, 164
   Canada, in 407
   character 6–7, 17, 48–9, 69, 131, 154–6, 175, 179, 230–1, 327, 376, 396, 400, 439, 464–5
   Churchill, relationship with 16–18, 31, 41, 43, 52, 54–6, 58, 65–6,

68, 70, 81–2, 129–30, 181–2, 251, 341–2, 361–2, 384, 388, 403, 406
death 447
declaration of war 31–3
depression 8, 85, 132–4, 356, 390, 413, 426, 459
destiny 11–12, 33, 128, 156
election (1943) 282, 356, 358, 360–2, 366–8, 374, 464
faith 136, 179, 250, 448
funeral 448
HMAS *Sydney* disaster 24–5
illness 69, 79, 85–6, 117–19, 230, 283–4, 362, 374, 393–4, 419, 427–9, 437, 438, 439, 459
Japan, relationship with 27–8
MacArthur, relationship with 154–5, 198–200, 205, 260, 267, 366, 374–6, 388, 399–400, 418–19, 439, 462, 465
media management 48–9, 86, 114–15, 116–19, 127, 177–8, 181–2, 189, 214, 269, 344, 357–8, 362, 367, 464
no confidence motion (1943) 358
Papua and New Guinea 222–3, 281, 341–2
Perth, visits to 85–6, 419
smoking 426–8
socialism 9–10, 11–12, 63, 250–1, 360, 376, 434, 463, 465
sport, and 39–40, 49–50, 188–9
UK, visit to 387, 394–407
USA, relationship with 18, 60–1, 150, 162–3, 251, 382–3, 384, 394, 462
USA, visit to 387–94, 407
writer, as 10, 11–12, 32–3, 55, 464
Cyrenaica *see* Libya

D-Day 398–9, 402, 405
Dalton, Hugh 405
Darwin 41, 44, 47, 78, 93–4, 110, 112–13, 133, 134, 144, 149, 204, 207, 282, 384, 412, 460, 464
attacks on, 122–6, 127, 140, 345, 349, 350, 357
defence of 115, 119, 361, 387
evacuation 47, 109, 126
RAAF base 124–5, 140
Deakin, Alfred 402
Dechaineux, Captain Emile 423, 425
Dedman, John 367
Deniki 221, 222, 226, 229, 298
Derrick, Sergeant Thomas 'Diver' 378–80, 442–3
Detmers, Commander Theodore 22–3
Dili 125, 135
Dill, Field Marshal Sir John 392, 399
disease 236, 242, 243, 273, 290, 341, 365
Donnelly, Bill 173
Donovan, Jack 181
Doorman, Rear Admiral Karel 137
Dougherty, Brigadier Ivan 290, 318, 321, 324
Drakeford, Arthur 293, 367
Drysdale Mission 372–3
Duffy, Des 75
Duke of Gloucester 403, 404–5, 434
Duncan, Val 416–17
Dunlop, Lieutenant-Colonel Edward 'Weary' 142
Dunn, Bill 424
Duropa Plantation 329–30, 335
Dutch 62, 71
Dutch East Indies 16, 20, 42, 44, 56, 66, 71, 96, 101, 106, 109, 116, 128, 138, 149, 388, 440, 454, 457
dysentery 236, 435

Earl Ridge 420
Eastern Front 381
Eather, Brigadier Ken 262, 264, 279, 285–6, 287, 312–13, 321, 371
Efogi 243, 244, 252–4, 256, 257, 258, 285
Eichelberger, General Robert L. 266, 321, 323, 331–2, 336–9, 371, 375
Eisenhower, General Dwight D. 36, 151, 402
El Alamein 345–6, 378, 442
Elliott, Sergeant Jack 286
Eora Creek 235, 242, 285–9, 290, 293–5, 303, 304

Evatt, Herbert 'Doc' 20, 29, 32, 40, 43, 48, 53–4, 73, 86–8, 89, 133–4, 176–7, 191, 343–4, 358, 361, 366, 382–3, 392, 413
Exmouth 145, 358

Fadden, Arthur 3, 4, 13, 17, 20, 121, 343, 358, 366, 387
Fairfax, Warwick 231
Far East 15, 19, 20, 22, 36, 58, 65, 74, 115, 132
Farncomb, Rear-Admiral H. B. 188
Farnsworth, Olga Ora 174
Farragut 187
'Fashions for Victory' 207
Feinstein, Calman 212
Fiji 93, 94, 186, 383
Finland 26
Finschhafen 143, 348, 371–4, 380
Fisher, Andrew 465
Florence D 122
football 49–50, 249–50
Forde, Frank 29, 47, 86, 89, 119–20, 127, 156, 290, 367, 382, 411, 427, 437, 440, 447, 448
Fourth Liberty Loan 40
France 13, 25, 381, 461
  Allied invasion 398–9, 402, 405
Francisco River 356, 359, 364–5
Francol 140
Fraser, Peter 400
French, John 247–8
Fuchida, Captain Mitsuo 112, 122–3
Fuzzy Wuzzy Angels 243

Galleghan, Lieutenant-Colonel Frederick 'Black Jack' 75
Gallipoli 5, 9, 14, 27, 64, 72, 75, 76, 87–8, 90, 95–6, 106, 166, 232, 241, 312, 319, 351, 353, 369
Garing, Group Captain Bill 'Bull' 237
Gemas 77, 84, 90
Gemencheh Creek 72, 75–6
Geraldton 145, 358
Germans 4, 5, 13, 25, 38, 42, 50, 55, 190, 237, 281, 399
  Blitzkrieg 26
  Japan and 72
  Kormoran 22–4, 25

Luftwaffe 26
  Middle East, in the 213
  move across Europe 13
Gilbert Islands 98
Gollan, Ross 362
Gollar, Diana 185–6, 194
Gona 219, 253, 256, 263, 270, 302, 303, 306–7, 309, 310, 312–13, 318–19, 322–8, 339, 348, 384, 460
Gorari 294–7, 300–1
Gourlay, Geoff 452–3
government
  federal and state power 63, 343
  money, appeals for 40, 117–18, 189, 197, 206
  referendum 413
  social reforms 343–5, 406
  tax reform 343
Gowrie, Lord 25, 40, 179
Grant, Corporal Max 124
Grant, MP Norbert 315
Greater East Asia Co-Prosperity Sphere 201
Greece 5, 14, 56, 73, 87, 116, 120, 134, 165, 248, 260, 271, 277, 324, 352
Guadalcanal 73, 185, 208, 219, 227, 238, 263, 265, 279, 318, 328, 340, 341, 349, 351, 382, 451
Guam 45, 451
guerrilla warfare 47, 113, 136, 139, 178
  Australians 191–2, 207–8, 216, 242–3, 288, 347

Haddy, Lieutenant Alan 323–4
Haig, Field Marshall Douglas 167, 381
Hainan Island 28
Halsey, Admiral Bill 350, 422
Hammond, Walter 407
Harcourt, Major Harry 311
Harding, General Edward 308, 309, 320, 321
Harrison, Hector 448
Hasluck, Sir Paul 32, 464
Hattori, Colonel Takushiro 94, 139

Hawaii 18, 28, 38, 43, 93, 116, 182, 191, 200, 201, 204, 206, 223
Heath's Plantation 370
Hei 122
Henderson, R. H. 159
Herring, Edmund 'Ned' 277–8, 285, 287, 323, 326, 327, 328, 335, 353, 357, 359
Hirohito, Emperor 16, 92, 93, 102, 108, 113, 138, 145, 195, 204, 263, 272, 302, 329, 337, 426, 436, 438, 441, 450–1, 455–6
Hiroshima 179, 450
Hiryu 122, 203–4
Hitler, Adolf 5, 6, 10, 13, 17, 42, 54, 55, 58, 66, 110, 117, 130, 152, 191, 342, 346, 361, 367, 381, 407, 441, 461
HMAS *Arunta* 423, 435
HMAS *Australia* 187–8, 423, 425, 435–6
HMAS *Bataan* 453
HMAS *Canberra* 196, 227–8, 230, 231
HMAS *Coonawarra* 122
HMAS *Geelong* 195
HMAS *Hobart* 187
HMAS *Kuttabul* 196
HMAS *Perth* 136–7, 139, 142, 416
HMAS *Shropshire* 423, 425, 435, 446, 454
HMAS *Sydney* 22–5, 28, 38
HMAS *Vampire* 37, 180–1
HMAS *Warramunga* 423, 435
HMAS *Yarra* 140–1
HMS *Electra* 37
HMS *Express* 37
HMS *Hermes* 181
HMS *Indomitable* 19, 37
HMS *Prince of Wales* 19, 37–8, 41, 43, 56–7, 93
HMS *Repulse* 19, 37–8, 41
HMS *Tenedos* 37
holiday periods, cancelling 40
Holland 144
Holmes, Lieutenant Besby 351
Holt, Edgar 362
Hong Kong 20, 43, 71, 109, 398

Honner, Lieutenant Colonel Ralph 260, 262, 322, 324–6, 327, 328
Honshu 450, 452
Hoover, Herbert 35–6
Hore-Ruthven, Patrick 40
Horii, Major General Tomitaro 222, 235–6, 238, 241, 252–3, 255, 257, 263, 265, 269–73, 279, 285, 290, 292, 296, 302, 303, 327
horse racing 21, 39–40, 49, 189–90
Hosking, Gladys 193
Hughes, Billy 9, 20, 21, 121, 159, 220, 222–3, 231, 260, 266, 267, 343, 360, 362, 366, 374, 387, 388, 404, 428–9, 465
Hull, Cordell 392, 394
Hungary 26
Hunt, Lance Corporal John 289
Hunter, James 7
Hutchison, Major Ian 291
Hutton, Len 407

Imita Ridge 261, 264, 265, 268, 270, 280
India 50–1, 57, 67, 82, 110, 130, 136, 183, 270
Indian Army
  9th Infantry Division 30
  Johore, defence of 77–8, 81, 83, 84, 87, 96
Indonesia *see* Dutch East Indies
industrial relations 40, 76, 177–8
  postwar reconstruction 405–6, 414, 433
  unions 76, 78–9, 117, 172, 177, 190, 346, 381, 433
Inoue, Admiral Shigeyoshi 26–7, 51, 90, 111, 187, 188
intelligence (military) 27, 44, 44–5, 73, 91, 98, 116, 187, 202–3, 220, 225, 237, 239, 246–7, 295, 303, 350, 381, 423
  code breaking 28, 187, 191, 201, 202
  Japanese 47–8, 74, 77, 84, 97, 103, 109, 125, 139, 180, 223–4, 229–30, 270, 296, 373
Ioribaiwa 261, 262, 263–5, 268, 270, 272, 279, 285, 296

Iraq 463
Isurava 229, 233, 234, 235, 238–9
Italians 4, 72, 281

Jacka, Albert 241, 378, 443
Jackson, John 158
Jackson, Les 158
Japan 25–6, 29, 51, 138–9, 182–4, 312–13, 387–8, 441, 456–7
   atrocities 84, 92, 107–8, 109–10, 142, 234, 243, 247, 259, 284, 294, 301, 309, 355–6, 366, 416, 435, 444–5, 446, 451, 455
   Australia, plans for 50–2, 72–3, 94, 102, 110–14, 138–9, 180
   capitulation 449–51, 454–5
   China, invasion of 4, 13, 14, 15–16, 26, 31, 43, 50, 66–8, 93, 109, 116, 138, 234, 456
   Germany and 72
   Malaya, in *see* Malaya
   Papua and New Guinea, in *see* New Guinea, Papua
   Philippines, attack on 35–7, 42, 43, 45
   railway building 16
   'sightings' 53
   Singapore, attack on *see* Singapore
   suicide attacks 425, 426, 428, 436, 441, 446, 453
   threat 13, 17, 20, 21, 31, 71
   USA, relations with 16
Java 66, 71–2, 101, 102, 106, 116, 137, 140–1, 142, 144, 184, 435, 445, 451
Java Sea, Battle of the 137–8, 141
Jellicoe, Fleet Lord 361
Johore 73, 77, 79, 80–5, 86–7, 95–6, 103
Joyce, Gladys 127, 133

Kachidoki Maru 415
Kagi 252
Kagu 122, 203
Kai-shek, Chiang 15, 66–7, 129, 376, 392
kamikaze attacks 425, 426, 428, 436, 441, 446, 453
Kanga Force 191, 208–10, 347, 354

Kawai, Tatsuo 26, 27
KB Mission 240, 247, 248
Keenan, Joseph B. 456
Kelliher, Private Richard 370
Kenna, Private Ted 443
Kenney, General George Churchill 266, 279, 311, 337, 348, 364, 384, 423, 429
Kensaku, Major General Oda 327
Keynesian theory 406
Killerton Junction 338–9
King, Admiral Ernest 392, 412, 413, 418
King, Mackenzie 402
King George VI 400, 402, 405
Kingsbury, Private Bruce 241, 248, 442, 442
Kinkaid, Admiral 422
Kirishima 122
Knox, Colonel Frank 58
Kobe 183
Kokoda Track 208–10, 221–3, 226–7, 228–9, 232–3, 235–6, 238, 242–3, 248, 253, 256, 257, 260–1, 270–2, 279, 280, 284–7, 289–90, 291, 294–7, 298, 304, 322, 384, 421
Komiatum 363–4
Kondo, Admiral Nobutake 50–2, 111
Koolama 109
Korea 26, 109, 463
Kormoran 22–4, 25
Kuala Lumpur 71, 72
Kuching 366
Kumusi River 296–7, 302–3, 322, 339
Kursk, Battle of 381

Labor movement 11
Labor Party *see* Australian Labor Party
Lae 90, 93, 142–3, 208, 340, 347, 348, 356–7, 364–5, 369–71, 383, 460
Lavarack, Lieutenant General John 101–2, 389
Laver, Major H. L. 365
Lawrence, Colonel T. E. 47
Lawrence, Max 207
Leach, Captain 38

Leonski, Edward Joseph 193–4, 216, 300, 347
Lewis, Essington 214–15, 463
Lexington 187, 188
Leyte 422–3, 425–6, 429, 451
Liberal Party 437
Libya 3, 5, 352–3
Lindwall, Ray 39
Lloyd, Brigadier John 281, 283, 288, 290
London 395–6
Long, Huey 36
Lowe, Charles 126
Ludendorff, General 167
Luzon 430, 436
Lyons, Joseph 174

MacArthur, Arthur 151
MacArthur, General Douglas 4, 64, 396, 399, 439, 449, 460
  Australia, in 149–56, 158–63, 177, 183, 184, 191, 198–200, 206, 211, 215, 293, 388, 418–19
  Blamey and 161–3, 164, 170, 176, 213–14, 266, 271, 280, 297, 298, 308–9, 311–12, 375, 408–9, 409–13
  Borneo, and 439–40, 445
  character 154–6, 166, 171, 248, 330, 376
  Curtin, relationship with 154–5, 198–200, 205, 260, 267, 366, 374–6, 388, 392, 399–400, 418–19, 462, 465
  Japan, in 453–6
  media management 152, 224–5, 280, 330, 337–8, 357
  military career 166, 170
  Papua and New Guinea 220, 222–3, 238, 239–40, 245, 253–4, 259–60, 267–9, 280, 287, 296–7, 310, 319–21, 327, 335, 348, 371–2
  Philippines 15, 35–7, 43, 57, 144, 149, 151, 159–61, 165, 245, 248, 268, 310, 341, 372, 375, 408, 410, 418–19, 422–5, 426, 428, 429–30, 433, 435–6
  Supreme Commander, as 55, 150, 162, 176, 251, 407, 409–12, 462
MacDonald, Ramsay 11
McEwen, John 'Black Jack' 121, 267
McGrath, Father John 122
Macindoe, Hugh 173–4
Mackey, Corporal John 441–2, 443
McLaughlin, Fred 136, 179, 250, 390
McLeod, Ivy 186
Madagascar 179–80, 181, 270
Madang 383
Maguli River 259
Mailey, Arthur 188
malaria 243, 273, 341, 365
Malaya 14, 20, 34, 37, 38, 42, 51, 57, 72, 111, 223, 325, 343, 398, 426, 451, 460
  Australian defence of 72, 75–6, 77, 80–5
  Japanese in 28, 29–30, 43, 44–6, 56, 71–2, 74–9, 92–3, 109, 116, 160, 234, 288
  withdrawal to Singapore 92–3, 94–5
Manchester, William 149
Manhattan Project 449–50
Manila 35, 71, 433, 435, 436
Mann, Tom 11
Mannix, Archbishop Daniel 428
Mansfield, Justice Alan 456
Markham, Corporal 226, 298
Maroubra Force 209, 232, 234, 238, 241–2, 245, 252, 256, 257–9, 262, 271, 298, 300
Marshall, Colonel Dick 151, 159
Marshall, General George Catlett 68, 150, 162, 192, 394, 408, 412
Marshall Islands 98
Martin, Private Stanley 311
Marx, Karl 11
Marxist theory 406
media 382
  Blamey and 172, 224, 261–2, 280
  censorship 77, 127–8, 197–8, 231, 315
  Curtin and 48–9, 86, 114–15, 116–19, 177–8, 181–2, 189, 214, 269, 344, 357–8, 362, 367, 464

media (*continued*)
  MacArthur and 152, 224–5, 280, 330, 337–8, 357
Melbourne 115–16, 152, 153, 183, 184–6, 211, 249–50
Melbourne Cup 21
Menari 256, 257, 261, 270
Menzies, Robert 3, 4, 12–13, 17–18, 20, 21, 38, 48, 58, 62, 68, 79, 119, 121, 159, 164, 168, 174, 175, 248, 260, 267, 343, 361, 366, 374, 387, 402, 414, 434, 437, 448, 465
Middle East 13–14, 17, 22, 34–5, 42, 46, 47, 50, 57, 66, 101, 102, 110, 119, 129, 158, 165, 174, 176–7, 200, 213, 232, 243, 248, 281, 286, 322, 345, 351, 378, 459
Midway 182, 186, 201–5, 205–6, 215, 219, 237, 259, 425, 460
Mikawa, Vice Admiral Gunichi 227–8
Mikuma 204
Militia Bill 342–3, 356
Miller, Lloyd 185
Milne Bay 225, 236, 236–7, 239–40, 245–8, 252, 259, 301, 308, 323, 341, 384, 460
Milne Force 225
miners' strike 76, 346
Mission Ridge 245, 252–4, 256
Mitchell, Major John 351
Moffat, Private 227
Monash, General Sir John 5, 27, 35, 102, 166–9, 170, 171, 172, 223, 225, 249, 260, 307, 463
Montgomery, Field Marshal Bernard 345, 402
Moorer, Lieutenant Thomas 122
Morotai 440, 451, 454
Morris, Major-General 209–10, 221, 227
Morrison, Ian 14
Morshead, Lieutenant General Leslie 352, 389, 440–1
Moten, Brigadier Murray 354
Mount Tambu 363–4
Mubo 354, 359, 364
Muirhead-Gould, Rear-Admiral 197
Mulholland, Jack 124–5

Murdoch, Keith 64, 344, 362
Myer, Sir Norman 153
Myer Warrender, Pamela 153
Myola 232–4, 238, 243–4, 252–3, 281, 287, 291, 292, 295

Nagasaki 450
Nagoya 183
Nagumo, Vice Admiral Chuichi 122, 180–1, 202–3
Nassau Bay 354, 356, 364
National Welfare Fund 343
Nauro 257, 261, 270
Nazis 51, 52, 55, 65, 70, 251, 381
Neosho 187
New Britain 26, 66, 68, 85, 88, 109, 115, 143, 343, 371, 373, 439, 451
New Caledonia 68, 94, 186, 187
New Guinea 18, 26, 44, 68, 73, 85, 94, 98, 109, 115, 116, 138, 142, 149, 158, 190, 191, 208, 215, 282, 361, 382, 384, 389, 398, 439, 451, 454, 460, 463
  Japanese invasion 219–24, 236–48, 249, 269–73, 278–80, 322, 328–9, 337, 355, 371–2
New Guinea Force 278
New Hebrides 68
New Ireland 26, 89
New Zealand 68, 72, 82, 110, 342, 382–3, 393
Nimitz, Admiral Chester W. 202–3, 350, 418, 422, 429
Nishimura, General 456
North Africa 13–14, 42, 174, 248, 281, 286, 322, 351, 373, 441
Northcott, General John 411
Northern Territory Force 278

Oiva 221, 296, 297, 300–1
Operation 1-Go 350
Operation FS (Fiji-Samoa) 73
Operation Matador 29
Operation Overload 398–9, 404, 405, 407
Operation SR 142
Operation Vengeance 351
Orcades 101, 142

O'Reilly, Bill 39
Osmena, Sergio 423–5
Ostreicher, Lieutenant Robert 123
Owen, Lieutenant-Colonel William 221–2, 226, 298–9
Owen Stanley Range 208–10, 220, 232, 236–41, 246, 259, 264, 265, 266, 295, 304, 310–12, 317, 324, 341, 348, 353, 421, 460
Ower's Corner 298

Packer, Frank 344, 362
Page, Earle 27, 58, 87, 91, 119–21, 128, 135, 150
Papua 52, 68, 73, 115, 116, 186, 219, 234, 282, 384, 398, 460
  'fighting withdrawal' 242–3, 254, 256, 257, 318
  Japanese invasion 219–24, 236–48, 269–73, 278–80, 322, 328–9, 337, 355, 371–2, 461
  military 220–1
Parit Sulong 80–3
Pattina 29
Patton, Major George S. Jnr 36
Pearl Harbor 28, 30–1, 33, 34, 35, 38, 42, 43, 45, 48, 50, 67, 93, 112–13, 116, 122, 160, 187, 201, 202, 204, 282, 350, 423, 460, 461
Penang, 46
Percival, Lieutenant-General A. E. 46, 83, 92, 96–7, 103, 105, 108, 114
Perkins 187
Pershing, General 307
Perth 115, 143–5, 178, 413, 419, 448
Pett, Corporal Lester 291
Philippines 15, 18, 42, 43, 45, 56, 82, 109, 149, 151, 159, 160–1, 165, 191, 201, 223, 249, 268, 341, 372, 375, 399, 408, 410, 418–19, 422–5, 426, 428, 429–30, 435–6, 451, 457, 461
Phillips, Admiral Sir Thomas 19, 37–8, 41, 44, 409
Port Headland 145, 358
Port Moresby 41, 52, 90, 93, 98, 115, 142–3, 158, 186, 187, 188, 190, 198, 208–10, 215, 225, 233, 234, 238, 244, 249, 252, 254–5, 258, 267, 297, 311, 318, 335, 384
  Japanese assault on 220, 221, 222, 223–4, 227, 229, 236, 243, 256–7, 264–5, 272, 280
Porter, Brigadier Selwyn 258, 259, 260, 321
postwar reconstruction 405–6, 414, 433
Potsdam Declaration 451, 456
Potts, Brigadier Arnold 232–5, 238–9, 241–5, 252–9, 262, 289–90, 298, 318, 322, 421
Power, Lieutenant Kevin 286, 287
Powers, Lieutenant J. J. 188
Prime Minister's War Conference *see* War Conference
prisoners of war (POWs) 197, 207, 284, 407, 414–17, 435, 443–4, 450, 452
  Australia, in 417
  liberation of 451–3
  treatment by Japanese 84, 92, 107–8, 109–10, 142, 234, 243, 247, 259, 284, 294, 365–6, 416–17, 435, 444–5, 446
propaganda 30, 74, 105, 152, 190, 215, 231, 265, 317, 330
public morale 49

Quezon, Manuel Luis 37, 153, 424

Rabaul 66, 85, 88–9, 115, 186, 191, 205, 220, 223, 226, 229, 298, 337, 339, 341, 349, 364, 369, 439
racism 157, 438
Rakuyo Maru 415–17
Ramu Valley 383
Ranau 435, 444, 446, 451
Rangoon 45, 120, 129, 136
Rankin, Lieutenant Commander Robert 141
Read, Major-General G. W. 167
Reid, Alan 47, 230
Richards, Corporal Billy 370
Rischbieth, Bessie 402
Robertson, Lieutenant-Colonel J. C. 78, 80, 389

Robertson-Glasgow, R. C. 188
Robins, Walter 407
Rodgers, Don 60, 127, 133, 374, 390, 394, 401, 405, 464
Rodgers, Warrant Officer 311
Rommel, Field-Marshal 5, 200
Romulo, General 153
Roosevelt, Eleanor 393
Roosevelt, Franklin D. 16, 27, 36–7, 64–5, 66, 120–1, 128–30, 151, 152, 155, 161, 181, 192, 230, 248, 251, 268, 341–2, 358, 361, 362, 382, 384, 412, 429, 459
  Churchill and, 42–6, 54–7, 66–7, 70, 131–2, 376
  Curtin's visit to the USA 387–94, 407
  death 438
  Japanese attack 29, 31, 33
  Pacific War 42–3, 46, 52, 54–7, 350, 418
Rosenthal, General Charles 260
Ross, David 216
Ross, Lloyd 47
Rowell, Lieutenant General Sydney 225, 233, 239, 244–6, 247, 248, 254, 256, 257–8, 261, 264–9, 271–2, 277, 285, 287, 306, 353
Royal Australian Airforce 69, 349, 358
Russia 9, 26, 42, 51, 53–5, 60–2, 94, 190, 206, 381, 461

Saidor 384
Saigon 28, 415
Salamaua 90, 93, 143, 208, 340, 347, 348, 353, 354, 356–7, 359, 364–5, 369–71
Samoa 93, 94, 186
Sanananda 219, 303–4, 306–7, 318, 320, 322, 326, 328, 337–40, 348, 384, 460
Sandakan 366, 435, 443–5, 446
Sattelberg Ridge 372, 373, 377–80, 442
Savage, Ellen 355
Savage, Gunner Russell 450, 452–3
Savige, Major General Stan 171, 351–5, 356, 359, 361, 363–6, 369, 384, 389, 411, 419–22, 451–2
Savo Island, Battle of 227–8
Scanlan, Lieutenant-Colonel John 88
Schroeder, Major Ed 336
scorched-earth policy 177–8
Scullin, James 361, 428, 434
Shackleton, Barry 185
Shaggy Ridge 372, 380, 383
Shedden, Frederick 13, 15, 20, 29, 32, 60, 61, 87, 127, 133–4, 174, 176, 192, 388, 408–12
  Curtin's visit to the US and UK 390, 395, 397, 399, 407
  War Conference, 163–4, 184, 198, 200
Shoho 187
Shokaka 187, 188
Simemi Creek 331–2
Singapore 13, 14–15, 17, 54–5, 56, 58, 68, 94–5, 110–11, 116, 133, 134, 136, 160, 199, 206, 223, 234, 257, 282, 288, 325, 398, 401, 414, 426, 460
  defence of 19–21, 37–8, 41–2, 46, 57, 79–80, 96–8, 361
  evacuate, plan to 87–8, 90
  fall of 105, 106–10, 114–15
  Japanese attack on 28, 43, 45
  siege 101–6
  withdrawal to 92–3, 94–5
Slim River 46
Solomon Islands 27, 68, 73, 94, 187, 190, 219, 227, 231, 238, 349, 439, 451
Somerville, Admiral 181
Songkhla 29
Songkhram, Field Marshal Phibun 43
Soputa 303, 307
Soryu 122, 203
South-West Pacific Force 422
Southwell, Belle 156, 179
Soviet Union 456
Spain 26
Sparrow Force 131
Spender, Percy 121, 260, 387
SS *Holbrook* 78
SS *Lurline* 390, 391, 410
SS *Nashville* 423, 429

SS *Phoenix* 423
Stalin, Josef 53–4, 55, 60, 62, 70, 117, 231, 367, 381, 399
Starcevich, Private Leslie Thomas 'Tom' 445–6
Stoke Poges 396
Stuart tanks 328–30
Sturdee, Lieutenant General Vernon 34, 47, 83, 115, 128, 133, 420–1, 440
Suikaka 187
Susumu, Captain Hosijimi 435
Sutherland, Richard 192, 198, 245, 408–9
Sweden 26
Sydney 111–12, 118, 179–80, 193, 197, 358, 460
  Japanese reconnaissance 193, 194
  Japanese submarines in the harbour 195–6
Symington, Captain Noel 226, 229
Syrian Campaign 165

Takuo, Captain Takakuwa 443, 444–5
Tarakan 71, 398, 440–2, 446, 447
Tarakena 338
Task Force South Pacific 59
Taylor, Brigadier Harold 104
Taylor, Leading Seaman R. 141
Templeton, Captain Sam 221, 226–7, 235, 270, 272, 296, 298–9
Teshima, Lieutenant General 454
Thai-Burma Railway 137, 142, 365–6, 414–15, 452
Thailand 28, 29, 31, 37, 43, 45, 93, 109, 111, 116, 160, 207, 223, 257, 325, 414, 451
Thanbyuzayat War Cemetery 457
Thompson, Pauline 186
Thornton, Lance Sergeant C. W. 77
Tiger of Malaya 110, 112, 426
Timber Workers' Union 7
Timor 41, 44, 102, 123, 125, 128, 131, 135–6, 140, 149, 160, 207, 216, 451
  Australian commandos 207–8, 216, 347
Tobruk 3–5, 17, 42, 116, 165, 174, 226, 260, 281, 318, 323, 330, 378
Tojo, Prime Minister 94, 110–12, 138, 145, 183, 197, 202, 204, 426, 456, 461
Tokyo 453–4
  Allied bombing 183, 201, 438
Tokyo War Crimes Trials 456
Tomioka, Baron 51–2, 139, 182–3
Tomitaro, Major-General 89
Tone 122
Toyoshima, Hajime 124
Tracey, Ray 433, 447
Trainer, Percy 448
Trocas 24
Truk Island 51, 180, 451
Truman, Harry 449–50, 453, 455
Tsukmoto Lieutenant Colonel Hatsuo 229
Tsuyou, Major General Yamagata 322

unions 76, 78–9, 117, 172, 177, 190, 346, 381, 433
United Australia Party (UAP) 3, 12, 20, 360, 374, 387, 437
United Nations 437
United States of America 15, 30, 42, 456
  Australia, relationship with 18, 57, 59, 60–1, 64–5, 112, 139, 198–200, 374–5, 394, 463
  Japan, relations with 16, 29
  military forces in Australia 143–5, 156–8, 162–3, 183, 184–6, 198–200, 211–12, 293–4, 313–17, 347, 461
  navy 308–10, 330
  Pacific War 57, 90–1, 98, 183, 219, 266, 279, 306, 309–12, 320–1, 328, 335–7, 375–6, 419
  Perth, military base in 143–5
Urbana Force 331, 336
USS *Bagley* 228
USS *Boise* 430
USS *Chicago* 187, 195–6, 228
USS *Ellet* 228
USS *Enterprise* 203
USS *Hammann* 204
USS *Hornet* 201, 203

USS *Houston* 137
USS *Lexington* 143
USS *Missouri* 454
USS *Mugford* 355
USS *Parrot* 144
USS *Patterson* 228
USS *Peary* 126
USS *Phelps* 188
USS *Pinegrove* 143
USS *Yorktown* 143, 188, 203, 204

Varley, Brigadier Arthur 103, 416
Vasey, General 245, 246, 254, 291, 292, 294–7, 302, 303, 306, 318, 320, 321, 338–9, 356, 370, 383–4, 389, 411
Vichy France 26, 281, 352
Vietnam 26, 28, 109, 116, 414, 451, 457, 463
Vita 181

Wairopi 296, 303
Waldron, Major General Albert 308
Walker 187
Wallace, Henry 392
Waller, Captain Hector 137
Walsh, Lieutenant Nick 281
war brides 317
War Conference 163, 184, 192, 198, 213
'war footing' 63, 114, 282, 360
Ward, Eddie 79, 190, 283, 346, 356, 358, 367, 381–2, 387, 410
Ward, Lieutenant Colonel Kenneth 239
Warner, Denis 436
Warren Force 307, 309
Wasserman, William Stix 213, 409
Waterside Workers' Union 78
Watson, Major Bill 220, 222
Wau 191, 347, 353, 356–7
Wavell, General Archibald 73–4, 79, 92, 97, 101–2, 104–5, 106, 129, 165, 166, 404

Webb, Sir William 456
Webster, Private Ed 315
Western Front 14, 101, 166–8, 241, 301, 351, 353
Wewak 364, 443
White Australia Policy 32, 374, 437–8
Whitfield, Colin 196
Whitlam, Gough 463
Wilkinson, Warrant Officer 229
Willoughby, Colonel 153
Wilmot, Chester 262, 298
Wilson, Alex 3
Windeyer, Brigadier Victor 369, 372, 373
Women's Employment Act 344–5
Wood, Dulcie 185
Wootten, Major General George 246–7, 323, 330, 336–7, 338–40, 356, 372, 373, 377

Yamaguchi, Admiral Tamon 204
Yamamoto, Admiral Isoroku 50, 52, 90, 110, 113, 138, 179–80, 182–3, 195
  assassination 350–1
  Battle of Midway 201–3
Yamashita, Lieutenant General Tomoyuki 235–6, 288, 456
  Australia, plans for 110–13, 138, 183, 184, 215, 460
  Malaya, in 28, 29–30, 44–5, 51, 71–2, 74, 77, 83, 92–3
  Philippines, in 426, 428, 429–30
  Singapore, attack on 94, 96–8, 102, 104, 106–10
Yamato 179
Yokohama 183, 453
Yokoyama, General 219
Yong Peng 82, 83, 84
Yorktown 187

Zedong, Mao 15, 392

www.ingramcontent.com/pod-product-compliance
Ingram Content Group UK Ltd.
Pitfield, Milton Keynes, MK11 3LW, UK
UKHW041300180426
11947UKWH00009B/588